# PLAIN
# FOLK'S
# FIGHT

*Civil War America* | Gary W. Gallagher, editor

# PLAIN FOLK'S

*The Civil War and Reconstruction*

# FOLK'S

*in Piney Woods Georgia*

# FIGHT

Mark V. Wetherington

THE UNIVERSITY *of*
NORTH CAROLINA PRESS
CHAPEL HILL

Designed by Kimberly Bryant
Set in Minion by Keystone Typesetting, Inc.
Manufactured in the United States of America

The paper in this book meets the guidelines for permanence and
durability of the Committee on Production Guidelines for Book
Longevity of the Council on Library Resources.

Library of Congress Cataloging-in-Publication Data
Wetherington, Mark V.
Plain folk's fight : the Civil War and Reconstruction in Piney
Woods Georgia / Mark V. Wetherington.
p. cm. — (Civil War America)
Includes bibliographical references and index.
ISBN 0-8078-2963-3 (alk. paper)
1. Georgia—History—Civil War, 1861–1865—Social aspects.
2. United States—History—Civil War, 1861–1865—Social aspects.
3. Reconstruction (U.S. history, 1865–1877)—Georgia.
4. Farmers—Georgia—Political activity—History—19th century.
5. Artisans—Georgia—Political activity—History—19th century.
6. Whites—Georgia—Social conditions—19th century. 7. Whites—
Georgia—Politics and government—19th century. 8. Georgia—
Rural conditions. 9. Georgia—Social conditions—19th century.
10. Georgia—Politics and government—1865–1950. I. Title.
II. Series.
E559.W48    2005
975.8′03—dc22        2005006284

09  08  07  06  05    5  4  3  2  1

*to My Parents and Mark*

# CONTENTS

# ILLUSTRATIONS & MAPS

This book explores the rural world of white Southern plain folk during the Civil War and Reconstruction in piney woods Georgia. Rather than blindly follow the dictates of class consciousness or the planter elite, a majority of the plain folk chose to secede from the Union, support the Confederacy, and fight again in the postwar era for what they determined to be their own self-interest. Although they lacked the material possessions of their wealthier planter and professional neighbors, they were prideful people. They believed that they could hold their own against the world despite the absence of railroads, the telegraph, towns of significant size, or a manufacturing base in their region. They were wrong. Four years of war left them beaten and humbled but determined to regain control of their neighborhoods through whatever means were necessary, including violence and political terrorism.

Presenting the plain folk's voice is problematic. This large and inarticulate mass of common people left few private papers that have survived. I have nevertheless attempted to reconstruct their world and give them a voice based on the sources available. I maintain that it is a story worth telling, despite arguments that another Civil War book is one of the last things Southern history needs. What happened to the wiregrass plain folk fills a gap in Civil War historiography, although the themes encountered in their experiences of war, death, defeat, and search for redemption are universal. Their fights—economic, social, military, and political—shaped their collective identity in a nineteenth-century rural world that they were unable to defend from change imposed on them from outside the forest.

In my search for sources I have received the help of many. I am indebted to Dale Couch and Anne P. Smith, Georgia Department of Archives and History, and Chuck Barber, Hargrett Rare Book and Manuscript Library, University of Georgia, for their assistance, as well as to the staff of the National Archives. For their willingness to share information and guide me to new sources I thank Keith Bohannon, Anne Marshall, Chris Trowell, and Julian Williams. I also wish to thank The Filson Historical Society, Louisville, Kentucky, for its support of this project through sabbatical time as well as members of the Filson staff for their encouragement, particularly Jim Holmberg, Judy Miller, and Brian Pollock.

From the proposal stage to the final manuscript this book benefited from the assistance of many other colleagues. No one has been more generous with faith in my project, leads on sources, and time than Stephen V. Ash, who read much of the manuscript. William W. Freehling made helpful suggestions at the proposal stage; Stephanie McCurry, Amy E. Murrell, and Christopher Phillips commented on chapters and offered many insights for improvement, for which I am deeply grateful. The readers for the University of North Carolina Press, editor-in-chief David Perry, and copyeditor Stevie Champion made this a better book.

Finally, I thank my family and friends, especially Glenna Pfeiffer, for their interest and support. This book is dedicated to my parents and to my son Mark.

# PLAIN
# FOLK'S
# FIGHT

Standing near the center of the white section of Orange Hill Cemetery, in Hawkinsville, the Manning family monument rises as a gray classical column that is broken off before reaching its full promise. It is a metaphor for the fate of the Manning family and the plantation South. Seaborn Manning was a prominent Hawkinsville planter-merchant who, as a lieutenant colonel of the 49th Georgia Infantry, led more of the lower Ocmulgee River's plain folk into battle than any other local officer. "Beloved" by his men, Manning died in 1862 from wounds received during the Battle of Cedar Mountain, Virginia. His wife Harriette saw to it that his body was brought home and buried. Stretching beyond the Manning plot are more grave markers for the town's antebellum elite, many of them slaveholders and professionals who, like Manning, led the yeomanry into battle but, unlike him, lived to return home and die there in old age.[1]

Conspicuously absent from Orange Hill Cemetery and most burial grounds along the lower river are graves of the plain folk war dead. Like Seaborn Manning they lost their lives, but unlike Manning their bodies never came home. They died and were buried far away. Occasionally, their final resting place was a cemetery like the University of Virginia's. It was there that

Second Sergeant Daniel Mason's remains were interred in 1861. A former store clerk at Hawkinsville, he lost his arm at First Manassas. Failing to recover from the wound, Mason died in the Confederate general hospital at Charlottesville a little more than two months later. He was neither the first nor the last member of the Pulaski Volunteers to be buried in the Charlottesville cemetery.[2]

In time, 1,093 more dead Confederates joined them. Mason and his comrades were tightly tucked into the ground in rows that evoke images of Africans packed into the hulls of slave ships. Almost 140 years after the Civil War, headstones distinguish only about two dozen graves. Without individual markers, the soldiers' names became disassociated from their bodies in one mass burial. We only know from measurements taken by men in the burial detail in 1861, for example, that Daniel Mason was put below ground about twenty-one feet from the entrance wall. The remains of Mason and his comrades represent the steady bleeding off of Southern white manhood that eroded the Confederacy's ability to win the war. Today we are left to ponder the meaning of the life and death of such plain folk with little physical evidence that they ever existed. A single monument erected near the cemetery's center in 1893 lists the dead soldiers' names by state and regiment and carries the inscription: "Fate denied them Victory, but clothed them in glorious Immortality." Over two hundred of Mason's fellow Georgians were buried in the cemetery, more than the war dead of any other Confederate state, including Virginia. They are the conflict's forgotten casualties.

Who were they? How did they find themselves fighting and dying hundreds of miles from home? How did their families respond to the war after the initial rush of excitement faded and four years of hard fighting followed? How did the veterans themselves deal with the changed world they found at home in 1865? The answers to these questions lie largely in the experiences of common people whose lives were forever changed by secession, the war, and its aftermath.

A number of key interpretive points frame this portrait of plain folk at war. Race consciousness, for example, had more influence in shaping plain folk ideology and motivation to support secession and war than class consciousness. By 1860 the piney woods were virtually surrounded by black belts with slave majorities. Although yeomen were increasingly engaged in cotton growing and slaveholding, they still saw their region's identity as distinct from the neighboring black belts. They feared the consequences of a Republican presidency and possible black emancipation, which would free former slaves to move into subsistence areas like the piney woods.

By early 1861 the wiregrass country had become a secessionist region. Its white people, motivated by obligations to defend family and home, ideals of white liberty, and fears of Yankee victory and black emancipation, mobilized at rates similar to those found in Georgia's cotton belt. They now identified with the new Confederate nation and did more than their share of volunteering and dying. Although mobilization thinned out the white men at home, this nonplantation area did not become a home front of white women and slaves where household authority was fundamentally altered, as has been suggested for the plantation South. The antebellum patriarchy remained in control and kept the home front functioning even as growing numbers of plain folk joined the new wartime poor. Sherman's march and widening divisions between Confederate patriot and anti-Confederate households were psychological blows that made it impossible by late 1864 to continue to effectively fight a two-front war in Virginia and at home.

Pulled between loyalties to the Confederate nation and their local neighborhoods, some of the same men who had led mobilization now called for an end to the war to preserve the human and material resources needed to rebuild their postwar communities. Many veterans believed that a rejection of cotton and a return to safety-first farming and livestock herding was the best pathway. New South deforestation and the expansion of cotton production and the crop lien system made this a difficult road to travel as the common range was fragmented. The veterans' most successful fight took place in the political arena, where ex-Confederates used paramilitary tactics and ritual violence to defeat freedpeople and their white Republican allies, preserving a white patriarchy that relied on ex-Confederate officers for a new generation of leadership.[3]

Who were the plain folk? As Frank L. Owsley wrote over a half century ago, the vast majority of Southerners belonged to a large and complex group of rural whites called "plain folk." According to Owsley, they formed a large middle class situated below the planter elite but above the poor whites and slaves in the South's hierarchical social structure. Most of them were "neither rich nor very poor." The vast majority of plain folk were nonslaveholding farmers who owned land and produced a self-sufficiency from farming and livestock herding. Owsley included small slaveholding farmers, farm laborers, squatters, and tenants in his narrowly defined group. Almost twenty-five years ago Edward Magdol and Jon L. Wakelyn called for a more inclusive definition of Southern "common people," one that expanded Owsley's group to include small planters, country store owners, urban mechanics, day laborers, and factory workers. More recently, Stephanie McCurry has defined the yeomanry as "self-working farmers" owning fewer than 150 acres of improved land and fewer than ten slaves.[4]

In this study "plain folk" and "yeomanry" are used interchangeably. However, because yeomanry implies lesser freeholders who cultivated their own land, I consider plain folk a more inclusive term that reflects the group's complexity. For purposes of this study, then, antebellum plain folk are defined as white households owning fewer than ten slaves and working less than 150 improved acres and more often under 100 acres. In the countryside landless farm laborers, overseers, storekeepers, and tenants joined the farmers and small slaveholders. Moreover, in a part of Georgia where the largest town, Hawkinsville, boasted a population of about three hundred in 1860, plain folk also included a long list of Southern-born commoners such as blacksmiths, brickmasons, carpenters, mechanics, and minor professionals, notably clerks, teachers, and shopkeepers, as well as unskilled laborers and teamsters who arrived from the countryside. Often recent arrivals from rural areas, they constituted important links between farming families and the town professionals who often employed them.[5]

In 1860 such plain folk accounted for about 90 percent of the white households along Georgia's lower Ocmulgee River. Far from being marginalized by planters and their enslaved African Americans, plain folk occupied the center of society in the piney woods. As such, they shaped its essential character, just as they did in the South's nonplantation regions. They defy stereotyping. Plain folk were bumptious and deferential, nonslaveholders and masters, evangelical, antievangelical, and unchurched, mostly Democrat but occasionally Whig. Largely small farmers, they aimed for economic self-sufficiency but embraced the market economy in varying degrees. As Jeffersonian republicans, they agreed that economically independent yeomen formed the bedrock of a moral and virtuous republic, but by the eve of the Civil War many of them were becoming increasingly involved in the cotton economy.[6]

Although often rankled by planter privilege, plain folk nevertheless agreed that white men had the right to own black slaves as personal property. Whites almost universally believed that biracialism was an essential element of Southern society. Surrounded by plantation belts with black majorities, plain folk were psychologically committed to defending racial slavery, an institution that elevated their own status as white folk and ensured social order, even when they did not stand to gain economically. At the same time, plain folk feared the uncontrolled expansion of plantation slavery into the piney woods, an area traditionally bypassed by the planter elite and one that offered the plain folk cheap farmland and seemingly unlimited access to the open range.[7]

Yet few plain folk households or neighborhoods were entirely self-sufficient. Some lower Ocmulgee counties in 1860 barely met levels of self-sufficiency in corn production, the basic food crop, even before troop mobilization began in 1861. In light of this deficiency, a surprising number of yeoman families shifted scarce white labor from the production of food crops for home consumption to cotton production for market. The yeomanry traditionally produced goods for market exchange, notably cane syrup and wool, but these commodities did not require the time and effort demanded by cotton, nor did they compete with corn for land and labor as did cotton. In short, some households that struggled to put food on the table turned to cotton in varying degrees to shore up their domestic economy.[8]

Cotton was not the only economic link between plain folk and planters. Indeed, about 20 percent of yeoman households owned slaves. The acquisition of slaves by yeoman farmers, particularly slave women and children, tied them directly to racial slavery. Often a majority of small masters' assets was invested in enslaved African Americans, as was the case with large planters. Moreover, plain folk and planters also shared mutual concerns in the open-range system of livestock herding. Unlike Georgia's black belts, where planters were limited in their expansion of plantation-scale cotton production only by their ability to buy more fresh land and slaves, the pine belt's natural land-scape restricted plantations to narrow bands of fertile soil, primarily along rivers and streams. As a result, the conflict between plain folk and planters over fence laws that was well under way in the cotton belt was minimized in the piney backwoods. Both planters and yeomen left large tracts of land unimproved, which served as mutually recognized common rangeland, and some of the area's largest livestock men included both yeomen and planters.[9]

Local plain folk and planters often shared something dearer to them than cotton, slaves, and the open range—common family ties. In a part of the South where planters large and small represented less than 10 percent of all households, intermarriage between the two groups was common. The relative newness of the lower river region played a role in this familiarity. Settled for only two generations at most by 1860, and in the case of territory southwest of the river for just over a generation, society was still in a state of frontierlike flux. Neighborhood boundaries and landscapes and populations, especially those west of the river, were still being negotiated. By black belt standards, there were few truly large planters in the lower river region; only three owned over one hundred slaves in 1860. True, some planters built two-story Greek Revival homes as displays of wealth and conspicuous consumption, but many, such as Jackson Coalson, who owned over ninety slaves in the 1850s, still lived in common log houses. In short, the plain folk character of society along the lower Ocmulgee extended beyond the households of slaveless yeomen and small masters and reached up the ladder of wealth as far as customs, kinship, and values were concerned.[10]

This story of Southern plain folk unfolds in southern Georgia's piney woods, part of a unique subregion that stretched along the coastal plains from North Carolina to eastern Texas. In southern Georgia the forest covered more than 17,000 square miles in the mid-nineteenth century. A borderland between the state's more fertile cotton belt and its tidewater, the piney woods were also referred to as the "pine barrens" and the "wiregrass country." Longleaf pine trees and a natural ground cover called "wiregrass" visually dominated the unique natural landscape. This perennial provided year-round grazing for livestock and, like the pine, lent its name to the region. Georgia's extensive longleaf pine forest formed the center of Dixie's larger pine belt, just as the lower Ocmulgee River occupied the center of Georgia's rolling wiregrass country. Five antebellum counties—Coffee, Irwin, Pulaski, Telfair, and Wilcox—bordered most of the lower river in 1860.[11]

Why explore this region? During the last decade, scholars have studied the Confederate home front from the standpoint of its Appalachian, cotton belt, tidewater, and urban communities, as well as from the perspectives of class, gender, and race. The Southern pine belt, geographically among the South's largest regions, has not received adequate attention. By shifting the focus from the plantation South to the Southern piney woods, *Plain Folk's Fight* explores a home-front heartland where Union soldiers were not seen by noncombatants until 1865. But the reactions of plain folk to the secession crisis and war mobilization were of great concern to contemporary secessionists and Southern nationalists. If the pine belt's inhabitants were to join those of the Border States or, for that matter, plain folk in northern Georgia as essentially anti-Confederate, then a new Southern republic would be vulnerable to Yankee invasion on both its upper and lower frontiers and to a civil war from within.[12]

Although it was unclear to Georgia secessionists at the time of Abraham Lincoln's election, they need not have worried about the piney woods. Despite its status as a poor region where 75 percent of the people were white and the average farm size was less than one hundred acres, the low-slaveholding wiregrass country was pro-secession by early 1861. A narrow majority of the lower Ocmulgee River's white men reflected this regional trend and voted for secessionist delegates. And despite conventional wisdom that the pine belt's plain folk joined northern Georgia's disaffected and unreliable unionists, about 60 percent of the lower Ocmulgee's military-aged men were in Confederate uniform before the end of the war's first year—more than its share. These volunteers spanned the social spectrum from plain folk like Daniel Mason to planters like Seaborn Manning.[13]

Ironically, Confederate soldiers such as Mason believed that defeat would mean their own degradation and unmanly submission to a hated enemy, thus making them "slaves" to Yankees. In a society where white supremacy and localist and states' rights doctrines were essential elements of plain folk ideology, Lincoln's election fulfilled white fears that the North was determined to wage a war of Southern subjugation and slave emancipation. It was the duty of all honorable men to protect their families and homes from Yankee domination. Evidence along the lower Ocmulgee suggests that plain folk were motivated to support secession and the war both by ideology and their own sense of honor and masculinity.[14]

*Plain Folk's Fight* plays on the phrase "rich man's war, poor man's fight," which implies that planter self-interest was responsible for secession, the war, and the Confederate defeat. By treating the plain folk as a monolithic group, however, historians emphasizing the importance of class resentment largely ignore the possibility that the war was fought for anything other than slaveholders' property. The plain folk's critical role in and responsibility for secession and the war are disregarded, as is their determination to fight for their own concept of freedom, white manhood, and nationhood. A majority of plain folk supported secession and did so for their own reasons, as we shall see.

In this study "fight" assumes meanings beyond its military references: secession was a political fight to preserve the plain folk's republican rights and social identity as white people, soldiers' families struggled for survival at home, and plain folk and freedpeople fought for self-worth in an impoverished postwar world. Unlike the wartime plantation belts, the piney woods home front did not become a world of white women and slaves, but rather a part of the Confederate interior where household authority and patriarchy exhibited considerable resiliency both during and after the war. More often than not, the inner conflicts exposed by the conflict were not between classes, but between individuals and within their own minds as they attempted to reconcile conflicted identities and loyalties on the household, family, and neighborhood levels.[15]

Several overarching themes run through their story. The localism that played out on the neighborhood level shaped the plain folk's attachment to people, place, and political movements. Wiregrass people clearly considered their part of the world different from the wealthy and densely settled plantation belts that surrounded them. Even within the lower Ocmulgee region, black and white belt neighborhoods lent diversity to the landscape that reflected differences in their soil quality, populations, and involvement in commercial agriculture. As a result, rural neighborhoods took on identities that were reflected in their politics and their stance during secession and war.

Race consciousness played a huge role in determining how plain folk sorted out their neighborhoods from others and from the rest of Georgia and the South. Although nine out of ten white households along the lower river belonged to plain folk, almost 30 percent of all households owned at least one slave. Thus, its image as a "barren" region belied a growing involvement in the institution of slavery and the cotton economy. Most white families had kinfolk or friends who were masters, usually of a handful of slaves, and frequently these were women and children. There is little evidence that such plain folk harbored guilt concerning slavery. They believed that whites were inherently superior to blacks and understood that their own slightly elevated social status was dependent on racial slavery.

There is abundant evidence that plain folk harbored deep fears about the black majorities along their borders and what would happen to their own world if the slaves were freed. Plain folk deferred to the planter elite not only because they were wealthier and better educated, but also because they controlled large numbers of enslaved African Americans and kept them on distant and more fertile lands. The local yeomanry may have resented planter privilege, but given the choice between slaves controlled by Southern planters and slaves liberated by Northern Republicans, and thus free to move into the "poor man's" country inhabited by the yeomanry, the plain folk sided with planters. Governor Joseph E. Brown understood these racial fears and insecurities and effectively exploited them to politically and militarily mobilize the yeomanry during the secession crisis and the war. Without plain folk votes, lower river communities would not have narrowly supported secession with a slight 51 percent majority, joining the larger wiregrass Georgia as a secessionist region.[16]

Although enslaved African Americans, freedpeople, and planters play important roles in this study, the Deep South's rural white plain folk supply the central voices in a complex story. Far from being manipulated, plain folk played active rolls in secession, mobilization, the war, and Reconstruction and were moved to action for their own reasons. Compelled to make choices—secessionist or unionist, Confederate volunteer or conscript, home-front patriot or deserter, postwar yeoman or New South advocate—they reshaped their identities as Southerners.

John K. Whaley was the Natty Bumppo of the lower Ocmulgee River. Like James Fenimore Cooper's fictional frontier character, he was a solitary man who lived off the land hunting, fishing, and foraging in the wild woods. A throwback to an earlier era, he hunted by "the light of a pine torch" and felt crowded by anyone who settled within five miles of his cabin. Whaley deeply resented the arrival of the acquisitive cotton planters who bought up the land, cut back the forest, tilled the soil, and fenced in their crops, making it difficult for plain folk like himself to find sustenance in the woods. By the late 1850s "Old John K.," as he was called, had had enough of the cotton planters and slaves who transformed Pulaski County's virgin forest into a cotton frontier. Despite his advanced age of sixty or so, Whaley packed up what little he owned and fled deeper into southern Georgia's pine forest. There, on the edge of the Okefenokee Swamp, he fished, hunted, and trapped for much of the remainder of his life.[1]

At the end of the antebellum period, the Ocmulgee River world that Whaley knew was vastly different from the one William Bartram had visited in 1778, when Bartram saw a verdant landscape of "fragrant groves and sublime forests." By the time Whaley was born in the 1790s, the postrevolutionary surge of westward migration across Georgia's fertile cotton belt was already under way. The landscape Whaley found after a series of cessions by the Creek nation between 1804 and 1821 still carried the marks of centuries of Indian occupation that Bartram had observed a generation earlier. As Whaley entered his teens, however, the sublime forests were already being cleared and planted in cotton. Indeed, following its organization in 1808, Pulaski County became part of a larger borderland where the rich cotton lands of Georgia's black belt gave way to the poorer sandy soils of the wiregrass region. Whaley lived on the edge of this commercial world until the final years of his life. Only then did he leave the Ocmulgee and move deeper into one of the wildest landscapes in the eastern United States.[2]

Muddy and sluggish, the Ocmulgee River rises in Georgia's upcountry and flows across its black belt, picking up volume and red silt before crossing the fall line at Macon. Near the town of Hawkinsville, approximately 70 river miles below Macon, the Ocmulgee leaves the humus-rich cotton lands and enters its lower section. For 133 river miles it cuts a winding channel through the wiregrass country before joining the Oconee River at a place called the Forks to form the Altamaha River. In Whaley's day, it took two days to travel overland from Hawkinsville to the Forks. It took as much as seven days to reach the Forks by steamboat from Savannah, running against the current up the Altamaha. After the arrival of steamboats on the river in the late 1820s, one of the plain folk described the Ocmulgee as "one of the smartest rivers for navigation in the southern states."[3]

Like any borderland, the ground where cotton belt met pine belt along the lower Ocmulgee formed a contested area that raised questions of regional identity and loyalty. After all, it was this transitional zone that separated, as one antebellum observer remarked, "the *black* labour from the *white* labour of the South." The longleaf pine belt's unique ecological system, with its peculiar flora and fauna, was responsible for its reputation as both a barren piney woods land in the opinion of commercial farmers and as a best poor man's country in the eyes of plain folk. But the region was also a mental construction of people living there, and its boundaries were largely set by their past experiences and emotional responses to the world around them. Plain folk saw their society as an expression of a country republican ideology that embraced Jeffersonian ideals of an economically independent yeomanry sharing common interests. They stereotypically regarded planters as aristocrats who dressed in store-bought finery, sent their children to academies, lived in painted mansions, and let their slaves do the work for them. In an increasingly commercial

Southern world, plain folk considered themselves marginalized within the thinly populated pine forest but understood that its free and open livestock range was the foundation of their self-sufficiency. From the woods they dealt with their growing involvement in the market economy and slavery on their own terms and to their own advantage. By 1860, however, the wiregrass country was virtually surrounded by plantations given over to the production of cotton and rice. Even within the forest, the boundaries between pineland and river bottoms were contested areas where negotiations between plain folk and planters took place over land use and slavery. This debate helped both define and unify plain folk, who saw their region threatened by the expanding plantation system. As one pinelander declared in 1861, it was the "piney woods against the world."[4]

Seemingly simple and static, the lower Ocmulgee was actually complex and dynamic. As John Whaley had recognized in the 1850s, economic and social forces were changing the region. Images of the piney woods as a homogenous region isolated from the Southern mainstream and populated by a monolithic and precapitalistic poor white yeomanry were themselves stereotypes, the inventions of abolitionists, writers of romantic fiction, and creators of travelogues. As Whaley doubtless understood, planters did not own all of the slaves and cotton farms. Plain folk entered the marketplace in growing numbers. In time, the lower Ocmulgee's landscape was transformed by nineteenth-century settlers into two clearly distinguishable patterns: piney white belts, where less than 20 percent of the people were enslaved, located in southeastern Pulaski County and in the backwoods of Coffee, Irwin, Telfair, and Wilcox Counties; and fertile black belts, where upward of 20 percent of the people were enslaved, situated in northern Pulaski County and down the river valley.[5]

Scattered across these landscapes were rural neighborhoods with populations and economies that varied depending on soil quality, crop specialization, the availability of labor, and access to markets. Black belt neighborhoods were more densely settled than those in white belts. Regardless of their location, neighborhoods—collections of households, churches, fields, mills, country stores, and woodlands—formed the foundation of local society. It was on this level that the plain folk collectively defined the characteristics that gave their communities identity and meaning. The county seat towns of Abbeville, Douglas, Hawkinsville, Jacksonville, and Irwinville were but wide places in the road and reflected the area's overwhelmingly rural nature. Not one person along the lower Ocmulgee lived in a locale of much more than three hundred people, the population of Hawkinsville, the area's major market town.[6]

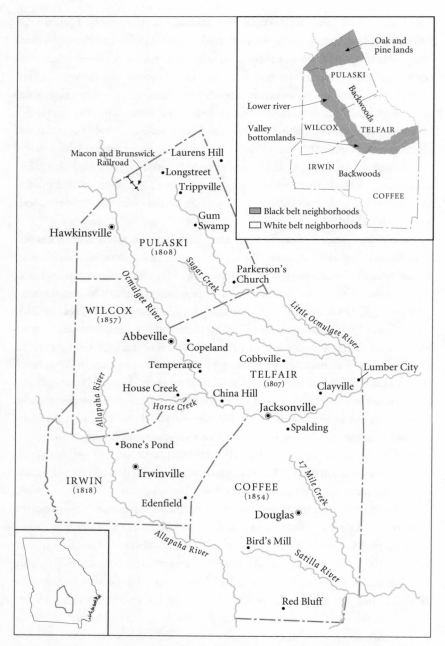

The lower Ocmulgee River region in 1860. Black belt neighborhoods were situated above Hawkinsville in northern Pulaski County and along the river flood plain until its confluence with the Oconee River. White belt neighborhoods were located in the more remote backwoods beyond the river valley.

There were few places in the antebellum South where country people were more predominant. Plain folk constituted the majority of white households in every neighborhood. Of the 2,090 white households along the lower river in 1859, plain folk accounted for nine out of ten. Even in a cotton-rich county like Pulaski, they represented eight out of ten white households. And despite its reputation as a black belt county, Pulaski alone accounted for 40 percent of the area's plain folk, the remaining 60 percent coming from the four "lower" counties of Coffee, Irwin, Telfair, and Wilcox. It was there, in a world where the longleaf pine shaded as much as 90 percent of the land, that slaveless plain folk and small masters raised livestock and farmed "small pieces of ground . . . by their own labor."[7]

A majority of plain folk—households working less than 150 acres and owning fewer than ten slaves—lived in backwoods neighborhoods. The white belt they formed accounted for well over one-half of the lower Ocmulgee's land area. The backwoods began just beyond the river valley's hardwoods and ran deep into the virgin pine forests of antebellum Coffee, Irwin, Pulaski, Telfair, and Wilcox Counties. Despite its overall size, the backwoods—unlike the black belt neighborhoods—was sparsely populated, often with less than five inhabitants per square mile. One could journey through the woods for ten miles and not pass a farm. A traveler recalled that in 1858 "only at long intervals did rude pine log huts present themselves . . . in all this vast solitude, save Nature clothed in the majesty of her glory." Planters did not find nature's "glory" impressive and avoided the pine barrens, leaving a landscape of virgin woodlands stretching "far beyond the range of human vision."[8]

The vast majority of the backwoods' plain folk were native-born Georgians. Ninety-seven percent of Coffee County's inhabitants—black and white —were born in state. Although land ownership was widespread in the pine belt, the actual amount of cultivated land was small. Fifty percent of the farms in Irwin, Telfair, and Wilcox Counties contained less than fifty improved acres. At the Bird's Mill neighborhood in Coffee County, two-thirds of the households worked fifty acres or less, about average for the county.[9]

Unlike reclusive John Whaley, most plain folk remained along the lower Ocmulgee and coexisted with planters and slaves in an increasingly commercial economy. Lucius Williams was typical of the slaveless plain folk who worked small farms with white family labor. In 1860 he lived with his wife Catherine Garrison Williams and son William in a white belt neighborhood where planters were exceptions. Their household depended on sixty acres of land and a two-horse farm to grow crops. In 1859 they harvested two hundred bushels of corn as well as sweet potatoes, beans, and peas. With about seventy cows, hogs, and sheep in the woods, they made good use of the open range.[10]

Without grown children or slaves to supplement the household's labor, Catherine joined Lucius in the fields year-round. Although elite Southern women felt that field work lowered white females to the level of slaves, plain folk households needed every available worker to help set out corn and cane, dig and bank sweet potatoes, hoe and pick cotton, and tend vegetable patches and livestock. Both husband and wife participated in the day-to-day management of the farm. Rather than compare such plain folk households to other groups of Southerners, a New Englander who spent months in the antebellum piney woods wrote that "generally they have but few if any slaves & live like N. E. farmers . . . by their own labor."[11]

When it came to devoting land and labor to crops, corn came first. Without fertilizer most farmers expected to raise about 10 bushels per acre on piney woods land, but the use of home fertilizers such as cow manure doubled the yield in a very good year. Farmers fortunate enough to own bottomland could make up to 50 bushels per acre. Since corn and cotton were planted at about the same time and competed with each other for labor, plain folk and planters made clear choices between planting corn for home consumption and cotton for market. On average, each Southerner consumed about 13 bushels of corn per year, corn bread, grits, hoecake, and hominy being common table fare. By 1860 the lower Ocmulgee's farms produced an average of 35 bushels per person, a level above the state average of 29 bushels but far behind those of the Upper South and the Midwest. Corn fodder—blades stripped from the stalk and cured in the sun—was an important source of food for cattle and a local substitute for hay. A corn crop of 100 bushels easily produced 1,000 pounds of fodder, which in times of hay shortage was bartered and sold on the local market for five to six dollars per stack in the mid-1850s.[12]

The lower counties' reputation as a region where corn replaced cotton was misleading. Many backwoods neighborhoods were more diversified than they first appeared. Although corn was the most conspicuous white belt crop, the plain folk's ability to meet and surpass levels of self-sufficiency in this critical foodstuff was limited. The amount of cleared land barely met their needs. Unlike the more fertile black belt, backwoods farmers worked marginal land with family labor, tilling soil described as "very poor in all the elements of fertility." In addition to poor land, the households of slaveless plain folk had limited access to farm labor, usually within their own kinship or communal neighborhood networks. As a result, in 1859 levels of corn production for Telfair County barely surpassed self-sufficiency and fell short in Wilcox, whereas upriver in Pulaski County, fertile land and slave labor yielded a surplus of corn. Corn country's prized crop was often in short supply in the lower counties, particularly if households devoted scarce labor to cotton.[13]

In an effort to diversify and produce something worth exchanging on the local market, plain folk turned to other crops. Sugarcane, because it could be converted into cane syrup and raw sugar, was popular. Although grown in small patches throughout the region, it was more abundant in the lower counties. As one antebellum traveler reported of southern Georgia: "Every one here raises cane for sugar enough for his own use only." But it was cane syrup, not raw sugar, that offered the greatest potential for trade. Cane was planted in the spring at about the same time as corn, rice, and cotton. Most farmers expected to get slightly over 100 gallons of cane syrup per acre. Telfair was the banner syrup county, producing over 11,000 gallons in 1859. Many lower Ocmulgee planters rationed syrup to their slaves. James Lathrop's slave Martha recalled cane syrup being rationed on his Pulaski County plantation along with "greens, meat, 'taters an' cornbread." But the black belt neighborhoods, while producing a surplus of corn, did not meet adequate levels of syrup production. Thus, plantations became markets for plain folk syrup just as they sometimes became the source of corn for needy yeoman households in times of grain shortages. The center of this exchange was the market town of Hawkinsville, where syrup was sold in stores by the gallon and the barrel.[14]

Although most often associated with tidewater plantations and slave labor, rice joined the plain folk's crop mix. Taken together, the white belt lower counties collectively formed a significant pocket of interior production. Together, households there grew as much as 60,000 to 70,000 pounds of rice per year in the 1850s, whereas Pulaski's cotton farmers grew less than 2,500 pounds in 1859. In some households, rice was a secondary grain crop after corn. Most plain folk practiced a form of dry cultivation and planted rice between rows of corn. Greenleaf Dearborn observed this method of rice growing in wiregrass Georgia in 1836: "Here they sew it on high land," he wrote, "& it looks more like oats than any other grain and grows about as high."[15]

At Irwinville and Bird's Mill, neighborhoods situated over twenty miles from the river, 28 and 41 percent of the households, respectively, grew rice, proportions even higher than those in river valley communities. Bird's Mill in southern Coffee County, whose proportion of slaveholding was among the smallest of all backwoods communities, boasted a higher proportion of rice growers than any other neighborhood. Several nonslaveholding plain folk grew over 1,000 pounds of rice, a significant amount when William Manning's plantation with one hundred slaves to work and feed produced 3,360 pounds in 1859. Among plain folk, adding rice to the crop mix was a matter of dietary preference, rice replacing on the tables of yeoman households in the lower counties the wheat often grown by farmers upriver. But some plain folk sold or bartered portions of their small crops to planters as slave rations or traded rice for goods at country stores such as McRae and McMillan, where rice was sold in amounts as small as five pounds and for a little over six cents per pound. Like cane syrup, rice was as good as money in the pockets of plain folk.[16]

Plain folk households that included young male farm laborers under their roofs were able to exceed levels of self-sufficiency and enter the market economy on a more ambitious scale. Archibald Campbell, for example, cultivated a 100-acre farm with the help of four sons in a white belt neighborhood of Telfair County. Together they grew 500 bushels of corn and tended 350 cows, hogs, and sheep. They also picked three bales of cotton in 1859.

The extent of cotton growing among plain folk households is surprising given the wiregrass region's reputation as corn country. Perhaps more than any other single endeavor, cotton production was an indication of the market economy's penetration into the heart of the forest. In Telfair County during the 1850s the cotton crop increased by almost 50 percent, only slightly less than the 51 percent rate recorded upriver in more fertile Pulaski County. Doubtless the expanding operations of small and large planters accounted for much of the increase in Telfair, but plain folk along the lower river continued to enter the market as well. Although the vast majority of these yeomen, like those in other parts of the South, traditionally placed food production for home consumption first, cotton's growing presence in the wiregrass was at odds with such concepts of household self-sufficiency but in step with growing plain folk involvement with the cotton market in Georgia's plantation belt.[17]

Indeed, by the 1850s many plain folk households in white belt settlements could not leave the fleecy crop alone. While slave labor and cotton growing was heavily concentrated in Wilcox County's river bottom neighborhoods of Abbeville, Cedar Creek, and House Creek, cotton growing spilled beyond the bottomlands into the piney woods. In the Gibbs and Snow Hill settlements, for example, almost 60 percent of the households grew one or two bales of cotton, a proportion not far behind the level of cotton production in parts of Augusta's hinterland. Almost all of the backwoods Wilcox yeomen worked fewer than one hundred acres, many fewer than seventy-five. Still, cotton growing made inroads in a county that did not quite meet levels of self-sufficiency in corn in 1859. Upriver in the Gum Swamp neighborhood of eastern Pulaski County, cotton growing was even more pervasive. There, 85 percent of the households grew some cotton and almost 40 percent cultivated one or two bales, which matched the production levels of small growers in black belt Glascock County. With only 15 percent of the Gum Swamp's households led by slaveowners, it is not surprising that 82 percent of the growers were nonslaveholding farmers. Among these small producers, a bale or two beyond the requirements of the household were grown and sold or bartered in Hawkinsville, where farmers picked up coffee, sugar, and other items.[18]

Although plain folk grew relatively small amounts of cotton compared to planters, their one or two bale crops should not necessarily be viewed as a highly cautious entry into the market economy. The wonder is that over 50 percent of the households in some neighborhoods grew cotton in any quantity above home needs, given the constraints of poor soil, small farms, and scarce labor. River valley planters enjoyed tremendous advantages over plain folk when it came to cotton growing. It started with the soil. In 1858 Wilcox County planter Norman McDuffie boasted in a letter to the *Pulaski Times* that 1,400 pounds of seed cotton was picked from a single acre on his plantation and "if not injured by storm or otherwise, I shall pick from the same acre, at least 1,500 pounds more." Although he suggested that McDuffie might be exaggerating, the editor noted that this was the best cotton yield reported in many years. McDuffie's output, however much he may have stretched the truth, pointed up the tremendous inequities of fertile land distribution and the shaping of the social geography that resulted. The mucky bottomlands routinely yielded from 800 to 1,000 pounds of seed cotton when fresh and continued to produce similar amounts for several years.[19]

The sandy soils of the piney uplands, on the other hand, yielded 500 pounds of seed cotton per acre when new ground, but dropped to only 100 pounds of lint cotton after a few years. Consequently, it took plain folk four acres to produce a single 400-pound bale of ginned cotton, at least twice as much land as needed along the river. Yeomen thus faced tough choices if they were determined to grow cotton at any level above that required to meet household needs. Unlike planters such as Norman McDuffie, most plain folk lacked the slave labor needed to both increase cotton output and maintain food crop production. Moreover, to get the highest cotton yield for their labor, and therefore the highest cash return, the cotton land needed to be their most fertile. From the standpoint of household self-sufficiency, it made no

A backwoods cabin with a mud and stick chimney typical
of those inhabited by plain folk. (Olmsted, *A Journey in the
Seaboard Slave States*, 385; courtesy of Audio-Visual Archives,
Special Collections and Archives, University of Kentucky
Libraries)

sense for backwoods yeomen such as W. T. Faircloth to grow two bales while cultivating only forty-five acres of land and raising two hundred bushels of corn. Too much of his land—possibly as much as eight acres—was going to cotton. Faircloth was not alone. In the House Creek neighborhood, where less than 10 percent of white households were slaveholders, plain folk tossed caution to the wind and increasingly turned to cotton.[20]

A yeoman's status could rise head and shoulders above that of his neighbors when he combined slaveholding with cotton farming. By doing so, he increased his household level of cotton production as well as his household wealth. The benefits of adding slave labor to white family labor was not lost on ambitious plain folk. Alfred Burnham, for example, was one of the wealthiest farmers in the Copeland neighborhood of Telfair County. With the help of four sons and the adults among his nine slaves, Burnham's three hundred improved acres produced twelve bales of cotton and two thousand bushels of corn in 1859. At age fifty-two, he was a solid member of a prosperous neighborhood of plain folk and small planters, almost all involved to varying degrees in cotton growing. Burnham's house may have remained unpainted, but, as his slave Easter Reed later described it, it was "a nice big one." Only the small planters in his neighborhood could boast farms of greater cash value than Burnham's.[21]

Alfred Burnham was not alone. He belonged to a diverse group of plain folk owning nine slaves or less; half of them owned fewer than five. They accounted for 70 percent of all slaveholders and 20 percent of all white households in 1860. Like Burnham, about one-half of all plain folk masters lived in the lower counties, while the remainder resided in Pulaski. Yeoman slaveholders represented a group that slaveless plain folk could realistically aspire to join. The odds were long—about twenty to one—that a local white head of household could become a planter. The odds were much better—about five to one—that that person could become a yeoman slaveholder. Unassuming and hardworking, most yeoman masters labored alongside their slaves and the white farmworkers in their families. A relative of yeoman master Abram Hargraves recalled that the Coffee County farmer "made a good plow hand in the field, as long as he lived." Hargraves was remembered as thrifty and unpretentious. "He wore a homespun shirt, carried a shot bag over his shoulders, a powder horn around his waist, and did not, in any way, have the appearance of being a well-to-do farmer." Despite his homespun look, however, the two slave cabins in his yard signaled to passersby that he was a farmer on the make.[22]

Unlike plain folk masters in black belt neighborhoods such as Copeland, those in the piney woods rarely claimed planters as neighbors. Consequently, there were fewer slaves in the backwoods and those who lived there belonged to plain folk. The proportion of slaveholding households in the white belts was as low as the 6 percent at Bird's Mill. Gum Swamp's 15 percent, which was close to the average, was one-half the proportion of slaveholding households found along the river valley's narrow band of black belt neighborhoods. Such enslaved African Americans were mostly women and children isolated from the larger slave communities. When slaves belonging to the estate of J. C. Young were put on the auction block in Irwin County in 1852, for instance, seven women and children were sold to six bidders, mostly plain folk. Slave women cost less than men and were thus more affordable to plain folk, who could expect a slave woman's reproductive labor to pay for their investment in the future.[23]

Because of their large numbers, kinship ties, and position in the social hierarchy, slaveowning plain folk were an important part of the economic and social fabric. They formed a middle ground between slaveless yeoman farmers and the planters situated on the white belts' edges. Together, yeoman masters and planters accounted for 30 percent of all white households. Marriages between slaveless plain folk, small masters, and planter families unified communities spatially and ideologically and lessened the social gap between the groups. Although 70 percent of white households did not own slaves, it was not uncommon for a family member to claim a slaveholder as blood kin or a relative through marriage. In the 1850s John Vickers, the son of slaveholder Rebecca Vickers, married the daughter of a small planter and John's brother Henry wed the daughter of a slaveless yeoman. By marrying up and down the social hierarchy, plain folk masters expanded the ideological foundation of racial slavery by introducing it into the households of nonslaveholders.[24]

Despite the gaggle of slaveless yeomen, small masters, and planters who often celebrated the Fourth of July together or met on militia grounds, plain folk and planters knew where the important boundaries were and their implications for the social geography. In his will, planter John Daniel not only stipulated that some of his land was "on the river," an important distinction, but he also described "a drain or hollow which divides the pine land and oak land adjoining." Daniel's hollow formed a boundary between black and white belt lands. By 1860 small planters and larger planters—owning ten to nineteen and over twenty slaves, respectively—were heads of 182 white households or 9 percent of the total. Just over 70 percent of these planters lived in black belt neighborhoods in Pulaski County or along the fertile river bottomlands between Hawkinsville and Lumber City, where the competition for land drove up prices. Writing from the Copeland neighborhood in 1843, yeoman farmer John Malloy sought a $600 loan from his brother in North Carolina to pay off his debt for land, noting that his soil was "as rich as ever a crow flew over."[25]

Although planters were a distinct minority in an overwhelming plain folk majority, their power and influence far outweighed their numbers. Their dominion over the best land and slave labor marked them as people to be reckoned with economically, politically, and socially. The unmistakable signs of their commercial endeavors were evident in the black belts, which were "very thick settled" by the early 1840s. Cotton fields stretched to the horizon, head-high rail fences surrounded crops, and the price of everything— especially land and slaves—was high. But the planters' investments paid off. The value of Pulaski real estate in 1860 was worth more than the combined value of all land in the four lower counties. Forty-three percent of the lower river's approximately two thousand white families lived in Pulaski, a testimony to fertile land's power to attract settlers. By 1860 this area was on the southern frontier of Middle Georgia's cotton belt. It was this world that John Whaley left behind.[26]

Good cotton land was the key to building an estate worth handing down to the next generation. When Pulaski County planter Cornelius Bozeman was asked his opinion of the quality of a tract in 1830, he frankly told an acquaintance that the property was "worthless and quite barren and out of the way." What Bozeman meant was that the land was "worthless" for growing cotton and "out of the way" as far as access to steamboat landings was concerned. In other words, it was a plain folk landscape, which Bozeman discounted in favor of richer plantation land. Generally, the richest black belt land was in northern Pulaski County and along the lower river valley. The unifying geological feature of much of this area was an underlying formation of soft or "rotten" limestone that enriched the sandy loams. The soil, variously described as "yellow loam" or "mulatto" land, was underlaid by clay subsoil that kept moisture near the roots of cotton plants. Such choice land was quickly taken over by slaveholders. Only ten years after Pulaski's formation in 1808, its tax rolls revealed a heavy concentration of slaves in black belt neighborhoods such as Longstreet and their near absence in white belt settlements such as Gum Swamp.[27]

Seaborn Manning was one of the lower Ocmulgee's big planters. In 1860, when he was thirty-eight, his estate was valued at $35,000 in real and $80,000 in personal property, including 5,500 acres of land and a store in Hawkinsville.

Manning's fifty slaves worked 1,500 improved acres and produced 179 bales of cotton in 1859. At an average price of ten cents per pound, he grossed around $7,000 on a single cotton crop. Such wealth allowed Manning and his wife Harriette to acquire the ottoman, piano, ornamental fireplace dogs, china, and silver tableware that graced their home and the jewelry that adorned her. The cotton boom of the 1850s benefited planters living in black belt neighborhoods like Longstreet, situated beyond Manning's plantation. Longstreet had all the makings of a village, including an academy, churches, mills, and a new railroad depot, but its driving economic force was cotton. Ninety-seven percent of the neighborhood's households grew cotton; one in four of them belonged to a planter.[28]

Despite the presence of some of the county's biggest planters, seven out of ten of Longstreet's cotton growers were nonslaveholding plain folk. Settled in cheek by jowl among the planters, the majority of them worked farms of seventy-five or more improved acres, larger than those of backwoods plain folk. Like yeoman farmers in Georgia's upcountry, they found cotton growing an attractive way to build estates and increase household consumption. Members of their own family worked their fields. With the arrival of the Macon and Brunswick Railroad at John Coley's place on the eve of the Civil War, greater access to transportation provided plain folk with opportunities to expand the domestic economy beyond cotton, home manufactures, and livestock. The railroad's tracks were soon lined with crossties, firewood, and sawmill lumber bound for Macon.[29]

The Pulaski County pattern extended southward along a black belt of fertile land formed by the Ocmulgee River's floodplain. Its mixed hardwood bottomland was covered by a dark, mucky soil, the timeless accumulation of mast and silt deposited by annual freshets. By the early 1840s river valley cotton farmers and planters could "hear the steam Boats constantly running," according to one yeoman. Neighborhoods with names such as Copeland and Spalding grew up along the river, but like Longstreet they were not the exclusive communities of planters. In 1860 only about one-third of all planters lived in the four lower counties of Coffee, Irwin, Telfair, and Wilcox. Nevertheless, the extent to which planter wealth dominated the narrow black belt neighborhoods was evident in the Spalding neighborhood of Coffee County. Planters large and small accounted for about one-fourth of Spalding's households. The leading planter in the four lower counties was William Manning, whose 100 slaves and 9,500 acres at Spalding comprised an estate rivaled only by Longstreet planters.[30]

The Ocmulgee River and its tributary creeks united most of the region and gave planters and cotton farmers access to coastal markets. (Courtesy of Georgia Archives)

Spalding's big cotton growers, landlords, and slaveholders clustered on the best soil near William Fussell's country store. Manning and six other wealthy planters produced almost half of the county's 1859 cotton crop and owned over half of the cash value of Spalding's farms. They also owned 35 percent of the county's slaves. Because of the concentration of large plantations at Spalding, its white inhabitants formed only a small minority of the neighborhood's population. They were overwhelmingly outnumbered by enslaved African Americans, whose presence created a narrow black belt within a predominantly white belt region. Beyond the planters, the white families at Spalding ran the gamut of Southern society. Approximately two-thirds were nonslaveholding plain folk who cultivated fewer than fifty acres of land. They included William Catoe, a poor white who worked one acre of land and existed off small quantities of corn and sweet potatoes. Most, however, were yeoman farmers such as George Pridgen, who grew no cotton but small quantities of corn and sweet potatoes.[31]

Local planters and plain folk masters owning more than five slaves belonged to a privileged group of Georgians that possessed perhaps 90 percent of the state's wealth while representing only one-fifth of its white families. Their economic ambitions, social aspirations, and investments in fertile land and slaves linked them to a community of interest that included Georgia's wealthiest planters. Whether local masters owned one or one hundred slaves, they too shared mutual interests and obligations: they exercised the right to own human property, they controlled and exploited slave labor, they could divide slave families at will, and they would lose significant amounts of wealth if their slaves died, escaped, or were freed. Collectively, they formed an economic and social middle ground between Georgia's cotton belt planter elite and the plain folk of the wiregrass country.[32]

Plain folk and planters shared concerns beyond slaveholding and the privileged status it brought to all whites, slaveholders and nonslaveholders alike. In a rural world where as little as 5 to 15 percent of the landscape was improved by 1860, the open-range system of livestock herding formed a critical part of the domestic economy. As one Methodist circuit rider observed of the plain folk, "most of the people . . . lived by raising stock." The relative values of livestock, as opposed to real estate, reflected the growing importance of herding over farming as one traveled downriver into the white belt. In Pulaski County, the value of livestock in 1860 represented only about 26 percent of the real estate value of all farms, while in Wilcox County it increased to almost 40 percent and in Telfair County to almost 70 percent.[33]

Southern livestock herding often has been associated with squatters and small farmers who grazed cattle on public lands, but the local picture was more complex. Although cotton belt planters and plain folk were increasingly at odds over the passage of fence laws, the enormous tracts of wiregrass range "recognized as free pasturage for all stock" diminished the competition between commercial farmers and livestock herders for land. Indeed, both plain folk and planters were heavily involved in local livestock herding, and both groups had an interest in the open-range system. In Spalding, for example, planters Jonathan Ashley and William Manning were by far the leading cattlemen, each owning almost four times the value of livestock held by the largest yeoman stockman. Collectively, however, the neighborhood's few planters owned half of all its livestock. Further, although planters owned much of Spalding's real property and farmed the most fertile bottomland, as much as 90 percent of their holdings remained unfenced and unimproved pineland—a common grazing range open to all citizens. Thus planters, who paid taxes on most of the river valley and much of the adjoining wiregrass range, shouldered most of the tax cost of the open-range system in neighborhoods where black and white belts met.[34]

The open-range system did more than put butter, milk, and pork on the table. It created market opportunities for range products. Sheep grazed on wiregrass year-round and were rounded up in pens and sorted by their markings. They were clipped in late April and early May. Wool was one of the most important range products and one the white belt counties dominated. Telfair County's grazing lands alone produced three times the wool clipped in black belt Pulaski County in 1859. The market price for wool often exceeded that of cotton, and wool production was much less labor-intensive. Plain folk and planters closely followed wool prices, selling to local merchants or wool buyers at the most advantageous time or hauling it to market in Savannah. Wool production allowed plain folk to compete with planters on an equal footing in at least one sector of the local economy. At Spalding, yeoman-herder households clipped 50 percent of the neighborhood's wool. Country and county seat stores became the centers of local exchange. Martha McRae bought alpaca, gingham, raisins, shoes, and tobacco at the neighborhood store in 1854. She paid off her account by the credit she received for bringing in 192 pounds of wool valued at sixteen cents per pound. Thus, "buying more land and sheep" was the plain folk answer to the planters' cry for more cotton and slaves.[35]

It is not surprising, then, that protecting the open-range system was a mutual concern of local plain folk and planters, a type of self-interested cooperation that shaped a sense of community. When traditional rights of grazing and gleaning so critical to the plain folk's domestic economy were threatened, citizens turned to the General Assembly to protect a natural resource that supported the domestic economy. In 1859, for instance, livestock men in Irwin and Wilcox Counties lobbied successfully for a law taxing nonresident herders five cents per head more than residents to curtail overgrazing of the range by outsiders. Laws were also passed to regulate firing the woods and to prevent camp hunting by outsiders, who used range fires to drive game into killing zones. As one piece of protective legislation observed, nonresidents were "running stock wild, and often destroying whole herds, . . . hunting deer and other species of game." Such callous disregard for the range and the commonweal was addressed through favorable statutes by local state legislators, who were often livestock raisers themselves.[36]

The timber growing on the range was another interest that plain folk and planters shared. After crops were harvested and the weather cooled, yeoman farmers and slaves headed for the woods to chop timber and raft logs to river valley sawmills or to Darien. According to one lower river farmer, his household's "main source of revenue was from timber." A few men such as Wilcox County raft pilot Joseph Covington made a humble living from the timber trade. But "getting out scab timber" was an important, albeit seasonal, source of income for many households. Yeoman farmer Allen Powell and his sons herded cattle, raised subsistence crops, and picked a bale of cotton in 1859, but in their spare time they cut timber to make ends meet. Planters Oliver Cook, John Dorminy, Samuel Fuller, Norman McDuffie, and Thomas L. Willcox also participated in the timber trade, using slaves as woodchoppers and raft hands. The business in lumber was so important that plain folk and planters gathered at local conventions and lobbied the General Assembly for legislation favorable to the timber trade, including the "laying out" of timber roads to river landings. In 1853 well over one hundred lower Ocmulgee timber cutters met at Lumber City, where they combined a Fourth of July celebration with the selection of agents to represent them in their negotiations with timber buyers. Keeping timber roads open and rafting streams cleared, along with the apprehension of log thieves, were ongoing concerns for those involved in the trade, regardless of social standing. In Telfair County, timber thieves caused "great injury and damage" to private lands by furtively cutting down trees and floating them to sawmills. Acting in the interest of an absentee owner, one agent in 1856 implored Jacksonville attorney William Paine to prevent the theft of timber "*so far as possible . . .* or make it so that the parties pay for the timber."[37]

Unlike plain folk and planters, one large group of people did not go to the lower Ocmulgee region voluntarily. By 1860 enslaved African Americans comprised 27 percent of its population. They were among the first settlers to reach the Ocmulgee. Most, like their masters, were native-born Georgians; many came from farms and plantations in the eastern part of the state. George Walker was one white person who played a role in the Ocmulgee's settlement. In 1817, as a young man, he brought four slaves into Pulaski County for his father, George Walker Sr. An Irish-born cotton farmer, George Sr. had moved from Burke County to Longstreet ten years earlier and began to clear land for his plantation. His son's importation of William, Isaac, Isom, and Susan raised Walker's total number of slaves to forty, making him the fourth largest planter in a county rapidly becoming a part of the cotton South. At the end of the antebellum era slavery was a vibrant and growing institution on the cotton frontier, the number of slaves increasing by 50 percent in the 1850s.[38]

Many slaves reached the Ocmulgee in coffles, chained together and sold by slave "speculators" at Macon and other places. The process of obtaining new slave laborers for lower Ocmulgee farms and plantations continued throughout the antebellum period. Slave coffles and auctions were common sights. Balaam Sparrow, for example, was born in North Carolina during the mid-1820s and sold twice before he became the property of a Pulaski County master. He left behind his mother Lizzy and several siblings. Sparrow's experience exemplified the antebellum pattern of the sale of Upper South slaves to Lower South planters and cotton farmers, a long-distance relocation that shifted as many as one million slaves to the interior of the Deep South.[39]

Most slaves were field hands. On large plantations like Seaborn Manning's, work was highly regimented and organized around gang labor. More common in the black belt neighborhoods where over half of the lower river slaves lived on plantations, gang labor divided the field hands into several groups that plowed, hoed, and weeded depending on the need. Because only three local planters owned more than a hundred slaves and only a dozen more than fifty, overseers were not used as extensively as they were in central Georgia. Planters or their sons frequently supervised the work themselves or used male slaves as drivers. Longstreet planter Thomas Walker, for instance, used slave Sarah Nance's father as a "Nigger Driver" or "sub-foreman or straw boss." On small plantations and farms, the task system was more common among small masters such as Alfred Burnham. There was little or no division of slave labor where whites and blacks worked together. One of yeoman Madison Snell's slave women "worked in the fields and also cooked for her Master," combining domestic and field work. On such farms the degree of contact and familiarity between masters and slaves inevitably increased. Burnham's slaves ate in his kitchen after the white family had finished. His slave girl Easter recalled: "Ours came out of the same oven an' pots that the white fokes used."[40]

Slave field hands included both men and women, as was usually the case among slaveless plain folk. Arthur Colson recalled that his mother Molly was a common "plow hand," while his father Ephram Taylor plowed, hoed, and split fence rails on Jackson Coalson's plantation. The heavy work—clearing new land and grubbing out roots—fell on the shoulders of prime male field hands. Because of their greater capacity for heavy work, prime hands were ranked at the top of the slave labor force and cost more than most other unskilled slaves. In 1855 Thully Williamson's prime hands Alex, Jack, Lige, Sampson, and Shade—all between the ages of twenty-one and thirty-three—were valued between $900 and $1,100. The ability to bear children and do field work pushed up the price of slave women, just as their value dropped dramatically when they passed the childbearing years. In 1850 the appraisers of Wilson Mobley's estate in Irwin County valued fifty-five-year-old Sally at only $150, whereas eighteen-year-old Jane and her four-year-old daughter were together valued at $1,000. Indeed, on both plantations and yeoman farms, slave children, who seemed to be everywhere, represented the future labor force for planters and plain folk.[41]

The practice of purchasing a slave woman and depending on her reproductive capability to increase the value of an estate was evident on farms of plain folk like Wiley Whitley. His single slave cabin was home to a twenty-seven-year-old mulatto woman and five children between the ages of one and seven. With the female slave performing as both field hand and house servant, Whitley's white family would have to work for a decade or more to feed, clothe, and shelter her dependent children before the oldest among them could carry their weight in the fields. But as a corn farmer and livestock herder who planted no cotton in 1859, Whitley could afford to wait. As he grew older, so too would his slave children, and their value would increase. Whitley was not alone. In fact, from 33 to 43 percent of all slaves, depending on their master's county of residence, were under ten years of age in 1860. In Pulaski County, where most planters and slaveholding plain folk lived, children under the age of fourteen accounted for 45 percent of the enslaved population. Yeoman masters viewed these young slaves as integral parts of a future domestic economy, as well as chattel of value on the slave market. Increasing cotton growing and slave ownership among plain folk created common ties between black and white belt neighborhoods, joining kinship and the common range as factors that eased tension between these communities.[42]

Just as livestock herding and timber cutting produced common bonds between plain folk and planters, slavery created economic and social ties between the two groups, often to a surprising degree. In 1860 almost 40 percent of Pulaski County's white households owned at least one slave, and 45 percent owned between one and five. Such plain folk had a substantial economic interest in slavery's future since a few slaves often accounted for well over half the value of a farmer's property. This was certainly true of Pulaski farmer Isaac Johnson. At the time of his death in 1856, Johnson's slaves Joe, Fanny, Mose, and Sam were valued at $3,250 and represented almost 80 percent of his total wealth.[43]

The lower Ocmulgee's social structure found slave men, women, and children at the bottom of a society arranged around white concepts of race, class, and gender. Above the slaves were white plain folk ranging from poor whites to yeoman masters. At the top were planters, who, though constituting a powerful elite, were nevertheless a small minority of the population. Everyone had a place or social standing in the community. As Governor Joseph E. "Joe" Brown, who was widely respected along the lower river, put it: The "*white* class is the ruling class." Regardless of their obvious differences in wealth, the white majority was bound together by race. A slaveholder himself, Brown believed that the very existence of racial slavery made all whites, including plain folk, members of the ruling class. A white person's elevated position in society, he wrote, instilled "pride of character and a shared heritage which prepared him to participate in the political affairs of the State."[44]

Brown's use of "him" reflected the privileged role enjoyed by adult white males regardless of class. White men were husbands, fathers, property owners, voters, officeholders, soldiers, and slave patrollers. The household, the basic unit of domestic production and reproduction, was normally organized around white male landowners, who controlled the dependent women and children living on their place. Members of society—male and female, slave and free—found their social station largely defined by the status of the male head of household. The control of households by white men was patterned after and reinforced by religious beliefs. There was biblical justification for male "authority" over the dependent women, children, and slaves living on their property. God, who in turn chose men to govern His earthly household, governed man. As ministers of the Pulaski Primitive Baptist Association noted in 1847 regarding white male authority, God "gave to each their respective charges saying occupy till I come." This privileged position brought with it responsibilities. A white man was "accountable for his [household] government or stewardship to God." In exchange for the obedience of women, children, and slaves, white men provided the basic necessities of life, including protection from want and physical harm. Honorable white men considered this relationship to be private in nature, with little or no interference in their rule of "their respective charges" by other people or government.[45]

As wives, mothers, daughters, and sisters, white women also had well-defined roles in society, ones that normally subordinated them to men. Many women found these roles delineated by religious beliefs. White women were to be dutiful and obedient helpers to the male governors of their daily lives. Primitive Baptists, who constituted a major community of faith in the backwoods, believed that the "sisters" were critical to the success of male "heads of families." Women were cautioned not to "usurp authority over man" but were encouraged to use "chaste conversation coupled with love" to support their men in household governance. Much "depends on you," a group of church elders declared to women, "for you can do more for their encouragement in the discharge of their duties than any other earthly instrument."[46]

Women literally were the instruments of childbirth, a key to economic independence among the slaveless plain folk majority. A woman's reproductive capacity was critical. More children meant more farm laborers. At seventy-seven, Robert Jones of Telfair County was too old to do much work himself. But a younger wife gave birth to four males in six years; in 1860 all of them were between the ages of fifteen and twenty, and all were described by the census taker as "farmer" or "laborer." For nonslaveholders like Jones, children were the means to household self-sufficiency and comfort in their old age. With limited opportunities for personal or economic advancement, most farmwomen took pride in their household management and their children, turning inwardly to domesticity for self-definition as men turned outwardly toward the marketplace and the political arena. Within their humble sphere, women were regarded as exemplars of modesty and virtue.[47]

Some women, however, were masters of slaves, a status that gave them a vested interest in the peculiar institution. Sixteen percent of Telfair County's planters were women, as were almost 20 percent of its small planters and 15 percent of its plain folk. Many women slaveholders were widows. Sarah Willcox, the wife of influential Telfair planter-politician Mark Willcox, came into

A common log cabin of the type inhabited by poor whites and slaves. (Hall, *Forty Etchings*, plate xxii; courtesy of Audio-Visual Archives, Special Collections and Archives, University of Kentucky Libraries)

possession of twenty slaves following his death in 1852. Married or widowed, such women were seldom fragile plantation belles. They were capable household managers who often took pride in their ability to oversee farmwork as well. In 1849, in a letter to her husband who was away in California, Charlotte Taylor wrote from Hawkinsville: "We shall commence planting the new ground next week. The negroes have conducted them selves very well and worked as well as I could expect them." Some slaveholders took special steps to ensure that women as well as men enjoyed the benefits of slave ownership. When Pulaski planter John Daniel died in 1830, he divided thirty-six slaves equally between his sons and daughters, making certain that daughter Mary, for instance, could expect the lifestyle of privilege to which she was accustomed. Mary became the owner of Caty, Silas, Clary, Caroline, and Henry "with the future increase of the females." In this manner, planters bequeathed the slave system they brought to the lower Ocmulgee to their children and grandchildren, a system that made white women in slaveholding households the beneficiaries of black bondage from cradle to grave.[48]

Despite the hierarchical nature of Southern society, the lives of country people—black and white, slave and free, rich and poor—were intermingled. Rural neighborhoods were distinguished by communalism, an interdependence of plain folk families to accomplish tasks that were beyond the means of individual households. The entire year was marked by such occasions as logrolling in winter, burning the woods in spring, sheep shearing in May, fodder pulling in August, and hog killing in December and January. These neighborhood rites engaged whites and blacks and were followed by eating, drinking, and dancing, the same activities that took place on prominent holidays like the Fourth of July and Christmas. Churches, however, were the most important social institutions beyond the family household. Such cooperation forged a sense of community among individualistic farmers and planters increasingly involved in a market economy.[49]

When the preacher had finished his sermon on a hot August evening in 1855, the backwoods Baptist congregation of Parkerson's Meeting House in Pulaski County stood ready to accept new members. The church's clerk recorded what transpired next: "After sermon by Brother Baker doors were opened for reception of members by experience. Came Sister Rebecca Wright and Sabra Cadwell, and were received; also came Abel T. Wright and was received by experience." During a three-day revival held just a month before, six more new brothers and sisters had been received into the church family. They were not alone. By 1860 about fifty log and frame church houses were scattered across the lower river landscape. To characterize this region as an evangelical society, however, would be an exaggeration. Church members probably accounted for no more than one-third of the adult white population. Moreover, these "good citizens" split into warring missionary and anti-missionary camps, a theological rift that reflected deeper economic and social divisions among the country people.[50]

Unlike the surrounding black belts where Episcopal and Presbyterian congregations were common, churches in the lower Ocmulgee were exclusively Baptist, Methodist, or Primitive Baptist in 1860. Although evangelical Baptist and Methodist churches are often associated with poor whites and slaves, the largest and wealthiest local congregations belonged to these faiths. According to one estimate, in the 1840s Primitive Baptists accounted for almost half of all churched people in wiregrass Georgia, compared to about a quarter each for Baptists and Methodists. These congregations often had fewer than fifty members. Yet they were the area's most inclusive social institutions, allowing both men and women, black and white, free and slave, poor and rich to walk through the open door of fellowship.[51]

Sabra Cadwell's family was typical of the households that gathered at white belt meetinghouses. Husband James and sons Martin and Thomas were farm laborers. Eight children fifteen years of age or younger lived with them. They were independent, hardworking corn and hog farmers who attempted to reach self-sufficiency using the white labor in their household. When Sabra's neighbor Rebecca Wright walked down the aisle to join the church followed by her husband Abel, a slaveholding farmer, the occasion reflected the significant role women played in evangelicalism.[52]

Indeed, by the mid-1850s women accounted for about 70 percent of Parkerson's Baptist members. Among Primitive Baptists, however, near–gender equality existed in some congregations. At New Hope Primitive Baptist Church in Wilcox County, women represented 51 percent of the membership in 1842, and at Young's Meeting House in Irwin County women accounted for 48 percent between 1836 and 1843. Though women often outnumbered men, white males ruled church life in the same manner in which they were the earthly governors of dependent women, children, and slaves in their households. Church elders were men charged with maintaining church discipline, thus finding in church governance the legitimization of their household authority.[53]

And just as women outnumbered men but found them ruling churches, so too did slaveless plain folk outnumber slaveowners but nonetheless repeatedly elected them to positions of congregational authority. This was true among

Primitive Baptist churches in both black and white belt neighborhoods. At Young's Meeting House, plain folk masters and small planters dominated the congregation. George, Jacob, and James Paulk, brothers in the familial and spiritual sense, served repeatedly as clerks and deacons, one taking up the mantle of leadership where the other left off. By 1860 George owned eight slaves, and Jacob and James were small planters. Members of their extended family intermarried extensively with plain folk and other slaveholders, as well as with the family of the Reverend Richard Tucker, a prominent Primitive Baptist leader. At New Hope Primitive Baptist Church, planter George Reid served as clerk almost constantly after 1842 and was ordained deacon in 1851.[54]

In wiregrass Georgia, Primitive Baptist congregations stood at the social center of their neighborhoods rather than at the margins, as was often the case of Primitives in plantation districts. As the dominant congregations, piney woods Primitive Baptists formed a major barrier to the efforts of evangelical black belt Baptists and Methodists to cooperatively transform antebellum society into a civil society by restraining self-serving individualism through such benevolent works as missions, Sunday schools, Masonic lodges, and temperance. Simply put, Primitive Baptists were highly individualistic and opposed benevolence. Calvinistic in outlook, they believed strongly in election, predestination, and people's inability to reform themselves. Unlike regular Baptists and Methodists, Primitive congregations such as the one at Young's Meeting House agreed in 1840 to "shut the doors against all preachers who are in favor of the institution of the day called benevolence."[55]

The Primitive Baptist faith was perfectly suited to white belt egalitarianism, localism, and self-sufficiency. The working farmers in Primitive Baptist congregations believed that each household was responsible for its dependents. "Good economy and industry are honorable traits of the Christian character," church elders reminded their charges in 1847. Indebtedness was frowned upon. In contrast to black belt Baptist and Methodist congregations where planter families filled some pews and the "ruffles and furbelows and feathers of fashionable ladies" were noticeable, plain folk in the backwoods were "nearly all dressed in homespun" and sat on "benches without backs." Comparatively few of their members were slaves. Their ministers were preacher-farmers who worked their own land and had no formal training. In fact, Primitives were suspicious of the better-educated evangelical clergy; "their preachers should not be such as are graduated in a theological seminary, which promote self-aggrandizement and the friendship of the world, which is enmity with God."[56]

By 1860 the Primitive Baptists were surrounded by black belt evangelicals who considered Primitive theology and practice outdated and useless. Simon Peter Richardson, a local Methodist circuit rider, maintained that Primitives "preached . . . a gospel that had no moral effect upon the lives of the people." In sharp contrast to the humble Primitive buildings, white frame Greek Revival churches such as Longstreet's Evergreen Baptist rose in plantation districts and down the river valley. Seated in their pews were mission-minded wealthy planters like George Walker III. His riches, which in 1860 included one hundred slaves, were greater than the combined wealth of all households that gathered in the backwoods church at Parkerson's.[57]

For Christian gentlemen such as Walker, slaveholding carried with it responsibility for the moral character of their human property. Writing to the *Christian Index* in 1855, "Observer" reminded planters and yeoman masters alike that slave ownership created a "multiplicity of . . . new relationships." Among those was the master's accountability to God for his physical treatment of the slaves he governed, as well as their spiritual development. Some slaveholders took this charge seriously. Planter James Lathrop sent his slaves in a two-horse wagon to Blue Spring Church, where they sat in the back of the room. "When th' preacher got through preachin' ter th' white fokes they'd leave an then he'd preach ter us," a black member of the congregation recalled. At Hawkinsville, domestic servants like Caroline Malloy occupied a "gallery especially built for the slaves and every Sunday found each place filled." The white preacher, another slave recollected, "baptized us just like he did the others." In some black belt congregations slaves outnumbered whites; at churches such as Evergreen Baptist the slaves in the gallery outnumbered all the plain folk at backwoods churches like Brushy Creek Primitive Baptist in Irwin County.[58]

Just as planters feared the bumptious irreverence and intemperance of plain folk at election time, yeomen were suspicious of the status of slaves in evangelical congregations. Primitives did not theologically object to slave membership—both Peggy and Tom joined Young's Meeting House in 1839. What worried them was the size of the African American congregations in black belt neighborhoods and the commitment to spiritual equality and salvation that evangelical leaders espoused starting in the 1830s. Since Primitive Baptist theology held that God's elect were numbered and chosen before the beginning of the earth, it considered the expansive nature of evangelicalism to be the theologically unsound workings of reform-minded meddlers hungry for "the friendship of the world."[59]

As long as evangelicalism remained in the cotton belt, local Primitive Baptists were less concerned with the message of deliverance and spiritual liberation that Baptists and Methodists brought to their black and white members. In 1843, however, wealthy lower river planters, including William Fussell and brothers Woodson and James L. Willcox, established a Methodist campground named in honor of Simon Peter Richardson, the circuit rider who questioned the legitimacy of Primitive Baptist theology. Richardson Methodist Episcopal Camp Ground was situated in the Spalding neighborhood, where it not only met the needs of the area's many slaves but also could attract plain folk from the adjoining white belt neighborhoods. It was a symbol of growing planter influence and expansive evangelism that threatened plain folk notions of social hierarchy and order. Writing in February 1861 of the need for missionaries in Georgia's piney woods, an evangelical minister noted that he was spending "most of my time in preaching to the destitute churches of lower Georgia . . . the most destitute region I know of."[60]

There were troubling signs that not all black belt masters were as concerned with their slaves' well-being as planters like Woodson and James Willcox. Among the "dreadful" consequences of slave mismanagement was inadequate supervision. Slaves with appetites beyond their weekly rations "will provide for themselves at the expense of a neighbor," warned "Observer," by stealing from nearby plantations and plain folk farms. Moreover, some slaves were left to their own devices on the Sabbath and congregated in large numbers, a specter that caused concern among plain folk accustomed to slaves in small numbers, and then mostly women and children. An incident in 1858 at Hawkinsville highlighted their concerns. The proprietor of a "floating grocery" sold a large quantity of "Professor Degrath's Electric Oil" to much of the "colored portion of the community." Gathered on the banks of the Ocmulgee River on Sunday, the slaves consumed the prescription, which quickly made "their locomotion exceedingly ungraceful." The grocer, who claimed to be a descendant of Virginian John Smith, was charged with selling liquor to slaves on Sunday and hauled into court. Remarkably, he was found not guilty by a jury convinced by an able defense attorney that there was reasonable doubt as to whether the bottles were filled with molasses or whiskey. Incredulous, the judge thanked the jury but warned that more verdicts like this one would "ruin the country." The itinerant peddler paid his lawyer and left town "under strong indications that Judge Lynch was about to open his tribunal." The incident revealed to plain folk a disturbing degree of agency among slaves, who not only earned money by raising crops in slave gardens or as skilled workers, but were free to gather and spend it on "red eye" so powerful that if an intoxicated man "were to fall into the water after drinking it, he would be dangerous food for the fish."[61]

Like increasing cotton production, slaveholding, and evangelicalism, railroad construction was another antebellum trend that threatened to make the wiregrass country more similar to the black belts surrounding it and in the process destabilize backwoods neighborhoods. Railroad construction pitted the interests of outsiders such as cotton planters and merchants against those of plain folk, who while increasingly involved in the market were determined to embrace it on their own terms. The construction of the Macon and Brunswick Railroad, which reached John Coley's farm on the eve of the Civil War, reflected local support for railroads by market-oriented citizens who saw the line as one of the building blocks of civil society. In 1857 a letter to the *Georgia Weekly Telegraph* noted: "There are many planters on your line of Road whose interest will be to aid in the construction of it, and as they are always alive to their interests, therefore, a liberal subscription may be expected from them." George Walker of Longstreet led this movement in eastern Pulaski County. He bought shares of the company's stock and joined its board of directors.[62]

To white belt plain folk, Walker, who owned almost $100,000 in land and slaves, embodied planter wealth, evangelicalism, large slaveholding, and greater market access that could undermine their neighborhoods. Among the Jacksonian-minded yeomanry, railroads were at best a mixed blessing and at worst a threat to economic independence and self-sufficiency. Like the yeomanry of Upcountry Georgia, many plain folk feared that railroads would chop up the countryside, kill livestock, start range fires, and give private corporations an unfair advantage over individual landowners. Moreover, white belt small farmers and livestock men were mindful that wherever railroads penetrated the forest, cotton farming, fence building, slaveholding, and timber cutting followed. Thus, railroads, with their power to construct civil society, also possessed the power to destabilize rangeland. As the value of real estate escalated, common ranges became fenced agricultural acreage, and railroad rights-of-way restricted the common rights of grazing and gleaning.[63]

The Macon and Brunwick Railroad was not the plain folk's first such experience. The idea of creating a route from the Atlantic to the Gulf of Mexico by building a canal or railroad between the Ocmulgee and Flint Rivers was floated by Thomas Spalding of Sapelo Island as early as 1827, when he received a charter "to cut a canal or construct a railroad of wood." Although little work was actually accomplished by Spalding, the General Assembly extended the Ocmulgee and Flint Railroad or Canal Company's charter throughout the antebellum period. Finally, under the direction of Abott Hall Brisbane, a South Carolina engineer, actual work on a horse-drawn wooden railway began in the early 1840s.[64]

Brisbane pulled together backers for the route to Albany, including $300,000 from "our slave-holding subscribers." But when the bottom dropped out of the cotton market in 1841 "the planters . . . ceased payment on railroad stock," Brisbane later complained. Desperate for laborers and with little working capital left, Brisbane, previously an engineer on the Western and Atlantic Railroad project, convinced unemployed Irish railroad workers there to "undertake with the company for stock" in lieu of wages. The Irish hands agreed, but only if Bishop England of the Roman Catholic Charleston Diocese, which included southern Georgia, paternalistically guaranteed "the value of the stock and validity of the Company." England gave his blessing to the project "on the condition that a white man should be provided, with his free labour, for every black man who should be furnished by his master in place of the installments which he owed on his stock." Thus, a railroad project funded by black belt planters, blessed by a Catholic bishop, and characterized by a racially mixed workforce began to cut a pathway through the piney woods.[65]

For two years Brisbane pushed the line through the forest "in handsome style" using one hundred Irishmen and one hundred enslaved African Americans. Soon he and the Irish workers announced that they planned "to locate ourselves for life" along the railway in a colonization scheme. Meanwhile, a rumor circulated among the white workers, one Brisbane credited to a competing railroad plotting to buy out the project "for a song," that the Irishmen would lose everything in an impending sale of the company. A "general row" among the disillusioned Irish workers followed, all work was suspended, and the railroad failed. In a report written in 1849 Brisbane blamed external forces for the railroad's failure, including low cotton prices, the withdrawal of planter support, and the enmity of Savannah, which feared that the line would drain away interior farm and plantation produce to the Gulf of Mexico. Only in passing did he admit that plain folk attitudes toward the railroad played a role in its failure, noting that the "great majority despise the idea of having settlers encroach upon them."[66]

Brisbane's project threatened plain folk notions of a moral economy in several ways, including their views on private property, localist identity, race, and social order. The Ocmulgee and Flint Railroad was granted an exclusive "right or privilege" to railroad or canal building within twenty-five miles above or below the railway line, opening up right-of-way controversies that plagued the company. Disputes between landowners and the railroad over the value of land "necessary for constructing and completing the said railroad or canal" resulted in an appraisal that was subject to appeal but ultimately had to be accepted by the property owners, most of them plain folk. Refusal to sell land to the railroad was not an option. For plain folk accustomed to their own ideas of dominion over their estates, such powers of corporate eminent domain were alien and threatening. Brisbane, ever the promoter, believed that the "sectional jealousy of the American States is beginning to exhibit itself on the score of comparative wealth" and that the South's commercial interests would be compelled by "jealousy" to "spare no expense to eclipse" the North in the race for wealth. Dixie's chance of success in this race "turns on the raw staple of cotton." The Ocmulgee and Flint Railroad was one way to efficiently move cotton to the coast and realize the planting elite's vision of the antebellum South.[67]

But there were limits to what the plain folk were willing to sacrifice in the name of "sectional jealousy." Although they participated more and more in cotton growing and slaveholding, small farmers in the white belt were unwilling to jeopardize their self-sufficiency and the stability of their neighborhoods for the economic interests of planters. In other words, they were unwilling to abandon their identity as plain folk and be subsumed by a larger cotton South. Moreover, racism and nativism joined their distrust of large planters, corporations, and the people who owned them. Irwin County was among the whitest and poorest of the white belt's counties. The one hundred or so adult male slaves employed by the railroad were equivalent to almost 40 percent of the county's entire slave population in 1840, a majority of whom were women and children. Such a large number of male field hands, many of them from outside the lower river region, seemed to imperil public safety and social control. The same could be said of the Irish Catholic workers, most of whom arrived in the United States during the 1830s and were not citizens. Virtually penniless, they worked for rations and shares in the railroad. White men, they nonetheless performed slave work. Such "Irish niggers" now announced plans to settle permanently along the railway. Intermarriage between the Irish men and local women was taking place as well, Brisbane reporting that "some five or six of our best young Irishmen" married locally. Further, as most of the Irish workers became naturalized citizens in 1841 and 1842, they gained the ballot, creating potential for a foreign-born Catholic voting bloc in a largely

Georgia-born Protestant population. When the railroad scheme failed, the Irish workers turned their anger and frustration on company officials in an action that could be described as a labor riot.[68]

Even before the railroad was completed, then, it destabilized the traditional white belt neighborhoods it crossed. Competition for land, deforestation, range fires, real estate speculation—all of these could be expected in the future, but the present was frightening enough for plain folk. The railroad's right of eminent domain, its foreign workers, its "labor riot," its potential to damage self-sufficiency and economic independence were enough to make "the great majority" of local whites "[throw] their weight in the scale against it." According to one account, the plain folk "were so much opposed to the road passing through their premises . . . [that] the laborers were met with sticks and staves . . . and dire threats of vengeance were made against them by the people." Such violence and warnings marked the degree to which plain folk were unwilling to accept expanding commercialism in the name of the plantation South at the expense of their own notions of economic liberty and the "good republic." Many were ready to embrace the market economy but on their own terms, growing cotton or some other marketable crop after meeting their household's self-sufficiency. Few were willing to hand over their rural neighborhoods—the source of their family's livelihood—to corporations owned by outsiders and operated for the benefit of black belt planters and merchants.[69]

Such was the lower river's economic and social landscape in 1860. Seventy percent of the white belt's inhabitants were nonslaveholding plain folk, the farmers and livestock herders whom Governor Joe Brown described as Georgia's "producing classes." As the antebellum era drew to a close, this white world was surrounded by a black belt devoted to cotton and rice production and dependent on slave labor. In the wiregrass country, whites outnumbered blacks three to one; along its borders enslaved African Americans formed black majorities. The cotton and slaveholding frontier continued to eat away at the white belt's borderlands, and railroad schemes such as Brisbane's and the Macon and Brunswick threatened to split it open. For people who abhorred being "encroached upon by settlement," plain folk found the late antebellum period one of economic change and growing anxiety in their own corner of an increasingly insecure South.[70]

Yet the plain folk had a hand in the growing commercialization. In wiregrass Georgia during the 1850s the average improved acreage and the number of slaves per farm increased, while the number of cotton bales per farm doubled. By 1860 civic-minded merchants and cotton planters had transformed Hawkinsville from two rows of dilapidated buildings into an enterprising interior cotton market with a railroad on the way. Planters were not the only people who understood that cotton and slavery were a means to wealth. Plain folk along the lower Ocmulgee were fully in step with their well-heeled neighbors. The antebellum landscape reflected an economy still in transition: from one composed of households and neighborhoods heavily involved in the market for cotton to those only marginally involved. In the process, plain folk made the lower river more like the surrounding black belts and blurred their own regional identity, but refused to surrender it. John Whaley saw it coming and left the area. The Indian frontier of his childhood had become the cotton frontier. Stereotypical descriptions of the lower river as a barren wasteland of poor white squatters and cow drovers were no longer accurate, if they ever were. But in 1860 the plain folk had not yet redefined themselves or their changing region within the larger South.[71]

n the first part of January lower river farmers usually broke new ground and prepared for the upcoming planting season. But as rain swept across Georgia on January 2, 1861, plain folk and planters left the fields to cast their ballot in the most important referendum in the state's history—the selection of delegates to the secession convention. Jacksonville lawyer and unionist William Paine argued that by holding the plebiscite secessionists were "precipitating the State into a revolution" and staunchly stood his ground. There were, however, approximately three thousand other men of voting age along the lower river who comprised about 27 percent of the white and 17 percent of the area's total population. The vast majority of them were plain folk. Those who bothered to vote were in a "predicament," according to Paine, for pulling Georgia out of the Union would leave the defenseless state vulnerable to invasion by the North. If plain folk votes were based purely on economic interests, as some secessionists feared, then the disunion movement in Georgia was doomed to failure.[1]

Although secessionists had no way of knowing it, by January 1861 piney woods Georgia had become a disunionist region. The ballots cast by lower river white men reflected a gradual shift in political identity in keeping with the region's economic transformation in the 1850s. Fifty-one percent of the voters supported secessionist delegates. In a part of the state where 70 percent of white households were led by non-slaveholders, plain folk did not, as secessionists feared, vote as a homogeneous block of unionists but weighed their choices and gave secessionists a slim majority. The arguments of influential secessionists such as Joseph E. "Joe" Brown and Howell Cobb convinced many plain folk that they must defend their honor and homes from Yankee insult and invasion and become part of the larger movement for Southern nationalism. William Paine and other local unionists now found themselves out of step with the majority opinion. Like its economy and society, the lower river's political identity was in the process of being redefined.[2]

Politics began at home. In many households the male head was the only person who voted. At Lumber City, blacksmith James Steele's family consisted of eight people, seven of whom were either female or sons under the age of twenty-one. Neither these individuals nor Steele's three slaves could vote, a privilege that enhanced his authority as well as that of all white male free-holders who were twenty-one or older. Such household settings constituted the most immediate forum for political expression. Fathers paternalistically watched over the political development of their sons, and party loyalty was often, but not always, shaped by the fathers' political leanings. Indeed, voting often took place in someone's house where the owner's party allegiance was well known. In 1845 Irwin County established election precincts at the homes of John Gibbs, Daniel Grantham Sr., Manassah Henderson, and Reuban Gay, as well as at William Pridgen's mill. Thus on election day these private homes became public polling places. In the spring of 1860 the county's inferior court ordered that both the "election precinct and law ground" for one of its militia districts "be moved to [the] house of Abraham P. Clements."[3]

In theory, plain folk and planters were political equals at election time. Each man had one vote. In practice, however, yeomen deferred to wealthier planters and slaveowners, the men who owned much of the open range and the gin houses yeomen used. Planters wore the mantle of political leadership. While politically deferring to wealthier and better-educated planters, plain folk expected to be treated as political equals and to be respected as honorable members of the community. In exchange for such political deference, planters were expected to safeguard plain folk interests on the state and national levels. It was a form of "consensual governance" in which the elite held power with the consent of plain folk, who believed that planters understood their needs and protected their interests, which at times were the same.[4]

Plain folk formed clear voting majorities in every county. Even in black belt Pulaski County, where seven out of ten local planters resided, slaveless plain folk accounted for about two-thirds of the white households. Planters, however, dominated Pulaski's political life. In the 1850s all of the county's state representatives except one were large or small planters. Of the justices of the inferior court, 60 percent were large or small planters, as were four of the five men elected sheriff during the decade. Even in white belt counties, masters of enslaved African Americans dominated political life. Although Irwin County counted fewer slaveowning households than any other county in the region, 85 percent of the men who served Irwin as state representatives and senators between 1830 and 1860 were either large planters, small planters, or small slaveholders.[5]

Although planters were repeatedly elected to the statehouse at Milledgeville, there were political leavings for small slaveholders and nonslaveholding plain folk at courthouses. This practice may have lessened political envy among the nonslaveholding yeomanry, who constituted between 80 and 90 percent of voters in the lower counties by 1860. County officeholding gave plain folk, including small masters, positions of authority and small salaries. Of the sheriffs elected in Irwin County during the late antebellum years, approximately 40 percent were yeoman masters owning three or fewer slaves. There were four slaveowners among the nine men chosen by their neighbors to serve as justices of the Coffee County Inferior Court in the late 1850s. Clearly, owning slaves was not a political liability even in the whitest backwoods neighborhoods.[6]

Indeed, there were unmistakable bonds between home, politics, and slavery that manifested themselves in ways beyond the election of masters to office in the white belt's whitest county. John Gibbs, Abraham Clements, Manassah Henderson, and William Pridgen—men whose homes and places of business were election precincts in Irwin County—were all small slaveholders possessing between one and five slaves. Thus, in a county where 90 percent of voting-aged white men were nonslaveholding plain folk, the majority of polling places were located on ground owned by slaveholders. On election day, a male ritual when voters exercised a right circumscribed by color and gender, nonslaveholders often cast ballots at homes where the head of household's authority included supervision of not only his white family members but also black slaves. A single slave cabin behind the yeoman master's house, as on Manassah Henderson's farm, was an ample reminder to plain folk that the political system and slavery were intertwined and had the blessing of local government.[7]

Moreover, the household-based political network linked slaveless yeoman families to those of more affluent officeholding planters. Intermarriage created powerful ties between families as well as classes, providing nonofficeholding small farmers with a sense of connectedness to wealthier officeholders, who in turn depended on kinship networks to form an effective political base of support. Such connections created powerful party loyalties that repeatedly returned the same person—or members of the same family—to office over extended periods. This was particularly true in countywide races for state representatives, where marriage alliances created pools of voters in different neighborhoods who united at election time to send their candidates to the state General Assembly.[8]

Household-based politics allowed women, although disfranchised, to play key roles at election time. At first glance Elijah Vickers, a yeoman farmer owning one slave in 1860, had little political clout beyond his single vote. But his mother, small planter Rebecca Vickers, was the sister of George Paulk, a slaveholder who represented Irwin County in the state senate from 1853 to 1856. She also was the sister-in-law of planter John Dorminy, the county's state representative in the 1840s and 1850s. A common denominator in this Dorminy-Paulk-Vickers political network was Rebecca, whose politically active brother and brother-in-law were linked to her sons through blood ties and marriage. The same family connections resulted in the election of her oldest son John as a justice of the Coffee County Inferior Court. Thus, women were not voiceless in a household- and neighborhood-based political culture. They were key elements in successful political barbecues and rallies, for office seekers were keenly aware that their attendance attracted impressionable young male voters and mixed politics with courting. Along with religious revivals and militia musters, such political events drew the largest crowds on the neighborhood level.[9]

If politics began at home, then political deference began in the neighborhood. Before the emergence of dominant national political parties later in the century, social gatherings and political meetings offered the best opportunities for men to take the measure of their neighbors and decide who was worthy of deference. Political office and slave ownership tended to run in the same families regardless of whether politicians were from black or white belt neighborhoods. The Willcoxes dominated political life in the traditionally Democratic Copeland neighborhood in much the same way that the Friers and Mannings did in the Whiggish Spalding neighborhood. Militia district lines and settlement patterns often determined neighborhood boundaries.

A rural Georgia patriarch and his sons. Such men often
influenced the political leanings of their households. (Hall,
*Forty Etchings*, plate xxvii; courtesy of Audio-Visual Archives,
Special Collections and Archives, University of Kentucky
Libraries)

For example, Copeland was part of the 339th Militia District, which extended from the river into the piney backwoods, but the neighborhood's center of population and wealth, as well as its churches, stores, and mills, was situated along the black belt river road, where the Willcox family controlled social and political life.[10]

Political traditions were reinforced on the neighborhood level by a prevailing sense of localism, a feeling of devotion to neighborhood—the place where family life, economic activity, and political discussion unfolded. In all spheres of activity, those taking place closest to home were most important. Politics was no exception. Justices of the inferior court, commissioners of slave patrols and roads, and justices of the peace all were elected or appointed locally, often on the militia district level. The militia grounds became the stage for political ritual and proved effective training camps for men with political ambition. During the Seminole campaigns of the 1830s, militia companies met regularly, elected officers, and placed troops in the field. At local churchyards and other public grounds, men from all walks of life—artisans, laborers, yeomen, and planters—participated in militia drills. Because fellow militiamen elected officers from the ranks, the elections were rehearsals for political campaigns and militia and civil officeholders often became one and the same. At Hawkinsville on May 30, 1836, forty-one men "came forward and voted" for "a Captain and other Commissioned and non Commissioned" officers. William Whitfield was elected first lieutenant, gathering more votes than any other officer candidate. Already a successful politician, Whitfield won a seat on the Pulaski County Inferior Court six weeks before the militia election and was destined for a seat in the General Assembly later that year.[11]

Militia elections were used to forge alliances, test political strategies, and smoke out the opposition. In 1845 Irwin and Telfair Counties held an election to choose a colonel for the militia regiment. Whig politician William Paine charged that the entire affair was tarred with chicanery and pointed a finger at planter Mark Willcox, a Democrat. The law required that notices of the militia election be posted by the captain of each militia district; voting was to take place at Jacksonville and Irwinville. But as Paine advised Governor George W. Crawford, this "was *not* complied with and at *least* two thirds of this county knew nothing of such election and I suspect half of Irwin." With most of the militiamen in lower Telfair and Irwin Counties left in the dark, Willcox proceeded "with his usual officiousness" to hold the election in "the upper district," which included the Copeland and Temperance neighborhoods where Willcox and the Democrats were virtually unbeatable. "I know not that he will have the presumptuosness [sic] to forward the returns of said election to your Excellency," Paine wrote in disgust, "yet he may do so and try to palm them off." To Paine, the election was an example of how a powerful local politician could derail the democratic process. As a result, militia officers had been "thrust upon" the men in a rigged election when there were at least three "gentlemen" whom the rank and file would have been pleased to elect.[12]

Along the lower river there was no better illustration of household- and neighborhood-based political power and plain folk deference than the Willcox family. The foundation for this influential kinship network was laid when John Willcox migrated from North Carolina to the lower Ocmulgee frontier and settled in the Temperance community. John's wife, Mary Lea Willcox, bore him fourteen children, eight of them sons who lived to adulthood. Six of them served in the state legislature. Democrats of the Jacksonian stripe, the Willcox family based its political power in part on wealth. Five of the sons became planters. Mark and Woodson were two of the leading slaveholders in Telfair County, the former setting up his household at Copeland and the latter near Jacksonville. By 1860 Woodson owned 42 slaves, while brothers Clark and John owned 22 and 23 respectively. Their brother James moved across the river to the Bowen's Mill neighborhood, where his slaves grew cotton and he ran a country store. He was described as "rich" and worth as much as $50,000 in 1859, although a critic warned creditors that he would "try to keep from paying if he can."[13]

The Willcox family was politically potent not only because of its wealth, but also because of its kinship connections and military reputation. John and Mary saw their numerous children marry the sons and daughters of prominent and politically active local planting families, thus bringing them into the fold as well. Mark married Sarah Ann Elizabeth Coffee, a daughter of General John Coffee, a neighboring planter and politician who represented Telfair County in the legislature and served three terms in the U.S. Congress. Two sons of John and Mary, as well as a daughter, wed children of nearby planter John Daniel, while three more sons married daughters of Thomas Swain, a prosperous small slaveholder and ferry operator at Jacksonville. With Mark settled at Copeland, brother Woodson near Jacksonville, and the remainder of their kin scattered along twenty miles of river between them, the family had a powerful political base that repeatedly returned its sons to the halls of government. The Willcox men had admirable military reputations to boot, a fact not lost on the plain folk. Masculinity mattered among the voters, and the Willcoxes were proven leaders. Mark fought in local skirmishes with the Creek

Indians and campaigned with his father-in-law, General Coffee, when the Seminole war spilled into Georgia during the 1830s. Moreover, the Willcoxes were not too proud to live in log houses, as did Mitchell Willcox, or marry the daughter of a small slaveholding widow, like John Coffee Willcox, who wed Elizabeth Swain of Jacksonville.[14]

Due partly to the influence of such black belt planting families as the Willcoxes, the lower Ocmulgee was an antebellum Democratic stronghold. As part of the "new" cotton frontier stretching beyond the Ocmulgee to the Flint, as opposed to the "old" lands east of the river, the lower counties formed a region where white majorities and backwoods farmers were dominant. They were solidly in the camp of John Clark, a politician who became governor in 1819 and owned land in Telfair County. Clark's faction represented the aspirations of piney woods farmers and nonslaveholders, as opposed to those of wealthier planters from the state's older black belt who formed the more aristocratic States' Rights or Troup faction. As a group, Clark's supporters were unionist in outlook and supported Andrew Jackson during the nullification crisis. In the 1820s and 1830s Irwin and Telfair returned over 75 percent of their ballots for the Clark faction's candidates. To plain folk seeking protection of their rights from infringement by Whig-style internal improvements and corporate privilege such as Brisbane's railroad, the Democrat's egalitarian ideology made sense. The Willcoxes might be planters, but as livestock men they understood the value of the open-range system and the customs of grazing and gleaning that supplemented plain folk domestic economy. From the mid-1830s to the end of the antebellum period Irwin, Pulaski, and Wilcox Counties never gave a majority to any but the Democratic Party in a presidential election.[15]

The vast majority of local Democrats were not black belt planters like the Willcoxes, but white belt farmers. William Brewer, who lived near Lumber City and owned one slave in 1860, was typical of the plain folk who voted Democratic. Brewer worked a forty-acre farm with his own hands, five dollars worth of farm implements, and a couple of horses. His livestock included two milk cows, fifty hogs, and fifty sheep. He grew enough corn to feed his wife and five children. Brewer depended more on the wool he sheared from his sheep for pocket money than on cotton. What linked the Willcoxes and their planter neighbors to Brewer and other yeomen was open-range livestock herding, slaveholding, and Jacksonian notions of egalitarianism, individual advancement, and the restriction of corporate privilege when it threatened such natural resources as the forest.[16]

The Democrats' hold on the lower Ocmulgee was also due to politically powerful Primitive Baptist congregations. Consisting almost entirely of plain folk, the Primitive memberships normally voted with such Jacksonian Democrats as the wealthy Willcoxes. Although they often remained publicly silent on political issues, the Primitives had an uncanny way of putting members of their churches into public office. Indeed, in Irwin County the question was often not whether a Primitive Baptist would be sent to the state legislature, but which congregation would claim the honor. In the 1840s and 1850s black belt New Hope and white belt Brushy Creek routinely sent one of their own to Milledgeville, including such prominent citizens as John Dorminy, George Paulk, George Reid, and Smith Turner. All of these men were slaveholders, and Dorminy and Reid were planters. While Union-minded planters like the Willcoxes reflected a spirit of nationalism along the lower river, the Primitive Baptist outlook demonstrated localism and traditionalism, although the two views were not mutually exclusive. Together, they posed a serious challenge to secessionist hopes to use evangelicalism to mobilize the yeomanry behind their cause.[17]

Church members had their own notions about the cults of honor, recreation, and conspicuous consumption associated with the South's social elite. Primitive Baptists considered gambling, horse racing, and fiddling, which were popular in elite circles, to be "vile practices." In a plain folk world, honor had less to do with individual status and more to do with family reputation. When the church met in conference to consider charges of unchristian conduct by members, shame was used to publicly punish the unrighteous and maintain social order. Church discipline at Brushy Creek during the 1850s and 1860s resulted in the excommunication of members for "drinking too much," using profane language, and joining a "Missionary church." The reputations of members were thus weighed by fellow believers and judgment rendered, reinforcing concepts of communal and familial rather than personal honor.[18]

Although Primitive Baptists rejected the evangelical promise of redemption, materialism, and worldliness often embraced by black belt planters, they did not renounce slavery. Indeed, Primitive Baptist leaders were often masters of slaves as well as masters of their households and congregations. And just as plain folk voters repeatedly elected these masters to political office, they frequently chose them as church officers as well, legitimizing their dual authoritarian roles in the religious and political culture of the backwoods. As strict constructionists of the Bible, Primitive Baptists understood that Christ did not abolish human bondage. In 1860 a church leader declared in the *Primitive*

*Baptist* that he had never known a member of the faith "who had any standing in the Church, or any character for orthodoxy, who was an abolitionist." Reflecting their distrust of formally trained evangelical clergy, one piney woods elder in 1861 blamed the secession crisis on "abolitionist priestcraft." Most Primitive Baptists were unionists first, "if it be indeed a Union of rights, interest, and honor," and secessionists only "as the last resort."[19]

Traditionally, Whigs formed the major threat to the Democratic coalition of black belt planters and backwoods plain folk and Primitives. Although the lower river was solidly Democratic, Whigs accounted for as much as 40 percent of its voters before sectionalism destroyed the party. Whigs were particularly strong in the black belt neighborhoods of Pulaski County as well as along the Ocmulgee's "big bend," although they rarely claimed a majority of the voters. Associated with high levels of commercial agriculture and slaveholding, Whigs usually came from more affluent and better-educated households. The largest planters tended to be conservative Whigs with more faith in their party's willingness to protect the status quo, including their own economic interests, than a Democratic Party of smaller masters and backwoods plain folk. In fact, Whigs harbored long-standing fears of Southern plain folk and their bumptious individualism and egalitarianism.[20]

Like Democrats, most voters were Whigs out of family loyalty and neighborhood tradition. Ironically, it was in Telfair County—home of the Democratic Willcox family—that the Whig threat was strongest, especially in the Spalding neighborhood. The difference between Democrats and Whigs, however, was one of degree rather than of kind. As the example of the Willcox family suggests, one could be a planter and slaveholder and still be elected by the plain folk. But it helped if you owned 20 to 40 slaves. If you were one of the few big planters and possessed more than 50 slaves, you were probably a Whig. William Manning, owning 100 slaves and a plantation that resembled a village, was a Whig, as were neighboring planters the Ashleys and Friers.[21]

Still, most Whigs like most Democrats were country farmers. As the aged Telfair County paterfamilias Jacob Fussell, some of them accumulated a life's estate that included slaves. Fussell, who owned nine slaves in 1860, was on the verge of becoming a small planter as he neared the end of his life. Virtually blind, he employed his slaves to tend livestock, grow food and a little cotton, and cut timber. Downriver at Jacksonville, Major Alexander Dopson, a small slaveholder, Mason, and Methodist churchgoer, joined local Whigs such as William Paine in opposing the Willcox-led Democrats. Although he boarded in the home of widow Rebecca Swain, whose daughters Susannah and Elizabeth married Woodson Willcox and John Coffee Willcox respectively, he may have had difficulty hiding his contempt for her Democratic in-laws. In the 1840s Paine accused their brother Mark Willcox of demagoguery by pandering to the plain folk's antirailroad prejudices. Although Mark voted for the Western and Atlantic Railroad bill, he represented himself as antirailroad to the yeomanry while tarring Whig George Crawford as a pawn of railroad corporations. "Among the ignorant he takes the ground that you are a strong railroad man, *which shows the man*," Paine declared.[22]

This was the political culture that opened the prosperous but tumultuous 1850s. Small and middling lower river planters, backwoods plain folk, and Primitive Baptists formed a political coalition that espoused democracy, unionism, and white supremacy. Rarely did the Whig minority threaten their political hold on the region. Because men thought of politics in terms of family and neighborhood rather than distant and impersonal national parties, politics was personal and tied to concepts of deference, honor, and masculinity. More dependent on local personalities than state and national leaders, the area's two-party system faced enormous challenges that soon destroyed the Whigs, left the Democrats without effective opposition, and altered the plain folk's political identity.[23]

As Northern censure of Southern society increased during the 1850s, the ideological gap between plain folk and planters narrowed internally, while the gap between plain folk and Yankees widened. Abolitionist attacks forced plain folk to align themselves with planters from the surrounding black belt or with distant Yankee reformers. Increasingly, an "us" versus "them" mentality took hold. Plain folk thought of themselves and others in terms of stereotypes. They saw themselves as children of the soil, dependent on all that grew on their small pieces of ground and all who worked it, slave and free. No matter how humble their station, farmland and rangeland were the sources of their identity, prosperity, and security. Yankees, they believed, were cut from a different cloth. Greedy and pushy, Northern merchants turned moneymaking and Puritan-style self-righteousness into a high art. Southerners were convinced that Yankee capitalists, the middlemen in the world trade for cotton, were taking advantage of them. Of course, not all Yankees were antagonistic toward the South. Local citizens knew from experience that Northerners who settled among them—men such as brothers James and Charles Lathrop from Indiana—married into local families, became slaveholders, and acquired sufficient Southernness to blend into the community. Most Yankees, however, were regarded as distant and faceless meddlers whose radical views became ever more threatening in the 1850s.[24]

Nowhere was this gap wider than over the issue of slavery. White liberty was based on race slavery, according to the plain folk's republican ideology; slavery made their own privileged status and social order possible. Heavy-handed control of enslaved African Americans was necessary to prevent anarchy. The decade had hardly opened when Georgians were confronted with problems that grew out of the Compromise of 1850. Supporters of the compromise such as Howell Cobb hoped that it would guarantee a degree of equality for the South within the Union, which many slave masters, especially conservative Whigs, saw as the best way to protect the institution of slavery. Cobb's thinking reflected the majority opinion along the lower river in 1850. Southern Rights men, on the other hand, saw the compromise as a sellout and an unmanly submission to the North, which they believed ultimately would lead to disunion.[25]

In an effort to rally Georgia's moderates behind the compromise, unionists called public meetings during the fall of 1850. "The Friends of the Union of Telfair," for example, met at Jacksonville in October and pledged their support for the compromise. Gathered that day were local men who, like Howell Cobb, were willing to set aside party and sectional loyalty for the good of the Union. Among them were conservative Whigs such as Spalding planters Joshua Frier and William Manning as well as Union Democrats such as Mark Willcox and James Rogers. Democrat or Whig, these men were respected, powerful community leaders who believed that slavery and the South's interests were best protected within the Union. Nonslaveholder Archibald Campbell, now nearing sixty, feared disunion and the consequences it could have for his family. County meetings such as the one at Jacksonville drummed up support for the compromise and nominated candidates to stand for election as delegates to a state Union convention in Milledgeville.[26]

The delegates who gathered in December 1850 were elected in a lively fall campaign. The selection of the lower river's six-man delegation (two from each county) was an exercise in paternalism and deference. Although chosen by a plain folk majority, the delegation consisted exclusively of affluent men from black belt neighborhoods. The slaveholding Willcox family sent three brothers (one-half of the lower river's representatives) to the convention. Yeoman slaveholder George Willcox (Irwin County) and Whig politician William Paine (Telfair County) were the only nonplanters. Mark Willcox (Telfair

County) was, like Howell Cobb, an old Jacksonian Democrat and opposed secession. Planters Norman McDuffie and Willis Reeves represented Pulaski County and James Willcox, Irwin County. As a group, the delegates reflected the conservative influence planters exercised among unionists and the trust plain folk placed in them.[27]

The majority of delegates at the Union convention opposed secession; nevertheless, they maintained that although the Union was revered, it was not sacred. Refusing to protect slaveholders' property anywhere or refusing to admit a slave state to the nation amounted to "dissolution of the Union." The people of each state, the delegates reasoned, had a right and a duty to resort to secession if it was deemed necessary "to effect their safety or happiness." The entire matter boiled down to whether the Federal government would uphold the Constitution's guarantee to protect the property of Southern citizens. If it would not, the republican "experiment has failed." Having finished their work, the delegates called on the voters "to sustain us in our efforts to save the Constitutional Union of our Fathers, and vindicate the honor and equal rights of the South." It was better to leave the national household "of our Fathers" than to become despised stepchildren within their own family. In what became known as the Georgia Platform, the delegates recommended that their fellow citizens accept the Compromise of 1850 as the last best hope of preserving the Union, but they warned that Georgians would secede and fight for their honor and rights if necessary. The only remaining question was whether the delegates and the voters were bluffing.[28]

In the decade following the Compromise of 1850, a series of events forced plain folk to adjust their political identities to new realities. For Whigs such as William Paine, it meant the death of their party and the search for a new political home. Paine became a Know-Nothing, then a Southern Democrat. By the spring of 1861 he was a recruiting officer for the new Confederate nation. Die-hard unionists and Whigs unwilling to join the emerging Southern Rights Party often found a home in the Constitutional Union Party, a refuge for conservatives who believed that slavery's best protection was the Union itself. Meanwhile, determined to protect the Southern Rights plank in the Georgia Platform at all costs, Southern Rights men attempted to transform the national Democratic Party into the party of John C. Calhoun rather than Andrew Jackson.[29]

Despite the political power and wealth represented by unionist planters like the Willcoxes, there was surprising opposition to unionism following the Compromise of 1850, which was revealed immediately in the gubernatorial election of 1851. Although almost 57 percent of lower river voters supported Howell Cobb and unionism, Southern Rights candidate Charles McDonald had strong local support. He received 72 percent of the votes in white belt Irwin County, which claimed fewer slaves and planters than any other local county. The fault lines separating the two camps were essentially those dividing black and white belt neighborhoods. Cobb's support was strongest in Pulaski and Telfair Counties, the older counties east of the river where the largest slaveholding and traditionally Whig neighborhoods were situated. There more than 60 percent of the voters were Constitutional Unionists.[30]

The Southern Rights camp's popularity in the wiregrass country, as in the upcountry, was due to a combination of frontier egalitarianism, regionalism, and racism. Despite the growing commercialism of the 1850s, most plain folk still valued frontier communalism and localism above the commercialism and nationalism that Cobb and the Constitutional Unionists represented. Neighborhoods of kinship and mutual assistance were the source of plain folk self-sufficiency, economic independence, and personal autonomy. These were dearer to them in the final analysis than expanding markets, transportation improvements, and a centralized and distant government. Moreover, the states' rights ideology of Charles McDonald appealed to many slaveless white men not because it protected slavery per se, but because it offered localism its best constitutional protection from overreaching outsiders and land-grabbers, be they Northern abolitionists or Southern railroad developers like A. H. Brisbane. Shorn of the right to own slaves, Southern white men became in their own minds less-than-equal partners in the Union. To white belt plain folk, slavery was a control issue: if emancipated, slaves would flee the black belt and settle in subsistence regions like the wiregrass. Though many plain folk lived at or near subsistence levels, they were free to own land and felt superior to slaves and landless immigrants, such as those who worked on Brisbane's railroad, whom they violently turned away from their neighborhoods.[31]

Seventy-five percent of the voters who turned out for the presidential election of 1852 supported Democrat Franklin Pierce, an early reflection of the Whigs' difficulty in holding onto their share of the ballots. Increasingly, Whigs who could stomach the Democrats joined them; others were attracted to the new American or Know-Nothing Party. Unionist in outlook, the American Party drew attention away from the divisive issue of slavery by declaring that the rising number of foreign immigrants posed a greater threat to the nation than slavery. By the mid-1850s old-line Whigs and Union-minded Democrats unwilling to join the more radical Southern Rights Democrats had joined the

American Party. The party ritual called on members to take an oath to preserve the Union and, like the Masons, included secret handshakes and signs. Although its detractors believed that the party was antirepublican because of its anti-immigrant stance and its secrecy, its defenders charged that immigrant voters controlled by Northern demagogues were already destroying the republic. The party was a safe political home for Southerners who were unwilling to tackle the dangerous issue of slavery head-on and who seriously thought that the American Party could clean up corrupt Northern politics. In addition to Jacksonville lawyer William Paine, Willis Reeves became a Know-Nothing. A wealthy Pulaski planter, Reeves was a state legislator during 1828–30 and 1851–52, as well as a delegate to the Union convention in 1850. In the late 1850s, as he approached the age of seventy, Reeves emerged as one of the county's leading Know-Nothings.[32]

The new party's "Second-Degree" pledge called for Know-Nothings to support only fellow party members in local elections, thus putting party above family and neighborhood loyalty and furthering its reputation as an antirepublican organization. Its secrecy undermined neighborhood localism and became a potent weapon against the Democrats. In Hawkinsville, dry goods store owner Warren Wood reflected the influence of merchants in the Know-Nothing Party's leadership, men who often were small slaveholders themselves with a stake in slavery's future and an interest in the market economy. Nevertheless, some yeomen were attracted to the party. Downriver in the old Whig stronghold of Telfair County, plain folk such as William Studstill and R. D. Wooten took active roles in the party's meetings.[33]

The rise of the American Party and persistent Unionism in Georgia troubled the Southern Rights wing of the Democratic leadership. With the Whig Party's breakup, Southern Rights advocates expected gains for their side. In time, however, they came to fear that their plain folk rank and file was disgruntled or alienated. Democratic leaders suspected that those leaning toward Know-Nothing's unionist ideology might be antislavery as well, especially in the low-slaveholding, white belt areas in Georgia's upcountry and wiregrass, where there were relatively few slaves. The new American Party thus had the potential to split the traditional Democratic alliance between planters and plain folk and upset the traditional power structure.[34]

Indeed, despite the lower river's tradition as a Democratic stronghold, the party experienced desertion in the region during the 1850s. In the 1852 presidential election, for example, 90 percent of the voters in white belt Irwin County, the most frontierlike of the region's new counties, voted Democratic.

Five years later, with the Know-Nothings on the rise, 79 percent supported the Democratic gubernatorial candidate. During the same contests, Democratic strength in Telfair dropped from 59 percent to 45 percent. Surprisingly, Democrats were losing ground in both black and white belt neighborhoods to die-hard unionists represented by men like William Paine, who were concerned with the seemingly reckless stance of Southern Democrats and threw their weight to the American Party.[35]

The Know-Nothing Party was not the only secretive organization that threatened the traditional Democratic planter–backwoods plain folk alliance. In the mid-1850s a Masonic lodge was formed at Irwinville. Masonic lodges had cropped up earlier along the river at such towns as Hawkinsville and Jacksonville, but these were black belt neighborhoods where evangelicals and planters like Alexander Dopson and Duncan McRae were prominent. The establishment of Irwin Lodge in the backwoods had an immediate impact on local politics, which was heavily influenced by Primitive Baptist congregations. Since Primitives denounced the Masons for their benevolence and ex-communicated their own members for joining Masonic lodges, Irwin Lodge quickly became a rival political center to Primitive meetinghouses. In the 1840s and early 1850s Primitive congregations had routinely sent one of their own to the state legislature. But in 1857, the year after the Irwin Lodge was created, one of its members, M. G. Faulkner, won a seat in the state senate, breaking a string of successful Primitive candidates dating back to 1849. Moreover, the following year fellow Mason George Young was also elected senator, an office he held until 1861. Along with the Know-Nothing threat, the rise of the Masonic lodge at Irwinville destabilized backwoods politics west of the river.[36]

Meanwhile, outside threats to "domestic security" in the late 1850s—including violence in "Bleeding Kansas," the *Dred Scott* decision, and John Brown's raid—eroded the political middle ground and drove many voters into the Southern Rights wing of the Democratic Party. One of its most visible leaders was Joe Brown, a yeoman-style lawyer, Baptist slaveholder, and staunch states' rights man from the hills of northern Georgia. Although he speculated in stocks and bonds and real estate, Brown's homespun image played well among Georgia's plain folk. The states' rights wing in Georgia hoped to hold onto traditional areas of voter loyalty in the upcountry by making Brown their leader. The strategy also worked in the piney woods, where Brown's popularity and troubled national events ended the erosion of Democratic strength during the critical period between 1857 and 1860, when

Georgia weathered an economic depression and increasingly moved toward secession.[37]

Brown reversed the trend of eroding Democratic strength along the river. There are several explanations for his appeal. His yeoman origins, folksy antimonopoly and antiaristocracy rhetoric, and Democratic affiliation were important. In the gubernatorial contest of 1857, he easily defeated Benjamin Hill, a Know-Nothing and unionist, receiving 55 percent of the votes in Coffee County, 66 percent in Pulaski, and almost 80 percent in Irwin. Brown's reputation as a self-made man made him immensely popular in the wiregrass country, as it did in the upcountry, where his reaction to the panic of 1857, particularly his rejection of pleas for relief by banks, won him plain folk support. As elsewhere in Georgia, the depression along the lower river disrupted the cotton boom, hurting not only large planters and merchants, but also cotton farmers and small slaveowners just entering the cotton market. Brown's depiction of relief-seeking bankers as spoiled children of privilege struck a responsive chord among plain folk suspicious of corporate power and privilege.[38]

Finally, market-oriented planters and cotton farmers endorsed Brown's state-supported economic development schemes such as the Western and Atlantic, which helped open the upcountry. Although plain folk relied heavily on local networks of exchange and trade, increasing cotton production and slaveholding may have convinced such market-oriented producers, especially former Whigs, to support Brown, and for good reason. Late in 1857 the Democratic leadership put before the legislature two state-supported railroad projects, each designed to win over voters to the party. One of these was the Macon and Brunswick Railroad. Its survey lines passed through eastern Pulaski and Telfair, the lower river's largest cotton-producing counties, where competition between Democrats and Whigs had been most intense. Macon's merchants had sought a competitor for the Central of Georgia Railroad, which had a stranglehold on the city's cotton traffic, while Brunswick's merchants were eager to tap into the cotton belt trade. Merchants in both cities, as well as in Hawkinsville, hoped to rid themselves of Yankee middlemen in the transatlantic traffic in cotton and finished goods. Among the railroad's civic-minded supporters at Hawkinsville were banker Orran Horne, planters Norman McDuffie and Cornelius Bozeman, merchant Simon Merritt, and planter-physician Thomas Ryan. As one of the railroad's engineers recalled: "What high hopes we all once had of the advantages of direct trade with Europe, especially from . . . Brunswick."[39]

Freedom from Northern middlemen and access to markets appealed not only to town merchants, but also to rural voters living along the railroad's proposed route. Due to the influence of planters such as George Walker III, one of the railroad's strongest local supporters and a member of its board of directors, the line ran near Longstreet and through eastern Pulaski County, a rich cotton-growing neighborhood. In Telfair, Archibald Campbell, Hugh McLean, and Mitchell Willcox were counted among the railroad's "friends." The line also had local support in the legislative halls. All four members elected to the General Assembly from Pulaski and Telfair Counties in 1859 stood to benefit personally from the railroad's construction. In Pulaski, George Jordan, the son-in-law of George Walker III, owned over $16,000 worth of land near the proposed line, while cotton planter Richard DeLamar lived on the east side of the river and also would gain from railroad access to markets. In Telfair County, planter-merchant Malcolm N. McRae owned property in Lumber City, where he operated a store and farm directly in the railway's path. William Paine, a Jacksonville attorney and former Whig–turned–Know-Nothing and now a Democratic convert, acted as an agent for absentee landlords and provided them with information and "ideas" on how the line would affect their land values. Fortunately for the Democrats, the railroad project did not threaten the extensive cow range southwest of the river in traditionally anti-railroad Coffee and Irwin Counties, where many plain folk who lived forty miles from the proposed route could support Brown without feeling threatened by the project.[40]

When voters cast their ballots in the gubernatorial election of 1859, one that pitted incumbent Democrat Joe Brown against the American Party's Warren Aiken, Brown enjoyed a distinct local advantage over the flagging Know-Nothings. Seventy-five percent of the votes went to Brown, many of them from the governor's "American friends [who] approve my administration." The erosion of American Party strength in both Pulaski and Telfair Counties, through which Brown's railroad project passed, was about 10 to 12 percent of the turnout during the presidential campaign three years earlier. Telfair's anti-Brown majority in 1857 had given unionist and Know-Nothing Benjamin Hill 55 percent, but now Brown received 60 percent of the ballots. In Pulaski County Brown won over 70 percent of the votes, and in Wilcox County he received an astonishing 94 percent. Brown's plain folk appeal and his states' rights ideology, as well as the Macon and Brunswick Railroad, were important elements in local Democratic consolidation, which was virtually complete by 1860. A once vibrant two-party political culture with a persistent unionist core had been transformed, at first glance, into an overwhelmingly states' rights political identity.[41]

The reshaping of plain folk's political identity did not occur in a vacuum. In addition to disturbing national events such as the undeclared war in Kansas and a rash of incendiary acts in Georgia, threats to "domestic security" took place closer to home. In the spring of 1858, for example, two female slaves on the Blevins plantation in neighboring Houston County attacked the overseer's sleeping wife with an ax. That two slave women could commit such "a dreadful crime" caused the "most intense excitement" among whites, who blamed abolitionist rhetoric for the incident. Three weeks later the *Georgia Journal and Messenger* declared that "this slavery agitation must cease, or there is no safety to the South." Slavery, the editor concluded in language that lower river inhabitants understood, "is purely a local and domestic question, with which the South will permit no interference from outsiders." The fear of slave revolt was one of the psychological costs of slavery for white society, which considered local control over slaves and white safety to be inseparable. That women took part in the attack was particularly unnerving for plain folk, whose patterns of slaveholding included the purchase of less expensive women and their children.[42]

The "safety" problem would not go away. Robert Toombs warned in 1860 that the tremendous increase in the South's slave population (from 800,000 to 4 million in two generations) spelled racial disaster for whites if new cotton frontiers were not found to disperse the slaves. "What shall be done with them?" Toombs asked. "We must expand or perish." Deep South white belts offered internal possibilities for the expansion of slavery, as increasing cotton production along the lower river had revealed in the 1850s. But expanding the peculiar institution into traditionally white belt areas had also meant spreading the "safety" problem when planters such as Samuel Fuller arrived from Bibb County in the 1840s and carved out a plantation from the Wilcox County bottomland. By 1859 Fuller had accumulated "a pretty Extensive property," including forty slaves. Although united in their race consciousness, plain folk and planters were of divided minds over the desirability of plantation-sized African American settlements in the white belt. As the decade ended, the question of how to spread slavery into white belt areas and safeguard domestic security remained unresolved. Abolitionist and Republican Party opposition to slavery's expansion into the territories increased white fears of insurrection within the growing slave population.[43]

This was the troubled frame of mind when Hawkinsville slaveholder and

Know-Nothing Frederick Brown gave a speech at a Fourth of July barbecue in 1858. The unsettled state of national affairs and the South's future clearly worried him. After a public reading of the Declaration of Independence, Brown stood before the audience at Wesley Chapel and reviewed the causes of the American Revolution and the history of the nation's founding. Then turning to a darker present, he "spoke of the fear he entertained of the decay of our Republic from party rage and fanaticism." The nation, like ancient Rome, was in peril. The middle ground represented by the Georgia Platform of 1850 had disappeared and Union-minded men like himself looked to the future with growing apprehension.[44]

The surreptitious landing of the slave ship *Wanderer* on the Georgia coast in 1858, only months after Brown's speech, placed before the public the highly volatile issues of the foreign slave trade and a burgeoning slave population. The smugglers' plot was soon discovered and the *Wanderer* seized, but not before some of the Africans were scattered, including a coffle headed through the wiregrass country. The incident had special meaning for residents along the lower river, as Federal authorities penetrated the interior to seize the slaves. In Telfair County, former Whig and yeoman master John F. McRae was sworn in as a deputy U.S. marshal and led a posse of plain folk slave catchers to intercept them. Some of the slaves were taken to Jacksonville and temporarily held at Woodson Willcox's plantation. The episode once again raised questions about Federal power to regulate the slave trade, on the one hand, and market-oriented plain folk's desires for cheaper "Ashantee prices," on the other. Although planters generally opposed reopening the trade, fearing that it would devalue their slave property, from a plain folk perspective the issue was a "democratic question" of making small masters of yeomen and democratizing slaveholding on the cotton frontier. Predictably, many Northerners viewed the *Wanderer*'s landing as the illegal and immoral reopening of the transatlantic slave trade and redoubled their anti-Southern rhetoric.[45]

Fifteen months after Frederick Brown spoke at Wesley Chapel, abolitionist John Brown launched his raid on the U.S. arsenal at Harpers Ferry, Virginia. Although Brown's plot to incite a bloody slave insurrection failed, the raid convinced many Southerners that they were no longer safe in a nation unwilling to uphold the South's constitutional rights and unconcerned for the personal safety of its white population. No aspect of slavery horrified Southerners more than slave revolts, as the local Blevins attack revealed. Brown's raid, described by the *Georgia Journal and Messenger* as a "wicked and rash outbreak of fanatical madness," was a wake-up call for the South "to exercise an increased vigilance in regard to domestic security." White collective anxiety and anger increased as abolitionists made Brown a martyr to their cause. In the spring of 1860 a letter to a Macon newspaper warned that John Brown's biography could be bought in a local bookstore and called for banning the "incendiary" book. Increasingly, plain folk saw themselves as citizens of a republic given over to what Frederick Brown labeled "fanaticism." That same spring, Frederick and fellow professionals at Hawkinsville organized a "musket" company and requested that they be equipped by the state armory.[46]

## Secessionists

In 1860 the leaders of Georgia's secession movement wondered if their state would again stall the disunion campaign in the Deep South as it had in 1850. They pondered what support, if any, they could count on among the plain folk. Secessionists such as Robert Toombs feared secretive Know-Nothings like Frederick Brown would appeal to the class interests of plain folk and divide the Democratic Party, thus ensuring a Republican victory in the presidential election of 1860. If Abraham Lincoln prevailed, secessionists feared that the plain folk majority might submit to Republican rule rather than support secession, thus setting the stage for a bitter internal civil war between hard-core secessionists and die-hard unionists. Would southern Georgia's plain folk vote their narrow class interests and derail the secession movement?[47]

Wiregrass Georgia, however, had seen its traditional unionist center erode to such an extent by 1860 that a secessionist victory there was possible. During the crisis of 1860–61, a majority of the white belt's plain folk set their class interests as nonslaveholders aside and supported disunion at the polls. Despite pockets of persistent unionism, especially among Primitive Baptists and old-line Whigs, Joe Brown's popularity solidified his party's strength in the region. Successful black belt planters such as Samuel Fuller now described themselves as "Brown" men, meaning states rights' proponents rather than Union Democrats. In the 1850s more and more yeomen forgot the Union nationalism of their fathers, joined planters like Fuller, and became Brown Democrats. Brown's own views on states' rights were entirely consistent with the plain folk's localist political tradition. Yeoman farmers boasting little in the way of material possessions treasured what their republican heritage had bequeathed them—economic independence and personal liberty. The right of white men to determine local matters placed plain folk in the same ideological camp as Georgia's states' rights planters such as Fuller, who repeatedly voted for Brown and would write him that he, Fuller, used his "influence in my county which has gone for you almost unanimously."[48]

By the end of the antebellum period, race consciousness outweighed class consciousness in the political culture of the plain folk. Racial slavery made all whites superior to blacks, and plain folk concepts of honor, liberty, and independence were dependent on racial domination. Although the yeomanry's republican sensibilities were often offended by examples of corporate privilege and planter power, bonds of whiteness were stronger than class division on the cotton frontier. Plain folk supported the the expansion of slavery into the territories not because they owned slaves or expected to resettle there, but because they embraced the constitutional right of individuals to take their property wherever they liked. Republican Party plans to block the expansion of slavery into the territories meant that the growing population of enslaved African Americans would expand internally into the Lower South's white belt. Even slave women, often the choice of yeoman masters, could not be counted on to remain docile given the increasing antislavery agitation, as the Blevin's plantation attack chillingly illustrated.[49]

Yet plain folk feared the specter of emancipation even more than slavery's internal expansion into its white belt. There were already instances of slave emancipation in the Western Hemisphere. On his way to California in 1849, Hawkinsville physician Robert Taylor had passed through Panama, where Simon Bolivar had freed the slaves. Taylor was disturbed by what he saw. Writing to his wife, Taylor declared: "This town & the country afford a strong illustration of the evils of freeing the blacks." Before emancipation, slaveholders "were living much in the style of the old Castilions," and their plantations were exemplars of "wealth & taste." But Taylor witnessed a post-emancipation landscape of decay and desertion, a frightening picture of one possible future for his South. Fields once highly cultivated now "present but slight traces of the hand of man"; slaves once "happy . . . in the hands of their owners are a filthy, lazy, & miserable set living almost exclusively on the spontaneous production of the land." Emancipation could destroy the plantation society established on the lower river, just as it had done in Panama. Freed slaves would move to the white belt and live on "the spontaneous production of the land," competing with whites for limited resources, just as they did where the black and white belts met.[50]

Domestic security, racism, and fears of a postemancipation world thus shaped the plain folk perspective during the presidential campaign of 1860. Fearful for their safety and further alienated by Northern attacks on the

Southern social system, Southern Democrats chose as their standard-bearer Kentuckian John C. Breckinridge, a man whom local Brown Democrats could get behind. They gathered at county courtyards and drummed up support for their cause and supported the work of the Baltimore convention. Southern Democrats, the "true hearted southerner," as locals described themselves, professed Unionism of the Jacksonian stripe and demanded that the Georgia Platform of 1850 be upheld. In Telfair County, they met at Jacksonville and endorsed Breckinridge as the legitimate candidate of the "*true* National Democratic party of the Union." They passed a series of resolutions that reflected their thinking: "[We] as a portion of the people of this Union, consider ourselves as entitled to equal rights with the people of any portion of it; that we have the right to carry our property into any Territory that has been, or may hereafter be, acquired by the United States." Emphasizing the need for the territorial expansion of slavery, they soundly repudiated the doctrine of "Squatter Sovereignty" as "political heresy." Equal rights for Southerners and the territorial expansion of slavery were the issues that the Southern Democrats at Jacksonville put first, before the Union if necessary.[51]

One of the leading Brown Democrats at the Jacksonville meeting was the oldest son of unionist Mark Willcox. John Coffee Willcox had grown up within the kinship circle of the county's most powerful family. Prior to his death in 1852, Mark Willcox owned more than fifty slaves and served at various times as county sheriff and state legislator. Privileged by his family's planter status and political connections, John was sent to Oglethorpe College near Milledgeville, where his father and three uncles—James, George, and Mitchell—served repeatedly in the General Assembly. John married the daughter of the respectable and propertied widow Rebecca Swain and settled next door to his mother-in-law near Jacksonville. Now a small planter, Willcox had a pretty wife—Elizabeth—who bore him four children in six years. Their eleven slaves worked his five-bale cotton and corn farm and, along with his white family, brought the total number of mouths to feed to seventeen.[52]

In 1860 John Willcox was thirty-one years old. As it happened, all of the "true hearted" Southern men who met with him at Jacksonville were relatively young, with an average age of thirty-one. Though certainly not wet behind the ears, they were younger than the men who had led the Union movement in 1850. Indeed, the passing of Mark Willcox from the scene and the arrival of his Southern Democratic son reflected a generational shift in local leadership as well as a hardening of anti-Yankee attitudes. At twenty-three, lawyer Erastus Smith was the youngest known participant at Jacksonville; John Daniel, another attorney, was twenty-seven. Planter-merchant Oliver H. Cook chaired the meeting, which, in addition to drafting the resolutions, selected three delegates to represent Telfair at the party's convention at Milledgeville on August 8. The delegates were Erastus Smith; William Brewer, a yeoman farmer who owned one slave; and Murdoch Willcox, a small planter from Temperance. John Coffee Willcox and his friends were not major planters, but rather a mixture of rising small planters, professional men, and yeoman slaveholders. When John's father and his uncles met at the Union convention in 1850 and headed off secession, John's fellow Southern Democrats were teenagers or just entering their twenties. In 1860 their careers were still largely ahead of them. They were ready to assume the mantle of political leadership and displace the fixtures of the political establishment represented by the older generation. Rather than following the example of their fathers, they admired men like Georgia politician Francis S. Bartow, who championed "the great principle of Congressional protection" for Southern Rights.[53]

Moderate voters with Know-Nothing, Unionist, or old-line Whig leanings rallied to the banner of the Constitutional Union Party in 1860. Like the Southern Democrats, they claimed to be unionists but were less likely to use secession as a threat. Unlike their opponents, who viewed the expansion of slavery into the territories as a critical issue, Constitutional Unionists considered it an "abstract question" used for partisan political purposes by both Southern Democrats and Republicans. The party chose former Know-Nothing John Bell of Tennessee as its presidential candidate and adopted a vague platform to uphold the Constitution and the Union. Old-line Whigs, Union Democrats, and Know-Nothings such as William Paine found the middle-of-the-road, wait-and-see philosophy of the party to their liking. Ten years earlier at the 1850 Union convention men of Bell's bent, including Paine, had been numerous and influential enough to forestall secession. But the divisive 1850s, which saw party fragmentation, abolitionist-inspired insurrection, and rising Southern insecurity, were not kind to their unionist views. Moreover, some of the lower river's most powerful unionists were no longer in positions of leadership or had literally passed from the scene. Mark Willcox and his brother George died during the 1850s, and James soon followed. All three had attended the Union convention in Milledgeville in 1850 as voices of moderation.[54]

If the presidential election of November 1860 was any indication, the political identity of most plain folk now resembled John Coffee Willcox's, not the Unionism of his deceased father. Almost 65 percent of the voters along the lower river cast ballots for Breckinridge, a significantly higher level of support than the approximately 50 percent he received statewide. The most rabid Southern Rights counties—those exceeding the average for the area and the state—were situated beyond the river in the more recently settled piney woods. A landslide 93 percent of the voters in Wilcox County, for example, supported the Southern Democrats, while 80 percent and 76 percent of the voters in Irwin and Coffee Counties, respectively, backed Breckinridge. Sixty-two percent of Pulaski's ballots went to Breckinridge. Southern Democrats were found in all neighborhoods, but the white belts dominated by plain folk and yeoman masters were the strongest Southern Rights communities in November 1860. Thus, the traditionally Democratic counties went to the Southern Rights candidate for president, as they overwhelmingly did throughout Georgia's wiregrass country.[55]

In contrast to Breckinridge's strong showing, only 33 percent of the lower valley's voters supported Constitutional Unionist John Bell, significantly less than his statewide following of 40 percent. Not surprisingly, the old-line Whig stronghold of Telfair was the only county that Bell carried, with 56 percent of the vote. Overall, the Constitutional Unionists received 10 percent fewer votes than the Whigs and Know-Nothings had won along the river in the 1850s. Joe Brown's "poor, honest laborers of Georgia" had returned wide Breckinridge majorities in four of five counties. The spirit of compromise that prevailed at the beginning of the decade was gone, and with Abraham Lincoln's election secession seemed more likely than ever.[56]

One day after the presidential election the General Assembly met in Milledgeville. Its members did not know the outcome of the national contest but expected the worst. In his address to the legislature, Governor Brown quickly advanced his pro-secession agenda. He recommended that Georgia secede immediately rather than wait for a convention of delegates from other Southern states to decide its future. Although the legislature failed to pass a resolution calling for immediate secession, it supported a $1 million appropriation to protect the state from Northern invasion. At Milledgeville, the General Assembly authorized Brown to accept ten thousand state troops and encouraged the organization of volunteer companies. Secessionists throughout Georgia approved Brown's actions. Moreover, support for secession increased after confirmation of Lincoln's election, an event described locally as a "tide of Black Republican fanaticism," spread into the countryside.[57]

Secession was, along with increased cotton growing and slaveholding and a more intense siege mentality, another step in the reshaping of plain folk political identity. The crisis forced plain folk to weigh the value of union against the possibility of an independent state. But to explain secession as a conspiracy of the slave power elite or strictly in terms of class consciousness reduces individual plain folk to political ciphers. Their status as voters in an American republic, their identity as Southerners, Georgians, and piney woods people provided a broader context that shaped their political decisions, as did family and neighborhood tradition. Plain folk believed that honor, so often associated with the South's social elite, was theirs as freeholders in a republican world if they managed their households wisely and used their power as family governors responsibly. What united yeoman secessionists was not a fear of planter power in the South—plain folk deference to planters in political matters had been long established—but their overriding fears of Yankee domination, Southern submission, and what this meant to their concept of honor and masculinity. The antislavery crusade and the rise of the Republican Party represented an external Northern money power conspiracy far more threatening to plain folk notions of equality, honor, property, and racial superiority than a slave power conspiracy. Planters might throw their weight around in Milledgeville, but they were people the plain folk knew, rubbed shoulders with at church or Masonic lodge meetings, and in some cases were family relations. Planters acknowledged the right of plain folk to vote, own property in slaves, defend their honor, and uphold their status as freeholders in a society based on racial slavery. On the other hand, plain folk feared that Republican Party–style emancipation would liberate slaves to move wherever they could find employment, including the backwoods. It would be better to secede and preserve slavery than to see the forests invaded by freedmen.[58]

It was the plain folk's Southern identity that spoke at the polls on November 7, 1860, and it was this identity that secessionists hoped would prevail in January. Without their support, secession would fail in Georgia. During the second week in November the state's most influential political leaders gathered in Milledgeville to debate the state's future. Now a leading secessionist, former unionist Howell Cobb played on white fears of slave insurrection, notions of white male honor, and the belief that if Southerners submitted to Lincoln's election they were little more than slaves themselves. Unionists countered that Lincoln's election did not threaten the South. The debate continued though the middle of the month and ended with the passage of a bill on November 20 calling for the election of delegates to a state convention beginning January 16, 1861, at Milledgeville. A group of twenty-four unionist legislators who opposed immediate secession—among them William Paine of Telfair and George Young of Irwin—requested that Hershel Johnson speak to them on this "perilous issue." Johnson reportedly told the group that while he deplored the Lincoln victory, he did not believe that Northern aggression was inevitable. Georgia, however, must be prepared to resist coercion. To unionists such as Paine and Young, Lincoln's election, secession, and the possibility of war were distinctly different things.[59]

As the campaign for convention delegates heated up in November and December, state senator William Paine became a minor thorn in the side of secessionists. Perhaps more than any other local politician, Paine refused to set aside the lower river's unionist identity. He opposed a bill to spend $300,000 of the $1 million state defense appropriation for an armory because he believed the measure would be ineffective. Despite a decade of growing sectional tension, Paine and other unionists argued that Georgians should be taxed for such purposes only when "the honor and interest of Georgia require it." In Paine's mind, that time had not yet arrived despite Lincoln's election. He openly declared that the secessionists had stampeded the state down the road of disunion without careful consideration of its implications for the public's safety. Paine attempted to turn the armory proposal against its proponents. Standing before the senate, he argued that secessionists were "precipitating the State into a revolution" without the means of protecting its citizens, as evidenced by the pro-armory faction's belated call to arms when few could be quickly manufactured or purchased. On December 14, 1860, when a house resolution called for Georgia to stand beside any seceding state coerced by the Federal government, Paine introduced an amendment. He called for all members of the house and senate to back up their secessionist rhetoric with action and "tender their services" to the state if such Federal coercion took place, at which time "the Governor [would] be requested to call out the members of the Senate and House of Representatives first, for the field." The amendment failed, but Paine had made his point.[60]

On the same day unionist legislators gathered in the senate chamber and called on Paine to serve as one of the meeting's two secretaries. Clearly, the antisecessionists wanted their position recorded and printed in the press. Paine hand-recorded the major outlines of the antisecession argument. Secession first and cooperation with other Southern states afterward was a "delusive policy"; such "hasty, ill-advised" action was doomed to failure. In words that would seem prophetic, the unionists looked into a future beyond secession and saw disaster: "We can see nothing but divisions among our people, confusion among the slaveholding States, strife around our firesides, and ultimate defeat to every movement for the effective redress of our grievances."[61]

The *Milledgeville Southern Recorder*, a unionist paper, declared secession a partisan issue with Georgians split along political party lines. The division among the people was obvious in the countryside. As the January 2 election of convention delegates approached, William Paine and others joined the Cooperation or "Union resistance" Party. It was a mixed lot comprised of conservative former Whigs and Know-Nothings, as well as old-line Union Democrats, all of whom opposed immediate secession. Many of them had supported John Bell and the Constitutional Union Party during the presidential election of 1860 and were surprised by the Southern Democrats' overwhelming victory. Although not all were unconditional antisecessionists, they were united in the belief that secession should be undertaken only in cooperation with other Southern states. A united South, they argued, was more likely to win concessions from the North and less likely to be attacked. Nevertheless, recalling the Georgia Platform of 1850, they still put Southern rights and Southern honor ahead of "submission" to the Union at any cost. The view of older men such as planters Joshua Frier, a former Whig, and George Reid, a Union Democrat, reflected this cautious approach, as opposed to younger secessionists like John Coffee Willcox. It was the lower river's unionist identity based on the traditional black belt planter and backwoods Primitive Baptist coalition that cooperationists hoped would reexert itself in January.[62]

On the other hand, the "immediate secession party" and its supporters were tired of waiting. Lincoln's election was the final straw despite assurances that his administration would not interfere with slavery in the states where it already existed. It was only a matter of time, secessionists such as Cornelius Bozeman believed, before the Republicans moved to further erode the South's "constitutional guarantees and safe-guards" and abolished slavery altogether. Lincoln's election, to their way of thinking, was like a Northern declaration of war on the Southern way of life. In the immediate secessionist mind, the choice for Georgians was clear: secede now or submit to Northern domination. Thus, the immediate secessionists assumed the mantle of protectors of Southern political culture. The virtuous republic created by their ancestors during the American Revolution had been ruined by Yankee corruption, greed, and misguided antebellum social reforms, especially abolition. As risky as secession seemed to plain folk, the movement's rhetoric appealed to their notions of local and regional pride, their right to pursue their own affairs without Northern meddling, and their white supremacist outlook. Secession might be "revolution," as unionist William Paine declared, but a revolution was necessary to separate a virtuous South from a decadent North that had "prostituted" the Constitution and elected Abraham Lincoln president. It was the plain folk's Southern identity that secessionists called on to make the revolution a reality.[63]

The months between Governor Brown's election in the fall of 1859 and the balloting for delegates to the secession convention in January 1861 were like one endless political campaign. The old Union Democrat coalition of black belt planters and backwoods Primitive Baptists was solidly defeated. The coalition was determined to win on January 2. Although there were fewer voters statewide than for the presidential contest in 1860, the reverse was true along the lower river, where turnout grew by 7 percent. Most of the increase occurred in the white belt lower counties, where Coffee and Irwin reported a surge of 30 to 40 percent. As a result, downriver cooperationists carried three of five counties. However, the total popular vote for delegates, which included ballots from the upriver black belt neighborhoods, gave secessionists almost 52 percent of all local ballots and reflected wiregrass Georgia's broader secessionist sentiment. It would have been impossible for secessionists to win this slight majority without the votes of plain folk.[64]

Although the lower valley was now narrowly of secessionist persuasion, a look at delegate selection reflects how strongly its traditional political culture—particularly the plain folk deference to slaveholders and the overrepresentation of black belt neighborhoods in political affairs—loomed over white belt areas even under the threat of disunion. When considered as one group, men standing for election as cooperationists or secessionists represented not only political identities, but also social status and neighborhood affiliation. Despite the overwhelming preponderance of nonslaveholding households (again, approximately 70 percent of white households in 1860), 75 percent of local delegate candidates were masters of slaves, with planters and small planters representing almost half of them. Given the predominance of slaveholders, it is not surprising that fully 70 percent of the candidates lived in black belt neighborhoods. Moreover, almost a third of them lived in county seat towns and worked at least part-time as professionals—hotel owners, merchants, and storekeepers. Thus, in the most important election in the state's history—unionist William Paine called it a "revolution"—plain folk did not abandon deference to slaveholders in the interests of class.[65]

Both cooperationists and secessionists relied on politicians from black belt neighborhoods to carry the election, yet there were telling differences between the two groups of candidates. The majority of secessionists, like most cooperationists, were slaveowners, but they represented fewer of their group's candidates (66 percent) than did their slaveowning cooperationist opponents (87 percent). Furthermore, planters accounted for less than 20 percent of the slaveowning secessionist candidates. Indeed, Cornelius Bozeman was the only planter who ran as a secessionist from the lower river's five counties. With thirty-one slaves and a total wealth of $51,000, he was one of the richest men on the campaign circuit.[66]

Small rising planters—a group conspicuously absent among cooperationist candidates—were well represented by secessionists. Thomas "Tobe" McGriff of Longstreet and Daniel McLeod of Wilcox County were small planters with an economic stake in slavery and continued expansion of the cotton economy. Both recently had entered the growing class of small planters from the ranks of the slaveowning yeomanry. In 1859 McLeod owned ten slaves and produced twenty-seven bales of cotton, more than some big planters. At the opposite end of the secessionist spectrum were two nonslaveholding candidates. One of them was James Hilliard, a Douglas hotel owner and clerk of the Coffee County Superior Court. A man of limited means who was described as "disposed to do right," Hilliard possessed a town and professional status that set him apart from plain folk in the countryside. Indeed, secessionist candidates such as Hilliard were three times as likely to live in town as cooperationists. Moreover, 80 percent of them resided in black belt neighborhoods.[67]

Like the secessionist candidates, most cooperationists were masters of slaves, only more so. Slaveholders comprised 87 percent of the men running as cooperationist candidates, compared to 66 percent among secessionists. And while secessionist candidates were masters from all levels of slaveholding— from big planters to small planters to yeoman masters—cooperationist candidates tended to be either big planters or small masters. Forty-three percent of the cooperationist candidates were planters, more than twice the proportion found among immediate secessionists. They included Spalding resident and former Whig Joshua Frier and former Know-Nothing leader William Mayo of Pulaski County. Men of wealth and power in a plain folk society, cooperationist planters were conservatives imbued with strong Union sentiments. Although distrustful of secession and its leaders, they recognized that disunion might be a necessity if the Southern rights outlined in the Georgia Platform were not protected.[68]

George Reid was typical of the cooperationist planters. As he stood for election that December, the old-line Union Democrat could look out his window and see six slave cabins, home to thirty-five slaves. He could watch overseer John McCall direct labor on his plantation in the Adams settlement. During the 1859 planting season, his field hands grew one thousand bushels of corn and fifteen bales of cotton, a comparatively small cotton crop for a middling planter. But Reid, like many plain folk, was a cattleman; his slaves tended over one thousand head of livestock. His lifestyle was comfortable but unpretentious, although his total wealth approached $50,000. A war could take more than these material possessions. At fifty-four, George was too old to fight, but three sons—Drewery, Henry, and George—would likely see combat if war came and lasted more than a year or two. Disunion and war could destroy all that Reid and his family had worked for. George and his wife Frances must have wondered what the new year would bring.[69]

The remaining cooperationist candidates were small masters and nonslave-holders who represented just over 60 percent of the antisecessionist candidates. Among the yeoman masters were James Williamson, of Telfair County, a Baptist preacher-farmer who owned six slaves; Manassah Henderson, of Coffee County, a farmer and small slaveholder; and Jacob Young, a farmer, small master, and store owner living at Irwinville. Rowan Pafford, the son of a Tennessee horse and mule dealer, was the only nonslaveholding yeoman running as a cooperationist candidate. With a total wealth valued at $6,500, he was among the least well-to-do of all candidates but nevertheless far better off than most of his plain folk neighbors. As a group, then, the antisecessionist candidates were more likely than their opponents to be planters and slave-holders but less likely to be small planters who resided in black belt neighborhoods and towns.[70]

In addition to well-known planters like Joshua Frier, the cooperationists relied on the support of another traditionally unionist group—Primitive Baptists—to win the lower counties. Manassah Henderson, George Reid, and Jacob Young were members of Primitive Baptist churches as well as unionists. The congregations of black belt New Hope Primitive Baptist in lower Wilcox County and white belt Brushy Creek Primitive Baptist near Irwinville looked to these men for leadership. Reid, for example, served as church clerk at New Hope while Young was a lay preacher at Brushy Creek. They posed a serious challenge to secessionist hopes to mobilize the plain folk behind their cause and were determined to recoup their political losses in the late 1850s to politicians with Masonic and states' rights credentials.[71]

When plain folk went to the polls a week after Christmas and voted for delegates to the secession convention, they had no idea what the outcome would be, but one thing was already clear. Neither a cotton oligarchy of planters nor a radical class of yeoman farmers would dominate the lower river's delegation. After all, only four planters were running in the five counties and only one of them was a secessionist. Unlike the planter-dominated delegation to the Union convention in 1850 where the Willcox family held half the seats, the delegates' voices in 1861 were much more diverse. After the votes were counted, it was evident that although secessionists won a narrow majority of the popular vote, they would send only four of the lower river's ten delegates to Milledgeville.[72]

The geography of secession, unlike that of the presidential election a few weeks earlier, redrew traditional lines based largely on slaveholding, cotton production, religious affiliation, and unionist tradition. Immediate secessionists won the seats in the upriver black belt counties of Pulaski and Wilcox. In Pulaski, cooperationist planter and former Know-Nothing William Mayo was beaten by planter Cornelius Bozeman, who was joined by Longstreet small planter and secessionist Tobe McGriff as the county's second delegate. Support for disunion in such neighborhoods was so strong that old-time unionist and planter Charles Taylor now described himself as "a Secessionist," although "not an active or very influential one." In Wilcox, with only six planters but plenty of up-and-coming small cotton farmers, voters remained consistent with their earlier support for Breckinridge and the Southern Democrats, just as secessionists hoped. Having given more than 75 percent of its votes to Breckinridge, Wilcox was a tough place for the unionist planter and Primitive coalition to prevail. Indeed, George Reid was defeated by a fellow member of the New Hope congregation, a secessionist named Smith Turner. A fifty-one-year-old storekeeper and small slaveholder, Turner repeatedly represented his county in the state legislature during the 1840s. He described his plain folk secessionism as "the honest conviction of a frail old man." With $15,000 in total wealth, he was far from poor but was worth only about a third of Reid's total assets. For the trip to Milledgeville Turner was joined by another secessionist delegate, small planter and cotton farmer Daniel McLeod.[73]

In keeping with its persistent unionist tradition, Telfair County elected two cooperationists. Both James Williamson and Hugh McLean lived in black belt neighborhoods along the river road and were small slaveholders. Williamson, a Baptist preacher-farmer, was at fifty-five the oldest delegate from the lower river region. "Uncle Jimmy," as he was fondly called, preached up and down the river at country churches and brush arbors. McLean, a yeoman master with seven slaves, lived in the Clayville neighborhood. The delegate count, however, was very close and suggests that the efforts of secessionist Democrats such as John Coffee Willcox were not in vain. The immensely popular Williamson defeated the leading secessionist by only twelve votes. Although cooperationists won the county, secessionist strength in Telfair rose from 44 to 48 percent of the vote in a matter of weeks.[74]

In Coffee and Irwin, which Breckinridge carried overwhelmingly in November, the resurgent coalition of unionist planters and Primitive Baptists swept four cooperationists into the convention by wide margins. In Coffee, former Whig planter Joshua Frier easily defeated secessionist James Hilliard, while Rowan Pafford joined Frier as Coffee's second cooperationist delegate. In Irwin, the most sparsely populated and least market-oriented of all, cooperationists Manassah Henderson and Jacob Young won. Both men epitomized the prosperous yeoman masters (both owned three slaves) who accounted for half of the lower valley's delegates, as well as the type of solid and respected Primitive Baptists who emerged as both civic and religious leaders on the county level. Henderson's name was synonymous with public virtue and the rule of law in antebellum Irwin County, where he served at various times as commissioner of the slave patrol, overseer of the poor fund, and sheriff. In addition to his farm, Young operated a store at Irwinville and served as clerk of the superior court throughout the 1850s.[75]

In the white belt cow counties of Coffee, Irwin, and Telfair, cooperationists thus gained the upper hand and created the type of unionist plain folk countermovement that secessionists feared, but one out of step with the wiregrass region as a whole. Two-thirds of lower river voters supported cooperationists, representing a significant reversal of the Southern Rights sentiment reflected in the plain folk votes for Breckinridge only weeks before. Thus, when push came to shove and secession as theory was tested in practice, conservative planter–style Union nationalism and Primitive Baptist–style localism were more important than Southern regional identity in the white belt backwoods. The importance of religious leaders and their congregations in reversing support for secession was significant. One-half of all cooperationists elected as delegates had leadership roles in Baptist or Primitive Baptist churches. Indeed, the family names of cooperationist delegates Manassah Henderson and Jacob Young graced Primitive meetinghouses during the antebellum period.[76]

But what did plain folk and Primitive Baptist support for cooperationists mean when weighed against their earlier endorsement of Breckinridge? One thing is clear. Plain folk votes for cooperationists were not votes against the institution of slavery or slaveholders. After all, five of the six local coopera-tionists elected by the plain folk were slaveholders even after the energized unionist planter and Primitive Baptist coalition increased voter turnout in January. Far from voting their own narrow class interests, yeomen continued patterns of deference toward masters of slaves even in the whitest of white belt neighborhoods. However, their unmistakable preference was for small mas-ters or conservative planters with unionist reputations who believed that slavery was best protected within the Union. Such men could counter the "hasty, ill-advised" actions of the radical secessionists who, as unionist Wil-liam Paine argued, had placed Georgia in a "predicament" and were now determined to destroy the Union.[77]

Looking over the delegates who gathered at Milledgeville, the editor of the *Georgia Journal and Messenger* saw "men of ripe age, experience and influ-ence." The lower Ocmulgee's delegates were certainly "ripe." Forty percent of them were in their forties, compared to about 32 percent of the convention's delegation as a whole. At thirty-five Rowan Pafford and Jacob Young were the youngest of the lower Ocmulgee delegates, and James Williamson was the oldest. If age brought "experience" the local delegation was in good shape, but if wealth was "influence" they were at a disadvantage. Without question, most of them were less well off than their fellow delegates. In terms of real and personal property, the area's delegates had average assets of $4,560 and $10,850 respectively, compared to the convention delegate average of $14,238 and $28,889, or about one-third of the average total wealth. And while plant-ers accounted for almost half of the entire convention, they comprised only 20 percent of the local delegation, although local delegates were slightly more likely to own slaves than the convention's delegates as a whole. Compared to the delegates the lower river sent to the Union convention of 1850, the most striking difference was the relative absence of lawyers, planters, and Willcox family members. The 1861 delegation, which consisted of plain folk, small slaveholders, small planters, large planters, a minister, and a storekeeper, was more broadly representative of the region's economic and social groups than in 1850.[78]

### The Secession Convention

On the morning of January 16 delegates to the convention that would decide the issue of secession gathered at the statehouse in Milledgeville. After roll call, Reverend James Williamson of Telfair County opened the gathering with a prayer. One of almost a dozen ministers among the 301 delegates, "Uncle Jimmy" was not the best educated of the clergymen and certainly not the wealthiest. But Williamson represented southern Georgia's slaveholding plain folk very well. He rose "to seek the blessings of God upon the deliberations" and addressed "the throne of grace in a fervent and patriotic appeal." His prayer may have been the high-water mark for cooperationists, for the delegates then chose by acclamation secessionist George Crawford as president of the convention. They spent the day listening to the pro-secessionist speeches of commissioners from Alabama and South Carolina, both of which had already seceded from the Union. Two days after the convention began, its doors were closed to all but the delegates, whose deliberations proceeded in secrecy.[79]

Planter and former Whig Eugenius Nisbet of Macon declared that it was "the right and duty of Georgia to secede from the present Union" and introduced a resolution calling for the state to join a "Southern Confederacy." In the form of a counterresolution, Herschel V. Johnson argued that although Georgia should not stay in the Union without additional assurances and concessions from the North that its rights would be protected, it should consult and cooperate with other Southern states before seceding. Nisbet's resolution for immediate withdrawal from the Union passed with 166 delegates for secession and 130 opposed. On the following day, when Nisbet introduced the Ordinance of Secession that officially pronounced Georgia's secession, cooperationist Benjamin Hill offered Johnson's resolution as a substitute, but this motion was defeated by a similar margin—164 to 133. Consistent in their secessionist views, the Pulaski and Wilcox delegates voted against Johnson's "wait-and-see" resolution, whereas the cooperationists from the lower counties supported it. The Ordinance of Secession was adopted by a final vote of 208 to 89 after many cooperationists switched their votes in a show of unity once the handwriting was on the wall. On January 19 Georgia was out of the Union and for all practical purposes an independent republic. One week later a southern Georgia unionist wrote in disgust: "We heard the unpleasant news, a few days ago, that Georgia is no longer attached to the union. . . . Our nation is being led by a set of unprincipled . . . fools."[80]

Most cooperationists who changed their vote in the final ballot came from wealthy black belt counties in central and coastal Georgia where black majorities were common. Many of them were former Whigs. The die-hard cooperationists who steadfastly voted against secession represented white belt counties with fewer slaves and less wealth, primarily in the wiregrass region and hill country of northern Georgia. With only one exception, the six delegates from the lower counties of Coffee, Irwin, and Telfair supported the cooperationist position to the end and left a legacy of unionist resistance that endured beyond secession. Manassah Henderson was the exception. He switched his vote in favor of secession and evenly split the region's ten delegates, reflecting the virtual tie in the popular vote for delegates that gave secessionists their slim majority. At forty-six, the former sheriff and county ordinary was chosen by the plain folk as a cooperationist to represent their views in Milledgeville. As the owner of three slaves, Henderson had a greater stake in the peculiar institution than most of his plain folk neighbors, but there was little to indicate that he would break ranks with the other local cooperationists. Based on what he produced on his one hundred acres of cultivated land, he is best described as a livestock man and sweet potato farmer. Unlike many of the farming households nearby, he produced no cotton crop of record. Henderson seemed an unlikely candidate to join wealthy cooperationist planters from the surrounding black belt by changing his stance.[81]

Perhaps Henderson, like fellow cooperationist Herschel V. Johnson, now believed it his duty to defend Georgia "against hostile invasion from any source whatsoever," a duty even the most die-hard cooperationists admitted. It is more probable that he, like Johnson, joined the secessionists in a show of state loyalty and unity. Henderson had differences with the immediate secessionists from other parts of the state, but they were all Georgians. When it came to a choice between submission or secession, the latter seemed to be the only course that an honorable man could take. Northern attacks on the Southern way of life, denounced again and again by secessionists during the crisis, made men such as Henderson more self-conscious of their Southern identity, as conflicted and malleable as it was. This nascent Southern nationalism required that he and other plain folk set aside their local identities for a larger cause—the Confederacy. What remained to be seen was whether their new Confederate identity would be tested by war. Telfair's state senator, William Paine, considered it likely. From Jacksonville early in March he wrote to Governor Brown: "Old Abe, talks a little saucy, and may get up a small war."[82]

t was midafternoon before Captain Thomas Ryan got the Pulaski Volunteers into formation and marched them from the Methodist church down to the Ocmulgee River ferry. The day, Thursday, May 23, 1861, was marked by emotional farewells, prayers, and a "sumptuous" dinner on the grounds. A thirty-five-year-old planter and physician, Ryan led the soldiers along narrow dirt streets lined with tearful well-wishers—mothers and fathers, brothers and sisters, wives and sweethearts. Like farming and politicking, war was a household affair. Families with names such as Budd, Coley, Bohannon, Fleming, and Sapp sent from three to five men to join the unit. In many respects the company was an extension of the community and reflected the families, kinship circles, and neighborhoods that made up the county. It was no accident that the first company of citizen soldiers to leave the lower river was organized in black belt Pulaski County, where six out of ten voters cast ballots for secessionist delegates. The company's creation was a manifestation of their new Confederate identity and the political motivations that shaped their patriotism.[1]

Under the watchful eyes of the kinfolk and friends standing near Simon Merritt's new cotton warehouse, the volunteers crossed over to the river's eastern bank. Buggies, carts, and farm wagons waited to carry them to Buzzard Roost, where they would entrain for Virginia. The men loaded their baggage and waved a final time, catching their last glimpse of Hawkinsville, its frame homes, stores, and warehouses hardly a generation old. As they moved across the gently rolling cotton fields and hardwood bottoms, some of the soldiers passed near their own farms. Toward the end of the day they stopped at Thomas Sutton's plantation and set up camp. There they spent their last night in Pulaski County. As the company moved away from home, emotions ranged from excitement to homesickness. Of their first bivouac, eighteen-year-old Private Daniel Fleming would recall: "Not until we became settled in our camps for the night did we fully realize what a sacrifice of home comforts we had made."[2]

Like politics, mobilization began at home. It was there that the fear, patriotism, and uncertainty of war was first felt. Like the secessionist convert Manassah Henderson, households collectively weighed the sacrifices of volunteering against their own commitment to the Southern cause. Such decisions were influenced by the strength of the new Confederate identity of adult household members, female as well as male. For while the essential act of volunteering was a display of Southern nationalism determined by gender, women like Private Fleming's mother supported or at least acquiesced in their men's decision to volunteer. The home that Fleming and his comrades missed almost immediately was what the war was all about. Antebellum concerns about domestic security from internal threats were joined by concerns for homeland security unleashed by "the tide of Black Republican fanaticism." Mobilization carried away sons, husbands, and fathers while at the same time their very absence intensified sentiments for people and place, as Fleming's words reveal. Defending home and family was perhaps the strongest initial motivation for fighting the war.[3]

Home meant different things to Captain Ryan's troops, but as the volunteers traveled farther away from the lower Ocmulgee, home became a mixture of emotions and images of the people and places that had been at the center of their lives. For most of the younger men still living with family, these people included their mother, father, and siblings who lived under the same roof. For married men like Ryan, his wife and children were closest. But for all the volunteers, these people included the relatives and friends who surrounded them on a daily basis, white and black. The places were as varied as the people, ranging from backwoods yeoman farms to plantations to villages. The home place itself was a collection of rooms and porches, yards, outbuildings, and fences. Beyond it stretched the fields and woods, paths and roads, creeks and rivers that formed rural neighborhoods deeply etched in their minds. The property they enjoyed, whether their own or their parents', included clothes and furniture, land and livestock. For some men such as Captain Ryan, the property also included slaves.[4]

The soldiers' wartime identity and loyalty began at home and moved out in concentric circles to the neighborhood, the county, the state, and the new Confederacy. Perhaps no single image of home was stronger than mother's. When Private Fleming lamented the lack of "home comforts" before his unit even left the county, he was expressing a son's loss of the household comforts that were largely created by his mother. Images of family and home were central to the volunteers' motivations. Women brought the soldiers into the world and nurtured them, women cooked their food and made their bedding and clothes, and women nursed them back to health when they were sick or injured. Domesticity in the form of wise household management smoothed over life's rough edges on the cotton frontier. Sitting around the campfire on Thomas Sutton's plantation that first night on the long journey to the Virginia front, Fleming and his comrades immediately sensed the value of domesticity now lost.[5]

Home and its sentimental images of people, places, and property existed within the broader context of the plain folk's heritage, the accumulation of customs, institutions, laws, rights, and traditions handed down "by our fathers," as Governor Joe Brown put it. In a region whose social structure was based on racial slavery, black servitude was the benchmark of plain folk's liberty within the broader social structure. In a message to the General Assembly in 1861, Brown stated Georgia's reasons for fighting in terms that plain folk understood: An overreaching federal government led by a "Black Republican" threatened this "priceless heritage" now embodied in the new Confederate republic by setting class against class and race against race in "a bloody revolution." It was the duty of "the Christian and the patriot" to rally to the South's defense without hesitation and turn back the Yankees. To "stop to count the cost" of defending home and family placed the freedom and lives of white Georgians in jeopardy. "What is my property worth when I am a slave?" Brown asked. "If we are conquered, our property is confiscated and we and our children are slaves to Northern avarice and Northern insolence." Saving their cultural heritage from Yankee conquest motivated men to fight. Peter Coffee, a small planter from the Copeland neighborhood, echoed Brown's rhetoric when he wrote of the formation of a volunteer company in Telfair County early in 1862: "A more determined & cheerful response were never displayed by a people determined to be free or sell their lives in the cause."[6]

Brown thus continued to use race consciousness to create a collective white household of mutual interest threatened by Yankee invaders to encourage volunteering, just as he had raised the specter during the secession crisis. White supremacy and masculinity depended on black enslavement. The unmanly submission culturally associated with slaves, women, and children was the opposite of adult white male freedom and manliness claimed by yeomen. Like other white Southerners, plain folk took black slavery for granted; it was the natural social station for African Americans. Few of them felt guilty about the institution's brutal impact on the lives of the enslaved. Shortly after Georgia seceded, one Macon newspaper editor put it this way: "That African servitude is right, has too long been viewed and discussed as an open question. The South, at least, is no place for those who have scruples on this subject." Indeed, secessionists believed that the creation of a "new Republic" was the best way to protect slavery and the social hierarchy it supported from the "baneful influence of outside intermeddlers," namely Yankee abolitionists. Brown's imagined Georgia household was a place "of perfect homogeneity of interest, where every class of society is interested in sustaining the interest of every other class." Honorable men had no choice but to defend their homes, their masculinity, and white supremacy from "military subjugation and social ruin." As F. H. Bozeman, a Pulaski County Civil War veteran, bluntly put it many years later: "The War was about the 'Nigger.' "[7]

Brown's own popularity and leadership along the lower river also motivated plain folk to volunteer and support mobilization. In May 1861 he painted a bleak picture of Southerners driven from a national home created by their ancestors by an administration that was little more than "a military despotism disregarding all Constitutional guarantees and restrictions." By calling for 75,000 troops to invade the South, Brown argued, President Lincoln had unleashed the dogs of war on white Southerners and was enlisting the lowest Northern rabble with cries of "beauty and booty." Brown left little to the imagination as he described the horrors that would follow if the Yankees were not turned back. Homes would be plundered, slaves incited to "insurrection and murder," women and children assaulted and killed. The plain folk's patrimony, their sense of connectedness to family, heritage, and place, made it a duty for men to voluntarily join the army.[8]

There was no greater motivation to fight than to have one's homeland and freedom threatened by the enemy. Even as the Pulaski Volunteers were break-ing camp at Sutton's plantation on May 24 for the long trip to the front, Yankees invaded Virginia and occupied Alexandria. Georgia could be next. When New York policemen seized rifles belonging to a Macon firm, Brown retaliated against the "unprovoked aggression" by capturing ships belonging to New Yorkers moored in the port of Savannah and held them until the Georgia-owned guns were released. This and other actions to defend the state's honor further solidified public opinion behind the governor. Former cooperationist and unionist William Paine was won over by Brown's decisive-ness. In a letter to the governor one month before the war began, Paine described the sentiment along the lower river: "Every one seems determined to sustain your Executive action—and the first act of aggression from any quarter will rally the people to you, to a man."[9]

Paine's own metamorphosis from unionist to Southern nationalist re-flected a broader transformation of identity in the wiregrass country. After Georgia's secession, Paine returned to Jacksonville and faced the rising tide of Confederate nationalism at home. A month before the Southern attack on Fort Sumter, he was a Confederate enrolling officer and reported to Governor Brown on stationery embossed with the new national flag. Although Paine admitted that recruiting was slow before hostilities began, the lower river mobilized at a rate that exceeded expectations based on its population base. Accounting for approximately 2 percent of Georgia's white people in 1860, the region sent about 1,000 men into Confederate service by the end of October, thus accounting for 4 percent of the 25,000 Georgians then in national service. Additional volunteers in the spring of 1862 brought the total proportion of local military-aged men in Confederate service to about 60 percent in the war's first year. As Telfair yeoman farmers H. T. Bussey and William Studstill wrote the governor in 1863 regarding their county's early mobilization efforts: "We felt that we were not behind any other portion of Georgia . . . and felt proud."[10]

Mobilization, which included assembling, equipping, organizing, and training troops, was not one frenetic movement limited to the war's opening months. It continued throughout the conflict. But the lower river region, like most of the South, was woefully unprepared for war in early 1861. Although volunteer military companies were fairly common in Dixie's cities, its agrarian society made them less likely outside of larger towns. The local militia occa-sionally met and drilled, but plain folk largely ignored the military aspects of musters except when threatened by the specter of frontier Indian attacks, slave uprisings, or larger national threats. When war with Mexico had loomed on the horizon fifteen years earlier, for example, a citizen informed Governor Crawford that no military organization had existed in Telfair County "for some years." Only the excited "state of our foreign affairs" made local citizens "feel it their duty to organise." Confidence in the militia as a fighting organization had not improved fifteen years later when, six months before the Civil War began, one of its own major generals warned Governor Brown that the public's war spirit was "incompatible with the reality of the militia."[11]

White Georgians responded to the state of unpreparedness by organizing military companies. Early in May the *Georgia Journal and Messenger* declared that the war spirit "is on the increase" and for good reason. "Multitudes are rushing to arms—leaving the plow-share for the sword and the pruning hook for the spear." Companies from throughout central Georgia passed through the city of Macon on their way to the Virginia front in a seemingly endless parade of Southern nationalism.[12]

Along the lower Ocmulgee the war spirit grew stronger, too. In the six months between the surrender of Fort Sumter and syrup-boiling time in November, neighborhood after neighborhood answered the governor's call for troops. By the end of October 1861 seven local infantry companies and part of another were organized and accepted into the new Confederate army by President Jefferson Davis. The chronology of infantry company organization early in the year reflected the geography of secession, beginning in black belt neighborhoods and moving downriver into the white belt backwoods. The war spirit was infectious. On behalf of the Irwin Cow Boys, Captain James Y. McDuffie wrote to President Davis from Irwinville: "We bring our own arms . . . and I think we shall be able to render, as riflemen . . . Effective service."[13]

With the largest white population and the strongest support for secession, Pulaski County led the way with two infantry companies—the Pulaski Volunteers and the Georgia Rangers—and a battery of light artillery shortly thereafter. The Wilcox County Rifles joined the vanguard during the same week in a county that gave a higher percentage of its ballots to secessionists than any other along the river. During the summer months Coffee, Irwin, and Telfair, although less enthusiastic about secession, fielded companies as well. The Telfair Volunteers were organized during the first week in June. Remarkably, Coffee County raised two infantry companies (I and K, 23rd Georgia Regiment) in late August, as well as contributing men to a third (Company F, 23rd Georgia Regiment) composed of recruits from Cobb, Coffee, and Spalding

Counties. The Irwin Cow Boys, formed in sparsely populated Irwin County, were in training camp by late August. Matt Ashley, a member of one of the lower river's largest planting families, organized a cavalry company. Late in August, from Ocmulgeeville, Ashley told Governor Brown: "We will be ready to march whenever and wherever ordered." About one thousand recruits representing almost 40 percent of all white males of military age comprised this first wave of volunteers.[14]

Events in Pulaski County set an example for mobilization. Even before Brown issued a call for volunteers, community leaders organized volunteer companies to defend Georgia and the Confederacy. By the end of March Dr. Thomas Ryan had formed the Pulaski Volunteers, the first company organized along the lower river. With more military experience than anyone else in the community, Orran Horne, a Hawkinsville banker, small slaveholder, and veteran of the Seminole and Mexican wars, became the town's drillmaster. Afraid that the war might end before they could get into the fighting, men and boys flocked to Hawkinsville to volunteer and elected Ryan as their captain. So many men turned out that a second company—the Georgia Rangers—was established and Horne was elected company commander. The men marched and countermarched, practiced the manual of arms, and went into camp in a grove of trees near the Methodist church. They waited for orders to the front, but none arrived. Rather than have their troops succumb to boredom, Ryan and Horne sent them home to wait for the recall signal—a blast from the town's old cannon.[15]

Several weeks later Captain Ryan learned from Governor Brown that their offer of service had been accepted. He asked Private Sam Stephens to signal the recall. Stephens loaded the cannon with an extra charge to make sure that the boom would be heard in the county's remote parts. Afraid that the old relic might explode, he leaned it against a large tree and reached around the trunk to light the fuse. Just as he feared, the cannon exploded with a ground-shaking boom, its rusty pieces falling to earth. The largest piece landed behind Seaborn Manning's store about three hundred yards away and hit a hog—the county's first war casualty.[16]

Not to be outdone by Pulaski's Confederate patriots in their enthusiasm for the "cause," men in the counties below Hawkinsville journeyed to Georgia's cities to volunteer rather than wait for the formation of local companies. George F. McLeod traveled sixty miles from Wilcox County to join the Macon Guards, while W. A. Willcox of the House Creek neighborhood went about thirty miles to Hawkinsville to enroll in the Pulaski Volunteers. As many as

Plain folk volunteers of the Irwin Cow Boys, Company A, 61st Georgia Regiment, in camp at Savannah in December 1861. (Courtesy of Chip Newman)

fifteen Telfair County men signed on with the Georgia Hussars at Savannah, including Charles, Jacob, and Locke Clements, the sons of Horse Creek planter Charles Clements.[17]

The first wave of infantry companies departed after the sheep were sheared and the corn was planted. The volunteers left harvesting the crops to the kin and friends who stayed behind. This favorable timing was purely accidental; in 1861 there was no master plan to raise and equip the companies. Confusion and uncertainty prevailed on the neighborhood level, in part because Georgia and the Confederacy raised troops simultaneously. Worried that Georgia would be invaded from the coast, Governor Brown organized his own army of state troops only to see them repeatedly called up for Confederate service. Bewildered citizens dealt as best they could with a multitude of questions that arose regarding enlistment, the entitlement of soldiers to Confederate equipment, the length of military service, and pay. Planter and state legislator Malcolm N. McRae was approached by Telfair County residents with numerous concerns about the organization of local infantry companies: How many men did it take to form a company? How long would they serve? Who was responsible for outfitting the men? Obviously frustrated by questions he could not answer satisfactorily, McRae wrote Brown: "We have exerted ourselves in the matter and there being a difference of opinion . . . I deemed it necessary to write to you on the subject." McRae's letter, composed shortly before the county's first infantry company was organized, was typical of those that reached the governor's office from confused citizens.[18]

People had questions for planter-politicians such as Malcolm N. McRae because they risked their most valuable possessions—their kinfolk—in the gamble for the new Confederate republic. Most of the soldiers were from plain folk households that depended on small farms and white labor for subsistence. Every white man who joined the army took one laborer from the fields and reduced crop harvests. Unlike Senator McRae, the households of slaveless plain folk could not fill the labor shortage created by mobilization with slave labor. But McRae and his fellow slaveholders had an answer: Their sons volunteered, too. McRae's son Alexander, his only child of military age in 1861, joined the Georgia Hussars just after turning eighteen. He left Lumber City for Savannah and signed up along with his uncle, John C. McRae, before a local infantry company was organized.[19]

Even in traditionally unionist Telfair County, a middle ground between the poorer white belt counties below and black belt Pulaski County upriver, slaveholders' sons voted for Southern nationalism with their feet early. After all, these households were responsible for bringing Telfair to within a handful of votes of a secessionist majority. Although the antisecession vote may well have been larger if the January 2 vote were for secession rather than for delegates to a secession convention, a solid core of pro-secession, slaveholding households formed the local vanguard for Confederate mobilization. In early June 1861, for example, eight extended slaveholding families provided between three and five men each for the Telfair Volunteers. These men alone accounted for 26 percent of the soldiers carried on the company roster. In fact, in instances where families sent more than three men into the company, slaveholding families accounted for about two-thirds of them. The slaveholders ranged from the sons of plain folk masters such as Alfred Burnham to the sons of Woodson Willcox, the county's largest planter. Planter Duncan McRae's household may have been the most ultra-Confederate of all. Four of Duncan and Jane McRae's sons joined the Telfair Volunteers. William, the youngest, was barely sixteen. When considered as a group, slaveholding families, which accounted for about 32 percent of the county's total white population, contributed at least 36 percent of the Telfair Volunteers in the spring of 1861. When it came to early mobilization, slaveholding households led by example.[20]

About two-thirds of the Telfair Volunteers were plain folk who volunteered from nonslaveholding households. Such men formed the overwhelming majority of the infantrymen in all companies. Some of them, such as Private William Jones, were described as a "farmer" or "laborer" in their parents' household. They worked long hours on the family farm or, as may have been the case with Jones, tenant-farmed another man's land. Others, like Private James Shelton and his brother, Third Sergeant Nathaniel Shelton, had left their parents' households by 1861. The Shelton brothers' aging father and mother, Methodist preacher Charles Shelton and Jane Boyd Shelton, led a hardscrabble existence on a small home place and claimed a total wealth of only $450.[21]

The recruits who filled out the companies' ranks as privates and noncommissioned officers were usually between eighteen and thirty years of age. William Jones, for instance, was about twenty when he left home. Most of the men who enrolled in the State Rights Guards early in 1862 were born between 1835 and 1844, making them somewhere between eighteen and twenty-seven at the time of their enlistment. Some boys managed to slip in under the eighteen-year age limit established by the Confederate army early in the war. Henry Tomberlin, who gave his birth date as 1844 and was listed as fifteen by the census taker in 1860, managed to stay on, perhaps because he worked as a farm laborer for the company's captain, Samuel Fuller, and lived in Fuller's home. Lafayette Griffin was one of the youngest volunteers in a local infantry company. He enrolled in the Pulaski Blues in October 1861 at age fourteen, only to be discharged as "under-age" after eight months at the front. William Paine admitted that he got into a "scrape" with the father of two minors he recruited. The boys, who had walked twenty-five miles to volunteer at Jacksonville, were "fine looking fellows and very anxious to enlist." But their guardians refused to sign the consent.[22]

It was easier to enlist if one exceeded the upper age limit of thirty-five originally set by the Confederate government rather than being under age. Merrill Peacock may well have been the oldest man in Samuel Fuller's company. Born in 1809, he was about fifty-three when the unit was organized. Ezekial Scaff, a year younger, was a close second for the honors of company "pappy." Sixty-nine-year-old James Argo Sr. may have been the lower river's oldest volunteer. Although born in 1792 and a veteran of the War of 1812, Argo refused to miss the opportunity to follow his only son James Jr. to Virginia with the Pulaski Volunteers, even if he only performed "camp duty" for the younger men.[23]

Because medical screening was inadequate early in the war, the physical condition of the men varied widely. Most soldiers were between five and one-half to just under six feet in height, so the exceptions over six feet were noticed. When he visited their camp at Buzzard's Roost, a reporter for the *Georgia Journal and Messenger* was very impressed with the physical appearance of the Pulaski Volunteers. His words conjured up images of the storied tall and sinewy frontiersmen. The company included "many fine specimens of manhood and soldierly mein," he wrote, with fully one-third of its members standing over six feet tall. One strapping yeoman stood out because of his extraordinary size. Jesse Scarborough was six feet, four inches tall and tipped the scales at 207 pounds. Nicknamed "Baby," Private Scarborough became the company's mascot.[24]

The economic background of the men varied, but most of them were farmers. William Paine described the plain folk as "accustomed to the use of the rifle from boy-hood . . . being 'back-woods' men." They were used to fishing, gleaning, and hunting to help put food on the table. Most recruits were single and still lived with their parents. Jesse and William Jones were typical of such "hardy sons of toil," as Governor Brown described them. Eighteen and twenty years of age respectively on the eve of the war, they plowed the fields and tended livestock along with their two younger brothers.

Such recruits had worked under their fathers' supervision and escaped the humiliating regimentation that enslaved African Americans experienced in the fields. John Ward, a Coffee County one-horse farmer, epitomized the married recruits. He lived on a farm of less than a hundred acres and raised corn, peas, and sweet potatoes primarily to feed his wife and two young sons. He owned no slaves and grew no cotton crop of record.[25]

In black belt villages and towns, the hotbeds of company organization and recruiting, the backgrounds of the volunteers were more diverse. At Hawkinsville, day laborers, clerks, merchants, and skilled tradesmen joined companies along with farmers from the countryside. Daniel Mason hung up his clerk's apron and joined the Pulaski Volunteers. At twenty-seven years old, he claimed a total wealth of $450 the year before he became the company's second sergeant. Private Alvey Goodson, the son of Captain Ryan's nurse, worked as a laborer and lived with his mother Amantha in Ryan's household. It is doubtful that Alvey was eighteen (he was listed as sixteen in the 1860 census), but like many other boys he was swept up by the "war spirit" and followed Captain Ryan to Virginia. The staff of the *Pulaski Times* closed up shop and went to war. Although most recruits were native Georgians, immigrants were among the volunteers at Hawkinsville. Scottish-born merchant John Young claimed assets of over $6,000 before he enlisted in the Pulaski Volunteers and was elected first sergeant.[26]

Regardless of whether the volunteers lived in town or in the countryside, there were few slaveowners among them. Of the 139 Wilcox County men who joined the State Rights Guards, only three (2 percent) can be positively identified as slaveholders. However, one-third of the soldiers in the State Rights Guards had the surnames of Wilcox County masters, suggesting that kinship ties to slavery were extensive and resembled those of slaveholding households that sent volunteers into the army elsewhere along the river as well as in the South. Twenty-three-year-old Moses Daniel, for example, worked as a "laborer" on his father's farm on the outskirts of Hawkinsville. He lived with his parents and five siblings, all under age fourteen, and worked beside the adult bondsmen among his father's nine slaves. Moses joined the Pulaski Volunteers and was elected fourth sergeant.[27]

Scattered among the white recruits were a few male slaves brought along by their master or their master's sons to serve as body servants, bringing to the front some of the comforts their owners were accustomed to at home. Slaves set up and broke camp, chopped firewood, cooked, and washed clothes. A man servant was a luxury that only a few could afford. One of these was Orran

Horne, the Hawkinsville banker recently elected captain of the Georgia Rangers. Although Horne owned six slaves in 1860, a small number compared to the gangs owned by Pulaski County planters, he took along his slave Henry as body servant. Perhaps Horne thought that it befit his status as a company commander, a veteran of the Seminole and Mexican wars, and a senior militia officer to be waited on by his Henry. As the first infantry companies left the lower valley, Horne was touted in the local press as a Southern military man who outranked General Winfield Scott, the Union army's commander. As Horne's company passed through Macon on its way to Virginia, one newspaper said of the Yankee general: "Here may he meet a *Horn* and a *dilemma* connected with it."[28]

Infantry companies like Captain Ryan's formed the foundation of the Confederate army. Because each company was raised in the same rural neighborhoods or county, it became an extension of the community's economic, social, and political character. Rather than freeing up the recruits to act as individuals in a company of new men, as has often been the case in our own time, the company imposed old community relationships on the men. In some respects the company became a large family, a white male household in absentia sent to the front to protect their families at home. Captains became the new fathers, whereas junior and noncommissioned officers became surrogate older brothers. Many of the men were blood relations. There were "more kin folks here than you ever saw," W. A. Studstill wrote home from camp early in 1862. The Telfair Volunteers included four brothers from the McEachin family alone. Group cohesion was strengthened by the presence of two, three, and even four biological brothers in the same infantry company, not to mention cousins and uncles. Bound together by common ties of kinship and neighborhood, companies became focal points of pride as did their regiments and the Army of Northern Virginia (ANV), in which 80 percent of local Confederates served.[29]

Although the vast majority of enlisted men were plain folk, infantry companies were frequently organized in black belt towns and neighborhoods where mobilization leaders lived and support for secession was strongest. Captain Ryan, the Hawkinsville planter-physician, was typical of the men who led local mobilization. His "spacious and inviting" home was at the opposite end of the architectural spectrum from the small farm or log houses occupied by yeoman farmers. Embellished by tall white columns, long panel doors, and floor-length windows, it was a house few plain folk would ever know firsthand. And yet "within its walls" Ryan and his friends organized the Pulaski Volunteers. It was a home that benefited from slaveholding and reflected the connections between masters, black belt towns, and pro-secession. Ryan owned five slaves who worked in town as house and garden help, while over a dozen more labored on his small plantation in the country. His house was large enough to accommodate not only his white and black families, but also his nurse and her son. Ryan's home lent authority to his planter and professional ambitions as well as to his status as a patriotic Southern nationalist.[30]

Plain folk elected their captains from among the same sort of men they had turned to for political leadership before the war—slaveholders. In theory, aristocratic planters, the natural-born leaders and the managers of slaves, were elected by the same deferential plain folk who voted them into political office. But the reality along the lower river was more complex. Of the thirteen infantry companies organized during the war's first year, before casualties and Confederate conscription altered the character of their units, the enlisted men elected four planters as captains. Only Captain Samuel Fuller of Wilcox County's State Rights Guards, however, pursued planting as a sole occupation. The others mixed cotton planting with professional activities. Oliver Cook and Seaborn Manning were planter-merchants who combined agricultural and mercantile ambitions; Thomas Ryan also practiced medicine. James McDuffie of the Irwin Cow Boys was the only small planter originally elected a company commander. Slaveless yeoman farmers such as Philologus Loud of Wilcox County closely followed the wealthy planter-professionals. They were elected the captains of three companies followed by a banker, two physicians, and a merchant, two of whom were slaveholders.[31]

Among company-grade junior officers, the role of planters decreased and that of plain folk increased, a pattern that mirrored the antebellum political tradition of sending planters to the state legislature while filling county level offices with plain folk. In time, this proved to be a significant aspect of company elections because first lieutenants were often selected as captains in the case of vacancies created by death, disability, or resignation. Slaveless plain folk accounted for 50 percent of the men originally chosen as first lieutenants, while yeoman slaveholders claimed 20 percent. Thus, they were often first in line to move up the company chain of command. Equal numbers of small planters, merchants, and professional men, some owning a few slaves, accounted for the remaining 30 percent. David McCall of the Wilcox County Rifles was typical of the slaveless yeomen elected second in command of half of the lower river's companies. A prosperous farmer, he worked 150 acres and grew corn, potatoes, and four bales of cotton in 1859. Prominent in public affairs and fraternal life, McCall served as county tax collector and senior warden of the Irwin Masonic Lodge. The representation of slaveless plain folk was even greater (almost 60 percent) among second lieutenants, while the remaining 40 percent was comprised of a hotel keeper, a small slaveholding professional man, a yeoman slaveholder, a small planter-merchant, and a planter. Richard Tucker, the Irwin Volunteers' second lieutenant and the son of a prominent Primitive Baptist preacher, represented this group of junior officers. A nonslaveholding farmer, he cultivated 50 acres with a horse and mule and raised 300 bushels of corn, but no cotton crop of record.[32]

Plain folk thus elected slaveholders to lead 60 percent of the infantry companies formed in 1861 and 1862. These were the men who led mobilization and showed appropriate enthusiasm for the cause. Meanwhile, nonslaveholding plain folk were elected as first lieutenants in 50 percent of the units. This arrangement honored traditional patterns of deference in the political culture that officers and men shared but gave plain folk a voice in the company's officer circle. Although most conspicuous as captains, planters were outnumbered as infantry company commanders by professional men and plain folk who, though often masters, were not members of the planting elite. It is clear from this trend, however, that plain folk were not antagonistic toward slaveholders at election time. They repeatedly chose slaveowners to lead them at the highest level. Such company-grade officers came from the same neighborhoods and counties as their men. When their roles were combined with the local mobilization leadership reflected in the high number of volunteers from slaveholding households, it is difficult to argue that planters and their families avoided Confederate service at the expense of lower river plain folk.[33]

Considering the region's overwhelmingly rural character, a surprising number of professional men were also elected first or second lieutenants. At the beginning of the war 28 percent of the company-grade officers were professional men in part or whole. Indeed, there were almost as many merchants and physicians among the captains and lieutenants as there were planters. In this respect, the local company-grade officer corps was similar to the Confederate leadership emerging in other Southern areas situated on the borderland of cotton-growing regions. Such leaders lived and worked along lines of commerce and communication and played leading roles in modernizing transportation and improving communications. In Pulaski County, for example, both Orran Horne and Thomas Ryan were counted among the "friends" of the Macon and Brunswick Railroad and attended meetings that supported its construction.[34]

This commercial impulse among local officers reflected a strong desire of the business elite for greater economic independence from the North. Within the professional class, economic freedom joined defense of home, family, nation, slavery, and white supremacy as initial motivations for enlisting. When the war broke out, many professional men were in their early thirties and thus older than most enlisted men. They grew up in an era of escalating antitariff and free trade rhetoric. They agreed with Governor Brown when he declared in 1861 that "no country has suffered greater wrong than has been inflicted upon the South for the last quarter of a century, under the unjust and iniquitous system of [tariff] legislation adopted by the government of the United States." Rising commission, freight, and insurance rates, all of which resulted in "the usual expense to us, and profits to the Northern merchant," was the price of doing business with Yankee middlemen in the transatlantic trade. These costs were passed along to the growing number of cotton farmers who traded at their stores. In Brown's view the South, and by extension their own state and neighborhoods, had been reduced to dependent commercial "provinces" in order to "build up and pamper the power of a haughty rival section."[35]

To Governor Brown and his pro-secession supporters, however, the war's aims were greater than the "political independence" and nationalistic ambitions expressed by secession and the Confederacy. They now included "commercial independence." Brown warned Georgians that to win political freedom without economic independence would leave the South "subject to Northern rule and our political destinies will soon be controlled by those who have our commercial interests under their power." By leading volunteer companies to the front, professional men did more than protect regional pride. They threw off the yoke of Yankee commercial domination and reclaimed their honor as independent men. In the villages and towns, merchants often led the way. At Hawkinsville, for example, Warren Wood and William Thomas joined the exodus of professional men when they joined the Pulaski Blues and left their partner Gabriel Coley at home to run their dry goods business. Wood was elected captain of the company. Even in backwoods Douglas, professional men led early mobilization. A country peddler, hotel keeper, and store owner directed the meeting to organize an infantry company in May 1861. James K. Hilliard, the hotel keeper and Coffee County's leading secessionist, was elected one of the company's lieutenants. But it is also evident that for some professional men joining the officer's corps had less to do with commercial independence than with practical considerations. Shortly before the shooting started, one local attorney admitted to the governor: "The law is very flat, nothing doing, and I think I acted wisely in accepting the position I hold in the army—I can always resign when times improve."[36]

Because of their social status as merchants, planters, physicians, and prosperous slaveholding farmers, the leaders of the mobilization effort could depend on another factor to work in their favor—neighborhood political tradition. In company elections, it was natural for enlisted men to follow political customs and for would-be officers to use their political party connections. By early 1861 this meant Joe Brown's Democratic Party machinery, which, like the national party, professed Southern rights, white egalitarianism, and white supremacy. In the decentralized and chaotic political landscape of the late 1850s, county-level party machinery formed the most stable political framework. Three out of four Confederate infantry companies raised in Pulaski County were originally commanded not just by Democrats, but by members of the party's executive committee, a small inner circle of political insiders. Such local party leaders were best equipped to use political motivators to recruit citizen soldiers into volunteer companies and keep up their morale. Orran Horne, Seaborn Manning, and Thomas Ryan all belonged to this relatively small clique that managed the party on the county level. All three men—each with commercial backgrounds—led infantry companies to the front during the war's first year. These same men had helped John C. Breckinridge win almost 60 percent of the votes cast in Pulaski County the previous November. The trend was the same in the lower counties. Oliver Cook, a merchant, planter, and states' rights Democrat who had recently won a seat in the General Assembly, was elected company commander by the Irwin Volunteers. Similarly, early in 1862 yeoman farmers in Wilcox County elected Samuel Fuller, another Joe Brown Democrat, captain of the State Rights Guards in a county that had led all others in the percentage of votes cast for secessionist delegates. By early 1861 such men were Brown's local political voice among the politically aware plain folk who were increasingly convinced that they had a stake in a new Southern republic.[37]

Mobilization's leadership on the neighborhood level changed after 1861. Enthusiastic town professionals, small slaveholders, plain folk, and planters who had expressed patriotic and political motives for forming companies were now replaced by men who had sat out the first wave of volunteering. By the spring of 1862 few doubted that the war, contrary to initial expectations, would be anything but a long and bloody struggle. More troops were needed. On February 11, 1862, Governor Brown's proclamation "To the People of Georgia" put them on notice that President Jefferson Davis needed twelve more regiments from Georgia to serve for "*three years or during the war.*" The local quota was five new infantry companies, or about 650 to 700 more men. When this local quota was combined with the soldiers already at the front, at least 60 percent, and in some neighborhoods more, of the military-aged men would be in the Confederate army. Broadsides distributed throughout lower Georgia encouraged men from the wiregrass region to continue their exemplary support of the war by volunteering.[38]

Although these new soldiers were officially volunteers, their enlistment had required some coercion, and the mood that surrounded their organization was somber in contrast to the war spirit of early 1861. On Tuesday, March 4, 1862, the military-aged men assembled at their muster grounds in response to Brown's proclamation. Standing before the ranks, their regimental militia officers asked for volunteers, who would receive a fifty-dollar bounty, transportation to training camp, and the right to elect their own company-grade officers. If, however, an insufficient number of volunteers stepped forward, the commanding officer was "directed to *detach* or *draft*" the balance of the number needed. The first men to be drafted were those who failed to turn out for the muster "except from Providential cause made known at the time." These conscripts lost both the bounty and the right to vote for company officers, which were reserved for the "brave volunteer." County justices of the peace, who attended the musters, recorded the names of absent men and forwarded them to the state adjutant general's office for action. The threat of conscription was needed to fill out the ranks of the new infantry companies.[39]

In this strained atmosphere of continued mobilization, the local planter elite assumed the mantle of military leadership. Though politically aware slaveholders played a significant role in raising companies during the early months of the war, they were generally small masters owning fewer than ten slaves or small planters and professional men. Now in the spring of 1862, after a full year of war and on the eve of Confederate conscription, some of the valley's largest planters were elected by the plain folk to lead them into battle. The war was now clearly a long campaign to preserve the Confederate nation, white liberty, and black bondage. In Pulaski County, Seaborn Manning was elected captain of the Pulaski Greys. Samuel Fuller, the third largest planter in Wilcox County with forty-one slaves, was chosen company commander of the State Rights Guards. And in Irwin County, Oliver Cook, the thirty-one-year-old planter-merchant and member of the Georgia legislature, was elected captain of the Irwin Volunteers. Men owning more than twenty slaves were elected captains for 60 percent of the new infantry companies, compared to none in 1861. Most of them were in their thirties and brought years of experience in political office along with them. Although the captains elected in the spring of 1862 were mostly planters and planter-merchants, men with professional backgrounds continued to set examples of leadership by standing for election as junior and noncommissioned officers. Asa Pipkin, a struggling merchant–turned corporal in the Pulaski Greys, described the officers of his company as "substantial business men of Hawkinsville."[40]

The most striking example of planter leadership was that of William Manning, who became colonel of the 50th Georgia, a regiment formed largely by companies organized in the poorer piney woods of southern Georgia. Unlike Southern Democrats Oliver Cook, Samuel Fuller, and Seaborn Manning, William Manning was a former Whig and unionist. With one hundred slaves on his cotton plantation in the Spalding neighborhood, he was the third largest slaveholder in the area and as close to the Southern planting elite as one came along the lower river. A visitor to the family plantation recalled china, damask table cloths, and mahogany beds. When he left home in March 1862, Manning left behind not only a mansion but also a highly productive agricultural village that rivaled the county seat of Douglas in size. His 1860 cotton crop alone, before deducting expenses, was worth almost $6,000. The Coffee County Guards, one of the companies in Manning's regiment, recruited heavily in the old Whig neighborhood of Spalding, and Manning's yeoman neighbor Alfred Smith was elected its first lieutenant.[41]

The emergence of planter leadership in the spring of 1862 suggests that some of the tensions that existed between plain folk and planters in the Old South were resolved in the name of wartime unity. In 1861 planters watched village bankers, merchants, and yeoman slaveholders rush off to an anticipated short and romantic war. In 1862 paternalistic planters stepped forward, including former unionist William Manning. Why? Too many men had died by March 1862 for planters in their thirties to avoid service, and the draft loomed on the horizon. Conscription was a coercive measure that divided rural neighborhoods and potentially reduced public support for the war. By volunteering to organize local companies and lead them into battle, planters united neighborhoods and encouraged plain folk to follow their example. It was also a test of manhood. As Governor Brown reminded men of military age who were willing to risk the draft: "I can not believe that the noble women of the State, who have done so much for the cause, would ever tolerate such delinquency." Women demonstrated their support of the war by sacrificing their men as volunteers and by permitting their own domestic space to be altered by the demands of a larger cause. Through such Confederate service, planters demonstrated their loyalty to the Confederate nation and the community, including its plain folk women. Rather than attending to their own narrow economic interests at home, men such as Seaborn Manning accepted the military consequences of secession and war that they helped create.[42]

The election of Telfair County physician James Humphreys as captain offers some insight into company formation early in 1862. Unlike Seaborn Manning and Samuel Fuller, whose black belt neighborhoods were secessionist in outlook, Humphreys lived in the traditionally Union Democratic neighborhood of Copeland. A forty-acre corn farmer and nonslaveholder, Humphreys was nonetheless a solid member of the rural upper middle class. By the time he was thirty-five his total wealth stood at almost $5,000. He was, like two other local captains, a physician whom people turned to in an emergency, a well-respected man entrusted with five slaves he managed for a minor heir. His household included his wife, three children, and Wiley Williams, a twenty-four-year-old Copeland merchant and boarder who signed on with Humphreys's company. In September 1861 the country doctor proudly informed Governor Brown that "my abilities" helped raise the company.[43]

Like many professional men who organized infantry companies, his initial motivations were mixed. He believed that the new Confederate republic was worth defending, but he was also challenged by community pride. By the time Humphreys seriously considered raising Telfair's second infantry company late in the summer of 1861, neighboring Coffee County, with about the same number of military-aged men, already had sent two full infantry companies to war. Humphreys took the lead in forming the new company in a county almost evenly divided on the secession crisis. Nevertheless, it would be a blemish on his community's reputation not to field a second unit. As the doctor told Governor Brown, he was "very anxious to have the county for its own credit sake" field another infantry unit.[44]

In August 1861 Humphreys advertised to enroll men and elect officers for the company, which was finally filled out only on the eve of the Confederate draft. Only about fifty men signed up. As the most highly motivated Southern nationalists in the county, they had volunteered the previous June. Humphreys was "unanimously voted for as Captain." Small slaveholder James Willcox was elected first lieutenant; William Hatton, a farmer and small master, was chosen second lieutenant; and nonslaveholding yeoman Lucius Williams was elected junior second lieutenant. The officers "drilled the men at two meetings" and "all profess to be satisfied," Humphreys informed the governor. The captain requested a commission for his officers and pledged that "the men will immediately prepare to enter a camp of Instruction at any point which you may direct." As he and other officers learned, the time-honored tradition of working the crowd at militia musters could result in one's election as an infantry company captain or junior officer. But Humphreys's unanimous election was also a tribute by farmers and small slaveholders for his service to the community as a physician and recognition of his reputation in the area.[45]

### "With No Stinted Hand"

On April 26, 1861, Mary Horne, wife of Hawkinsville banker and drillmaster Orran Horne, addressed the Pulaski Volunteers. The occasion was a flag presentation, a patriotic ritual that took place up and down the valley as company after company departed for the front. Mrs. Horne presented the banner made by women in the community to Private W. W. Williamson. She spoke briefly but to the point: "Take it, soldiers! and return with it to your homes with honor, or die beneath its folds in defence of Southern Rights and the independence of the Confederate States." White women such as Mary Horne recognized that their own destinies were now inextricably bound to a cause symbolized by homemade colors that had political meaning.[46]

Home, honor, independence, and rights—these were the words Southern nationalists like Mary Horne used to explain why their men left to fight and why the community sent them off with fanfare. Female participation in mobilization gave women a political voice in the conflict and stamped them as "Southern nationalists." James Humphreys's wife Rebecca Daniel Humphreys at least acquiesced in his role as soldier, company commander, and community leader. While managing their household, she and other patriotic women hoped to extend the positive influence of domesticity to the battlefront by collecting and forwarding food, sending personal items such as locks of hair and photographs, and writing letters to their soldiers.[47]

Flag presentations were the most public displays of female patriotism. Virtually every social group participated in the ritual, including plain folk, planters, and enslaved African Americans. Caroline Malloy, a domestic servant who belonged to lawyer Frederick Brown and his wife Fanny, joined her "white folks" at Hawkinsville for "a big celebration given for the Confederate soldiers." A yeoman farmer's wife attended a send-off in the Hopewell neighborhood and brought along Easter, a slave child who vividly recalled the excitement: "I never had heard such noises in my life. I hadn't never heard a fife or a drum, so when the band started playin' I got under Ole Miss's skirt an' stayed there." At a flag ceremony in Jacksonville, "many ladies" turned out to "bid the soldiers a hearty God-speed to the front." Among them was Miss Sadie Bussey, a symbol of virtuous Southern womanhood, who presented a flag to the Telfair Volunteers. In the audience were women, children, and slaves. Julius Boyd, recently employed as a storekeeper by his planter cousin, stood in the ranks of the Telfair Volunteers as its new first lieutenant, aware that "all the plantation and a great many people from other homes in Coffee went over to see them off."[48]

More than any other public event, flag presentations and farewell rituals were vivid reminders that women as well as men embraced the Southern cause. The defense of home and family, women and children, were key elements in the ideology of secession and mobilization. Defeat, Governor Brown asserted, would "transmit a heritage of bondage" to the children of white Southerners. Women were centrally involved in the ritualistic passing of banners to companies of men departing for battle. Such public displays were fraught with symbolism. In the summer of 1861 Private Luke Campbell, a member of a plain folk household who accepted a flag on behalf of the Telfair Volunteers, declared before the gathering at Jacksonville: "Ladies, we duly appreciate the gift you have offered. 'Tis wrought by the hand of fair woman— consecrated by her touch—hallowed by being associated with her in its conception, its construction, its presentation." Mary Horne's call for death before dishonor at the Hawkinsville flag presentation brought a manly response from Private W. W. Williamson, who ascribed ideal woman's virtues to the flag: "We pledge to defend that proud banner in all its pristine purity and loveliness, unsullied and untarnished, with our lives, our fortunes and our sacred honors." Made by female hands, the flags were raised above the crowd and carried forward into the struggle not only as the "proud, high, haughty emblem—of our youthful Republic," but also as symbols of white Southern womanhood.[49]

Not only the flags, but also the soldiers were literally the creation of women. Just as Northerners considered their mothers of warriors the source of virtuous sons who defended the Union against rebellion, Southern patriots viewed their women as good republican mothers. The rhetoric of Southern nationalism enlisted the image of the faithful, patriotic mothers of the Revolutionary generation for the new cause of the Confederacy and encouraged its women to become "worthy descendants of the matrons of '76." At flag presentations, mothers bid farewell to their sons and to their sons' boyhood, both sacrificed for the new nation. Thus, sending a son to war with her blessing was a political statement. Standing before the crowd at Jacksonville in 1861, twenty-one-year-old Luke Campbell said it best: "The hearts of the Southern mothers are in the cause, and they are willing to give up their last brave-hearted son, not even sparing the youngest. She has with a heart-rending struggle and self-sacrificing spirit . . . embraced and kissed for the last time her brave boy, and sent him away to fill a soldier's post—maybe a soldier's grave."[50]

As young Campbell understood, joining the Confederate army was a rite of passage to manhood for the "boy." But, for women, it was one fraught with the possibility of the loss of their sons and husbands and their growing dependency on the state and county for sustenance, thus becoming a passage of their own to a more public worldview. This event was made all the more exciting for young men by the presence of young women, who had frequented political rallies before the war. The attention of girls and women confirmed the boys' masculinity, while military service made them more eligible for the women's favors if their wartime conduct met community expectations. The female ideal of battlefield valor was clearly understood by the soldiers at Jacksonville. Having accepted the flag from the hands of Sadie Bussey, Campbell admitted as much when he turned to the "Kind and Patriotic Ladies" and said: "We know full well that we dare never turn our footsteps homeward—that we dare never look upon your smiling faces—till Victory has perched upon this banner; for if there is one crime upon which woman frowns with more awful displeasure than another, it is that of cowardice." Failure to measure up to the standards of "female patriotism," Campbell warned his comrades, "will forfeit the smiles and affection of woman."[51]

At a meeting in the courthouse at Douglas in May 1861, Confederate patriots encouraged young men to enlist by holding out the promise of female affection as a reward. Merchant John Spivey stepped to the rostrum and called on the "young ladies" to convince their "lovers" to volunteer if they had not done so. Young women, Spivey continued, should tell their men "to sign their names as volunteers and defend their homes and firesides, and when they returned, they would love them for the remainder of their days." Eligible men who refused to serve should be ostracized and forced "to go to some other lady, for they would not unite with a coward." The meaning of "unite" in both conjugal and marital terms was unmistakable. Moreover, questions of female dignity and patriotism were implied, for honorable and patriotic women joined with volunteers, whereas only "some other lady" stooped to "unite with a coward." In the context of mobilization, selecting a "lover" became a political statement by women.[52]

Leaders of the mobilization obviously appreciated the sexual connection between male volunteerism, on the one hand, and female patriotism and the "affection of woman," on the other. They used this form of community pressure to meet their county's soldierly obligations. Able-bodied, military-aged men unwilling to volunteer were publicly shamed into service. Shaming was necessary because both personal honor and community reputation were at stake if a neighborhood or county failed to field its share of infantry companies, as Captain James Humphreys recognized. Newspapers played a role in the humiliation. They published alphabetical lists of counties with three columns beside their names that indicated the number of voters, the number of infantry companies fielded, and the number of volunteers in Confederate service. Counties that did not meet their quota based on these statistics were publicly chastised.[53]

The centrality of Southern women and their human relationships in the public discourse of local mobilization is evident. The patriotic mother sent her sons to war, the patriotic young woman sent her lover to the front, and the patriotic wife sent "the father of her children . . . to the tented field, and do or die for herself, her children and her home." No honorable female would do less than support her man for the sake of her own reputation, that of her family, and that of her county. In return for womanly patriotism, soldiers at the front and the patriarchs at home vowed to protect their women from Yankee invaders. As one pinelander wrote in June 1861: "The women and children of the piney woods can't suffer where this spirit of enlarged patriotism is abroad in the land."[54]

Community leaders also understood the power of religion in mobilizing neighborhoods for war. According to abolitionists, slavery was a sin and slaveholders were sinners. To white men in the Lower South, this was an insult to both their religiosity and their sense of equality within the nation. Honorable men could not let such slights go unanswered. Private Luke Campbell combined the powerful images of feminine virtue and heavenly guidance on behalf of the Telfair Volunteers when he declared: "We firmly believe God is with us, and we know that woman is; and it is for this reason that we have our abiding confidence in the success of our holy struggle for constitutional liberty."[55]

At flag presentations and public farewells, citizens sought God's blessings on the troops and their crusade. The rituals had a spiritual quality if for no other reason than they often took place in churchyards. On May 23 Hawkinsville bid farewell to the Pulaski Volunteers and the Georgia Rangers with a dinner at the Methodist church. Men and women, children and slaves gathered at the companies' camps in the churchyard. In such settings, God's cause and the South's were inseparable. "We know the great strength of our enemy," an infantryman proclaimed, "but Southern chivalry will prevail, for we have Right as our 'pillar of cloud by day, and a pillar of fire by night.' " It seemed only fitting that clergy play a prominent role on these occasions. Longstreet minister George McCall traveled to Hawkinsville and gave the farewell address to the volunteers in front of the Methodist church. After several hours of prayers, speeches, and socializing, a collection was taken up and more money subscribed to equip the infantry company. The double blessing of womanly virtue and providential favor made some soldiers confident of victory. As Luke Campbell so eloquently affirmed: "Oh, God, can it be that Thou ever intended that the land which gave birth to such noble, patriotic women, should be conquered by the vile, ruthless Goths and vandals of the North? Never! Never! Heaven itself would forbid it."[56]

As the first companies left the lower valley in the spring of 1861, confidence and hope filled the hearts of the men and women who took part in the nationalistic flag presentations and farewell rituals. Watching their men and boys march down the dirt streets toward railroad stations and steamboat landings, those remaining behind witnessed the departure of an extension of their community, still complete and whole as it passed bearing aloft colors "wrought by the hand of fair woman." None had yet been killed or wounded by enemy volleys, friendly fire, or self-inflicted wounds; none had yet succumbed to disease, their bodies wracked by pneumonia or rheumatic fever in filthy military hospitals. Despite the overwhelming odds against it, victory over the "vandals of the North," as Luke Campbell described the enemy, seemed within their grasp.[57]

A dozen years after the Civil War, Mary White, a seventy-nine-year-old Coffee County widow, knitted 175 pairs of socks and stockings in twelve months while "doing other domestic work." Her exceptional accomplishment was noted in a newspaper. The socks and stockings were probably intended for her grandchildren and great-grandchildren who numbered 132, the equivalent of a Confederate infantry company. White's aging but busy hands exemplified the productive potential of mid-nineteenth-century women in the rural South, where home manufactures remained both a necessity and a matter of female domesticity and pride. Home manufactures, particularly homespun cloth, were traditional symbols of plain folk's domestic economy and independence. During the Civil War, they became symbols of women's political commitment to the Southern cause.[58]

The lower valley's households were immediately called on to support the war effort, not only by sending their men and boys into Confederate service, but also by putting their women to work outfitting soldiers. Governor Brown invoked male honor to encourage white men to volunteer and defend their Revolutionary heritage. In June 1861 he challenged white women to match the Revolutionary War record of their female ancestors by producing one home-made uniform of any kind or color. By July the Ladies Relief Society at Macon had collected from rural and town households all sorts of clothing, including coats, drawers, handkerchiefs, hats, shoes, and socks, as well as blankets, pillowcases, and sheets. Boxes bound for the front also contained an assortment of domestic products—bandages and soap, along with lemons, jellies, and wine. Conspicuous in their material support of the troops were black belt planters. In the fall of 1863, for example, Longstreet planters sent provisions of every description to sick and wounded soldiers in Macon's hospitals, including baskets of chickens, sides of beef, sacks of crackers, meal, potatoes, red peppers, rice, and dried fruit.[59]

These material contributions were inspired by more than female patriotism. Sentimental Victorian-era Americans were preoccupied with family and home. Despite an increasing tendency toward individuality and the pursuit of personal happiness in that era, family bonds and obligations still prevailed. Households were the primary source of the emotional, material, and moral support that the soldiers needed as they faced annihilation in a modern war. Thus, family sentiment became an important force in mobilization, a critical adjunct to female patriotism. Balanced by parents' and siblings' "sense and judgment" of what their trooper "would need away from home," family sentiment stimulated the collection of resources of every description to sustain their men. Concern for the welfare of family members in the Confederate army encouraged households to re-create as much as possible "home comforts" at the front. Women met weekly in sewing circles and formed the foundation of relief work. In praising the women of one Ladies Relief Society, a Macon newspaper noted that "every one's natural affection" for her brothers, husbands, and sons would result in an outpouring of support "with no stinted hand." Women of the Soldiers Aid Society in Pulaski County rolled up the carpets and rugs from their floors and sent them to Virginia to put something between the cold ground of winter camp quarters and the bodies of their men. Prominent planters like George Walker III served as local agents for the Battlefield Relief Association and collected supplies for companies at the front. Such attempts to equip and comfort the troops were public acts of Southern nationalism.[60]

Early in the war the need for domestic labor was most pressing to meet the demand for uniforms and personal items. During the summer of 1861 women were called on to produce the winter clothing needed to keep soldiers from a humid, subtropical climate warm in northern Virginia. Each household was expected to supply two pairs of heavy brown or gray-mixed jeans lined with domestic cloth; one army jacket of the same material reaching four inches below the waistband and large enough for a shirt or vest to be worn underneath; one vest of jeans or linsey; an overshirt; and one or two pairs of drawers, heavy woolen socks, an overcoat or hunting shirt with belt; and one good blanket. Gray and blue flannel shirts were preferred over red, as red shirts "present[ed] an excellent target for the enemy." In addition, families were required to provide their soldier with a comb, pocketknife, small tin cup, iron spoon, knife, and fork. The ability of households to meet these demands depended largely on the spinning, weaving, sewing, and knitting skills of women. There were also financial incentives early in the war for families to make homespun clothing for their soldiers. In a circular issued on May 18, 1861, A. C. Wayne, Georgia's adjutant general, announced a Confederate commutation to reimburse soldiers who clothed themselves. The commutation was sent to their captain, who served as company agent and purchased the clothing "from home."[61]

Some studies of elite Southern women suggest that their participation in domestic cloth production "seems to have been actually of very limited scope." Privileged women's "traditional identities," notes one historian, "conflicted with the campaign for home textile production." A decline in home manufacturing in planter households, the lack of a textile-producing tradition among elite women, and the association of such work with slaves are among the reasons cited to explain why a "homespun revolution" did not materialize. But most Southern women were not members of the privileged and educated slaveholding class. They were plain folk, especially in white belt neighborhoods, where they formed the overwhelming majority of households. Plain folk regardless of gender knew their economic independence depended on the hands of white family members, whereas planter households could rely more on slave labor.[62]

The ability of families to support their soldiers with the production of homespun varied from household to household and from neighborhood to neighborhood. In black belt Pulaski County, where 70 percent of the region's planters resided and the market economy was more entrenched, the value of home manufactures dropped by over 40 percent in the 1850s. Although the importance of households as centers of production declined in the North and in black belt areas such as Pulaski, the white belt continued to produce home manufactures (defined as all nonagricultural articles of personal property made by the family "whether for home use or for sale"). Despite the inroads of the market economy upriver in Pulaski, the production of home manufactures increased downriver by about one-third in the 1850s. Clearly, white belt neighborhoods placed a higher value on self-sufficiency and were more dependent on home manufactures to meet family needs than were planting districts.[63]

In white belt neighborhoods, then, white women's identities were shaped by farmwork and the production of home manufactures. Like the men in their families, plain folk women were accustomed to working with their hands. Among the home manufactures, they produced coarse clothing that, while suitable for dress and work on farms, was considered unfashionable and uncomfortable among elite families. In most plain folk households, women had little choice but to make the textiles themselves. It is unclear whether farm wives considered spinning and weaving degrading simply because elite whites associated such work with slaves and poor whites, although they made as much use as possible of small carding and spinning mills to relieve them of the drudgery of thread production. In antebellum Coffee County, "much of the cloth" was woven at home, but people "came from near and far" to have their carding and spinning done at Kirkland's mill. The "ladies of the household" in Irwin County mixed white and black dyed thread, "making as pretty gray jeans cloth as could be found." In the 1850s Telfair County families traded at McRae and McMillan for calico, gingham, and "northern" homespun, but the country store sold local homespun and jean cloth as well.[64]

White women along the lower river were the keepers of a domestic cloth tradition and the teachers of its finer points. According to local slave narratives, white farm wives and plantation mistresses played important roles in domestic cloth production before and during the war. One former slave recalled that after the fighting started and supplies of foreign cloth dried up at Hawkinsville, thread "had to be spun at home . . . by the negro women" who were "supervised by the mistress." When women of plantation households did not possess knowledge of textile production, white women taught them these at "sewing frolics." Similar to quilting bees, these gatherings took place from time to time to instruct white and black women in domestic textile production. "Good seamstresses would come and spend the day and make the clothes for the family and slaves. Then the mistress would go to the other plantations and help her neighbors sew," one female slave remembered. On his cotton farm in Telfair County, yeoman master Alfred Burnham's daughter Sara Jane taught the female slaves to spin, starting one girl's training at the age of eleven or twelve. In plain folk households of the lower counties, domestic cloth production remained one of women's duties and skills.[65]

In rural areas, the wartime "sewing frolics" were publicly organized patriotic acts of women to meet the needs of mobilization. This was a highly symbolic declaration of independence from outside sources of cloth that dated back to the nullification crisis. Homespun cloth was critical for uniforms in 1861, before the Confederate quartermaster department could clothe the hastily organized regiments. Governor Brown's call for the creation of a homespun revolution to meet this need may have fallen on deaf ears among some elite white women, but no revolution was necessary among plain folk, only increased production. This was accomplished by reorganizing domestic labor through such public group action. As Captain James Humphreys informed Brown from the Copeland neighborhood, the volunteers "are having their Clothing Spun & wove at home." The term "homespun" signified his men's sense of regional pride and independence as well as the political expression of Southern nationalism among women. According to the *Georgia Journal and Messenger* in October 1861, Telfair women emulated the female patriots of 1776 by setting "an example of patriotism worthy of all imitation" in domestic cloth production. The mothers, sisters, and wives of ninety-one men in one company forwarded to each a complete winter outfit consisting of an overcoat, vest, pants, drawers, and shirt. The only parts of the uniforms not made in Telfair were the buttons. "We call this practical independence," the newspaper's editor asserted, and urged other female patriots to do the same.[66]

Reasons beyond female patriotism and familial duty stimulated homespun production. Writing from the Temperance community in December 1861, small planter Peter Coffee cautioned Governor Brown that the price of homespun, like that of everything else, was out of control. It had climbed from ten to seventeen cents per yard in nine months. Thus, there was a compelling reason to produce homespun cloth as a purely economic endeavor, to create something to sell in an inflationary marketplace, and to bring income into a war-strained domestic economy. In the process, some women simply wore out their cotton cards. In 1864 a Pulaski court recommended that the county buy both cotton cards and yarn from the state and distribute them among soldiers' wives by lottery. Having seen many of their men off to war, however, women struggled with a new reality—food shortages. The manpower drain created by mobilization threatened their ability to feed *and* clothe their own households. Given the choice between working in the fields to produce food or sitting at spinning wheels and looms, women out of necessity chose food production over cloth production, ultimately leaving the homespun industry to those with surplus labor, usually slaveholders. The decision of plain folk women to decrease homespun production after 1861 had nothing to do with a lessening of support of their men in the Confederate army and everything to do with the survival of their families at home.[67]

Secessionists narrowly carried the lower river in January 1861, but their fears that plain folk would become the enemy in Georgia were not immediately realized. Once the war began, black and white belt neighborhoods closed ranks and mobilized. By March 1862 about 60 percent of military-aged men in the area were already in Confederate uniform, a rate of mobilization comparable to that of black belt communities. The governor appealed to the plain folk's sense of Southern honor and race consciousness as he exhorted them to defend their homes, families, and property from Yankee invasion and emphasized the consequences of a Northern victory—emancipation. Men from all walks of life voluntarily answered the call, joining local infantry companies organized primarily by Democratic Party leaders of the Brown stripe. The yeoman rank and file continued their traditional pattern of deference to the planting and professional elite by electing company officers from this group. For die-hard Confederate nationalists like Norman McDuffie, mobilization and the Southern cause became a new civic project embraced by the "friends of our country," people determined to preserve their state and nation.[68]

Women, then, were among the new country's friends and played a critical role in mobilization. Female patriotism and family sentiment were manifestations of a larger sentimental culture in which women championed enlistment and advocacy for the war as a test of manhood. Such encouragement, as well as the many public and private acts to support the soldiers, was a political expression of their own Southern nationalism. Flag presentations were public rituals whereby women linked the private and personal world of home and the new Confederate nation. Flags made and publicly presented by female hands personalized the associations between the front lines and the home front. Support for the war extended beyond secessionist politicians and soldiers to ordinary white women and children in every neighborhood who sacrificed the men of their households for a larger public good—the war effort. Despite the divisions revealed during the secession crisis, the war created a remarkable degree of unity in 1861, and the soldiers were confident of their ability to whip the Yankees. The lower river not only met but also exceeded its expectations for mobilization during the war's first year. Writing from the piney woods in May 1861, a resident reported: "The feeling is all right out here in the Wiregrass country, and each one of us feel that we are more than a match for a dozen of [Lincoln's] hirelings."[69]

**E**ight weeks after the Pulaski Volunteers left their first bivouac at Thomas Sutton's plantation in piney woods Georgia, they arrived in Manassas, Virginia. They were hundreds of miles from home. Each step of the journey had taken them farther away from familiar faces and places and into strange surroundings—Macon, Wilmington, Petersburg, and then Howard's Grove on the outskirts of Richmond. Their stop was not an accident. Even before departing Hawkinsville, the men of Captain Thomas Ryan's company had "directed our officers to tender our services to President Davis, with the request that we be assigned to the regiment . . . being formed by Hon. Francis S. Bartow" at Howard's Grove. A planter, Yale graduate, and one of Georgia's representatives in the new Confederate Congress, Bartow was a staunch states' rightist from Chatham County, Georgia. The company's officers put their request before Governor Brown, and he approved it. Rather than trust their fate to a faceless military bureaucracy, the citizen soldiers of the Pulaski Volunteers picked their company officers, their regimental commander, and their place to fight—the Virginia front.[1]

In late May the Pulaski Volunteers got their wish and mustered in as Company G, 8th Regiment, Georgia Volunteer Infantry, at Howard's Grove, Virginia.

Although infantry companies formed the Confederate army's core, soldiers took pride in regiments like Bartow's 8th Georgia. A regiment usually consisted of ten companies containing at full strength about fifty officers and one thousand enlisted men. Only days after its organization, Bartow's regiment was sent to Harpers Ferry, the scene of abolitionist John Brown's raid. There they became a part of the Second Brigade of General Joseph E. Johnston's Army of the Shenandoah, one of four infantry brigades guarding the Shenandoah Valley.[2]

As an approach to the Confederacy's capital at Richmond, the Shenandoah Valley was strategically important to the city's defense; moreover, from that position the Confederates could attack the flank of the Union forces invading northern Virginia. It was in the valley that, as a private in the Pulaski Volunteers recalled, the men first "experienced real war," but not what they expected. After destroying much of Harpers Ferry and abandoning it to the enemy, the Confederates retreated toward Winchester. They burned valuable military supplies, along with railroad cars and locomotives, on the tracks. Retreating and camping in the fields and groves left the troops weak and vulnerable to disease. At Winchester, one of them wrote, "We suffered much from sickness." By the time Ryan's men were ordered to Manassas, a junction of the Manassas Gap and the Orange and Alexandria Railroads, one of his men remembered, "nearly half of our company was unfit for duty." From Winchester, Bartow's regiment marched twenty-seven miles over rough terrain, forded the Shenandoah River, and reached the Manassas Gap Railroad at midnight. The march, wrote one who made it, was "fatiguing in the extreme."[3]

The regiment then endured a "slow, tedious" train ride of about eight hours to cover the thirty-five miles to Manassas. Most of the Army of the Shenandoah detrained from cattle and freight cars at Manassas late on a Saturday morning. The 8th Georgia marched over three miles to "camp in the woods, without tents, and without food." It was now under the command of the hero of Fort Sumter, Pierre G. T. Beauregard, and attached to his Army of the Potomac, which stood between Richmond and Brigadier General Irvin McDowell's invading Union army. Beauregard established an eight-mile-long defensive line along the southern bank of Bull Run River about three miles north of the railroad depot at Manassas Junction. An attack by McDowell's forces was expected at any hour. The timely arrival of the Army of the Shenandoah now brought the Confederate total to about 22,000 men, roughly equal in size to the Union forces.[4]

On the morning of Sunday, July 21, Ryan's men rose before sunrise, prepared breakfast, and at about 5:00 A.M. heard gunfire to their west. The first great battle of the Civil War had just begun. Believing that the Yankees would strike in the direction of Manassas Junction, Beauregard placed most of his army on the Confederate right, including Bartow's regiment, which was in reserve behind the defensive line. The men now heard cannon fire in the direction of Stone Bridge, where the Warrenton Pike crossed Bull Run several miles upstream. Not long afterward, as day "broke brightly over the fields and woods," a scattering of "musketry fire" convinced Beauregard to shift his reserve brigades to the Confederate left. Bartow's men, along with those of South Carolinian Barnard E. Bee and Virginian Thomas J. Jackson, were ordered to move toward the Warrenton turnpike. To the worn-out men, it was a "circuitous, wearisome, and at times double-quick tramp of between ten and twelve miles." Ryan's infantry company of farmhands, clerks, laborers, and merchants moved along narrow lanes through a countryside of oak and pine thickets broken by corn and wheat fields. As they approached the Warrenton Pike, the noise of musket and cannon fire grew louder. The fight that Captain Ryan and the Pulaski Volunteers had been looking for since the war began was almost upon them.[5]

Across the Warrenton Pike and on the Confederates' extreme left, Colonel Nathan Evans's South Carolinians needed all the help they could get. Unexpectedly, the Yankees had launched an all-out attack on Beauregard's left flank a few miles above Stone Bridge. By 9:45 A.M. Yankee soldiers were pouring from the woods into the fields in front of Evans's outnumbered regiment on Matthews Hill. The Federals attacked across open fields, only to be driven back by rifle volleys and grapeshot. In a second assault the Yankees sent Ambrose Burnside's entire brigade against Evans's thin line. The Confederates were pushed back into a thicket, where they continued to fire at the enemy for about an hour. Evans called for reinforcements.[6]

Bee's and Bartow's men watched the fight from a plateau on the turnpike's southern side, where they had taken up a reserve position. They were separated from the rail fences and farm buildings on Matthews Hill by a hollow. Yankees swarmed over the farmyard buildings, fences, and haystacks. "Generously yielding his own better judgment to Evans's persistence," Bee ordered his and Bartow's brigades across the turnpike and through the hollow to attack a Federal battery from the shelter of a thicket. Under heavy artillery fire the men advanced. They took up position on Evans's right and, in Beauregard's words, "extended forward at a right angle and along the edge of a wood not more than 100 yards from that held by the enemy's left." Colonel William T. Sherman's brigade anchored the Union left.[7]

Along with the rest of the 8th Georgia, Captain Ryan and the Pulaski Volunteers found themselves in the thick of the battle. "Desperate fighting" took place in the thicket. Ryan's men fired volley after volley as the regiment took in return what one soldier described as "a fierce, concentrated, murderous, unceasing" fire. As one eyewitness described it, "It was a hell of a bullet-rain in that fatal grove.—The ranks were cut down as grain by a scythe.—Whole platoons melted away as if by magic." Beauregard characterized the fighting along the right angle formed by the 8th Georgia as "short range . . . sharp and deadly, bringing many casualties to both sides." Men could hear the balls hitting their comrades. Bartow's horse was shot from under him; his adjutant was mortally wounded; and Lieutenant Colonel W. M. Gardner, the 8th Georgia's commander, fell to the ground with a shattered leg. Among the Confederates in the thicket, "shot whistled and tore through trees and bones. The ground became literally paved with the fallen."[8]

After eight or ten volleys the 8th Georgia was ordered to withdraw from the thicket toward the Warrenton Pike. The men fired three more volleys— walking, turning, firing, and reloading—as they retreated across open ground and through the smoky thicket. In the confusion, some of the soldiers were separated from their colors and "a horrible mistake occurred at this point.— Their own friends taking them for the enemy, poured a fatal fire upon their mutilated ranks." For two hours the Confederates slowly gave ground to a force twice their size and gradually pulled back toward the Warrenton Pike. Even among seasoned veterans, retreat under fire was a tricky business. The withdrawal by the amateur soldiers shot up by both enemy and friendly fire turned into a rout, the men "fleeing in disorder" across the Warrenton Pike and into the farm of a bedridden widow named Judith Henry.[9]

Generals Beauregard and Johnston arrived on the hill behind the Henry house and tried to rally the men. It was at this point that Brigadier General Bee either said admiringly, "There is Jackson standing like a stone wall! Rally behind the Virginians!" or, having seen his own men cut up while Jackson's stood in reserve, angrily shouted, "Look at Jackson standing there like a damned stone wall!" Jackson's men had arrived sometime before 11:00 A.M. and now marched from the woods behind the hill of the Henry house, where many exhausted and wounded men of Bee's and Bartow's brigades fled. According to Beauregard, the thought "came to me that if their colors were planted out to the front the men might rally on them, and I gave the order to carry the standards forward some forty yards, which was promptly executed by the regimental officers, thus drawing the common eye of the troops." Encouraged by Jackson's brigade and the sight of their regimental flags and officers, the men formed on the line of their colors with Jackson's men in the center.[10]

Throughout the hot and humid afternoon the armies fought on Judith Henry's farm. By midafternoon the Yankees had lost momentum. At this point, Beauregard counterattacked with everything he had. Jackson's regiments smashed the Union center yelling "like furies," men on both sides hearing for the first time the "Rebel yell." The Yankees were slowly pushed from the hill, but not before Bee was mortally wounded and Bartow killed leading his remnant 8th Georgia back into the battle. In a final effort to retake the lost ground and win the day, McDowell ordered yet another Union strike shortly before 4:00 P.M., but fresh Confederate reinforcements attacked his right and sent his army into retreat. By 5:00 P.M. the battle was over and the Union withdrawal, like the earlier Confederate one, turned into a rout. The South had won its first significant victory and Richmond, and perhaps the Confederacy as well, was saved.[11]

It had been a deadly day for the Pulaski Volunteers. They helped win the battle but, along with their fellow Confederates, paid a heavy price. Except for Bee's and Jackson's brigades, Bartow's 8th Georgia suffered more casualties than any other army regiment—almost 20 percent of the Confederate casualties at Manassas—and earned the moniker "Bloody Eighth." As General Beauregard passed through the regiment's "remnants" after the battle, he raised his cap and, according to Private Daniel Fleming, said: "Gallant Eighth Georgia, I have the honor to salute you."[12]

What did it mean to Ryan's men to stand in the thicket under fire, sight down the barrel, pull back the hammer, and pull the trigger? Most of the Pulaski Volunteers were backwoodsmen accustomed to firearms. They had hunted in the oak thickets and piney woods of southern Georgia for wild game. How did it feel to stand in the trees "carefully loading, steadily aiming, unerring, firing, and quietly looking to see the effect of their shots?" What were their feelings when they saw their own neighbors dropping around them in the thicket? How did they reconcile in their own minds the "horrible mistake" of friendly fire cutting down some of their comrades? "Mere boys fought like veterans—unexcited, save with that stern 'white heat,' flameless exhileration [sic], that battle gives to brave spirits," wrote one soldier. But was that possible, given the greenness of the troops and the fear and confusion of battle? Each man struggled to give meaning to his first battle based on what he did, felt, saw, and thought.[13]

Captain Ryan struggled as well with what happened in the deadly thicket. Slightly wounded, the company commander reassumed his civilian role as physician and took stock of the casualties. Among his men, a dozen or so were severely wounded and needed immediate help. A. R. Coley, the son of one of Pulaski County's leading planter families, was so badly injured that he was soon discharged; Sergeant Daniel Mason's arm had to come off; and Thomas Boatwright lingered for an agonizing twenty-four hours before dying. But there were five more men and boys beyond help, citizen soldiers who scarcely two months earlier had marched from the Methodist churchyard through Hawkinsville's streets and off to war. Found dead in the thicket "weltering in their heart's blood," as Private Fleming described them, were the infantry company's "Baby" Jesse Scarborough and John Lowery, who only a year earlier had been a student. W. M. Bowen and John Carruthers Jr. were laid out beside them. All of these deaths troubled Ryan, but one other was deeply disturbing. The body of Alvey Goodson, the teenage son of Ryan's nurse Amantha Goodson, was also found in the thicket. The boy had grown up in Ryan's own home and followed him to the battlefield. How would Ryan tell his mother that Alvey was never coming home?[14]

During the eight-month lull in the fighting after First Manassas, Ryan's men and those who soon joined them in Virginia had plenty of time to think. The battle taught them that a war they had romanticized from a distance was a horrifying and bloody game of chance. Why had they ended up on Matthews Hill that Sunday while the Georgia Rangers, leaving Hawkinsville a few days after the Pulaski Volunteers, never appeared on the battlefield? What but bad luck could explain their late arrival on the Confederate right as a seemingly safe reserve brigade, only to be shifted to the extreme left and thrown into the breech? They also realized that relatively few men in the company did the actual fighting, if Manassas was any indication of what was to come. Because of sickness and fatigue, only thirty-six of one hundred men had entered the battle at Manassas. Incredibly, half of these soldiers became casualties. And what but fate could explain why Alvey Goodson, one of the youngest, and Jesse "Baby" Scarborough, one of the biggest and most beloved, died in the thicket in their first fight, to be stretched out among the lifeless bodies at twilight, while half of the men walked away unscathed?[15]

The Georgians also quickly learned that war was fraught with long periods of boring camp routine broken only rarely by minutes of battlefield excitement and terror like those at First Manassas. As one Coffee County soldier recorded in his diary: "Mostly all quiet and rumors of Yankees." Early in 1863 A. R. Taylor would implore his sister in Virginia to send long letters on any subject because they would "relieve to a great degree the dull monotony of Camp life." Camp routine, however, was broken by the arrival of fresh volunteers from home. By the time of First Manassas, Orran Horne's Georgia Rangers and Philologus Loud's Wilcox County Rifles had mustered in as companies in the 10th Georgia. The summer and fall of 1861 saw the arrival of the Telfair Volunteers, led by physician Henry Smith, storekeeper Julius Boyd, and planter John Coffee from the Copeland neighborhood. They were mustered into Confederate service as Company H, 20th Georgia. In Irwin County, small planter James Y. McDuffie led the effort to mobilize an infantry company. By the third week in August, McDuffie's Irwin Cow Boys were drilling at Camp Stephens near Griffin, Georgia. That summer Coffee County sent two infantry units to the Army of Tennessee: Companies I and K of the 23rd Georgia. Then in October Pulaski County fielded a third infantry company—the Pulaski Blues—mustered into Confederate service as Company F of the 31st Georgia. The Pulaski Blues, along with the Telfair Volunteers, joined the lower valley units that had already become a part of the Army of Northern Virginia (ANV). Two cavalry companies, one organized by James Leith, a small planter and member of Pulaski County's Democratic Executive Committee, and the other by planter-merchant Gabriel Coley, entered Confederate service as Companies G and H, 10th Confederate Cavalry. In addition, a battery of light artillery was formed in Pulaski County by Thomas Dawson and Ruel Anderson and sent to the Army of Tennessee.[16]

## "They Can Not Get Hearty"

Fresh recruits were needed following First Manassas not because of fighting, for the men were engaged in little but picket duty and rare skirmishes. The new men were required because of the tremendous attrition that wore down infantry companies during months of monotonous camp life. By the time the 49th Georgia Regiment and its four lower river companies reached Virginia early in 1862, the local companies that preceded them had been at the front from six to ten months. Although most of the troops were accustomed to outdoor work, month after month of camp life and constant exposure to the elements took a tremendous toll. One soldier wrote: "I believe I will die with Ennui. If I don't kill time[,] time will kill me." Before long, he and his comrades realized that life in camp could be deadlier than combat.[17]

The experience of the Telfair Volunteers illustrates this point. They entered Confederate service during the summer of 1861 with 104 men. Less than a year later, on May 1, 1862, the company's officers counted only 48 soldiers present for duty. As Captain John Coffee looked over the muster returns that morning, he saw that, if ordered into battle, he could depend on only 39 privates, 6 noncommissioned officers, and 3 commissioned officers. For a variety of reasons—resignations, disease, and disability discharges—the company was slightly less than half its full strength. Men came and went with alarming frequency, including officers. By the time the weather warmed up that spring, Captain Henry Smith had resigned to serve in the medical corps and the men had elected Second Lieutenant John Coffee as their new captain. Two days after Coffee's election, typhoid fever claimed the life of Luke Campbell, a former college student who had accepted the flag on the company's behalf at Jacksonville's farewell barbecue. In November First Sergeant William Rogers received a disability discharge, and two days after Christmas Larkin Ball died of pneumonia at Richmond. The following February, Thomas Willcox, a son of planter Woodson Willcox, became one of the few men who hired a substitute. Few of the soldiers were killed in action or died of combat wounds. The truly hard fighting had not begun; yet, even if everyone returned from hospitals, leaves, and furloughs that first week in May 1862, only two-thirds of the company's original members would be present for duty.[18]

Disease was the major culprit. It must have seemed ironic to Ryan's men that their first deaths came in the solitude of camp at Winchester, Virginia, where William Budd, J. T. Fleming and John R. Willis died and were quietly buried soon after the company left the Shenandoah Valley for Manassas. It was a deadly pattern that became all too familiar. Before 1861 ended, three of Ryan's eight noncommissioned officers died of disease or indeterminate causes; a fourth—Daniel Mason—succumbed to complications that resulted from an amputated arm; and a fifth was discharged "on account of rheumatism contracted in 1861." Only three of the original eight sergeants and corporals remained with the company by Christmas 1861. Among these survivors was Daniel Blue, who between May and September moved up the ranks from fifth to first sergeant due largely to the disease-related deaths of fellow noncommissioned officers. Alarmingly, almost 20 percent of Ryan's men died in 1861, with disease claiming twice as many men as battle-related fatalities. Like rifle balls, disease did not respect class, rank, or physical condition. In June

1862 William A. Barker, a private in the State Rights Guards, told his wife in Wilcox County: "I stand soldiering better than I expected to do. There is a great many strong hearty looking young men that does not appear to get along any better than a little weakly fellow like myself."[19]

Draining companies of men faster than they could be replaced, disease took a terrible toll for a number of reasons. Like much of the rural South, the wiregrass country's relative isolation shielded its people from the epidemics and childhood maladies that often swept through seaports and interior railroad towns. Thus, the recruits had little natural immunity to communicable diseases once they left the piney woods. Largely fought along lines of transportation like those converging at Manassas, Civil War battles brought soldiers into the mainstream of communicable diseases, which could attack their systems with deadly results. Moreover, the soldiers were accustomed to rural neighborhoods where the population density was in some cases as low as six people per square mile, and problems of household and human waste were dealt with individually by household. In army training camps and winter quarters, recruits were crowded into artificial towns where raw sewerage, impure water, and rotting garbage created cesspools that bred disease. The troops were particularly vulnerable after major battles, when rotting human and animal remains created acute sanitation problems.[20]

All soldiers encountered this environment, but the young and the old who went into service before physical examinations were required were especially vulnerable. Furthermore, the Confederate quartermaster department was unable to meet the army's need for basic necessities like blankets, clothing, food, and shelter. Thus, elderly men like James Argo Sr. who signed up in 1861 quickly discovered that their aging bodies could not take the beating of camp life. Argo was soon discharged "on account of age." One of the most common complaints of soldiers—second only to hunger—was their almost constant exposure to the elements. From spring through fall men often slept on the ground with little or no protection from bad weather. Private Barker wrote his wife that he was well "except a very bad cold. I feel rather dull and sluggish on account of the exposure I have to undergo." Daniel Smith, another member of the State Rights Guards, believed that his knee wound would have healed sooner if he had not been "more than wore out from lying in the weather and Being exposed." Unable to depend on the army for adequate shelter, soldiers used captured Yankee tents. In March 1864 Lieutenant William Smith, a member of a Coffee County infantry company, wrote shortly after the Battle of Ocean Pond, Florida: "Rained last night but I slept dry under my new Yankee

Fly." The cumulative effect of months of exposure left men fatigued and vulnerable to disease. As one private from Wilcox County admitted to his wife three months after volunteering, "I am tired of living the way we have to live. . . . We have not had any tents to sleep under since we left Goldsboro in N.C."[21]

Men from the Lower South expected that the Upper South's harsh winters would take a toll, but adverse weather conditions persuaded them that climate was an even greater killer than the Yankees. As early as August 1861, a Macon newspaper warned mothers and wives to prepare winter garments and blankets for their men in service. But there were never enough blankets, tents, and warm clothes to ward off pneumonia and rheumatism. At night, the sounds of hundreds of men coughing and groaning rose from regimental camps. A petition of officers from one Georgia regiment sent to Governor Brown from Manassas in January 1862 declared that "owing to the great change of Lattitude," its officers and men had been "unfit for duty ever since we have been here." Twelve men had died from exposure since their arrival. The officers sought Brown's help in getting their regiment transferred to Georgia or any other place in the Lower South. Redding Pate, an assistant surgeon for the 49th Georgia, knew firsthand the terrible harm inflicted by Virginia's winters. After serving with the Pulaski Greys of the 49th Georgia through the spring and summer campaigns of 1862, Pate was stricken by chronic bronchitis and rheumatism. He left the regiment in November and returned to Hawkinsville before the harsh winter set in. A week after Christmas, in a letter to Governor Brown, he offered himself as surgeon of an infantry regiment being organized for "State service." By "remaining in a Southern climate," Pate wrote, he could still be of service to the Confederacy, but not in "so Severe a climate as Va."[22]

Plain folk soldiers did their best to protect themselves from the elements with what was issued to them and what they found. They started in the basic training camps such as Camp Davis near Guyton, where the 49th Georgia was organized, or Camp McDonald near Kennesaw. If they belonged to the first companies that arrived in these camps, the men literally created new neighborhoods, a process that resembled frontier conditions, and one they repeated throughout the war as winter camps were set up. In June 1861 a recruit at Camp McDonald wrote to a friend at home: "It is for me to tell you of the numerous *new grounds* we have had to clear up; the wells we have had to dig; the springs we had to clear & put troughs in, and the arbours we have built in front & rear of our tents. We have worked very hard since our arrival." For recruits more accustomed to clerking in stores, the work was exhausting and their first introduction to the hard nature of soldiering.[23]

When they went into winter quarters, the soldiers at least had a roof over their heads. Although this customarily took place in November or December, winter camp might not be established until well after Christmas, forcing the men to sleep on the ground before then. Sergeant William Fisher of Coffee County recorded in his diary that his regiment did not go into barracks for the winter until the latter part of January 1862. He noted, however, that he was pleased with the arrangement: "Went into Winter Quarters that we built ourselves of pine loggs[;] we had snug cabbins with brick chimney." Such log huts became the soldier's standard winter home in the Upper South. Usually, four men dug out a six-by-twelve-foot rectangle about a foot deep. Then they raised a log crib four to five feet high, chinked the cracks, and roofed their new home with whatever material was at hand. A small chimney of split logs and sticks was constructed using the same technique. Rough planks, packed clay, or straw served as a floor. Except for the sunken floor, it was a smaller version of a log cabin. Fisher described his hut as "snug," and some men affectionately named theirs. But the wooden "cabbins" rarely kept the cold and dampness entirely at bay. Despite depicting camp conditions that sounded almost ideal, Fisher noted nine days later: "I [have] taken a congestive chill."[24]

Months of prolonged exposure, inadequate supplies, and poor shelter wore down the troops' resistance to disease. Given their rural backgrounds, the fact that many volunteers were physically unfit, and a harsh climate, it is not surprising that the death toll from disease was horrific. Men died like flies as epidemics swept through the camps, killing soldiers and permanently reshaping neighborhoods at home. For example, of the 139 soldiers in the State Rights Guards from Wilcox County, forty-seven men—or one-third of the company—died of disease, compared to 11 percent killed in action. Eleven men and boys from the Gibbs family left with the unit early in 1862; eight never returned. Measles, pneumonia, smallpox, and typhoid fever sent five of them to their graves. Losses to disease were only slightly lower in the Irwin Volunteers, where almost 29 percent of the men died of a variety of ailments compared to the 5 percent killed in action. Some units were simply unlucky when it came to disease, while others, such as the Telfair Volunteers in the 49th Georgia, were more fortunate. Though it belonged to the same regiment as the Irwin Volunteers and the State Rights Guards, the Telfair unit lost only 12 percent of its men to sickness and disease.[25]

Childhood maladies were usually the first to strike. In the first summer of the war, as many as one out of seven Confederates serving in northern Virginia came down with measles, which "prostrated" almost half of the Pulaski Volunteers at Winchester. The disease claimed more men after a second round of volunteering in the spring of 1862. John Gibbs lasted only ten weeks in the State Rights Guards before he died of measles. David Hunter of the Irwin Volunteers died of measles at Wilmington, North Carolina, only six weeks after he enlisted. Others followed. Reuben W. Clements, the first lieutenant of Hunter's company, resigned his commission in July 1862 due to poor health caused by an outbreak of measles. From camp at Goldsboro, North Carolina, in May 1862, Clements informed a friend back home: "I have not been able to drill five days since I've been in camp." The company had been racked by sickness, with men scattered in hospitals—twelve alone at Goldsboro, where "they have not recovered from the measles and mumps." Fifteen men had been in hospitals for over a month, Clements wrote, "and I can not tell how much longer they may remain there." At times soldiers turned to home for medical help. In September 1861, six months before he had raised his own company, country doctor James Humphreys from the Copeland neighborhood was called to Fairfax Courthouse by the disease-ridden Telfair Volunteers. He planned to spend three weeks treating them, "or until they somewhat recover from their present sickness some 60 of them being down."[26]

Diarrhea and dysentery were the most common ailments and put large numbers of men on the sick list. Loose bowels struck recruits' digestive tracts as they tried to adjust to new diets. Less than three weeks after leaving home, Private Stafford Thigpen of the Coffee County Guards wrote his parents from Chatham County that a digestive ailment had swept through the entire company: "I have had the Diarrhea so severe that I scarcely could go at all and all the rest has been the same way." Bad food, filthy camps, and contaminated drinking water made diarrhea a principal killer. Abel Moore, a private in the Pulaski Blues, was so debilitated by chronic diarrhea that he was discharged from service, only to die in a Richmond hospital three weeks later. M. J. Peacock, a sergeant in the State Rights Guards, survived battle wounds but not the chronic diarrhea that took his life at Richmond six months after he enlisted.[27]

Pneumonia was another major killer among the lower river soldiers and for good reason. Accustomed to a humid subtropical climate with mild winters (the average monthly temperature at Hawkinsville between December and February was in the mid-forties), soldiers were vulnerable to the Upper

South's harsher weather. Its winters were more severe and snow was more common. Often the ground would be frozen for days at a time. For the poorly clothed and quartered Georgians, it was difficult for men to "get hearty" and remain so, as Reuben Clements put it. For these men, pneumonia became a deadly foe. In some infantry companies, pneumonia killed more men than any other disease. Thirty percent of the troops who died of disease in the State Rights Guards succumbed to pneumonia, usually during the colder months between November and April. Pneumonia killed 10 percent of the company and claimed only slightly fewer fatalities than combat. In December 1862 the Telfair Volunteers lost First Lieutenant William Hatton to pneumonia at Lynchburg, Virginia, only two months shy of a year in service. Sergeant James Fleming died of pneumonia in Macon's Ocmulgee hospital during November 1864; of his parents, the *Christian Index* noted that this was "their second son who has given up his life in this terrible struggle for independence." Army doctors did not know what caused the outbreaks. Some considered it an "inflammation" and resorted to bleeding their patients, which further weakened them. Opium and quinine dosages helped, but in the blockaded South these drugs were scarce. Home remedies of all types, including mustard plasters, were tried as well, but nothing seemed to rouse the sluggish men.[28]

Crowded camps, impure water, and raw sewerage created problems that quickly became deadly. Contaminated water and poor food made typhoid fever, after pneumonia, the second major killer in the State Rights Guards. Thirsty men drank water unfit for livestock. As a result, outbreaks of the disease swept through entire regiments, typhoid claiming more than 17,000 Confederate deaths over a single eighteen-month period. Typhoid killed nine men in the State Rights Guards, taking 19 percent of all soldiers who died of disease to their graves. It struck so swiftly that G. C. Ball and Robert Land never saw combat, both men dying at Camp Winder near Richmond in July 1862. Thomas Dixon of the Irwin Volunteers succumbed to typhoid at Goldsboro, North Carolina, eight weeks after joining the company. He never reached the Virginia front. Dixon lasted longer than a fellow member of his company, twenty-one-year-old William Luke, who died of typhoid during basic training at Camp Davis, four weeks after enlisting.[29]

"He limps very bad in walking," First Lieutenant Reuben Clements wrote of one of his privates in the Irwin County Volunteers, but his words were an accurate description of the entire company. Clements admitted that "there is 200 returned sick in the Regiment every morning upon average so the Adjutant told me this morning, our men are not dangerous but it appears they can not get hearty." Thomas E. Lee, who joined the Pulaski Greys in March 1862, wrote his wife five months later from a camp near Richmond: "The health of this regiment is very bad[.] Thair is a good deal of Sickness here." Shortly after entering service, W. A. Studstill reassured his family, "I am still in the land of the living," but added: "There is not half a dozen men in the company but what has been Sick already." Confiding to his uncle shortly after the Battle of Chancellorsville, Captain Wiley Williams noted that his company was so worn down by disease and fatigue that he took only fifteen men into combat.[30]

The disease, disability, and casualties sustained during the intense fighting in the summer of 1862 made it impossible for many companies to maintain adequate strength levels. This was now a hard war, a fact that Stephen Roberts of the 23rd Georgia noted in 1863, when he wrote home: "They will fight in Virginia and they fight to kill[;] that is decidedly the worst part of the war according to my experience." A gendered division of dying hit the home front on a scale unimagined before the war. The Pulaski Volunteers lost 40 percent of its men to death, disease, or disability after only fourteen months in the field. Disease or death in camps and hospitals claimed one-fourth of all the men who died, but almost 20 percent of the fatalities occurred on the battlefield. Thirteen percent were listed as having simply "died," with no cause of death recorded. The Coffee County Guards had been in Virginia only six months as the summer of 1862 drew to a close. It had lost 36 percent of its troops, 22 percent of these through death from disease and 32 percent through wounds.[31]

Volunteering alone would never fill the gaps in the ranks created by combat fatalities, disease, disability discharges, or debilitating wounds. New soldiers were needed to join the veterans at the front. The South's answer, with President Davis and General Robert E. Lee's encouragement, was the first conscription act in U.S. history. Passed on April 16, 1862, by the Confederate Congress as a public defense measure, the act obligated all able-bodied white males between the ages of eighteen and thirty-five to perform three years of involuntary service. Soldiers who had already enlisted for one year were required to serve an additional two years.[32]

A primary goal of the Confederate Conscription Act was to stimulate volunteering. Governor Brown's February 1862 proclamation "To the People of Georgia" put them on notice that the state needed to field twelve more regiments before March 15, in large part to replace soldiers whose terms of service would expire that spring. In 1862 the Confederate Army realized a net gain—after casualties—of about 200,000 men, with more than half of them volunteering but with the threat of the draft hanging over their heads. Without these troops it is likely that the Confederate nation would not have survived the bloody battles of 1862.[33]

These gains, however, were offset by the alienation and disaffection that conscription caused at home. The Confederate draft was not popular in Georgia or along the lower river. The governor bitterly opposed it. Many Georgians considered conscription unconstitutional and an affront to their patriotism. It was one thing to volunteer to defend the Confederacy, but it was another thing altogether to be coerced into fighting. The draft seemingly contradicted secessionist rhetoric that extolled individual liberty, localism, and states' rights while rejecting the type of centralized authority conscription represented. Antidraft sentiment was evident along the lower river even before the war began. A month before the Confederate attack on Fort Sumter, William Paine wrote Brown from Jacksonville: "Some of the boys are having some fun with the fears of the people, and have summoned a few to appear to stand a draft—A draft seems to be the terror of the women both old and young—and some of the men are worse than the women."[34]

Their "fears" were based on uncertainty. Who would be drafted? Who would die? What would happen to their women and children at home? These fears, however, were not evenly spread across the population. Conscription did not apply to all military-aged white males. Men of means, especially planters and professionals, could hire substitutes from those ineligible to stand the draft. Moreover, a broad group of civil officials, railroad workers and riverboat pilots, clergymen, telegraph operators, and teachers, to mention a few, were exempt from the draft. Deciding who deserved exemptions was often left to county officials who were dominated by slaveholders and wealthier men. Such inequities alienated many yeomen and poor whites.[35]

Conscription undermined the sense of unity that existed on the home front during the war's first year. Volunteering had allowed highly committed Southern nationalists to enter Confederate service and permitted less enthusiastic men to stay at home. The call for new infantry companies early in 1862 under the threat of a draft forced the fence-sitters to make a choice. They could volunteer, wait and be drafted, or evade the draft. We may never know how many local men would have avoided service altogether without conscription. When James Humphreys wrote Governor Brown in the fall of 1861 expressing the desire to raise a new infantry company in traditionally unionist Telfair County, he reported that he had approximately 50 men willing to volunteer. When Humphreys's company took to the field in March 1862, it contained 131 recruits. It is worth speculating that over half of them may have volunteered under the threat of a draft rather than being branded a "laggard in responding to the call now made."[36]

Almost immediately citizens found reasons to oppose the draft beyond the usual arguments against its unconstitutionality and coercive nature. Home-front security headed the list. One Coffee County yeoman believed that conscription would empty the piney woods of its military-aged men and leave the forest vulnerable to slave insurrection. Some counties maintained that they had done their fair share and that others should bear a greater burden of supplying troops. Telfair had only about one hundred men, who were weighed down by "infirmity of age & disability," two plain folk reported in July 1863. The county had met its previous quota of conscripts and to draft even more men would leave it "defenseless."[37]

Years after the war a draft dodger from Pulaski County recalled how he had told a man of similar leanings: "I carry my exemption in my pocket." He then pulled out a buckeye ball, slick and black from long use, supposedly the remedy for an ailment. Disabilities real and imagined became a popular way for men to avoid both conscription and being "disgraced by the presence of a DRAFTING OFFICER." Indeed, one of the most valuable qualities of a Telfair County surgeon recommended to the governor as medical examiner for the Fifteenth Senatorial District was, "He can look at a man straight in the face and say 'NO' whenever it is necessary." Disability papers literally were life-savers, and physicians were called on to render opinions. Local citizens also sought the views of state officials to prevent conscription. Early in 1863 John L. Driden of Coffee County contacted the state adjutant general's office to complain that although he was disabled, he feared being drafted by Confederate enrolling officers. The office wrote back: "It would seem that if you have a discharge for permanent disability, so stated in certificate, you would not be liable to conscription."[38]

Conscription forced citizens to take positions that often placed them at odds with their neighbors and Confederate authorities. Henry Grantham's disability was mental, not physical, but community opinion weighed heavily in deciding his fate. In 1864 Grantham was described as "an insane person going at large without a Guardian." But he was also considered by Confederate authorities to be "subject to conscription." When Grantham was taken into custody by a Captain Mitchell, the Confederate enrolling officer, justices of the Pulaski County Inferior Court originally supported Mitchell. Only weeks later, however, they reversed themselves and ordered Mitchell to release Grantham and "let him run at large." In the intervening days, the community had apparently convinced the inferior court that Grantham was truly insane and incapable of military service.[39]

A far more common means of avoiding conscription was election or employment as a minor civil official. In November 1863 Daniel Newbern, a Coffee County militia captain, asked the state adjutant general's office if bailiffs were "liable to conscription." Writing on behalf of state authorities, L. H. Briscoe assured him that they were not and that the enrolling officer who "seeks to coerce them" exceeded his authority. Newbern was informed that he was on solid ground if he told Jonathan Davenport, the enrolling officer, that bailiffs "will be justified and upheld in disobeying any order looking to his conscription." When militia ensign James Fletcher was tricked into volunteering by John Sinclair, a Confederate enrolling officer who told Fletcher that Governor Brown had "given up all of his militia officers to be conscripted," the young man who had expected "no fraud" traveled to Milledgeville on the "advice of friends to lay his case before the Governor."[40]

Another way to avoid the draft was to receive an exemption as a worker in one of the large group of protected occupations under Confederate law. In 1864 Stephen Daniel applied for an exemption on the grounds that he in effect served as an overseer for another man's slaves. The master was too sick to supervise the field work himself, and his old overseer had been "ordered . . . up to Macon." Charles F. Clarke, the enrolling officer, was accused of holding up Daniel's application and ordered by the local court to release Daniel, who claimed "to be illegally detained by you together with the cause of such detention." Apparently, Daniel's efforts did not pay off. Less than two weeks later Clarke appeared in Hawkinsville with orders signed by William Brown, commandant of conscripts, that pronounced Daniel subject to conscription.[41]

Resistance to coercion was not limited to Confederate authority. Once the pattern was set, disaffected men found ways to escape service in Governor Brown's state forces as well. In the waning days of the Confederacy, Edwin R. McPhail asked Brown if he was subject "to youre militia." McPhail had served for over a year in the Confederate army as well as some weeks with militia in the field as General William T. Sherman's army besieged Atlanta. But he had since "taken Sick" with dyspepsia and wanted Brown to detail him as a state-exempt hatter, a status he previously held under the Confederate War Department. McPhail argued that he had several brothers in the army and he was "the last one in the state." He could do more service at home making hats at a "reasonable price" for Brown's own troops. Moreover, he added, "I will work for Soldiers and Soldiers familys at any price you are amind to put on Such Hats." McPhail closed his letter with a plea: "Gov I wish to know what course to persue[.] I am always willing to do according to Superior Authority." Despite this avowed deference to authority, McPhail played out his case for eight months and effectively avoided further service. He dated his last letter to Brown on Sunday, April 9, 1865, as General Lee surrendered his army at Appomattox.[42]

Edwin McPhail was twenty-three in 1865. Doubtless he believed that he had done his part for the Confederacy by fighting for over a year in Virginia. He also assumed that the men who remained at home in Pulaski County backed him. McPhail had bragged to Brown that he could get every man in the county to sign an exemption petition if necessary. His boast says much about the men who remained at home in 1864 and 1865 and the limits of the coercive power of Confederate and state authorities. McPhail personally was not coerced by the militia calls, and some white belt neighborhoods collectively ignored what they perceived to be authoritarian threats. In July 1863 the state adjutant general's office warned George Young that due to Irwin County's failure to "supply her small quota" of men, "arrangements are in progress to enforce obedience where invitations and appeals fail to accomplish anything." The sense of unity that had characterized the war's first year was eroded by Confederate conscription and state efforts to field the militia as Sherman's army entered the state.[43]

Without question, the substitute hiring provision in the draft law had the potential of increasing class tension among plain folk who were unable to hire substitutes. Just how many people used substitutes to avoid military service completely is difficult to say, but the number of men already in Confederate service in the spring of 1862 who subsequently hired substitutes was insignificant. Some men in this group volunteered to avoid the stigma of being conscripts. Edwin McPhail may have been one of them. He admitted to Governor Brown that he had hired a substitute to fulfill his remaining obligation because of poor health. Of the 530 local men who served with McPhail in the 49th Georgia, only 13 (less than 3 percent) engaged substitutes, a proportion similar to that of enlistees in black belt Greene County, Georgia. The number varied from company to company. Six men used substitutes in the Pulaski Greys, a unit organized in a black belt county. Only two men in the Irwin Volunteers, however, employed substitutes and returned home to a white belt county. Not one man in the State Rights Guards hired a substitute, despite the company's high casualty rate.[44]

Though rare in all counties, substitute hiring was more common among soldiers from wealthier black belt neighborhoods. Backwoods soldiers who retained substitutes usually came from slaveholding families. The impact of substitute hiring on morale depended less on numbers and more on the black belt and slaveholding pattern. Both Irwin County Volunteers who hired substitutes belonged to families with ties to slaveholding, whereas those of their replacements did not. The son of a small planter, Reason Paulk engaged Andrew Jackson Barton as his substitute only two months after enlisting. The same could be said for James Whiddon, whose small slaveholding father may have helped him employ James Petty as his substitute on the same day that young Whiddon enrolled in the company. Brothers Alathia and J. A. D. Coley hired substitutes on the eve of the Battle of Second Manassas, left their comrades in the Pulaski Volunteers, and returned home. The scions of a prosperous planter, each brother claimed $10,000 in personal property in 1860. Though less well off, Josephus Carruthers retained a substitute and paid him fifteen dollars per month. Like the Coleys, Carruthers came from a slaveholding family, although on the small planter–yeoman scale. Thus, a few men privileged by the cotton-slave nexus and their family's wealth bought their way out of service while men from nonslaveholding families could not. It was little wonder that a substitute such as John Ray, employed by John Polhill of the Pulaski Greys on June 16, 1862, promptly deserted the next day.[45]

Hiring a substitute was expensive. One month after the draft became law, Irwin County farmer Jehu Fletcher faced conscription. In an attempt to avoid service, and possibly misunderstanding the substitute provision, Fletcher sent his son Joseph to Goldsborough, North Carolina, to take his place. But Joseph himself was draft-eligible, thus making him ineligible as a substitute. Jehu's friend, First Lieutenant Reuben Clements, wrote Fletcher that he had "done all I could to get Joseph in your place, but it was all in vain." Colonel Andrew Jackson Lane, commander of the 49th Georgia, ruled that Jehu had to "send a man that was exempt from the conscript law that was sound, he could take your place, if not you would have to come yourself immediately." But as Clements warned his old friend, the going price was steep: "Some men have come here since the conscription law became enforced and brought substitutes and paid them as high as $500 to take their places." Josephus Carruthers was bothered not only by the high cost of hiring a substitute, but also by the questions people asked him regarding his status as a former Confederate soldier. He complained to the governor that he would never "suffer" the draft while paying a substitute "out of my own pocket." If he was subject to any draft after being honorably discharged from the Confederate army, conscription represented "a bad law or bad men who administer it."[46]

Just why Jehu Fletcher avoided conscription is unclear, but it was not because his family opposed the war. Brothers Elbert and Horton Fletcher joined the Irwin Cow Boys in 1861 and brothers John and William enlisted in the Irwin Volunteers in March 1862. Thus, the family tradition of Confederate service from an overwhelmingly white belt county marked the Fletchers as Southern nationalists. Moreover, Jehu's son Joseph was now eligible for the draft. Perhaps it was for this reason—that the Fletchers sent so many men into Confederate service while other households had not—that Jehu sought ways to avoid the draft. Why should one family send so many men to the front and its women and children at home sacrifice while other households escaped? Why should he lose his independence and autonomy in the army, where he would be subordinate to men he considered social equals? Hiring a substitute would be difficult for a slaveless 100-acre corn farmer and livestock herder. In any event, Jehu Fletcher never joined the Irwin County Volunteers, but in closing his letter to his friend, First Lieutenant Clements informed Jehu: "Joseph has concluded to join this company." Undoubtedly, Jehu's son believed that it made little sense to return to Irwin County only to be drafted and sent back to Virginia. Like many other men, Joseph preferred to be a volunteer rather than a conscript. This would have brought small comfort to Jehu Fletcher, who soon learned that Joseph died of disease in Virginia ten weeks after he enlisted.[47]

For the troops who survived at the front, electing their own company-grade officers was one way to exercise some control within the broader chaos of modern war. As Reuben Clements's letter to Jehu Fletcher reveals, such fatherly officers not only handled the day-to-day business of leading and running infantry companies, but also kept open lines of communication to families on the home front. Clements described the company's health, the arrival of new recruits, the sickness of the regimental chaplain, and conscription and substitute hiring. Officers like him were involved in negotiations between men who were both willing and unwilling to join the company and their superior officers and often served as the plain folk's advocates. Clements told Fletcher: "I went to him [Col. Manning] and done all I could to get Joseph in your place." Clements's role as counsel for his friend contradicts the image offered by historians who argue that internal divisions between plain folk and their officers became a major cause of Confederate defeat.[48]

Based on the backgrounds of the officers elected by the plain folk, there is little evidence to support that conclusion for units organized along the lower river. Indeed, the almost routine election of officers by plain folk was an important combat motivation. Common soldiers influenced command choices at the level nearest to them and assured the reliability of their leaders. In choosing company officers, enlisted men repeatedly voted for members of all levels of society, including planters, political party insiders, professionals, yeoman slaveholders, and nonslaveholding plain folk. No doubt some plain folk resented fighting a "rich man's war" that made provision for hiring substitutes and planter exemptions and objected to wealthy political officers higher up the chain of command. But if "rich" meant owning slaves, this was not a liability when the time for company elections arrived. Sixty percent of the captains originally chosen by their men to lead local infantry companies were slaveowners in a white belt region where the level of slaveholding was lower than for Georgia as a whole. Plain folk's frequent election of slaveholders to officer rank suggests that the role of class conflict in undermining the popular will to fight has been exaggerated. Most plain folk shared the strong ideological convictions and pro-slavery motivations of slaveholders to fight, not because of property in slaves, but because of their concerns about the future of white liberty and supremacy if they lost the war. "If you would not be slaves, strike!" declared a recruitment broadside in the wiregrass country.[49]

Even if slaveless yeomen resented the status that came with an officer's rank, they did not have to wait long to make a leadership change on the company level. By 1863 death, disease, disability, promotion to regimental staff, and resignations had democratized the company-grade officer's corps to such an extent that plain folk often officered plain folk. High turnover created an officer's version of musical chairs whereby the faces constantly changed on the company and regimental levels. For instance, among the captains originally elected to lead the four local companies in the 49th Georgia, the average length of service was fifteen months, with sixteen months being the longest tenure. First lieutenants, a group dominated by yeoman farmers and small slaveholders such as Reuben Clements, were the logical source for new captains as vacancies arose, while noncommissioned officers and privates formed the reserve pool for first and second lieutenants.[50]

The experience of the Pulaski Greys illustrates the democratization of the company officer's corps, a process controlled by plain folk. Captain Seaborn Manning's election as lieutenant colonel of the 49th Georgia only three weeks after the company was organized created an immediate vacancy at the top of its command structure, where three out of four officers were slaveholders in the spring of 1862. Manning, a planter, was replaced by small slaveholder and former merchant Henry Whitfield, the company's first lieutenant. When a disability forced Whitfield to resign two months later, small planter and merchant John Pate, originally second lieutenant, was elected captain. About a year later Pate was elected major in the 49th Georgia, and Origen Americus Vespucius Rose, a former store clerk and private then serving as first lieutenant, became captain. Such frequent turnover at the top of the company and regimental command structure created a draft effect that pulled plain folk up through the ranks to positions of leadership. By 1863 three out of four officers in the Pulaski Greys were nonslaveholders.[51]

Infantrymen elected officers who were concerned for their welfare and willing to lead by example. Thus, physicians such as James Humphreys, Thomas Ryan, and Henry Smith, older men who possessed medical knowledge, were good officer candidates. Their education, community status, and history of care for the welfare of neighborhood families gave them a paternal image and an aura of coolness in times of emergency. The bonds between company officers and their enlisted men began at home. Since the officers and their troops came from the same rural neighborhoods, towns, and counties, they often had known each other before the war. In the field, officers were concerned with almost every aspect of their soldiers' lives, including their health, hygiene, willingness to follow orders, and punishment for transgressions. Usually older than the average soldier—James Humphreys was thirty-seven when elected—officers assumed fatherly roles in camp. In this way captains and regimental colonels became the patriarchs of large male households, handing down decisions that sometimes pleased or displeased their troops, decisions that had implications both in camp and back home.[52]

But privates and noncommissioned officers also voted for men who had displayed courage and could be expected to put their lives on the line in battle. The common danger that officers and enlisted men faced together in combat emotionally unified the small groups of men who formed companies that were reduced in size by casualties and disease to often less than fifty men. When Private Thomas E. Lee was elected second lieutenant of the Pulaski Greys shortly after Gettysburg, the nonslaveholder was philosophical about his election as an officer, writing to his wife: "I will be killed as a private as quick as I would be if I was an officer & an officer as quick as private." Lee knew that Yankee bullets were no respecters of rank. Indeed, his own rise into the officers' ranks was dependent on the death, disability, and disappearance of men who previously had been his superiors. And when James Humphreys resigned as captain of the Telfair Volunteers a little over four months after the company was formed, the men elected First Lieutenant James Willcox their new captain. At the time Willcox was only twenty-one, but he was a member of the prominent Willcox family, which accounted for one-third of the county's planters. There was little doubt about his willingness to lead men into combat. On August 10, 1862, only six weeks after his election, he was "severely wounded in breast and arm" at the Battle of Cedar Run and died less than two weeks later.[53]

The death of James Willcox found the Telfair Volunteers voting for a new company commander on the same day, their second captain's election in eight weeks. Again, the plain folk turned to a member of a slaveholding family rather than rejecting him outright because of his privileged background. His name was Wiley Williams. Wiley's father, planter Joseph B. Williams, had died in the explosion of the *S. M. Manning* in 1860; his mother, the former Sarah Fletcher, ran the family's corn and cotton plantation with twenty slaves. On the eve of the Civil War Wiley operated a store in the Copeland neighborhood and boarded with James Humphreys.[54]

The Williams family had more than its share of Southern nationalists. Six members enlisted in infantry companies organized in Telfair in 1861, and five joined James Humphreys's company in March 1862. Yeoman farmer Lucius Williams, Wiley's cousin, was elected second lieutenant when the company was formed. But Wiley enlisted as a private. He probably resembled the members of wealthy Southern families called "gentlemen privates," whose sense of pride and personal honor led them to enter military service in the enlisted ranks rather than seek commissions. In July 1862 Wiley Williams was elected first lieutenant, due largely to resignations and sickness among the company's officers. He served in that rank less than one month before becoming captain. His status as the son of planter parents did not hurt his chances of advancement among the plain folk. Moreover, the subsequent hiring of substitutes by two Williams men—one of them Wiley's older brother Fletcher—did not hurt his chances for promotion to major in February 1863 and ultimately to lieutenant colonel of the 49th Georgia in March 1864. Men were willing to follow Wiley Williams into battle because he led by example, he watched out for their interests, and they trusted his judgment.[55]

The argument that enlisted men resented officers because of class differences was even less convincing as the war continued into 1863 and 1864, when the gap between the socioeconomic backgrounds of company-grade officers and enlisted men narrowed. By late 1862 and early 1863 many of the wealthier men originally elected captains were gone due to wartime attrition. Their elected replacements were men from humbler, although by no means poor white origins. When Wilcox County's State Rights Guards organized, the unit elected wealthy planter Samuel Fuller as captain. He resigned because of a disability shortly after the Gettysburg campaign. Eventually, the men chose as their new captain a former first sergeant and first lieutenant named Alexander McLennan. Unlike Fuller, McLennan came from the ranks of slaveless plain folk. No McLennan household in Telfair County, where he was born, or in Wilcox County, where he resided, owned a slave in 1860. He was a solid member of the upwardly mobile group of yeoman cotton farmers that emerged in the 1850s. Plain folk trusted him because he was one of them and had demonstrated courage in combat. McLennan began his service as first sergeant in March 1862. Wounded at the Battle of Cold Harbor the following June, he was elected first lieutenant in August. Wounded again at Fredericksburg—this time in the right thigh—he was elected captain in July 1863.[56]

To summarize, plain folk chose men from both humble and prominent backgrounds to lead their companies. A man's reputation mattered more than his social status and wealth. Yet the tradition of deference to slaveholders persisted until the war's final months, when plain folk resentment against men from slaveholding households arguably should have been the greatest. This conflict was mitigated to some extent by the fact that both officers and enlisted men were usually volunteers who heard the same secessionist and nationalistic rhetoric and shared many of the same political values. In February 1865 the small band of survivors in the remnant Pulaski Greys needed a new captain. They selected Robert Sanders Anderson, the son of a prominent planter. Anderson had enlisted as a private when the company was organized and, after being wounded at Mechanicsville, became second lieutenant. He led the company until its surrender at Appomattox two months later, when "only a corporal's guard" remained. The plain folk may have admired such men for a number of reasons: their economic success as slaveholders and cotton farmers, their political leanings, or even their Masonic affiliation. Above all, soldiers chose as their leaders men who were most likely to get them through the bloody and seemingly endless war alive.[57]

### "If I Live"

Returning to Virginia with Lee's army after the disastrous Pennsylvania campaign, Lieutenant Thomas Jefferson Smith sensed that something momentous had happened. Writing a month after the battle, he described passing through the "ever memorable field of Sharpsburg [Maryland]" and seeing the "many graves there." The mounds of earth and crude grave markers were mute but "sufficient evidence of what a bloody field this was." Nevertheless, Smith concluded: "I think Gettysburg will take its place among the bloodiest battlefields the world ever saw." Blood and death seemed inescapable after the summer of 1863. As the war entered its third year, many soldiers believed they would be killed before it ended, particularly after the enormous losses at Sharpsburg and Gettysburg. Fear and uncertainty about their own lives combined with constant shortages of food, shelter, clothing, and medicine—and few furloughs to relieve the stress—took a heavy psychological toll. Shortly after the slaughter at Gettysburg, Thomas E. Lee confided to his wife: "I still think that if I live untill next winter that I can get to come home again."[58]

"If I live" was one of the questions that preoccupied the thoughts of plain folk officers such as Second Lieutenant Lee, as well as the men they led. As one chaplain wrote early in 1863 from the 49th Georgia's winter camp near Fredericksburg: "So many of their number have fallen victims to the unpitying instruments of war, that they almost regard life as a shadow." Death's appearance caused men to become introspective and ponder life after death or, as Lieutenant Smith described it, the "last sleep that knows no waking." Death had a way of taking the young and affable, leaving the rest to deal with the guilt and uncertainty that followed. One of the losses that troubled Smith was that of Fifth Sergeant Robert Jones. Like seven thousand other wounded Confederates, Jones was left behind at Gettysburg "in possession of the enemy" when Robert E. Lee's army retreated. Despite the medical attention of Yankee doctors and nurses, Jones died in a New York hospital. Smith wrote: "He was one of our best soldiers and a fine clever fellow. He will long be remembered by all who knew him." Only twenty-three, Jones, a farm laborer before the war, left his twenty-two-year-old wife Mary at home with no means of support.[59]

Surrounded by the destructive power of modern warfare, many soldiers turned to religion and their Heavenly Father to sustain them as the war progressed. Recent studies of revivalism in the Confederate army suggest that common soldiers, their officers, and chaplains used religion in different ways. For the common foot soldier, evangelical religion and the promise of eternal salvation provided the psychological assurance needed to survive in a "shadow" life of gloom and sadness. Formerly independent men accustomed to controlling their own lives, the now subordinate soldiers turned to God to relieve them of their own emotional distress in a brutal war that threatened their very existence. As Second Lieutenant Lee wrote after Gettysburg: "I beg god to spair my life." Men too proud to beg for anything in civilian life now found themselves at the mercy of their Maker.[60]

For the officers, religion offered a means of social control in companies and regiments composed of individualistic men who had elected them as their leaders. Most of the soldiers came from rural neighborhoods where a man's household was his to govern without questions of his authority. Army life, on the other hand, required ordinary troops to subordinate themselves to officers in a centralized and disciplined military regime, one that expected them to place their lives in harm's way. Evangelicalism, which called upon its followers to voluntarily set aside their individualism and walk obediently in the footsteps of Jesus, helped men transition into military life and face the horrors of combat. This was especially true when the officers themselves—men such as division commander A. P. Hill and local officers like Ruel Anderson—were ardent Christians. Anderson, for example, joined the Baptist Church when he was seventeen.[61]

For chaplains and missionaries, the war offered opportunities to nurture the spiritual life of the troops, which increasingly lifted their morale. Despite the critical role that evangelical religion played in the secession movement, the Confederacy did not supply chaplains to their regiments in 1861. Chaplains, when finally approved by the Confederate Congress, received only a private's pay and rations, compared to the compensation of a cavalry captain received by clergy in the Union army. Thus, early in the war well-meaning but less-than-qualified chaplains motivated by patriotism and the righteousness of the "cause" found they could not bear up under the hardship. Writing from Dirt Town, Georgia, in the summer of 1863, E. H. Warren, a missionary to the Army of Tennessee, warned that only strong preachers, both physically and spiritually, should go to the front. Those with "inferior powers" should stay home. When he joined Braxton Bragg's army at Tullahoma, Tennessee, Warren was entirely on his own. Thomas Dawson and Ruel Anderson, both officers of a Pulaski County artillery battery, helped the missionary get established. Board was a prohibitive five dollars per day in town, so Warren was forced to find housing in the camp of the "destitute regiment," where he busied himself "rallying the pious."[62]

In 1861 and early 1862, when religious indifference was high, not much "rallying the pious" was done. Sunday services were irregular, few ministers reached the front, and Bibles and religious tracts were scarce. If the truth were known, the rougher soldiers often considered Christians somewhat unmanly, especially during the first two years of the war. In a rural world ruled by the honor code, a man who turned the other cheek in Christian love was not much of a man. Evangelicalism was the pursuit of benevolence-minded women who, along with slaves, often outnumbered men in black belt churches. Pious Bible and tract-reading men, often ridiculed as "parsons" and "weaklings," might become cowards in the heat of battle. In February 1862 Reverend J. A. Garrison, chaplain of the 20th Georgia, wrote that he was "disappointed in the reception given to his labors as chaplain" and urged soldiers' families to send Bibles, religious newspapers, and tracts to their men at the front.[63]

A series of bloody battles—Sharpsburg, Fredericksburg, Chancellorsville, and Gettysburg—changed the way Confederate soldiers and their families viewed evangelicalism. Men were dying in numbers few thought possible in the war's first year, and there were few able-bodied men left at home to replace them. A. P. Hill's Light Division, which included the 49th Georgia, sustained more casualties at Chancellorsville than any other ANV division. Soon after the battle Chaplain John James Hyman visited every company in the 49th Georgia, met with the troops, and led frequent religious services. Hyman could not help noticing the empty places in camp created by the high casualties, writing "my heart was often saddened in finding so many of the boys that had so often met at the place appointed for worship of God, gone."[64]

"Gone" was the operative word. Hyman's observations were supported by the grim statistics of war. By the end of July 1863, Company F of the 49th Georgia (the Irwin Volunteers) barely resembled the unit that had left home sixteen months before. Almost 40 percent of the unit's original 122 soldiers were dead. Disease alone killed one out of four men, claiming responsibility for a staggering two-thirds of all deaths. Approximately three-quarters of the Irwin Volunteers had left the company at some point during those first sixteen months, either permanently—dead, captured, disabled, resigned, transferred out, or replaced by a substitute—or temporarily, most often due to wounds. James Dorminy, the son of planter and former state legislator John Dorminy, survived his wounds at the Battle of Cedar Run in August 1862 but died of typhoid fever in June 1863, even as Chaplain Hyman moved through Camp Gregg, Virginia, and ministered to the men. E. B. Barrett, another chaplain with the 49th Georgia, wrote toward the end of May 1863 that war and disease had decimated the ranks of both the Confederate and Union armies to "a fearful extent." Northern Virginia, he wrote, "may safely be called the graveyard of two powerful nations. Their bones lie bleaching in her soil."[65]

The great revivals that swept the Confederate army began after the battles and heavy losses that crippled companies like the Irwin Volunteers. They were first noticed in the fall of 1862 as the ANV retreated from the tremendous slaughter at Sharpsburg and were in full swing by the summer of 1863. From Camp Gregg early in June 1863, Chaplain Hyman wrote that the interest in personal salvation he saw rising before Chancellorsville had not dropped since the battle, but increased due to fatiguing marches and hard fighting that pushed the troops to the breaking point. Religion became a powerful means of sustaining motivation and the will to fight. Prayer meetings were held nightly, a Christian soldiers' association was established, and the regiment's troops constructed their own baptizing pool. Hyman personally baptized eighty soldiers in one month. The scenes he witnessed were emotional ones. Soldiers with tears streaming down their faces sought salvation and the prayers of God's people. These spiritual outpourings "would have caused the hearts of all pious mothers, fathers and sisters to leap with joy," Hyman declared. If their soldier was killed in battle, the "pious" family could still look forward to a reunion in heaven.[66]

Chaplains like Hyman often devoted their attention to nonbelievers, hoping to bring them to personal salvation before they died "unsaved" and spent an afterlife in hell. Without question, their work had a tremendous impact on the men. Even before Hyman's banner 80-man month, he reported that the 49th Georgia could count about 150 Baptists in its ranks. Baptist chaplains preached day and night to "large congregations," whose members "are asking for the prayers of the people of God, and three came out last night, in the face of their comrades, and asked to unite with the people of God." According to their chaplains, the soldiers seemed detached, shell-shocked, lost in the "shadow" life. They were "poor weather-beaten" men willing to "sit down, even in the cold, misty rain, for nearly half an hour, listening patiently to the words of God's ministers," wrote Chaplain Barrett, adding: "Undoubtedly the severe trials of this cruel war have had the desired effect upon their hearts."[67]

Late in June 1863 William Fisher of Coffee County noted in his diary that "43 persons mostly soldiers were baptized in New River." Exhausted and traumatized, many lower river men were now more receptive to evangelicalism than before the war. "I find them not only ready and anxious to listen attentively to the teachings of God's holy word, but are serious in regards to the salvation of their souls," Chaplain Barrett reported from a camp near Fredericksburg. William Smith, another member of a Coffee County infantry company, provided insight into the effectiveness of ministry among the men. In the summer of 1864 he listened to a sermon by a Primitive Baptist chaplain who used Romans 5:21 as his text: "That as sin hath reigned unto death, even so might grace reign through righteousness unto eternal life by Jesus Christ our Lord." The war had been brought about "by sin," and, as the children of Adam, all people were guilty of sin. Eternal life was available only through Jesus Christ, all others being "forever lost." In the fall of 1863 near Brandy Station, Barrett had noted that "hundreds of wayward transgressors" were coming forward, particularly after the enormous casualties at Gettysburg; they "are now rejoicing in the pardoning love of Jesus." In the 49th Georgia, sermons were preached in the morning and prayer meetings held at night, resulting in "a precious season" for soldier-converts.[68]

Like Christ, the men themselves were fatalistically laying down their lives to pay for a sinful war, if the Primitive Baptist minister did indeed "preach the truth," as, according to William Smith, he claimed to do. By sacrificing themselves on the field of battle, the men hoped to save their families at home and do God's will at the same time. This was the duty of the good Christian soldier: to fight unflinchingly in the face of death and die without fear if necessary. This was what his Christian family, his "social circle" back home expected of him. Even by dying of colic in camp, a soldier born in Telfair County "showed to the world that he was willing to die for the beloved Jesus who loved him so much." On the other hand, one religious newspaper reminded its readers that draft dodgers would be "tabooed by the men, and despised by the women." Inspired and supported by their faith and fellow believers, Christian men became model fighters rather than cowards. W. M. McDuffie, who joined Sardis Church and became the congregation's clerk before the war, was recognized for his "Christian walk and talk" both at home and at the front. He "was not ashamed to own his Jesus anywhere." Before he died of colic in 1863, his life "showed to the world that he was willing to die for the beloved Jesus who loved him so much." For men like McDuffie, the South's cause became God's cause, one and inseparable, sin reconciled through Christ's love and life through grace extended beyond death.[69]

But the high rate of killing that put fear into the hearts of men and created a "precious season" for chaplains caused others to doubt. Thomas E. Lee, like Fleming and McDuffie, had been a Christian before the war, and, like many Christians, the war tested his faith. After two years at the front, Thomas told his wife that "I will try to hold out to what little faith I have got" and asked her to get in touch with a friend at home: "Tell him to pray for me as I feel the kneed of pray[er]." By late July 1863, after a year of intense fighting, he was fatalistic about the future, predicting that the war would end during the

TABLE 1  Significant Events Permanently Ending Service in Local CSA Infantry Companies

| Infantry Company | On Roster | Killed | DOD | DUC | DIS | POW | DES | SUB | At Appomattox |
|---|---|---|---|---|---|---|---|---|---|
| Co. G 8th Ga. | 134 | 23 | 3 | 35 | 22 | 7 | 1 | 5 | 24 |
| Co. G 10th Ga. | 115 | 4 | 4 | 9 | 24 | 18 | 1 | 2 | 1 |
| Co. H 10th Ga. | 102 | 1 | 12 | 12 | 12 | 19 | 7 | 0 | 3 |
| Co. H 20th Ga. | 119 | 10 | 11 | 17 | 28 | 4 | 2 | 1 | 27 |
| Co. I 23rd Ga. | 93 | 5 | 5 | 16 | 10 | 11 | 4 | 0 | 9* |
| Co. K 23rd Ga. | 99 | 8 | 6 | 10 | 8 | 1 | 12 | 0 | 6* |
| Co. F 31st Ga. | 124 | 20 | 6 | 20 | 26 | 16 | 2 | 0 | 14 |
| Co. B 49th Ga. | 131 | 7 | 15 | 20 | 18 | 22 | 0 | 5 | 22 |
| Co. E 49th Ga. | 139 | 16 | 47 | 16 | 22 | 6 | 0 | 0 | 11 |
| Co. F 49th Ga. | 122 | 7 | 34 | 20 | 25 | 15 | 3 | 2 | 5 |
| Co. K 49th Ga. | 139 | 7 | 3 | 40 | 27 | 16 | 2 | 6 | 17 |
| Co. C 50th Ga. | 142 | 8 | 17 | 22 | 20 | 21 | 0 | 0 | 2 |
| Co. A 61st Ga. | 90 | 9 | 12 | 4 | 13 | 14 | 0 | 0 | 6 |
| Total | 1,549 | 125 | 175 | 241 | 255 | 170 | 34 | 21 | 132 |
| Percent of Total | | 8.07 | 11.30 | 15.56 | 16.46 | 10.97 | 2.19 | 1.36 | 8.52 |

*Source:* Henderson, *Roster,* 1:963–72, 2:45–58, 817–24, 1071–82, 3:620–28, 5:210–18, 235–53, 279–88, 303–12, 6:203–8. See also Chapter 3, n. 10.

*Key:* DOD = Died of Disease; DUC = Died of Wounds or Unknown Causes; DIS = Discharged/Disability; POW = Prisoner of War;
  DES = Deserted; SUB = Hired Substitute

*Surrendered at Greensboro, North Carolina.

coming winter with "the hardest fighting that ever has bin." With a sense of foreboding, he concluded: "I think they will destroy our army or theirs." Lee did not suggest who would win, only that the men of one army or the other would be annihilated.[70]

The catastrophic gendered division of dying had a profound effect not only on soldiers at the front but also on their neighborhoods at home. From a demographic perspective, these communities would never look the same. Of the eleven Gibbs family members from Wilcox County who enlisted in 1862, only Isaac and William Gibbs went home after the war. Richard Gibbs had been discharged earlier for disability, and eight men died of disease or wounds at the front. As Table 1 indicates, 35 percent of the Confederate infantry soldiers in piney woods Georgia were killed, succumbed to disease, or died of unknown causes and never returned to their families. The horrific death toll forced some desperate Confederates to urge the use of slaves as soldiers, an action approved by the Confederate Congress but too late to alter the war's outcome. In March 1865 company commanders of the 49th Georgia, including lower Ocmulgee officers Robert Sanders Anderson, Albert G. Brooks, Charles Walden, and Lucius Williams, requested that "our companies be permitted to fill up their ranks with negroes." Plain folk fears of male slaves and their potential for violence were overcome in part by localism. Under their plan, each soldier in the regiment would "furnish a list of relatives, friends, or acquaintances in his county of whom it is likely that negroes may be conscribed." Rather than depend on the Confederate military bureaucracy to handle the delicate issue of black conscription, plain folk themselves recommended both the slaveholders and slaves to be included on the lists, with the prospective black conscripts judged "from [their] former acquaintance with the men." Although General Robert E. Lee commended "the spirit displayed by this regiment," the surrender at Appomattox was only two weeks away when their request reached the top of the chain of command.[71]

The families of planters and slaveholders did not abandon these plain folk, at least not if the continuing service of their brothers, fathers, and sons mattered. Private George Reid Jr., the son of planter and unionist George Reid, surrendered with the State Rights Guards, as did yeoman slaveholder Charles Walden, now a second Lieutenant. Jonathan Fortner, Elijah Hunter, Joseph Rollins, and Jacob Smith—all in their late teens or early twenties—stacked their arms at Appomattox along with Isaac and William Gibbs. These 8 soldiers were all who remained of the 139 men who left with the company in the spring of 1862. Just as the ANV came to symbolize the larger Confederate cause for Southerners, the same could be said on the county level of the remnant companies who surrendered. People at home knew who had died and which families were represented at Appomattox. The sons of plain folk and planters gathered in ever smaller groups of survivors whose primary cohesion was shaped by mutual ties to people, place, shared political values, and ultimately their loyalty to one another. Their common experience and the sacrifice of their kin and friends unified them by, as Governor Joe Brown put it, "sealing their offering upon their country's altar with their life's blood." They were unwilling to abandon each other.[72]

Why anyone remained at the front is a question worth asking. Beyond their loyalty to each other and the plain folk officers they increasingly elected to lead them, some survivors still held onto the ideals that initially motivated them to join the Confederate army. From Richmond in November 1861, volunteer John M. Warren wrote a letter to his son "Jimmie" in Wilcox County that his infant child was as yet "unprepared to read." If Warren died, the letter remained to explain to young Jimmie why his father had left home. "Though the hardships are heavy," Warren wrote, "yet I feel blessed to be able to go into the contest for my country." To Warren, a deeply religious man and member of the Friendship Church congregation, "my country" was the cause worth his own personal sacrifice. It was in this new "country"—not the United States—that Warren believed his son would grow to manhood. Jimmie would, "when you shall have grown old enough to read and reflect upon it," learn of the "bold southern boys" who defended the Confederate nation. When such ideals of white independence were combined with religious faith, the war became a holy cause. Three years later Warren penned a letter to his pastor and the "brethren and sisters" at Friendship Church after he learned that the regiment was being moved to Fredericksburg. Warren feared that "this may be my last letter" and referred to the Book of Timothy: "I hope to be able to have the undying testimony that I fought the good fight. I've kept the faith[;] hence forth there is a crown laid up at his right hand that fadeth not away." For plain folk like John Warren, fighting the good fight for God and the Confederate nation was a blessing that had its rewards even in death.[73]

Some soldiers continued to fight because they believed that they were better than the Yankees and could beat them or end the war with a negotiated peace. This was true not only during the early years of the war, but also well into 1864. Captain Alfred A. Smith of the Coffee County Guards thought that victory was still within the Confederacy's grasp in June 1864. Writing from the breastworks at Gaines Mills, Smith boasted to Private Zean W. Kirkland, then at home on wounded furlough: "We are getting along with Mr. Grant finely. We have thrashed him in Every Engagement as yet. & he has not tried us since the 3rd and we left a old field blue with his ded." Smith expressed "great hope" that the war would end after the present campaign. The overall morale of his men was high. He concluded: "Every Soldier has got Bran new life in him." For a civilian population that placed General Lee and the ANV on a level similar to the one held by George Washington's troops during the American Revolution, high morale at the front was critical to high spirits on the home front, where Lee's army was the bellwether of the Confederacy's fortunes. As late as March 1865, a die-hard Confederate in Pulaski County stated that he and like-minded men were determined to rally to "our government and its cause."[74]

An even deeper underlying commitment of front-line soldiers was to defend family and home. Plain folk concepts of masculinity demanded that able-bodied men join the army to be worthy of the privileges of men, including the affections of female patriots. Personal and family honor demanded that soldiers meet expectations of manhood, finish the fight, and fulfill their obligations to their kin and neighbors at home, especially women and children. In this respect localism—an excessive devotion to a neighborhood and its people—became a powerful inducement to fight not only for broader national goals, but also for the protection of specific people and places. Letters from soldiers at the front are filled with references to people, places, and activities that formed the fabric of daily life during peacetime, a world they returned to in memories. Thomas E. Lee was delighted to receive the letter containing a lock of his wife's hair. In subsequent communications he repeatedly advised her not to send him items that he knew were in short supply at home. He could buy them at the front cheaper than she could in Georgia. "I don't want you to Suffer for any thing in this world if I can help it," he declared shortly after the Battle of Gettysburg. Soldiers wanted to know how the crops looked, feared that their livestock would be harmed, asked their children to be mindful of their mothers, and were concerned about the "spread of misery and want" at home. The underlying meaning of their own defeat and what it meant for the future of their families—submission to Yankees and equality with emancipated slaves—transformed the war into a struggle for Southern white freedom.[75]

For the lower river's Confederate soldiers, the war was a rite of passage and a test of manhood. Men joined the army to defend those they considered defenseless—the women and children they most frequently associated with at home—and their own privileged place in society. They believed they would win. But the infantry companies that left the lower valley with over one hundred men gradually dwindled. The deadly pattern of battlefield slaughter that hit home at First Manassas continued for almost four years. Deadlier still were the diseases that wasted the plain folk in horrifying numbers. Faced with annihilation, some men who once considered evangelicalism an affront to masculinity turned inward in desperation and became Christian soldiers for the Confederate war. The remnant companies that survived represented the families of both plain folk and planters. These men increasingly elected company-grade officers from plain folk ranks. Such soldiers remained at the front and fought because they found meaning in their emotional and physical suffering for the cause and each other, and within themselves. William Barker wrote his wife in Wilcox County: "I am tired of living the way we have to live, but I am willing to stay and try to bear my part with the rest of my fellowmen." As in the case of so many others, his willingness to remain and fight cost him his life.[76]

"I represent the war with six sons," proudly wrote "HOMESPUN" less than two months before the Confederacy collapsed. Despite being "pulled out of the Union against my will," four years of hard fighting, and the death of one son, the patriarch was still stirred by "strong emotions of patriotism" for Southern nationhood. Now was not the time to cry "whipped," he declared; it was the time for each family to throw every resource at hand into the war for "our independence." Presently in his early sixties, the former antisecessionist turned die-hard Southern nationalist was willing to see all nine of his sons "sacrificed upon the altar of liberty and independence" before his nation suffered "submission, subjugation, reconstruction, or peace on any terms." Indeed, he promised to send his three sons still at home into war "in their rotation of age," including the one "a little over sixteen years old." And if necessary, he would "steady" his own "time and care-worn frame upon my musket" and "mix my blood with my children's." Although anxious for peace, HOME-SPUN believed that losing the war to such a "relentless, cruel, and hated foe" would render his son's death meaningless and spell disaster for the South. The Yankees, he concluded, would "take what we possess, and then make us their slaves," overturning the white Southern construction of manhood based in part on racial slavery. This Confederate father wholly embraced the secessionist rhetoric and justified the death that touched his family as a necessary sacrifice for "the noble and glorious cause of freedom."[1]

There were, however, multiple meanings to "I represent the war." HOMESPUN's male family was well represented in Confederate service, but because of its gendered nature, his female family was invisible at the front. That the patriarch never mentioned his wife, the mother of their nine sons, and her equal claim to representation by their service, says much about the writer's view of his household. HOMESPUN governed a family in which sons in Confederate service represented their father—*his* household, *his* estate, and *his* name. Their "faithful" performance resulted in *his* "gratification."[2]

But his female family could also claim to "represent the war." Indeed, soldiers' mothers exemplified the conflict even more than their husbands. As soldiers' mothers, women such as Amantha Goodson literally gave birth to the Confederate army and doubtless maintained—as HOMESPUN put it—"I reckon I love my children as well as any person." For Goodson, the death of her son, who was killed at First Manassas, would have been an unimaginable sacrifice only a year earlier. As the conscience of the Confederacy, white female patriots urged their men to enlist and fight in a moral crusade to protect both home and the fledgling nation from Yankee invasion. By encouraging men to join the army, patriotic women became a powerful force for the state, insisting that the willingness to enlist and fight was a measure of manhood. HOMESPUN's wife may have been equally gratified that her sons, as her husband put it, "have all acted honorably and faithful as far as I know or believe." After all, their sons represented—in life and death—the connection between the family and the Confederacy, between citizen and state.[3]

*Soldiers' Fathers*

The gendered call to arms has left us with an image of the Southern home front as "a world of white women and of slaves." Ultimately, the Confederate army that had been mobilized to protect white women and children drained the interior of so much manpower that it became vulnerable to slave insurrection and the loss of paternalistic rule. Such descriptions of the Confederate home front, however, are drawn for the most part from the experiences of elite planter households living in black belt regions where slave majorities were common. Although it is true that blacks constituted 59 to 66 percent of the population along the upper Ocmulgee, no county claimed a black majority below Hawkinsville.[4]

Interpreting the home front as a world of women and slaves simplifies a complex story by restricting the possible narratives for the vast Confederate interior along gender and geographic lines. It also sets aside the significant home-front image of soldiers' fathers and denies wartime neighborhoods the duality represented by soldiers' wives and mothers, on the one hand, *and* soldiers' fathers on the other. This is not to suggest that rural neighborhoods in the Southern plantation belt did not become largely worlds of femininity, but it reminds us that the Southern home front could vary from region to region and from one neighborhood to the next. Soldiers' wives, widows, and children became the major symbols of the state's new constituency of wartime dependents, but they were not alone in the piney woods. Along the lower river, enough men remained on the county level to not only preserve the paternalistic social order, but also expand its prerogatives as a wartime necessity.[5]

Although as much as 60 percent of the military-aged white males left the lower valley to defend the Confederacy by the summer of 1862 and as much as 80 percent of them saw some kind of action at the front, enough men remained at home to preserve the framework of patriarchal society. This was possible for several reasons. Older white men were exempt from military duty for much of the war. In 1861 and 1862 the upper age limit for Confederate service was thirty-five, and though the limit passed forty-five and even reached fifty early in 1864, many of those affected still remained at home. A variety of state, home guard, local militia, and police companies became places of refuge for men of all ages, especially those over forty. Moreover, some of the military-aged men qualified for exemptions as county officers, including justices of the inferior courts, justices of the peace, and constables. In the 1850s the median age of justices of Georgia's inferior courts, administrative bodies that came to symbolize home-front patriarchy, was forty-three. Estimates of their number statewide ranged from 15,000 to 25,000. Finally, a reluctance among anti-Confederates to take the field as militiamen in 1864 made it acceptable for military-aged men who placed loyalty to family above the Confederacy to stay at home, especially in white belt neighborhoods. In time, anti- and pro-Confederate fathers populated a home front that became as divided as it had once been unified.[6]

There were always military-aged men at home. The boundary between home front and battlefront was porous. Soldiers moved back and forth, some returning home on temporary furloughs and some to stay. For example, 20 percent of the Pulaski Volunteers went home to stay over the next four years for a variety of reasons. More than half of the returnees received disability discharges. They included A. R. Coley, "disabled and discharged," 1861; Luke Sapp Jr., "discharged, 1862, on account of age and infirmities"; J. D. Bohannon, who lost an arm at Gettysburg and was "discharged 1863"; and Z. J. Redd, "discharged, 1864, on account of old age." The remainder of the returnees hired substitutes or, in the case of officers, resigned their commissions. Indeed, three out of four of the company's officers elected in 1861 had resigned by 1863, joining a steady flow of men heading home for perfectly legal reasons.[7]

Although the Victorian-era mother was instrumental in shaping a son's view of home and family worth fighting to protect, the father was equally influential in forming the male youth's sense of honor, manliness, and valor. These were the qualities that made men capable of defending home and country. The political indoctrination of young soldiers coincided with their own individualization during an era that saw the rise of sectional strife, the Republican Party, and secessionist sentiment. Boys were introduced to the activities that tested honor and manhood—fighting, gambling, hunting, wenching—in the company of male peers. It was within this household world that young Confederate soldiers had first learned about politics and the issues that divided and united citizens. Inevitably, they were exposed to the political traditions of households and rural neighborhoods, which through the years backed prominent local families and national political parties. Boys did not necessarily follow their father's lead in all things political, but his example and family politics were often their introduction to political ideology. If a Confederate father was "deeply mortified" by the specter of Yankee victory and its consequences, he, as the leader of his household, established an ideological reference for his sons.[8]

The emotions of Confederate patriotism burned hotter in the "bosom" of some families than in others. Some households were more willing to fight to protect home in all of its manifestations—household, state, and nation. In 1861 the most patriotic households tended to send men and boys—often more than one at a time—into the Confederate army. The owner of sixteen slaves in 1860, small planter Henry Campbell of Telfair County was typical of soldiers' fathers who repeatedly bid farewell to sons leaving for the Virginia front. Forty-eight years old when the war broke out, Campbell lived with his wife, a daughter, fourteen-year-old Charles, and three military-aged sons, all farmhands. Luke, the second oldest son at twenty-one, joined the Telfair Volunteers two weeks after his younger brother George signed up with the infantry company. Luke's enlistment followed the suspension of classes at William and Mary College, where he was pursuing an education against his father's wishes. Campbell's oldest son, William—twenty-two, married, and still living in his father's household—joined the army as well. The patriarch watched three sons march off to war during the conflict's first summer while his overseer, twenty-four-year-old John Mims, stayed at home, not serving until he accompanied Charles, the youngest Campbell son, into the field in 1864 as members of a militia company. In the households of such ardent Southern nationalists, belief in Confederate victory and a willingness to fight continued until 1865.[9]

The willingness of the Campbell family to contribute four sons to defend the Confederacy is a clear statement of its Southern nationalism. Young Luke's views on the war and the duty of white men to defend "our altars and our fires" are also unmistakable. When chosen to deliver the farewell address to the "Kind and Patriotic Ladies" at Jacksonville on behalf of his infantry company in the summer of 1861, Private Campbell revealed the extent to which sectional strife and secessionist rhetoric influenced his youthful thinking. The war was nothing less than "our holy struggle for constitutional liberty," he declared, a struggle to defeat "the vile, ruthless Goths and vandals of the North." Obviously, the connection between family obligation and duty to "our youthful Republic," as well as woman's crucial role, were uppermost in his mind. The men and boys of the Telfair Volunteers left their families and traveled to the front to "represent Georgia" and "do honor to Telfair County." Only woman's "female patriotism" and "self-sacrificing spirit" permitted sons and husbands to leave their mothers and wives at home. In exchange for such patriotism, women were entitled to the same protection they had come to expect during peacetime.[10]

Once at the front, some soldiers depended on their fathers, as well as other men in their neighborhood, to take up the slack on the farm and to protect their families from want and physical harm. Private Nathaniel Gibbs wrote his wife in Wilcox County: "Elen, tell . . . father I want them to shir my sheep and mark the lams." Although Gibbs was fighting in Virginia, he instructed family and friends on the mechanics of shearing sheep and selling wool, his household's major source of cash income. Writing from camp in 1863, Thomas Jefferson Smith sought a Telfair friend's support on the social front: "Bill I want you to cheer up the girls and keep them in heart. Some of us will get back home some of these days, and when I get back I want to find things all right. If you can take time, court a little for me as you know I am very bashful."[11]

But individuals could do only so much to balance the competing demands of battlefront and home front. On the county level, the inferior court became the place where the military and political goals of the state and the day-to-day necessities of families intersected. As members of the most significant local governmental bodies in antebellum Georgia, the five elected justices of the inferior courts possessed administrative, judicial, and legislative powers. Once the war began, their authority expanded, and the courts became the equivalent of a county-level war resources board. Recognizing their clout, Governor Brown repeatedly turned to inferior courts to drum up support for troop mobilization as well as manage home-front economy and society. The justices organized patriotic meetings, collected shotguns and country rifles, and formed home guard units. Moreover, they not only set the county tax rate that raised funds to support the wives and children of soldiers, but also selected the men who compiled the lists of indigent soldiers' families. They also decided who traveled to Macon to pick up cotton cards and salt for the "needy" families they approved. When smallpox broke out among the slaves of planter and fellow Pulaski County justice Richard DeLamar, they posted a guard on his plantation "to prevent the spread of the contagion." Far from collapsing, patriarchal institutions such as the inferior courts assumed wider powers with the blessing of state government.[12]

In many respects the five male justices of the inferior court formed a collective image of soldiers' fathers in the popular imagination. Indeed, in many cases soldiers' fathers actually were members of the court. Yeoman and small slaveholder Aden Scarborough, a justice of the Pulaski County Inferior Court from 1861 to 1865, was the father of Jesse Scarborough, the Pulaski Volunteers' lumbering "Baby" killed at First Manassas. Planter Cornelius Bozeman's son, Cornelius Jr., served as a private in the Pulaski Rangers while his father sat on the court with Scarborough. Inferior court justices were vital links between the Confederacy's military demands and the needs of home-front households. The courts' actions created ties that bound individual citizens and their families to the nation's fight for survival.[13]

Soldiers' fathers such as Cornelius Bozeman and Aden Scarborough not only regulated home-front economy and society, but also enlisted the help of other patriarchs to extend their authority into the wartime households of younger men in the Confederate army. Soldiers' wives, widows, and children "in needy circumstances" were entitled to the protection of the state in the absence of their men, but the precise measure of that need was determined by people like James Pugh, appointed by Pulaski County justices in August 1863 to compile the indigent list. Named by the justices of the court in each county, these agents of the inferior courts entered soldiers' households and determined the needs of their women and children. In peacetime, this action would have undermined white male authority to govern his dependents since it called into question a man's ability to "keep" his family, a question heretofore largely restricted to poor relief cases. But as the war progressed, state and local officials were compelled to deal with women and their children now dependent on the state for support.[14]

By early 1862 the inferior courts charged committees of older men with the oversight of soldiers' families. The paternalistic language used by the justices to describe the committees' responsibilities reveals the invasive nature of the courts and suggests the extent to which soldiers' fathers challenged coverture by reaching into the homes of their wives and children during their absence. Family government by committee, to a large extent, replaced the husband as head of household. In Irwin County, older and politically powerful men such as planter John Dorminy and yeoman slaveholder Reason Paulk were chosen by the court to "superintend and look after the wants of the wives and children of the Volunteers." Telfair County's committee members were required to "inquire [into] and supply the wants of the familys [sic] of the Volunteers now going into Service." Inquiring, superintending, and supplying—these were the prerogatives and responsibilities of husbands under coverture in peacetime. The state's new power projected the authority of older white males beyond their own homes and into households recently controlled by younger men, most of them plain folk.[15]

The inferior courts and their committees went far beyond compiling indigent lists and rationing cotton cards and salt. They made life-and-death decisions that preserved some households and shattered others, causing women and children at home to suffer even greater losses. The Telfair County Inferior Court appointed boards of physical examiners consisting of male residents who were considered "worthy, patriotic, and intelligent citizens." These boards reviewed the applications of men who wanted to be detailed to perform essential duties at home rather than go to the front. In July 1864, as Sherman's army closed on Atlanta and Governor Brown issued a cradle-to-grave call for militiamen, the Telfair court pronounced William Burch and J. B. Anderson exempt from military service because they operated gristmills; small planter Michael Durr, James Humphreys, and J. J. Johnson were declared Telfair's exempt physicians. In neighboring Pulaski County, the justices used the "great depletion of the able Bodied portion of the population of the

County under your late call for the militia force" to petition Governor Brown to exempt fourteen men from service so they could maintain slave patrols for "keeping the negro population in proper training."[16]

Naturally, when making appointments to committees and local posts the courts turned to men of similar backgrounds. The votes of these appointees kept the justices in office and, more often than not, out of the Confederate army. When the slaveholder-dominated inferior court of Pulaski County petitioned the governor in July 1864 to exempt men from militia service to perform patrol and overseer "duty" at home, 60 percent of the applicants were masters, including Charles Taylor, the county's leading planter. And when the justices of white belt Irwin County chose men to furnish supplies to impoverished soldiers' families at government rates, all of those selected were also members of the committee to superintend soldiers' families; two out of three were masters in the low-slaveholding county. Through their appointments and exemptions, then, inferior court justices created a tightly controlled and self-perpetuating circle of older, wealthier, slaveholding soldiers' fathers who remained at home to look after public "needs," including those of the ever-growing numbers of soldiers' wives, widows, and children.[17]

Rather than losing their patriarchal grip on Southern society, soldiers' fathers expanded their roles on the home front. Respected as venerable community leaders and heads of prosperous, often slaveholding households, the older paternalists became the embodiment of home-front authority. The war and its demand for military-aged men arrested the customary political advancement of a new generation of male citizens. Men like Seaborn Manning, who in peacetime assumed the mantle of political leadership as county court officers and state legislators, had resigned to provide military leadership on the battlefield. For plain folk soldiers less well-to-do than Manning, army service meant surrendering their customary household authority to agents of the state as never before. The patriarchal justices and committeemen charged with caring for the "wives and children of the Volunteers" and "the indigent poor women" engaged in a type of social fathering of soldiers' households.[18]

### Soldiers' Wives: The New Poor

On the home front, the image of the Confederate soldier's wife dominated all others. None was more emblematic of the new republic's struggle than the figure of the dutiful soldier's wife plainly dressed in homespun, tending the hearth fires, and providing for her children while her husband held the Yankees at bay. The prewar cult of domesticity and the popular literature of wartime prescribed quiet roles of sacrifice for patriotic Southern women, who must put their soldiers and the new nation above all else. Elite women in particular were expected to unite behind the Confederate cause by actively supporting mobilization and organizing soldiers' aid societies.[19]

Women and children, the dependents of adult white males, comprised the vast majority of the white population in the lower counties. In Telfair in 1860, for example, women and children accounted for about 70 percent of all whites and one-half of the total population, free and slave. White men were expected to protect all of their property, which in a sense included their wives, for "property in women," or the right of a husband's exclusive sexual access to and control over his wife's body, was the core of male perceptions of household dominion and masculinity.[20]

Governor Brown and fellow secessionists repeatedly painted vivid word pictures of rapacious Yankees "threatening to violate your homes," including their women. A "Call to Arms" broadside distributed throughout the piney woods in early 1862 declared that the "voice of your wives and children call upon you" to volunteer and "repel the hireling hordes that swarm upon our borders." By freely associating violations of the South and its households with the possible fate of white Southern womanhood, secessionists created a threat to white Southern manhood that transcended social class. Brown was master-ful at turning phrases that linked the defense of Georgia to its "noble women" and suggested that the willingness of men to protect women was a mark of white male virility. Shortly after Union forces invaded northern Georgia, the governor called on home guards to help drive "the vandals from our borders," challenging them in unmistakable language: "Will you not rise in your might and put forth all your manliness for this glorious consummation?" Failure to engage the enemy, Brown warned, would result in unmanly submission and the "deepest degradation and the most abject poverty"—a fate worse than death. In a special message to the General Assembly late in 1862, he avowed: "If we are subjugated, let it be only when we are exterminated."[21]

To the threat of Yankee violation of the sanctity of home and Southern womanhood was added the specter of male slaves turned loose on white women and children. Describing himself as a "friend" of the "volunteers & their wives and childrens," W. B. Overstreet of Coffee County, in the spring of 1862 warned the governor: "The negroes is choosing out the young damsel for wives as soon as the war is over." The language of mobilization required that volunteers hasten to the front lines to protect "the hearth-stones around which cluster all your cherished endearments," but the internal threat of slave insurrection seemed ever more likely as white men continued to leave the forest.[22]

Having set aside his obligation to protect his family in order to become a Confederate soldier, the new recruit looked to the state to assume that role in his absence. But by linking duty to protect the Confederacy and duty to the family in an effort to garner the widest possible support among the plain folk for secession and war, leaders such as Brown planted the seeds of Confederacy's destruction from within. The state's ultimate inability to adequately care for soldiers' families created contradictions between the demands of battlefront and home front. Ultimately, the soldiers themselves weighed their national duty against their familial obligations.[23]

Realizing the potential for disaster inherent in such conflicting demands, local planters and county officials pledged to care for the families of absent soldiers. Planters—those with the most to lose in terms of property—vowed to renounce cotton and to plant more food crops to better support soldiers at the front and their families at home. At a meeting in March 1862, planters resolved to plant corn, potatoes, and peas "so that we may be able to assist in sustaining our Government, and feed our armies in the field." Their second resolution called on other civilians to support soldiers' families "in the best possible manner that we can, and nothing shall deter us from doing the same so far as lies in our power."[24]

The obligation of local government to care for soldiers' wives was evident early in the war. During its July 1861 term, for example, the Pulaski County Inferior Court levied a tax of $6,000 to aid its volunteer infantry companies "at the seat of war" and provide for the volunteers' families who "are in want of assistance." During its May 1862 term, the same court ordered the county treasurer to pay out "to the wifes of soldiers[,] Mothers[,] or their families ten dollars a piece to those that are entitled." On August 30 the court ordered that ten dollars per month be paid to soldiers' wives "in needy circumstances" and one dollar to each child.[25]

But the very image of soldiers' wives that emerged as the war continued revealed the inability of government on all levels, as well as planterly noblesse oblige, to shield them from war's privations. In the early fall of 1862, eighteen months after the fighting started, one south Georgian painted a word portrait of wartime white women that was meant to emphasize their wartime ingenuity, but one that suggests a collective failure to care for them. Tattered homespun bonnets shaped by wiregrass fillings, threadbare dresses, and homemade shoes adorned these plain folk. Leather was so scarce that they replaced coarse hides used under their mattresses with homemade white oak mats. The hides, previously deemed unsuitable for clothing, were hauled to local tanners and shaped into shoes for fifty cents a pair. Their tattered appearance did not necessarily translate into low morale, for such displays of homemade clothing were frequently ascribed to female patriotism, as the writer intended, but it nonetheless underscored a declining home-front standard of living for common white women and children.[26]

When it became obvious that the planter elite and county government could not end the suffering among Confederate soldiers' households, Governor Brown and the General Assembly created a program of state welfare that offered direct financial aid to needy families. Established by statute on December 13, 1862, the Indigent Soldiers Family Fund consisted of a state appropriation of $2.5 million. Inferior court justices administered the fund on the local level. Families in "needy circumstances" were listed and divided into categories, including "Widows of Soldiers," "Disabled and Discharged Soldiers," and "Women Dependent upon Disabled or Deceased Soldiers or Those in Service." The lists were created on the militia district level. They were based in part on the names of needy families already used by the courts to distribute county funds, such as those raised in Irwin in 1861 from a tax set at 40 percent of the state tax rate and "levied for wives and children of volunteers."[27]

Updated by the inferior courts until the war's end, the lists for the Indigent Soldiers Family Fund are the best evidence available to measure the dependence of soldiers' families on state welfare. Most county returns were received by the first week in March 1863; they were then used by the fund's administrators to determine each county's share of the state appropriation. Obviously, a county's share was heavily influenced by its rate of troop mobilization and the number of dependents left at home. Thus, Pulaski County, which by March 1863 had fielded four infantry companies, an artillery battery, and several cavalry units, received the largest share—$18,782. It claimed a total of 632 state beneficiaries, including children, an astonishing rate of dependence in a county that normally administered a small poor relief fund. On the other hand, sparsely populated Irwin County received only $2,496 based on a total of 84 beneficiaries. Assuming that each widow and each woman dependent on "disabled or deceased soldiers or those in service" represented a family, the proportion of all families dependent on state support can be estimated. Irwin County, with the fewest number of beneficiaries, counted approximately 11 percent of its families in "want of assistance" by the spring of 1863, whereas

Coffee County reported about 24 percent. Casualty rates, as well as rates of mobilization, influenced the number of beneficiaries in a county. Wilcox County, for example, counted almost 40 percent of its families on the indigent list by March 1863, reflecting in part the high number of deaths in its infantry companies such as the State Rights Guards.[28]

Because the lists of destitute soldiers' families were maintained for the remainder of the war, it is possible to determine approximately how many families fell into the category of the "new poor" as the conflict progressed. Pulaski County, for instance, reported 183 dependent women in the spring of 1863, or approximately 20 percent of all white families. By January 1865, however, 337 soldiers' families were on the list, representing almost 40 percent of all white families. In just under two years, the number of impoverished families in Pulaski almost doubled. It is important to remember that these figures include only those families that sent soldiers to the front. They exclude prewar indigents supported by poor law relief or the households of families with no military-aged men living at home, often the aged or infirm. Both groups struggled to feed themselves on a home-front market reshaped by dwindling manpower and food shortages. As a result, the total number of indigent families was higher than the proportion represented by soldiers' families.[29]

The direct relationship between Confederate mobilization, military service, and growing poverty was visible as early as 1861 and addressed by the legislature late in 1862. The departure of men and boys, most of them farmhands, created a labor shortage and changed the familial roles of those left behind, including the women who took charge of their households. "For every man who took a gun there was a woman or a child who took a hoe or a plow and went to the fields," one Coffee County resident recalled. The manpower shortage became even more critical in the wake of Confederate conscription. G. W. Slaughter declared that he no longer had "a force sufficient to carry on his Milling operations to advantage to himself or the community" and put his business up for sale.[30]

The consequences of mobilization were not felt uniformly. Slaveless yeoman women with husbands at the front and small children to feed were the most vulnerable and joined the growing number of new poor first. Women of elite Southern households may have fretted over their new responsibilities for slave management, but it is doubtful that less fortunate plain folk women had much sympathy for them as their own standards of living slipped. The Jacksonville district of Telfair County offers a compelling illustration. As early as August 1863, one-third of its households were headed by soldiers' wives or widows already on the county's indigent list, the majority of them non-slaveholders.[31]

Yeoman farmer John McCrimmon was typical of the Jacksonville district's slaveless family heads who left home to fight. The McCrimmons were no better off than many of their plain folk neighbors, claiming $700 in total wealth in 1860. On a two-horse, forty-acre farm, he and his wife Christiana raised two hundred bushels of corn and some vegetables crops and tended a few hogs and sheep. This was more than enough to meet their needs—at least for corn during normal times. As the war got under way, Christiana must have felt fortunate. John did not join the initial rush of volunteers in the spring and summer of 1861, letting the more adventurous men and boys take the lead in defending the new Confederate nation. These included three of John's younger brothers, all of whom joined the Telfair Volunteers in June. For almost a year McCrimmon stayed at home and his household remained intact. But when additional infantry companies were organized in March 1862, more men signed up. Among them was John McCrimmon, who enlisted in James Humphreys's infantry company and became a first sergeant in his first year of service.[32]

At home, twenty-year-old Christiana McCrimmon and her two small children joined the nonslaveholding soldiers' families whose self-sufficiency slipped away. It was a difficult, humiliating experience for families accustomed to economic independence. If she had managed to raise half of the corn that she and John grew together, she would barely have reached the level of household self-sufficiency in the crop. But she could not do even that. August 1863—seventeen months after John left home—found Christiana and twenty-nine other women from the Jacksonville district on the list of indigent soldiers' families. Neither her husband's promotion to sergeant nor her father-in-law's status as a small planter prevented Christiana and her children from joining the group of new poor that grew with each passing month.[33]

Up and down the river the plight of soldiers' wives became common knowledge and a source of neighborhood concern. Another unfortunate woman was Elender Fountain, who in 1849 had married Nathaniel Gibbs, one of the eleven men from the Gibbs family who joined the Wilcox County's State Rights Guards. A thirty-five-year-old slaveless yeoman farmer, Gibbs's total wealth in 1860 was $819, less than one-fourth the average for Georgia's free adult male heads of households. Nevertheless, Nathaniel and Elender made do on a fifty-acre, one-horse farm. In the best of times it was difficult to feed themselves and their six young children (in 1860 the oldest was ten and baby James was ten months old). In 1859 the family had raised eighty bushels of corn, some tobacco, and a crop of vegetables, which was just enough to get by.[34]

After Nathaniel left for the front, the burden of farmwork fell on Elender, who could expect only limited help from her children and neighbors. Nathaniel worried about her and from Virginia sent instructions on the upkeep of their farm. In March 1863 he asked "if you have planted anything" and reminded her, "You must have the cows pened." Making matters worse and further undermining his traditional role as primary provider was Nathaniel's inability to offer financial assistance: "I hant drawn no money yet," he wrote, a common complaint among Confederate soldiers. Without her husband to break ground, plant and cultivate the crops, and round up and pen the cows, in addition to her usual duties of running the household and caring for her children, Elender and women like her had more than they could handle.[35]

If soldiers' wives such as Christiana McCrimmon and Elender Gibbs became major symbols of the Confederate "cult of sacrifice," then the "Widows of Deceased Soldiers" occupied the holy of holies within the cult's temple. Women who had lost their husbands to battlefield wounds or disease were the most needy of protection on the home front and more likely to fall quickly into indigence. They had lost not only their partners—and in many cases, the men who had fathered their children—but also all hope of their men returning home and regaining self-sufficiency. Left to the new widows was the messy business of settling estates and a mourning process seemingly without closure. Moreover, the unending worries of feeding and clothing their family without slave labor—"the women and children has the work all to do," some wiregrass women reminded Governor Brown late in 1864—placed widows in extremely trying circumstances.[36]

At the beginning of March 1863 twelve women were listed as war widows in need of support from the Indigent Soldiers Family Fund in Telfair County. Sixteen months later the number had more than doubled to twenty-nine. Pamela Brantley was one of the Jacksonville district's "Widows of Deceased Soldiers." Before the war she and husband Thomas had worked a twenty-acre, one-horse farm and had $600 in total wealth to show for almost fifteen years of labor. The single bale of cotton they produced in 1860 was their primary source of cash income. In March 1862, when Thomas Brantley joined James Humphreys's infantry company as a volunteer, along with John McCrimmon, he was forty-two years old, well over the conscription age limit. Thomas may have enlisted for patriotic reasons or for the $50 bounty, or for both. He left Pamela, who was almost his age, at home with four children. On his death during the Confederate retreat from Gettysburg, Pamela already depended on her children, ranging in age from nine to sixteen, to tend the fields and livestock. Even before her husband left, the family grew only about one hundred bushels of corn per year, barely enough to feed them. Their son James, now almost thirteen, was the family's only male plow hand. In all likelihood, the couple had not been self-sufficient in the months before Thomas enlisted, and the Brantleys were probably on the indigent list before the news that he had died. His military service deprived the family of his labor temporarily; his death did so permanently. Within a month his dependents' names appeared on the indigent list and remained there for three years. Pamela and her children, along with hundreds of others, joined the war's new poor.[37]

### Family Structure and Household Authority

The paternalistic home front governed by soldiers' fathers and characterized by growing numbers of indigent soldiers' families unfolded within the context of neighborhoods changed by mobilization and casualties. Historians are not the only ones who described the home front as populated by white women and slaves. During the war, residents of white belt neighborhoods skillfully invoked the image of defenseless black belt white women and children and applied it to their own communities. In 1862 W. B. Overstreet urged Governor Brown to "do something with the Negroes in our States." Black men would "slaughter" white women and children, Overstreet warned. He added that soldiers' wives were "uneassey" because "they husbands . . . have to lieve them Exposed to the Negroes."[38]

In Overstreet's white belt county, only one in five households owned slaves. His neighborhood, called Bird's Mill, was more than twenty miles from Spalding, which claimed the county's densest slave population. Moreover, most of the few slaves in Bird's Mill were women and children. Adult male African Americans accounted for only 20 percent of the slaves in Coffee County and less than 5 percent of its total population. Overstreet conjured up the image of defenseless white femininity and applied it to one of the whitest places in piney woods to support his objections to the Confederate draft. If conscription were enforced and more men went to the front, he wrote in April 1862, soon after the law went into effect, "wo bee the women & children." Overstreet thus created an imagined Bird's Mill home front patterned after the black belt, where conditions demanded that men like himself stay home to protect soldiers' families from slave insurrection.[39]

How did troop mobilization affect household structure and authority relationships along the lower Ocmulgee? Was the exodus of soldiers so massive that the wartime lower river became "a world of white women and of slaves" whose paternalistic society was threatened by "the departure of the men who served as its organizing principle"? The Jacksonville district of Telfair County formed a middle ground between wealthy Pulaski County and the poorer white belt counties below. Almost one hundred households lived along the river road between Clayville and China Hill, which passed through fertile black belt fields and poorer pinelands. The district embraced small farms ranging from twenty to two hundred improved acres as well as a few plantations. Its inhabitants—about 40 percent of whom were slaves—gathered at Jacksonville's frame courthouse, around common log churches, at country stores, and at corn mills to socialize and trade.[40]

During the first two years of war, the Jacksonville district contributed no more or less than its share of soldiers to the Virginia front when compared to others along the lower river. This burden, however, was not equally shared among Jacksonville's households. Almost half of its households (47 percent) were headed by people unfit for military service due to their age or gender. Moreover, approximately 40 percent of those households not only were led by overaged men or women, but also contained no males of military age. For example, seventy-year-old Margaret Hulett's family consisted of herself, her daughter Margaret, and Margaret's fourteen-year-old daughter Elizabeth; ninety-year-old householder William Hatton and his wife Mary resided with a white woman and two slaves. In nearly half the district's homes, mobilization and military service had no direct impact on household authority.[41]

Almost 60 percent of the households led by men ineligible for military service or women sent someone under their roof—sons, sons-in-law, boarders, or hired farmhands—into local infantry companies. Seventy-eight when the war began, slaveless yeoman farmer Robert Jones Sr. was obviously too old to serve, but his sons William and Jesse, both farm laborers in his household, entered the Confederate army, William signing on with the Telfair Volunteers in 1861 and Jesse joining James Humphreys's company in 1862.[42]

Obviously, the greatest change in household structure and authority came when a white male head of household—the family's governing voice and representative in the larger body politic—joined the Confederate army. In the

Jacksonville district, 29 percent of all heads of households joined military units. In these households, soldiers' wives became responsible for all that took place in the home. This included their traditional domestic obligations and the management of farmwork, including, occasionally, slave labor. For Mary Fussell, whose landless husband Jacob joined the Telfair Volunteers in 1861, this meant providing for herself and five children, all under the age of nine, with little property of their own to sustain them.[43]

Like most of the other married men enrolling in Confederate or state units, the vast majority of those in the Jacksonville district lived on farms, growing food crops and tending livestock. These citizen soldiers ranged from Oliver Cook, a prosperous planter-merchant, to Thomas Brantley, a slaveless one-horse corn and cotton farmer. They also included landless farm laborers and tenants such as Minor White, who left his wife alone at home when he volunteered. More typical was Lucius Williams, a yeoman farmer who worked sixty acres of improved land with the help of his wife Catherine. On their two-horse farm, the couple raised two hundred bushels of corn and forty hogs in 1859.[44]

Of the 29 percent of all heads of households in the Jacksonville district who served in the conflict, 61 percent left a wife and at least one child behind. Yeoman farmer John Walker had the largest immediate family under one roof—his thirty-eight-year-old wife Mary and eight children who ranged in age from one to sixteen. About 17 percent of married soldiers had a wife at home alone. Approximately the same percentage, however, left a wife and children at home with an older adult man or woman, individuals who provided badly needed household and field labor. Uriah Watson was apparently the only male head of household in the district who left an elderly person alone in his home when he volunteered: sixty-six-year-old Nancy Watson, probably his mother.[45]

About one-fourth of the district's household heads were white males of military age who for one reason or another did not join Confederate units. This does not mean that these men did not see some military service, either in the state militia or home guard. But it does suggest that if they were away from home at all it was for relatively short periods—weeks or months, perhaps, rather than years. Disabilities real or pretended and exemptions from service excused many of these men. To this group must be added a significant number of returnees from the Confederate army who were discharged for disabilities or, in the case of officers, resigned their commissions. Over the course of the war these numbers mounted. Indeed, almost 20 percent of the men in the two

Confederate infantry companies heavily recruited in the Jacksonville district became returnees. Such was the case of Captain Humphreys, who resigned his commission four months after arriving at the Virginia front and was declared exempt from militia service because he was a physician. Ironically, by the spring of 1865 returnees in Telfair County approximately equaled the number of original volunteers who remained with their companies to surrender at Appomattox. When joined with the patriarchs and the military-aged men who did not serve in the Confederate army, these returnees comprised a significant male presence on the home front. Indeed, writing in the summer of 1864, planter and militia company captain Samuel Fuller believed that he could raise a cavalry regiment of "minut men" in lower Georgia "out of the men that is now at Home."[46]

To summarize, as many as 70 percent of the Jacksonville district's household heads remained on the home front during the war. They did so for a variety of reasons: age, gender, and exemption from service. Soldiers who returned home because of disability, substitution, or resignation joined them. The male exodus in the district was undeniably significant, as the number of female heads of households increased by almost 30 percent. Continuity characterized household authority in large measure because the burden of soldiering fell on young men and boys living with parents, in-laws, or employers, who accounted for 57 percent of the district's infantrymen. The older men and women, the soldiers' fathers and mothers, as well as military-aged men who avoided Confederate service, continued to direct the farm labor of both whites and blacks. Certainly mobilization left vacant chairs at home, but not in every house and not at the head of most tables. Whether or not this pattern was unique to the region is a question awaiting further research. But it does suggest that one reason for the South's ability to wage war for four years, at least in low slaveholding areas remote from the front, may well have been the stability of its patriarchal social order despite mobilization.[47]

## "Managing My Estate"

Regardless of the overwhelming whiteness of the local population, mobilization tended to make black belt neighborhoods blacker, creating along the lower river the type of challenges for slave management found in the cotton belt. This was especially true in the cotton districts of Pulaski County, where 47 percent of the population was black, and in black belt neighborhoods along the lower river valley, where enslaved African Americans often formed one-third of the population, most of them living on plantations.[48]

Concerns about "keeping the negro population in proper training," as Pulaski's inferior court described the problem, were shared by planters and plain folk in neighborhoods where relatively few white men remained. Writing to the Confederate secretary of war in the summer of 1863, a group of Irwin County citizens petitioned for the "reliece" of Private William Wilcox of the Pulaski Volunteers from Confederate service. Wilcox, who traveled to Hawkinsville from the House Creek neighborhood in 1861 to join the lower river's first infantry company, was now needed at home. Anxious citizens wanted him "to take charge of slaves that [are] left in the county without any one to watche them." These plain folk were afraid of what eighty-seven slaves might do "which is on different plantations[,] two without a white man person."[49]

The petition of Irwin's citizens reflected the long-standing fear of black belt slaves harbored by plain folk residing in backwoods communities. Slaves could and did become runaways and plundered yeoman farms. It mattered little to these whites that only eleven black males over age eighteen lived on Thomas Willcox's plantation in the House Creek neighborhood. What worried them now was that mobilization had left slaves with no "white man person" to watch them.[50]

Their concerns were largely unfounded. For unlike the thousands of runaways who left the occupied South and joined the Union army to help defeat the Confederacy, local blacks did little to openly win their freedom. Deep within the interior, they waited on farms and plantations for freedom to come to them. Despite later claims to the contrary, local slaves knew that their "white folks" were locked in a deadly fight to break free from the North and keep them in bondage. Martha Everette recalled that the overseer on James Lathrop's plantation "enlisted in the army very soon after War was declared." She also remembered that her master "did often have food and stock feed sent to the soldiers." Mobilization reduced the number of military-aged white men in their neighborhoods and, according to one former slave, a "good many men slaves went with their masters" as body servants. As the war wore on, some enslaved African Americans sensed that impending disaster hung over the valley. Looking toward the horizon, one woman saw "blood on the edge of the sky" and knew "blood was being shed."[51]

The slave population was far from immobile, although it is difficult to determine the war's impact on slave movement. Planter Joseph M. White, who resided near the Pulaski County line, estimated late in 1862 that Confederate and state officials had "impressed & taken 20 pr ct of the slaves away from their owners." He was indignant that the "risqué & labor necessary" to prepare defensive works under General Mercer's call for impressments had unfairly burdened "a few poor counties" while "wealthier counties stand aloof & do nothing at all." White's complaint was not motivated by class conflict between planters and plain folk, but by his regional identity as a slaveholder on the borderland of the forest. He wanted his slaves returned, declaring as "a loyal citizen of this confederacy" that "a government that does not protect its subjects in the enjoyment of their property, so far as it lies in its power, is not the kind of government to command respect, or encourage the feelings of patriotism."[52]

It was on plantations such as White's that slave field work allowed a much higher rate of white male mobilization than would have otherwise been possible. Moreover, in a part of the South where cotton and corn regions met, the wartime shift to greater corn cultivation, which required less agricultural labor and in turn theoretically gave black belt slaves greater agency, was less dramatic. Much of the lower river was already corn country, and wartime production increased. By the spring of 1863 steamboats were hauling mostly corn and other produce to markets above and below Hawkinsville. A visitor to the town wrote that little cotton was cultivated by slaves, and farmers were planting peanuts and sugarcane. A small "oil manufactory" equipped with a hydraulic press made seventy gallons of peanut oil per day and marketed it as machine oil. Thus, a crop formerly considered a "contemptible article" consumed by children and slaves was now being planted on a large scale.[53]

As the war persisted and the plain folk's plight increased, the advantages of slave ownership became more pronounced. It was the labor of common field hands such as Arthur Coalson, who continued to work after his "young master enlisted and took one slave with him," that kept the households of slaveholders off the list of indigent families. According to one interpretation of elite women on the home front, plantation mistresses were often compelled to take over slave management in the absence of their men. Unaccustomed to the task, they sensed their limitations and doubted their abilities. Moreover, Southern patriarchs lost "their power as white males, as masters of families of white women and black slaves" because of their inability to protect women. Considering the general continuity in domestic authority along the lower river, the extent to which white women assumed responsibility for managing slaves after slaveholding men left for military service is worth exploring.[54]

How widespread was this new and burdensome duty of slave management among white women of the lower Ocmulgee? In the Jacksonville district, where masters led a third of all households (a level slightly higher than that of the lower valley as a whole), half of the masters were men too old for military service. Approximately 7 percent of the slaveowners were white males of military age who did not serve in regular Confederate infantry units. Moreover, white women accounted for 20 percent of the district's masters in 1860. They formed a significant group of primarily widows who had become accustomed to slave management before the war. One of these was Mary Dopson, the wife of Major Alexander Dopson, of Jacksonville, an old-line Whig, Mason, and Methodist layman whose total wealth amounted to $9,000 in 1860. When he died at age sixty-three, four months before the war began, his widow became the head of a household that included nine slaves. Taken together, then, almost 80 percent of the masters living along this stretch of the lower river remained at home during the war. In most cases, the fundamental authority relationship between slave and owner, regardless of the owner's gender, remained unchanged.[55]

The greatest change in master-slave relationships occurred in the 20 percent of slaveholding households in the Jacksonville district where wives were left to manage enslaved domestic servants and field hands after their husbands departed for the front. The scale of this task varied considerably from one household to the next. Catherine Anderson, for example, possessed a single slave, whereas Rebecca Cook, the wife of Captain Oliver Cook, now managed twenty-three. Greater access to slave labor ultimately meant that Cook's wartime household escaped serious privation, whereas Anderson found her name on the list of indigent soldiers' families by 1863. Clearly, women like Rebecca Cook had a higher commitment to and dependence on slave labor during both wartime and peacetime, an interest that shaped the status of her household and set it apart from those of plain folk.[56]

Along the lower river, authority relationships between masters and slaves were not fundamentally altered by wartime mobilization. The fountainhead of domestic authority—the head of household—experienced little change within the vast majority of slaveholding families. Older white men still ruled at home, but so did white women, who accounted for one in five of the district's masters in 1860. When the war started, half of these women had no men of military age living at home, so mobilization did not strip their households of the male dominion often considered an essential part of slave management. Only Christiana Clements, the widow of John Clements Sr., was left alone with slaves and no adult white males because of mobilization, but this was not unusual among slaveowning widows. In any event, mobilization did not significantly shift the "essential political act" of controlling slaves from men to women in the Jacksonville district.[57]

Since most slaveholding families maintained a higher standard of living, it is not surprising that the names of slaveless plain folk appeared on the lists of indigent soldiers' families first. The difference between the haves and the have-nots was especially apparent in the white belt backwoods, where the estates of masters were a marked contrast to the hardscrabble farms of the yeomanry. This inequality derived from more than just the labor advantage that even one or two field hands gave masters over nonslaveholders, for soil fertility was a key factor in the wartime struggle for self-sufficiency just as it had been in peacetime. In river valley neighborhoods such as Copeland, alluvial "low grounds" and "Bay lands" produced more than fifty bushels of corn per acre, while the poorer sandy backwoods lands yielded eight to twelve bushels of "good corn." Even without the advantage of slave labor, a soldier's family that worked more fertile river land outproduced a similar family toiling on poorer land.[58]

Less fertile land and the absence of slave labor made it increasingly difficult for soldiers' wives such as Elender Gibbs to keep the home fires burning. The task was much easier for women like Mary Dopson. On the other hand, maintaining self-sufficiency was even less demanding for female planters like Sarah Willcox, the widow of former unionist Mark Willcox. At fifty, she was the matriarch of a household that consisted of twelve whites and twenty blacks in 1860 on her plantation near Copeland. In 1859 the estate had produced two thousand bushels of corn and forty-five bales of cotton. Based on an average annual consumption of thirteen bushels of corn per person, the Willcox place harvested three times the corn required to feed its people. Moreover, as cotton production decreased, slave labor allowed planters such as Sarah Willcox to diversify by growing sugarcane and other crops traditionally produced and marketed by plain folk.[59]

The wives of slaveholders too old to fight fared better than their younger counterparts, who had to fill the void left by their absent soldier husbands. The older male heads of household remained at home throughout the war and spared their wives the burden of slave management. Fifty-year-old yeoman Alfred Burnham owned an estate worth $12,000, over ten times the value of Nathaniel Gibbs's place across the river. In 1860 Burnham, his sons, and his slaves harvested two thousand bushels of corn, almost ten times the crop needed to feed the ten whites and nine blacks living on his farm. Although Alfred and his wife Mary sent three sons into Confederate service, they could recover from the loss of labor because they owned nine slaves. Even without their adult sons, the Burnhams' level of production guaranteed a comfortable margin of self-sufficiency barring crop failure. The Burnham household was as patriotic as the next when it came to putting men into Confederate uniforms, but with slave labor it took the economic and physical hardships of war longer to erode the family's standard of living than it did their slaveless plain folk neighbors'.[60]

Whether female or male, small slaveholder or large, the masters of the lower Ocmulgee enjoyed benefits that only increased during the conflict. Their estates became islands of stability and surplus in a sea of wartime privation. The rewards they reaped from slave labor did not stop with crops of grain consumed by family or livestock, but included any farm product sold or traded on the inflationary market. Justices of the inferior courts were forced to regulate the local economy as best they could by setting price limits for the food that indigent soldiers' committees bought for the wives and children of troops. Thus, the slaves of planters became the major source of plain folk's food. Planter Norman McDuffie, for example, sold the Confederate government corn, fodder, and almost $1,800 worth of lard. Furthermore, slave labor itself was hired out on the severely strained Southern labor market. In 1863 three planters from Pulaski and Wilcox Counties were secure enough in their levels of food production to collect income from the Confederate government "for hire of slaves employed at Savannah"—this while plain folk families went hungry due to labor shortages.[61]

### "No Country Outside of His Pocket"

Beyond the gates of the estates of planters such as Sarah Willcox and prosperous slaveholding yeomen like Alfred Burnham was a rural economy unraveling at the seams. This was not because the patriarchy collapsed, or because slaves actively or passively undermined the peculiar institution, or because women at home became disaffected and stopped supporting the war effort. Basically, it was because the lower river's economy, which in some counties had barely reached subsistence levels in corn before the war, never recovered prewar manpower levels in the wake of mobilization and the horrific casualties that followed. It was only because most slaves continued to work that the local production of foodstuffs allowed the area's white people to fight for four years. With the impact of mobilization added to wartime shortages of virtually every commodity, the wiregrass economy eventually collapsed under the weight of the Federal blockade, runaway inflation, and speculation. The collapse made it even more difficult for plain folk because the burdens of wartime privation, like those of mobilization, were not equally shared from one household to the next.[62]

The republican simplicity and self-sufficiency that characterized backwoods society was based on popular perceptions of what was legitimate and illegitimate in the marketplace. The availability of critical foodstuffs such as corn in local markets was closely monitored, particularly in times of drought and crop failure. Families and neighborhoods struggled through hard times by assisting each other as best they could. Yeoman farmer Dunk Douglass of Coffee County and Primitive Baptist layman and storekeeper Jacob Young in Irwin helped war widows and orphaned children. Their willingness to share provisions was common knowledge in their neighborhoods. Hoarding and profiting from shortages, on the other hand, violated customs of equity and trust. Wartime hoarders, in the eyes of patriots, challenged Confederate authority and the home front's moral economy. As hard money dried up and resources grew scarce, "heartless speculators," as Governor Brown called them, seized the opportunity to make quick profits at the expense of their less fortunate neighbors by purchasing the property of debtors "at almost nominal prices" and by hoarding food and other supplies. By controlling essential commodities, Brown charged, "these Shylocks" weakened the Confederacy from within. These "hard-hearted and unpatriotic" speculators undermined the Confederate community—as a nation of states, as an army of men, as a home front of soldiers' families. Their "wicked avarice" reduced formerly self-sufficient families to "actual suffering, on account of their inability by their labor to purchase the necessities of life."[63]

Corn was a critical home-front commodity. Six months after the war began, corn traded on the Macon market for seventy-five cents per bushel. On the eve of Confederate conscription, justices of the Telfair County Inferior Court set the price of corn purchased for the families of soldiers at $1.00 per bushel. By January 1865 Confederate impressments agents were paying $3.50 per bushel, and speculation drove the price well above that. As early as November 1861, wrote one observer, cries of "Bread or Blood" were "worthy of consideration" on the home front, where basic "articles of subsistence" were already scarce. The efforts of inferior courts to regulate the price of corn and other commodities met with little success. Joseph White, a Laurens Hill planter, believed that local attempts to regulate prices were doomed since "the man whose soul is married to money" simply ignored them. With twenty-five slaves in his fields, White grew far more corn than he could use. Indeed, in the fall and winter of 1863 to 1864 he sold as many as five thousand bushels at the Confederate rate of between $1.75 and $2.00 per bushel out of a spirit of patriotism. But this was about half the price that some of his fellow planters and farmers got for their corn from less patriotic speculators.[64]

Common folk customarily depended on paternalists like Joseph White to control such "unprincipled public plunderers," who, as the Confederate patriot charged, recognized "no country outside of his pocket." Explanations of Confederate defeat that emphasize class conflict as the primary factor stress planter indifference to the wartime plight of plain folk as a key to disaffection among the yeomanry. Yet evidence suggests that some planters along the lower valley were fully aware of plain folk privations and attempted to fulfill their traditional role as paternalists in the moral economy. At the end of 1861, for instance, Telfair County small planter and inferior court justice Peter Coffee, with two sons already in Confederate service, charged that unpatriotic Hawkinsville merchants hoarded two thousand sacks of salt and charged prices that "poor people . . . cannot afford to pay." Coffee believed that such "wile speculation" created "extreme suffering" in the "farming part of the community" and called on Governor Brown "for protection against these speculators." Far from being indifferent to suffering among the yeomanry, planters like Coffee challenged the state to curb the speculation that exploited soldiers' families and other "poor people."[65]

Joseph White was, like Peter Coffee, a Southern nationalist who backed up patriotic rhetoric with action. He realized that speculation created an unequal distribution of wartime sacrifice. When a "poor neighbor" needed provisions, White sold them at government prices because he considered it his duty as a paternalist and patriot. He could certainly make more money if he sold bacon and corn to speculators, but, he maintained, it was important to lead by example in order to "check the spirit of speculation in my neighborhood." White was motivated not only by noblesse oblige but also by his commitment to the Confederate cause. "The less you bear the burdens of war," he admonished unscrupulous traders, "the greater you make the burden fall upon me." For White and other patriotic planters, the success of the Confederate experiment was now less about immediate financial returns and more about the long-term future of black slavery and white freedom. "I am willing to make any sort of pecuniary sacrifice," he wrote, "if it can save my country and my children from the fate of a subjugated people."[66]

White's commitment to the "success of our cause" was all the more remarkable because he suspected his practice of selling provisions at government rates made him vulnerable to his "poor" neighbors. Some plain folk, he believed, "emptied their [corn] cribs in the lap of speculators" at four dollars a bushel and turned to him to refill them at the lower government rate of two dollars per bushel. Nonetheless, White continued to sell provisions at lower rates. Although planters and merchants are often associated with wartime hoarding and speculation, Joseph White reminds us that citizens of all classes participated in speculation in ways large and small. Their collective actions, White warned, were "stabbing at the very vitals of our country" regardless of whether the speculators wore broadcloth or homespun. The example of planters such as White and Peter Coffee also remind us that while there were undoubtedly wealthy men who were indifferent to the plight of plain folk, there were also planters who used their community status and political connections to address the needs of the wartime poor and fulfill their traditional role as patriarchs. In Coffee's case, he, as the soldier's father, helped direct the home front through his service as inferior court justice while his son, Captain John Coffee, led the brothers, husbands, and sons of soldiers' families into combat in Virginia. For father and son, the privations of plain folk both at home and at the front became mutual concerns.[67]

### We the Undersigned

On January 31, 1865, the Pulaski County Inferior Court faced a crisis. Dwindling manpower, crop failures, and drought had undermined the county's capacity to feed its people. The reduced yields made it "impossible for us to procure corn by purchase," the justices concluded. The almost complete loss of the 1864 wheat crop worsened the grain shortage. Half of all soldiers' wives, representing 168 families and 354 children, "have not nor can they purchase corn for bread" in the lower river's wealthiest and most agriculturally productive county. The justices gloomily calculated that 1,500 bushels of corn was the least "we could do with."[68]

The inferior court then proposed a radical solution. Government corn collected as the previous year's Confederate tax-in-kind should be given to soldiers' wives and children rather than forwarded to the front. In recommending this course, the justices understood the growing political significance of soldiers' wives and families. The designation of "soldiers' wives" or "widows of deceased soldiers" gave such women a new political identity, one that entitled them and their children to government recognition and support. By placing their needs above those of the flagging Confederacy, the justices—most of them slaveholders—symbolically reversed the direction of home-front support without being disloyal to the cause. The soldiers' fathers decided that the war was unwinnable if the foundation of rural society—self-sufficient households and sustainable neighborhoods—was destroyed in the process. Increasingly, plain folk women looked beyond the Confederacy to a future in which they reconstructed their households in a postwar world. But this would be possible only if they preserved enough wartime resources to begin again.[69]

The soldiers' families in Pulaski County represented a growing home-front constituency that was dependent on the state and the inferior court. It was within the context of neighborhood survival and county politics that the wartime politicization of women took place. The emerging "cult of sacrifice" among Confederate women may have made them reluctant to dwell on their suffering in letters to their men in the field, but as their responsibilities became increasingly burdensome, they were less restrained in their appeals for help to local and state authorities. By the summer of 1864 it was doubtful that "many farmers" would be able to provide "a sufficient support for their families," as one petition signed by women attested. With the foundations of rural neighborhoods eroding, plain folk women became more assertive in demanding that local, state, and Confederate authorities address home-front problems.[70]

Never entirely relegated to the private sphere as far as public opinion was concerned, Southern white women exercised growing political influence as the secession crisis had unfolded and demonstrated increasing support for the Confederacy as war neared in 1861. They, too, had a heritage that seemed to be threatened, a heritage of protection by men and superiority to blacks, whatever their own social class. Moreover, the slaveholders among them, such as cotton farmer Mary Barnes, had a direct economic interest in the defense of slavery. White women of all classes, especially those of slaveholding households, had a stake in the struggle and were vocal in their defense of Southern rights. Writing in January 1861 after witnessing the formation of local military companies along the lower river, John McRae declared: "The women here appear to be more strongly interested in the cause than the men. I would infer from the tenor of their conversations that *they would be willing to join the Company themselves.*"[71]

The war, however, propelled women beyond the assertions of Confederate nationalism, as reflected in their symbolic public roles at flag presentations, and into more practical politics. The shift began on the neighborhood and county levels with the singular action of individual women. Some wrote letters and urged the governor to exempt their men from military service. The wife of William J. Bennett, who described herself as "uneducated," sought to have her husband excused from conscription on the grounds that he was "afflicted" and that her family was "depending on his labour for suport." Without his income, the family would become dependent on the state.[72]

The real political power of women, however, came when they joined together, and often with men, to petition the state as groups of constituents, just as they had done before the war. Unlike Bennett's wife, these women went beyond the needs of individual households to address the larger concerns of neighborhoods on the brink of disaster. During the spring, summer, and fall of 1864, when most such petitions were circulated and signed, the home-front economy was on the verge of collapse. Moreover, the invasion of Georgia and Atlanta's fall required the governor to call up all available men and boys for militia service, a further demonstration of the Confederacy's inability to protect its citizens at home. This emergency resulted in a series of proclamations that threatened to strip rural neighborhoods of previously exempt men who played important roles in their communities. Almost without exception, the petitions of women continued to seek exemptions from service for men— blacksmiths, mail carriers, shoemakers—on the grounds of "publick convenience" and their general usefulness "in the community & county."[73]

Soldiers' wives and mothers as well as patriarchs like Peter Coffee recognized the delicate balance between the manpower needs of battlefront and home front. Only a healthy home front could adequately support their troops. Thus, they collectively petitioned government authorities when they believed that the human infrastructure of agricultural production was threatened. In many respects, blacksmiths became the symbol of localism and neighborhood survival in farming communities. Exempt from Confederate service for most of the war, blacksmiths were in the eyes of farming women and men a "public necessity." They mended and sharpened agricultural implements, shoed working livestock, and operated shops where, as one group of petitioners described it, "we can have our old irons worked to an advantage." Petitioning Governor Brown shortly after his May 1864 proclamation directed the militia into the field, over fifty "citizens and soldiers' wives of Pulaski & Wilcox county" requested an exemption for blacksmith Robert C. Smith. If his shop closed down, farming families would be forced to haul their implements ten miles upriver to Hawkinsville or "25 miles below."[74]

Petitioners made similar arguments on behalf of other skilled workers, especially shoemakers. A group of Telfair citizens sought the exemption of shoemaker and tanner Duncan Graham, noting that he was in "very feeble & delicate condition" and "in all probability would result in but very little if any good at all to our army or cause." On the other hand, the county's men, women, and children needed shoes and Graham, although sixty-four years old, continued to work "for the public, and at *very moderate prices.*"[75]

Drafters of petitions were careful to mention that the men they wanted detailed from the Confederate army or exempted from militia service possessed a sense of duty and personal obligation to soldiers' families, therefore assuming some of the state's responsibility for their care. Robert C. Smith, for example, not only was a much-needed blacksmith, but he also displayed "great kindness towards the families of soldiers in working for many of them for nothing." Smith used a sliding fee structure for his services, charging the families of soldiers little or nothing and "those of property very reasonable." His sense of obligation and justice made him all the more valuable on a home front wracked by inflation, speculation, and shortages. As some Telfair County petitioners maintained, "a man of strict integrity & morals and much inclined to do all the good he can as a citizen" was needed more than another soldier at the front. Helping the home front helped the nation. Citizens fought to hold onto such men not out of disloyalty to the Confederacy, but out of the realization that without their services the local economy would grind to a standstill.[76]

The signatures of soldiers' wives lent both authority and legitimacy to the hundreds of petitions that Governor Brown received. This fact was not lost on men—including local politicians who were in many cases petitioners as well. They also recognized the validity of petitions signed by soldiers' wives and widows. Women accounted for 30 percent of the signatures of the "citizens & soldiers' wives" who petitioned on behalf of blacksmith Robert C. Smith. At times women were carefully identified as "Soldiers wido" or "Soldiers wife" to emphasize the sacrifices their households had made to the Confederate cause.[77]

The petition to exempt James T. Branch from military service in May 1864 offers insight into neighborhood petition making as well as what might be termed the "genealogy" of petitions. Branch lived in the remote backwoods of Irwin County on the Alapaha River near a ferry bearing his family name. Like most plain folk in his white belt neighborhood, Branch owned no slaves and worked fewer than one hundred acres. In 1859 his small farm produced corn, one bale of cotton, and the third largest rice crop in his neighborhood. A prosperous yeoman, Branch played a role in the public life of his militia district and served as both road commissioner and slave patrol commissioner in the 1850s. His sister-in-law, Millie Fletcher Branch, was one of a handful of small masters in the neighborhood. In 1860 she owned four young slaves.[78]

The extended Branch clan's support of the Confederacy was highly regarded despite its plain folk roots. When the county's first infantry company—the Irwin Cow Boys—was organized in the summer of 1861, four Branches volunteered, placing the family in the vanguard of local Southern nationalists. In March 1862 James T. Branch and a number of relatives joined the Irwin County Volunteers of the 49th Georgia. Branch soon transferred to Company A, 61st Georgia, an infantry unit that included many former members of the Irwin Cow Boys, where he served for over two years. In early 1864 Branch, now in his mid-forties, returned home "on sick firlow" because "old age and afflictions" made him "wholy unfit for field Service." By that time, James and his wife Ruthie had four sons "in the Service of his contry."[79]

Almost immediately, Branch was commissioned a justice of the peace in his militia district, an office that exempted him from Confederate service. He soon took a "grate interest in ministering to the assistance of the indegent woman and children," becoming the distributing agent of corn and meal for "soldiers familys" in his neighborhood. But a threat to his useful home-front service soon arose. Irwin County's enrolling officer believed that Branch should respond to Governor Brown's call for militia to turn back Sherman's army. In a petition to Brown, his family and friends charged the enrolling officer of "interupting" Branch's "assistance" to local soldiers' families and called for his exemption on that ground. Of the twenty-seven signatures on the petition, two-thirds were those of neighborhood women. Significantly, more than half of these women were related to Branch by blood or marriage, including his mother-in-law, sister-in-law, and a niece. The petition on behalf of Branch clearly reflects the internal conflict created on the neighborhood level by the need for men in military service and the growing concern for neighborhood protection, part of the seemingly endless struggle between localism and Confederate nationalism. An expression of the growing political voice of plain folk women, the petition declared in effect that there were limits to women's support of the war when their families' survival and the future of rural neighborhoods hung in the balance.[80]

After all, by the spring of 1864 James T. Branch was one of nineteen soldiers from an extended family of plain folk in the county's two infantry companies. These men had served the Confederacy well and paid a high price. Of the eleven who joined the Irwin County Volunteers along with Branch, six had died—most of disease—and another was permanently disabled by the time James arrived home. The end of the war was not in sight. The language of the petition is revealing. For over two years, Branch had "belonged to" the "Confederate States Service." Now he was home and performing "grate" service as a justice of the peace and as a district committeeman charged with "ministering" to the needs of soldiers' families. He "belonged" to his neighborhood. These people included his own large household: "a wife and 12 children yet with him[,] 8 of which is under 12 years of age[;] he has over 10 in family that is dependent on him for seport." Ironically, the petitioners now asked the governor to "protect" Branch from the war so that he could protect them from poverty, a service more important than any he could render at the front. Branch had done his military duty and the neighborhood had made its sacrifices. In the minds of plain folk women, Branch now rightfully belonged not to the Confederacy but to them and their children at home. Their petition was not an expression of disloyalty to the Confederacy, but instead a plea for justice.[81]

The circumstances of James Branch and his family complicate our understanding of the Civil War home front. Branch's experiences were varied and so were his identities. It is impossible to categorize him neatly. A soldiers' father, he watched his sons leave for the front in 1861. He then became a soldier himself in 1862 and a civil officer by 1864. His family hoped that his position as a member of the home front's ruling patriarchy would spare him further military service. His wife Ruthie was both the mother of soldiers and a soldier's wife. Her wartime household included twelve children, most of them too young to help in the house or on the farm. She was certainly among the soldiers' wives who needed Branch's protection, although her name does not appear on the petition. Thus, for Branch and his family and neighbors, the war created a complex, messy world of multiple roles and conflicting loyalties.

Although soldiers' wives and widows became major symbols of wartime sacrifice, the local community did not become a world of white women and slaves. Enough men remained at home to preserve the paternalistic social order. Indeed, during the war the powers of the inferior courts expanded along with the authority of soldiers' fathers. In a majority of households continuity characterized family authority and structure, and the relationship between household heads, regardless of gender, and their dependents, both white and black, did not change. Most soldiers were unmarried men and boys who still lived with their parents. After their departure, soldiers' fathers continued to govern most families. Mobilization did have a profound impact on the ability of households to remain self-sufficient, especially among the non-slaveholding plain folk. Unable to depend on slave labor to replace departing farmworkers, plain folk soldiers' families were the first to join the wartime new poor and become dependent on state assistance.

Women became increasingly concerned about the sustainability of their households and neighborhoods given the war's human and material costs. Their politicization, which began in the antebellum period and grew during the secession crisis, became even more pronounced during the war but unfolded within a patriarchal framework still shaped by men. The petitions of soldiers' wives, mothers, and fathers to Confederate and state authorities for the exemption of critical workers did not necessarily reflect disloyalty or class conflict. Strong, stable neighborhoods supported the Confederate war effort better than weak and disintegrating ones. Moreover, the loss of loved ones in the struggle against the Yankees and the privations on the home front united plain folk in their hatred of Abraham Lincoln and his "hirelings." Ultimately, however, if the war destroyed the neighborhoods it was intended to save, nationalism was displaced by localism. The multiple identities and conflicting loyalties of people who claimed "I Represent the War" such as James Branch's were real, but their differences were lessened by a common fear among soldiers' wives, fathers, mothers, kinfolk, slaves, and the soldiers themselves—the fear of death.[82]

"When the War started, white or colored, rich or po', all of us was scared," Easter Reed recalled. One of nine slaves owned by Alfred and Mary Ann Burnham, Easter watched four of her master's sons leave the farm near Hopewell Church to fight the Yankees. What frightened her and others along the lower Ocmulgee was a fear she expressed this way: "We was scared they'd be killed." As her words remind us, the fear of wartime death transcended both race—"white or colored"—and class—"rich or po'." Far from unified before the war, the lower river's people were further divided by the war into Easter's "we," the whites and slaves remaining at home, and "they," the men and boys fighting the Yankees. As the war went on, both "we" and "they" were forced into a new reckoning with death.[1]

Ultimately, the death toll was greater than the Burnhams or anyone else along the river could have imagined in 1861. The conflict claimed three of Alfred and Mary Ann's sons: James, John, and Thomas; only Miles survived military service. At least two of the boys managed to return to Hopewell and die in the house of their childhood. As Easter remembered: "When they come home they was sick an' I had to fan the flies off'n 'em." The Burnham boys' sacrifice on the Confederate "altar of liberty" did not keep the Union army out of Georgia or even out of their father's yard. The aging Alfred proved powerless to hold the black and white members of his household together in war and defeat. Early in the summer of 1865, Easter watched as the Yankees told him to call his slaves together, and then "master told them they were free to go where they liked."[2]

Her recollection is ultimately a story of black liberation, but it offers us a moving glimpse of the wartime suffering and sacrifice of a white Confederate household. During the Confederate nation's short life, soldiers' deaths became the political expression of Southern nationalism. Citizen soldiers along the lower river understood that death might be the price they paid for "love of country." They understood that blood traditionally was demanded to preserve liberty, from the Revolutionary War down to their own time, but they believed that "victory and freedom are worth the sacrifice." As Governor Brown reminded his fellow Georgians, "The rivers of blood which have been drawn from the veins of our fathers, brothers, husbands, and sons and other relatives by the hands of our cruel enemies form an impassable gulf between us and our wicked invaders." The mounting death toll thus legitimized the Confederate nation and raised the level of hatred toward Yankees. In a special message to the General Assembly late in 1862, Brown declared: "We were born free; and though it be upon the battle field, we should die free." On another occasion he warned that surrender and reunion were out of the question for dead soldiers' survivors, because "the blood of their brethren, who have fallen martyrs to our glorious cause, would cry to them from the ground, and rebuke the dastardly deed."[3]

None could claim to "represent the war" more truthfully than the wives and parents, brothers and sisters, sons and daughters of dead soldiers. Their ultimate sacrifice unified families along the lower Ocmulgee and shaped the collective "we" consciousness that Easter Reed recalled. Every class of Southern white society ultimately claimed to represent the war through death. Often interpreted by historians as a divisive force that fragmented the home front along class lines—"a rich man's war and a poor man's fight"—the staggering death toll ignored traditional distinctions of social class and reached though kinship networks into virtually every family. As Barnabas Williamson wrote home to Wilcox County late in 1863: "This horrible war seems to spread misery and want, broadcast, over the land." The greater the loss, the more embittered Confederate patriots became toward the enemy.[4]

Seeing grieving widows, children, and parents reminded the community of the human cost of the Confederate war and conjured up poignant memories of faces never to be seen again "in the Flesh." The hardships of a soldier's wife, hardships that a patriotic Confederate woman was expected to bear with a stiff upper lip, might end when the war was over if her soldier came home. But his death and the death of his comrades at arms transformed households and precluded their worldly reunification, imposing on many survivors a burden of "misery and want" that altered their views of themselves and the war. Death dispossessed deceased soldiers' wives and children of the necessities and security they had always known and diminished their family circle. Survivors searched for meaning in tragedy on a scale never before experienced. As the Reverend Richard Tucker of Brushy Creek Church observed at an associational meeting of Primitive Baptists held two months after the Gettysburg campaign, his people were living "in the midst of gloom and sorrow on account of our great calamities."[5]

The Civil War challenged traditional expectations about who should die, when and where death should take place, and the circumstances surrounding death, burial, and mourning. Death was commonplace in the antebellum South, particularly among the very young. Wilcox County planter Samuel Fuller and his wife Sarah Jane Bowman Fuller, for example, were privileged by slaveholding and other advantages, including the physician who was boarding under their roof in 1860. Nevertheless, despite their wealth and access to medical care, they had lost five of their six children in infancy. If a person made it through the deadly early years, however, he or she could normally expect a life that reached at least into middle age.[6]

But the epidemic of death that broke out in 1861 and continued for four years altered expectations of who did the dying. The war brought on an unaccustomed gendered experience of death. Men died in frightening numbers while women mourned their loss. Men feared death itself while women feared its consequences, a life without their loved ones and the security they had known. The departure of men for extended periods of time changed the social reality and meaning of home for the women left behind. As one Pulaski County wife wrote to her absent husband prior to the war: "Before you went away I loved home because you were here[;] now I love it because all that reminds me of you is here." The absence of soldiers intensified their families' sentimental feelings for both the people and the places they now associated with a safer and more secure prewar world.[7]

Ideally, then, death in the antebellum South came after a relatively long and fruitful life. Moreover, it took place at home, in bed, with family and friends close at hand. For just as the household was the center of life and work, so too it was the place of death. On the household level, women nurtured the sick back to health. One Pulaski County slave recalled that her plantation mistress "knew the best remedies" for illnesses, treating the afflicted with "worm food" made from weeds and teas brewed from sage and thyme. When the healing failed, the family gathered and waited to hear the "dying declarations" of their loved one. These last words might give insight into his or her spiritual condition and offer hope that the soon-to-be-broken circle would be reassembled in heaven. Relatives and friends held death watches that lasted night and day, observing the passage from life to death, awaiting signs or statements revealing the soul of the soon-to-be-deceased, and often writing these down.[8]

Country people coped with death through traditional burial practices that involved family and friends in communal displays of grief and mourning. Such neighborhood rituals placed the body in death within the same circle it had inhabited in life. Adults were accustomed to seeing and dealing with corpses and were involved in rituals that ensured that the remains were treated with dignity. Once the spirit departed, the ritual of caring for the corpse began. The body was placed on an improvised cooling board, often a wide plank resting between two chairs, and covered with a sheet. Washing and dressing the body by family members, often women, followed. The corpse was then placed in a front room or parlor, where it was watched for signs of life during a "wake" that ensured that the person was actually dead before burial. Meanwhile, men constructed a coffin from carefully selected boards, covered the outside with black cloth, and lined the inside with cotton and white linen. The body remained at home, usually from one to two days at most, as neighbors and distant relatives arrived to pay their respects. Large home funerals found virtually every room crowded with mourners, who spilled out onto porches and into the yard.[9]

In the rural South, the procession from the house of death to the field of burial was an informal part of the rite. The coffin was carried by wagon to a grave prepared by neighborhood men. Kinfolk and neighbors walked or rode behind the coffin. At the cemetery or family plot, the minister spoke a few words, a funeral hymn or two was sung, some Scripture was read, and the coffin was lowered into the grave. A simple service thus symbolized both continuity and closure for family and community. If a deceased man was a Mason, fraternal rites and death notices might be added to the ritual. Often a person made the passage from cradle to grave in the same neighborhood, even in the same house and grounds. Tobe McGriff, one of Pulaski County's delegates to the secession convention, lived and died "upon the place and in the house in which he was born" and was buried with his parents in the Longstreet neighborhood. On the eve of the Civil War, the landscape was dotted with scores of small, rural burying grounds. Their sandy yards were often swept clean of grass, and crude limestone walls occasionally surrounded family plots. Simple gravestones, fieldstones, and pine boards marked the final resting place of two generations.[10]

Those who passed into the afterlife at home peacefully and willingly, surrounded by family, with burial by kin and friends among ancestors in familiar ground, achieved what Victorians described as the "Good Death." The experience of Polly Ann Dykes McGriff in 1862 reflected the art of "dying well," the only exception being that she died young. A member of one of the most prominent families in Pulaski County, she was the daughter of planter Burrell Dykes and his wife Nancy Simpson Dykes, the mother of eleven children; shortly before the war she married Patrick McGriff, a small planter and Tobe's brother. Polly Ann died at home, surrounded by relatives and "a weeping husband," and was buried in a neighborhood cemetery. Reassuring signs in both her life and death suggested that the young woman would be waiting to greet her family in heaven. One of the "most lovely of her sex," she was a member of Evergreen Baptist Church and "consecrated herself to Jesus" in her late teens. She had remained a "consistent" member of this evangelical congregation of planter families and their slaves throughout her young life. According to those present at her deathbed, her foundation of faith rendered her unafraid to die.[11]

But there were "Bad Deaths," too, such as those of the thirteen black and white men killed by the explosion of the steamboat *S. M. Manning* on the lower Ocmulgee in 1860. The circumstances of their deaths—sudden and unexpected, with no chance for family and friends to comfort them in their final moments or hear their dying words—deeply troubled their survivors. Moreover, they died away from home, beyond the family circle. Indeed, the fact that the men met their end within a few hours' journey of "home, sweet, home" somehow made their deaths all the more difficult to accept and underscored the "uncertainty of life." Not only had these loved ones been unexpectedly snatched from their family circle, but also the violent explosion that "dreadfully scalded" and "horribly mangled" many of the bodies—in some cases, "their friends can hardly identify them"—violated the ideal of a Good Death and the sanctity of the corpses. For the family of Telfair County planter

Joseph Williams, coming to terms with his death was especially difficult, for his body was lost in the river, whose waters, as one visitor to the scene wrote, "seem to sing a requiem for the dead."[12]

The Civil War brought to the inhabitants of the lower Ocmulgee an endless stream of Bad Deaths. These fatalities occurred far from home, without the comfort of familial support or familiar surroundings. Like the steamboat disaster, however, the deaths united the community in mourning something "fatal and awful," as Jacksonville lawyer William Paine described the explosion's consequences. Death no longer visited the community as a natural occurrence. Death was now extraordinary in its brutality and frequency; it punished and transformed both the soldiers who died and the families who mourned. The wholesale killing made death a communitywide experience shared across neighborhood lines. In the first twelve months after the fighting began, the Pulaski Volunteers alone lost thirty-seven men (28 percent of the unit) to combat and disease, men drawn from virtually every neighborhood in the county.[13]

Cries of "a rich man's war and a poor man's fight" implied that a secessionist slaveholding elite had led Dixie out of the Union but avoided paying the conflict's human costs. In fact, men from all walks of life and all social classes fought and died while serving in the Confederate army. Death's scythe cut down the sons of planters and yeomen and village merchants. Their numbers grew with each bloody battle and disease-ridden encampment. By examining the soldiers who joined two infantry companies from Telfair County's Jacksonville district in 1861–62, we can get a clearer picture of who actually did the dying on the neighborhood level. As might be expected, the majority of the dead men came from slaveless yeoman and poor white households. About 70 percent of them were either heads of, or sons in, these households, a proportion close to the percentage of slaveless plain folk families along the lower river and in the South generally. Typical of these men was Private Joshua Smith, a landless poor white who joined the Telfair Volunteers in August 1861 and died of wounds at Gettysburg. Approximately 30 percent of the dead, however, were from slaveholding households, a proportion close to the percentage of slaveholding households in the Jacksonville district as whole. Dead men in this group included Lieutenant William Hatton, the son of a prosperous yeoman slaveholder and himself the master of two slaves, who died of pneumonia at Lynchburg, Virginia, in 1862.[14]

In rural neighborhoods like Jacksonville, slaveless plain folk accounted for the great majority of the Confederate dead, but not in disproportionately high numbers. Slaveholding households also paid a high price in human terms, one that corresponded to their numbers in the community. The family of small planter Henry Campbell, a prosperous man by any measure in his neighborhood, certainly did not avoid the war's human cost. His son Luke died of typhoid fever in 1861. Luke's death fulfilled a prophetic line in his own speech before the "Patriotic Ladies" of Telfair County less than four months earlier in which he evoked the image of the patriotic Southern mother who lovingly "embraced and kissed for the last time her brave boy, and sent him away to fill a soldier's post—maybe a soldier's grave."[15]

In rural neighborhoods, where grieving followed death after death year after year, families were united by receiving the worst possible news—their soldier was dead. The loss of privileged young men such as Private Luke Campbell made it difficult for the families of plain folk like Private Joshua Smith to claim that it was a "poor man's fight" on the neighborhood level, where families of all "grades" lived and mourned the mounting losses. Women especially were depicted as possessing a "self-sacrificing spirit," willingly buckling on "a brother's armor, and impressing fondly a last kiss prayer, 'God be with you,' in defending the right and avenging the wrong." In Private Campbell's representation, the mothers, sisters, wives, and widows of soldiers blessed the struggle for Southern independence by the sacrifice of their men and in return assumed an elevated place in the hierarchy of mourning.[16]

The dead soldiers' families were also united in their struggle to make sense of the carnage and somehow reconcile traditional views of death with the shocking wartime losses. The destruction of the *S.M. Manning* and the death of its passengers had been accidental, a singular disaster that some people doubtless explained as fate or God's will. The enormous wartime loss of human life, on the other hand, was planned, state-sponsored violence to achieve political goals. Rather than a single event that family and friends could grieve over and then put behind them, the Civil War would continue until either North or South prevailed or peace was negotiated. No one knew how long this would take. The men and boys must be dying for a worthwhile objective, their survivors told themselves, or else the slaughter was meaningless. Sacrifice for a transcendent cause, such as Southern nationalism, rendered an otherwise Bad Death a truly Good Death. In the larger sense, the soldiers fought to defend their new national home, the Confederacy, against invasion, defeat, and subjugation. Joining the Pulaski Rangers in May 1861, Private Charles Mason fought for "the great cause of Republican independence—a cause dearer to him than his own life." As for Private Luke

Campbell, the war became a "grand drama for freedom's cause, and the rights of mankind."[17]

But this new national home—"our youthful Republic," as Luke Campbell described it—was a recent political creation based on the old nation's states and counties, themselves comprised of neighborhoods formed by households, the homes of soldiers and their families and friends. These country people and home places also were at the core of the "cause." The language of soldiers' letters expressed not only Confederate nationalism but also neighborhood localism. Private William A. Barker, who joined the State Rights Guards early in 1862 and died in Staunton, Virginia, before the year was out, mentioned in a single letter his "pretty little boys," his "loving wife," "family," and—repeatedly—his home: "If Pa lives to come home"; "I do hope and trust to God that it will be my lot to return safely home to you"; If peace comes, "we can return to our happy homes again." In defense of home, nation, and his "fellowmen" at the front, Barker would do his part, although it ultimately cost him his life.[18]

Whether the cause was defined in terms of nationalism or localism, men died Good Deaths if they combined military duty with religious conviction and became Christian soldiers. Sergeant James W. Fleming was one of the men whose family, in remembering him and in giving meaning to his death, linked his Christianity and the Confederate cause. Fleming was "born again," joining Cedar Creek Baptist Church just before the war started. When he was hospitalized at Macon because of illness near the end of the war, his father traveled to his bedside. Happily for the family's peace of mind, Fleming's father heard his dying declaration. James voiced his "unwavering faith in the precious Savior" just as his spirit stepped across the threshold of eternity at the moment of his death. These words were profoundly reassuring to a father who had lost another son in the "terrible struggle for independence." A dutiful "Christian soldier" and the "idol of his family," Sergeant Fleming died near home, close enough to be carried there for burial, surrounded by his family and friends in a community of mourning. By Civil War standards, he died a Good Death.[19]

A soldier's readiness to give up his life, particularly in a valorous ending, suggested a Good Death. Even if death was sudden, the knowledge that he had been prepared and willing to die was comforting to his mourners, for it meant that he had experienced the "dealings of the good Lord with my soul," as one soldier put it. Shortly before artillery fire ended his life at Spotsylvania in 1864, "ardent secessionist" Charles Mason publicly professed his fervent desire "to

A piece of southern Georgia plain folk furniture—a cowhide-
bottomed chair—from the period 1840–70. The vacant chair
on the home front symbolized soldiers lost on the front lines.
(Courtesy of Atlanta History Center)

fight through the war and if it were the will of providence that his country should be subjugated he wished to die in the last battle." Although his survivors mourned his loss, they were consoled by Mason's belief in the cause and his readiness to abide by "the will of providence." The next of kin of Second Lieutenant Erastus Smith of the Pulaski Greys found solace not only in his willingness to die, but also in the valor with which he "fought the good fight." At Frazier's Farm near Richmond on June 27, 1862, he was wounded rallying the 49th Georgia, which had been "thrown into confusion" by enemy fire. Smith "seized the colors, bore them ten paces ahead of the regiment, and in the act of planting them and rallying his comrades, received the wound from which he died" after lingering for over a month.[20]

Published obituaries such as those of Private Mason and Second Lieutenant Smith served the same purpose as letters of condolence to family members. Some were written by kinsmen of the deceased, some by comrades who had been eyewitnesses to the death or had heard descriptions of the dying soldier's last moments. These accounts offered testimony of his noble character for the benefit of those on the home front. Mason's obituary noted: "Charlie was while in the army a general favorite with both officers and men, always cheerful, ever ready to oblige, and never shirking duty, truly he was a model soldier." One of Mason's comrades said of him: "His glory centered in on one sole object, the redemption of his afflicted country."[21]

Printed testimonials and memorials like these helped survivors construct a Good Death for their dead soldier. Although editors of the *Milledgeville Southern Recorder* found the notices "impossible to crowd into our paper" and questioned the necessity of wordy "Army Obituaries" and "sympathizing resolutions" drafted at company meetings purely "*for the newspapers*," they missed their deeper meaning. When death occurred away from home, beyond the family circle, "a formal company meeting" was as close to a proper burial as many soldiers received. The resolutions were funeral sermons and remembrances published and read on the home front, a substitute for the burial ritual that would never take place there. The same was true for Masonic rites. Members of Lodge No. 212 at Irwinville, for instance, were repeatedly "called on to mourn the loss" of their "much beloved brethren . . . who departed this life in Virginia in defence of our government."[22]

According to his obituary, Charles Mason's body "sleeps far from his youthful home beneath Virginia's crimsoned sod." So, too, did the remains of the vast majority of the lower Ocmulgee's plain folk soldiers. For almost four years, households, rural neighborhoods, and towns lived under the shroud of death. If soldiers died the Good Death as Christians and Confederates, then on women fell the primary responsibility for becoming good mourners. The new, troubling dilemma of wartime casualties, however, was that the faces of soldiers like Private Mason were never seen again, at least "Not in the Flesh." James and Sabra Cadwell's seven sons left for war from the neighborhood of Parkerson's Meeting House. Five of them died from wounds or disease too far from home to spend their last minutes with family members and too far away for burial in Parkerson's graveyard. Rare exceptions were soldiers like the Burnham boys or James Fleming, who died at home or in nearby hospitals, surrounded by family and buried in familiar ground.[23]

Most men died in distant hospital wards or in the confusion of battle, not at home. Because a huge number of deaths occurred before the availability of inexpensive embalming procedures and before the funeral industry made it possible to transport bodies home prior to their decomposition, prevailing ideas about what constituted a proper interment were often violated. Local customs and the soldiers themselves set the standards for their burial. To be interred in the "neet and christian like manner" that Hawkinsville merchant John Young requested in his will two days before enlisting as a sergeant in the Pulaski Volunteers was a reasonable enough request in peacetime. It was difficult to fulfill at the front. Because Young was killed at Gettysburg while serving as the company's captain, his body was left on the battlefield, like thousands of others, to be hastily submerged in mass graves by Yankee burial details.[24]

Among family members such deaths were difficult to accept, not only because of their brutality and suddenness, but also because they profaned the reverential nature of the traditional mourning and burial process. The violation of prewar burial customs, one that did not strike Young's family for more than two years after he left Hawkinsville, confronted some families almost immediately as new recruits succumbed to disease in training camps. But its magnitude and implications for the community did not sink into the collective consciousness until the fighting heated up. At the Battle of First Manassas, for example, nine members of the Pulaski Volunteers were killed in action or died of wounds. The high spirits and romanticism that characterized the war's first months quickly evaporated after the first major battle, as the doorways of plain folk and men of standing were shrouded in black. The breach of burial ritual troubled family members more than it did the soldiers, who became hardened to the sight of hasty battlefield and hospital burials as the war progressed. Initially, however, the burial of comrades away from home and the family circle bothered soldiers, too. When Private Richard Lott of the Coffee County Guards died of "brain fever" in Savannah less than ten weeks after joining the company, some of his companions wanted to carry his body home for burial. It was not an unreasonable request, Private Stafford Thigpen wrote his parents, but the regiment's officers "would not let no body carry the corps." Lott's new family of soldiers interred his remains in Savannah.[25]

The treatment of a soldier's corpse, especially on the battlefield, was a far cry from the care and reverence it would have received at home, although the deceased's comrades did their best. Rapidly deteriorating bodies made burial a nauseous and unhealthy task that the men abhorred. Most soldiers killed in battle were buried in their uniforms near the spot where they fell, sometimes rolled up in a blanket and usually placed side by side into a shallow trench. A few words spoken over mass graves by friends or the regimental chaplain was the most that could be expected. Perhaps the worst death scenario for soldiers' survivors unfolded at places such as Gettysburg, where defeat on enemy soil was followed by the army's hasty retreat. Virtually every lower Ocmulgee infantry company in the Army of Northern Virginia was engaged at Gettysburg. In retreating, the army had no choice but to abandon its dead and severely wounded to the enemy. Left to the care of Yankees, the remains of Captain John Young were interred in a mass grave. So were the bodies of First Sergeant George Gamble and Privates Samuel Jackson and Thomas Lupo—all killed on the first day of the battle.[26]

Information on battlefield casualties was slow to reach the home front and was often unreliable when it did. It was slightly over a month before the Telfair Volunteers learned the fate of wounded comrade Robert Jones, also left on the field at Gettysburg. He died on July 17 despite the efforts of Union army doctors to save him and was buried by strangers, far from his comrades and family. Many of the dead soldiers had just begun their productive and reproductive lives, which were now unnaturally cut short. The mourning of their passing, mostly among women, was difficult. Alvey Goodson was barely eighteen when killed at First Manassas. His single mother was left to mourn his loss in a home owned by Goodson's captain and her employer, Dr. Thomas Ryan. His body was never returned home. As anxiety about the fate of their kinsmen's remains during the war's first year grew, one Georgia newspaper turned the attention of troubled families to more comforting images of peaceful antebellum Good Deaths and quiet "family grave yards." There "the sleepers repose among kindred, from the grandsire to the tender infant." Although a comforting word picture, it was a resting place that most soldiers' bodies never found.[27]

More often than the families of plain folk, those of wealthy officers managed to bring their dead home for a decent burial within the circle of family and friends. Lieutenant Colonel Seaborn Manning knew the personal risks of war when he volunteered to lead the Pulaski Greys in March 1862. In his will written at Goldsboro, North Carolina, two months after he left Hawkinsville, Manning recognized that his service in the 49th Georgia might "at any moment" cause him "to be summoned before my maker." Witnessed by fellow officers Henry Whitfield, John Pate, and Erastus Smith, the will requested that Manning be buried in "a decent and christianlike manner." On August 9, a little over three months after drafting his will, Manning led the 49th Georgia into battle at Cedar Mountain, Virginia. There, as a member of the Pulaski Greys recalled, the regiment was "in the thickest of the battle" and "some of our best men" were killed and wounded. One of them was Colonel Manning, "beloved" by his "followers." Severely wounded in the right arm, he lingered for a month. Because of his wealth and prominence, his family could afford to transport his body home. It was laid to rest in the family plot in Orange Hill Cemetery at Hawkinsville. Manning's burial allowed his family—unlike those of his less privileged troops who died at the front—to follow the customary practices of interment, witnessed by his children and friends, all under the watchful eye of his widow Harriette, who was determined that her husband's desire for a Christian burial be carried out.[28]

Coming to terms with Seaborn's death stirred thoughts in Harriette's mind about her own mortality, about the impermanence of life and the frailty of family during war. Even before her husband died, the family circle was broken by the loss of her mother, Mary Wheeler, in March 1862 at age sixty-six. Widowhood was difficult enough in peacetime, but the steady erosion of Harriette's familial and material world in wartime made it harder still. Two years after her husband's death, after much reflection, Harriette was ready to express her own "views," as she put it, on the future of her family. Though it had been torn apart by the war's brutality, she planned to keep it together in death. In her will, which she made in the early summer of 1864, she directed her burial "by the side of my beloved husband" in a family plot "walled in with rock and when practicable a wire fence be placed upon the top of the wall." Enough room was to be left for the graves of daughter Minnie and sons Seaborn, George, and James, all then under the age of twelve. A "suitable monument" was to mark her and her husband's graves. Perhaps as she wrote these instructions she sensed that her own end was near. Harriette Manning died on June 19, 1864, leaving the couple's four orphans in the care of relatives.[29]

Wartime deaths sent shock waves not only through the lower Ocmulgee's households, but also through its economy. In places such as Hawkinsville, business houses as well as family circles were broken. Among the dead were clerks, merchants, and professional men. Their loss made it impossible to continue long-standing business partnerships. Sometimes new partnerships were born out of death; sometimes businesses dissolved entirely. The dry goods firm of Coley, Wood, and Thomas, for example, lost two of its three partners during the war's first two years. William Thomas died of pneumonia in a Confederate hospital during the summer of 1863; Captain Warren Wood of the Pulaski Blues succumbed to wounds later that year. The deaths of men like Seaborn Manning and Warren Wood reflected the high death rate among company-grade officers drawn from the slaveholding and professional classes.[30]

The death of men of property and standing prolonged the mourning process because it required yet another community death rite—the settlement of estates. Newspapers were filled with announcements of the impending administration of dead soldiers' estates, symbolic death notices proclaiming that their life's work in the form of property would soon be scattered. Indeed, in cases where local burials were impossible, estate settlements were often the only communal farewell to the dead on the local level.[31]

Captain John Young's will directed the administrators to sell his Hawkinsville store property, pay off his debts, and send the balance to family members in his native Scotland. Private Jesse Scarborough, though his total property was worth only $275, took care to see that his "beloved sister" Mary received what remained of it after the settlement of his debts. In the absence of a will, and if sufficient property was involved, three or four court-appointed neighbors would perform an inventory and appraisal of the estate in preparation for a public sale.[32]

These neighbors gathered at the home of the dead soldier, walked though the house, outbuildings, and fields, and recorded the value of crops, furnishings, land, livestock, and slaves. The inventory and appraisal might take place as early as two months after the soldier's death, but they were frequently delayed. Private Richard Smith of the Irwin County Volunteers died of disease at Keysville, Virginia, in September 1862; the inventory and appraisal of his estate did not take place until January 1863, almost four months later. The subsequent sale at auction of some or all of the deceased's belongings brought family, friends, and neighbors together in a neighborhood redistribution of property. The death of Captain James Y. McDuffie of the Irwin Cow Boys, for example, resulted in the dispersal of his cows, hogs, and sheep, his cooking lard and bacon, his goblets and plates, and even his sword.[33]

The death of white males such as Captain McDuffie had profound implications for enslaved African Americans. McDuffie's personal property included sixteen slaves. A master's death raised among slaves immediate questions about their own fate. In the settlement of his estate, would they be sold and their families broken up? The death of slaveholders' sons removed them from the future list of potential new masters once the household head died, but the demise of men like McDuffie opened up entirely new possibilities regarding their slaves' future. As the war dragged into 1862 and 1863, newspapers routinely carried notices of the settlement of estates of soldiers and small slaveholders like Lieutenant William Hatton. These called on people indebted to the deceased to "make immediate payment" and on those with claims against the estate to present them to the administrators.[34]

As chattel, slaves were subject to sale or hire in order to satisfy the debts of estates or help the survivors make ends meet. Following the death of Hawkinsville lawyer and slaveholder Frederick Brown early in the war, his widow Fanny found it necessary to hire out her slave girl Caroline, a highly valued domestic servant, to the Confederate commissary agent at Hawkinsville. In some cases, soldiers' wills dictated the fate of slaves. Clifford Lee, "being a soldier of the Confederate armes [sic] and being exposed to death in many ways," specified that his slave boy Esau be turned over to his mother for her use and then sold after her death. Seaborn Manning directed his wife Harriette to keep the slaves and plantation together to be worked for the "joint and mutual benefit" of his family until their youngest child reached age twenty-one, at which time the slaves were to be divided equally among his children.[35]

In some cases, slaves were genuinely moved by the death of white men who had grown up before their eyes. In others, where the relationship had been antagonistic, the slaves' reaction to the death may have been more ambivalent, serving only to remind them of their own mortality and of how much their status as chattel had bound together their lives and that of their master. Slaves on the home front were not just concerned about the fate of their masters and the implications of their death for both black and white members of slaveowning families, as some slave men went to the front as body servants. Orran

Horne's slave Henry accompanied him to Virginia, where Horne served as commander of the Georgia Rangers until his resignation on Christmas Day 1861. Planter Jackson Coalson's slave Arthur recalled that his "young master," who took charge of the estate after his father's death, "enlisted and took one slave with him"; both "fortunately, came back uninjured." Naturally, body servants at the front were exposed to the same diseases, harsh weather, and unsanitary camp conditions as their owners, and their families at home, to the same emotional strain concerning the fate of their kinsmen.[36]

Concern over the fate of their kinfolk at the front, as well as that of their masters, brought African American beliefs about death into play. The Africanization of white mourning practices, especially among masters' children exposed to the beliefs and superstitions of domestic servants, provided whites and blacks with additional psychological means of confronting death beyond the churchyard. In a part of the South where plain folk had their own system of signs and superstitions, as well as folk medicine, the interpretation of portents and the use of charms and cures may have been widespread, especially when under siege and dependent on every resource at hand to cope with it. With death hanging over the region like a dark cloud, there was little margin for error, little reason to tempt fate by not taking every possible precaution to keep death's black shroud from the doorway.[37]

Not all blacks were superstitious, but many slaves along the lower river believed in certain "signs of death." The screeching of an owl and sneezing while eating were considered by some as sure indications of impending death, as was "the bellowing of a cow and the howling of a dog after dark." Martha Everette, a slave on James Lathrop's plantation, rejected "that sneezin' while eatin' bizness," but recalled: "I heard a preacher say once that if you hear a cow bellowin' you could look out fer a death in a week er two." Arthur Colson believed in only one death warning, "a bell ringing in his ear," first heard on the night of his grandfather's death. He interpreted this as a "warning of coming sorrow." Signs of bad luck were to be avoided at all costs by those who recognized them lest they bring ill fortune on themselves or loved ones. Easter Reed tried "not to see the new moon through the trees for the first time," regarding this as a "sign of bad luck." When a death occurred, some slaves insisted on specific rituals. "If there is a death in the house," said Easter, "the clock should be stopped and a cloth should cover the mirrors." Doorways were draped with black bunting.[38]

The ritual favored by Easter Reed was impractical for most soldiers' families. They did not hear of their loved one's death until days or weeks afterward, and rarely did they learn precise details like the time of death. The purpose of such ritual in mourning and burial was to help the departed spirit on the journey to its final home. Without proper rites, some folk believed that the soul could not find its way to heaven or hell and was damned to an everlasting life of wandering the earth, haunting the households and neighborhoods it loved in life. Moreover, the belief that spirits often inhabited the bodies they occupied in life conjured up specters that the deceased's kindred could be visited by horribly mutilated apparitions—disemboweled, headless, limbless—representing the souls of dead soldiers seeking their final resting place. The images of the dead men and questions on their last minutes on earth haunted their survivors for years. Did they suffer? Did they utter last words and, if so, what did they mean? What did their bodies look like in death? Did they receive the neat and Christian-like burials requested in their wills? Such unanswered questions made mourning all the more difficult and prolonged the grieving process.[39]

Without a body to prove a loved one's death, some families held out hope that their soldier was still alive, especially when listed as missing in action. Equally distressing were seemingly senseless and unexplained deaths. What truly happened to Private Lewis Nobles of the Pulaski Blues after he was captured in a Richmond hospital on April 3, 1865? Only four days later he died of a gunshot wound to the head. And why was Corporal Abraham Walker, of the Irwin Volunteers, wounded and captured at Gettysburg, mortally bayoneted by a Federal prison guard? In time, the survivors' feelings of emptiness diminished and their memories dimmed. Sarah married Henry Townsend on June 2, 1859, she recalled many years later, but the details of his death at Cedar Mountain, Virginia, became as remote as the place. She told Wilcox County's ordinary: "[I] don't remember the date killed." Struggling to understand the war's brutality and its consequences at home, many families turned for spiritual guidance to the valley's leading social institutions—its churches.[40]

On Sunday, May 4, 1861, the congregation of Cedar Creek Baptist Church gathered in a modest building on a sandy hill where Wilcox County's river road crossed Cedar Creek. It was clear that troubling national events such as secession and the Confederate attack on Fort Sumter were on members' minds. After some reflection on the events of the past few months, the church clerk entered the following words in the minute book: "We pray to almighty god for wisdom to direct our course in this hour when the dark cloud of war is Rapidly gathering over us Threatening the overthrow of the most happy people and greatest nation of the world." On that Sunday, war was already a reality, but the death and destruction it would cause were still unknown. Indeed, on leaving the service the congregation's collective voice was one of prayerful hope that death and disaster might still be averted. Church members still believed that the "most happy people and greatest nation of the world" were merely threatened by "overthrow" rather than already irrevocably engaged in bloody warfare.[41]

Evangelicals played an important role in the secession movement and Confederate mobilization. Southerners believed that they were the most religious Americans and that their position in the national debates over slavery and secession was sanctioned by God, who gave whites "the right of holding another in involuntary servitude." In an interdenominational send-off of infantry companies at the Methodist church in Hawkinsville, for example, Baptist preacher George McCall delivered the farewell invocation from the church steps. The hat was passed and cash and subscriptions were collected in support of the cause. In the minds of many soldiers and their families, God's cause and the Confederacy's were one and the same. At an October 1862 meeting in Coffee County, the Smyrna Association led by local Baptist light John G. Taylor resolved to observe a day of "fasting, humiliation and prayer" the next month, believing that "God in his providence would remove those troubles and distresses that now surround us as a people." In search of a deeper understanding of their place in God's plan and a revelation of God's will as revealed by the fortunes of war, plain folk and planters sought spiritual guidance and solace to ease the emotional trauma that the "dark cloud of war" brought down on them.[42]

Personal convictions on the justness of a war to defend white liberty and Southern rights were supported by religious texts and repeated by the rank and file. Private Luke Campbell described the war as nothing less than a "holy struggle." The Confederacy was a revelation of God's designs for a chosen people. Seeking spiritual assurance in the face of death, many "lost" soldiers and backsliders were "saved" at emotional camp revivals while in the Confederate army. They believed that their sacrifices would fulfill Jehovah's plans now and in the hereafter.[43]

But along the lower valley there was an alternative theology to the one represented by the planter- and slave-filled evangelical churches of black belt neighborhoods, the settings of the first farewells for local infantry companies. In the backwoods, plain Primitive Baptist churches stood as opposite theological poles to the self-conscious, Greek revival buildings erected by planters. Their plank benches were largely filled with the families of nonslaveholding yeoman farmers, and antisecessionist preacher-farmers often held forth from their pulpits. Collectively, they rejected the elite's benevolence, conspicuous consumption, and worldliness. As manifestations of extreme localism, Primitive Baptist congregations were independent of any church hierarchy. Although they often banded together in small associations, just as often they disbanded over bitter doctrinal disputes.[44]

Despite their faith's opposition to mixing politics and religion, the Primitive Baptist leadership entered the local political arena to fight secession. Manassah Henderson, George Reid, and Jacob Young all ran as cooperationist delegates; all but Reid won seats at the secession convention and opposed Georgia's immediate withdrawal from the Union. Although against immediate secession, these men were not antislavery in ideology or practice. Henderson and Young were yeoman masters and Reid was a planter. As Primitive Baptists they felt little guilt over slavery, believing it a God-sanctioned institution. Strict constructionists when it came to interpreting the Bible, they maintained that slavery's acknowledgment in Scripture justified its earthly existence.[45]

In addition to the conspicuous pro-Union ideology demonstrated by their leaders during the campaign for secession convention delegates, the Primitive Baptists presented other challenges to the Confederacy's evangelicalism. Primitives rejected benevolence and "missionism." According to them, mission work that stirred wartime revivalism and helped create the Confederacy's Christian soldiers was theologically unsound. Back in 1855, the Reverend Richard Tucker, leader of the Brushy Creek Church in Irwin County and a spokesman for the lower valley's Primitives, had ridiculed such evangelical work. The "idea of the preaching of the gospel being the ordinary and extraordinary means in the hands of God of giving life to sinners," Tucker wrote, was "absurd" because it relied on man, not God, for salvation. Tucker and other devout Primitives considered the nonelect to be "sleeping dust" incapable of salvation regardless of the "means" employed by evangelicals. Indeed, the true purpose of "Preaching the Gospel," Tucker reminded his followers, was simply "the gathering together and feeding of the flock of Christ." Such a rigid and conservative theology had no interest in advancing the secular interests of the Confederacy. By denouncing the promise of everlasting life for thousands of Confederate Christian soldiers won over by revivalism, Primitives dashed the hopes for heavenly reunions held dear by their families in mourning. Christian soldiers might make better fighters, but in the minds of Primitive Baptists the size of their ranks was predetermined by God and thus inelastic.[46]

That conflicts would arise within Primitive Baptist congregations affected by the wartime slaughter was inevitable. Many, perhaps most, Primitives held firm to their beliefs during the war despite the enormous Confederate casualties and growing evangelical work among the troops. When the elders of the Primitive Pulaski Association met in September 1863, they reaffirmed their belief in the "eternal and particular election of a definite number of the human race chosen in Christ before the foundation of the world"; in 1864 they rededicated themselves to the rule that no member of the faith "has any right to join themselves to any worldly institutions of the day," including benevolent societies such as the Masons and Sons of Temperance, Bible and tract societies, and Sunday schools. All of these were major means of proselytizing among Confederate troops.[47]

Like all others who professed a faith and lost a soldier, George Reid and his wife Celia Reeves Reid turned to religion to see them through their grief. Their twenty-three-year-old son Henry was cut down in his prime at Second Manassas in 1862. Both George and Celia were longtime members of New Hope Primitive Baptist Church, and George served as clerk and deacon. If George Reid was a stalwart Primitive Baptist, then he subscribed to the church's predestinarian and antimission doctrines. There is evidence, however, that Reid's faith in such proscriptive and fatalistic beliefs had faltered by mid-1864. In May of that year, New Hope's church elders brought charges against Reid for affiliating with the Irwin Masonic Lodge. In June, shortly before the aging Reid led the Wilcox Grays—a State Guard cavalry company—into the field against Sherman's army, he was excommunicated from the congregation. Although the evidence is inconclusive, it is possible that Reid's effort to make sense of Henry's death led him to seek answers and comfort among the more "worldly" and benevolent Masons. They, too, were in mourning for the war dead among the lodge's membership.[48]

George Reid's excommunication reminds us that wartime death, which unified neighborhoods in mourning, never completely covered their deeper tensions. In the minds of Primitives, Reid's "affiliating himself" with the Masonic lodge was further evidence of the susceptibility of wealthy planters to a benevolent empire based on evangelicalism and social reform. Reid's wealth, political power, and social standing set him apart from most plain folk. His benevolence made him vulnerable to attacks from within the New Hope congregation, which by 1863 numbered only twenty members. Churches like New Hope were politicized during the secession crisis, and rifts among their members continued. In 1861 a fellow New Hope church member, secessionist Smith Turner, defeated Reid, a cooperationist candidate to the secession convention. Politically powerful, Turner, like Reid, had represented Wilcox County in the General Assembly. The political victory in 1861 of the small slaveholder and Abbeville merchant carried over into church polity as well, when Turner in May 1864 was elected clerk of New Hope, a position that Reid had held off and on for many years. Reid and Turner, antisecessionist and secessionist, planter and small slaveholder, found political support from within the same congregation, but Turner emerged victorious at approximately the same time that the elders brought charges of Masonic affiliation against Reid.[49]

A unionist in an overwhelmingly secessionist county in 1861, George Reid had become a Confederate by 1864, when he led his militia unit into the field. His family closed ranks with others and supported the war effort, the planter saying farewell to sons Drury, George, and Henry when their infantry company left for Virginia. The war changed Reid. Confronted by a mounting death toll that included his son and by the invasion of Georgia, Reid discarded his old-time Unionism and became a Confederate nationalist. One of the soldiers' fathers, Reid led a militia company comprised of older men and boys into the field as Sherman's army stormed the state's interior. Perhaps unable to reconcile the Primitives' antibenevolent and Calvinist beliefs with the evangelicalism that lent legitimacy and hope to the Confederate cause, Reid moved away from Primitive localism and embraced the more worldly Masonic ideals.[50]

For Reid's household and many others, the war brought death and mourning home. The bad news arrived on a scale unimagined before the war, and its very nature violated traditional assumptions regarding death's meanings and rituals. Young men were cut down in their prime far from home, never to be seen in the flesh again. The carnage cut across class lines and united neighborhoods in a common culture of wartime mourning. The reminders of death's aftermath—orphans, widows, rituals, and reconfigured estates—were commonplace. Families searched for answers that would somehow turn the seemingly endless Bad Deaths into Good Deaths. Some survivors took solace in the belief that their kinsmen had died in a "glorious struggle" for liberty and Southern nationhood. Others took heart in knowing that their dead Confederate was a Christian soldier whom they would see again in heaven. Still others questioned their traditional religious beliefs in the face of the wholesale human slaughter and embraced new ones that held out a promise to redeem their lost soldiers, and perhaps themselves as well.

**B**y the spring of 1864 inhabitants of the lower river had been at war for three years. No one knew when the fighting would stop. They did know, however, that the conflict had made "breastworks of our bodies," as a group of Wilcox County citizens put it. The battlefront, once situated in the remote Upper South, had moved to upper Georgia. Like a collapsing house, the Confederacy's walls were falling on its people. It seemed unlikely that conditions would improve. Yankee generals such as William T. Sherman believed that Southern civilians were as hostile as Confederate soldiers. They, too, must pay for the long and costly war. In the summer of 1864 a Macon newspaper cautioned that the Yankees assumed that "all rebels were beggars alike—had nothing in the world, and would be treated alike." It was now the official policy of the Union army to "break the spirit of the people" by "reducing them to the most abject condition of poverty, destitution and dependence."[1]

In its final year the war hit home like never before. Citizens faced seemingly insurmountable challenges as the battlefront and home front merged. Sherman's army was driving southward on Atlanta, the Yankees held Georgia's sea islands, and Union incursions into northern Florida resulted in bloody battles such as

Ocean Pond across the state line. As the year progressed, the piney woods were virtually surrounded by hostile forces. Increasingly, the white men left at home were called to fight the Yankees as militiamen in support of regular Confederate troops on Georgia soil. Each militia call extended the age limit of service and further "drained" the countryside "of its white male population," making it difficult for some neighborhoods to "make bread for the helpless women & children." A disastrous militia attack on hardened Union soldiers at Griswoldville in November changed the meaning of the war for soldiers' fathers at home and had deep psychological consequences. As 1864 ended, citizens in every county faced tough choices that forced them to redefine their loyalties to the Confederacy, Georgia, and their neighborhoods. A prevailing spirit of localism led "the people" to take matters "in hand themselves" in an attempt to end the Confederate war at home before it ended on the battlefield.[2]

Holding the Georgia front had reached critical proportions. In early May 1864 Confederate secretary of war James A. Seddon wired secessionist Howell Cobb that "we are in the very crisis of our fortunes." He asked Cobb to gather and organize "every trained soldier that can be Spared for service in the field" as militia reserves. Many militiamen mobilized in response to Governor Brown's subsequent appeal "To the People of Georgia" on May 28. The governor employed the same verbal imagery and racist appeals that he had used successfully to rally plain folk during the secession crisis and wartime mobilization. As Jeffersonian republicans, the yeomanry understood that they enjoyed the right to own property and vote because they were free white men. Defeat meant the loss of white liberty and their subsequent enslavement, Brown warned. Unless Sherman's army was defeated, "the property and homes of thousands must be destroyed, and they driven out as wanderers in destitution and beggary." Duty and honor demanded that the militia turn out and drive "the vandal hordes" from Georgia soil. "He who remains at home now will soon occupy it as a slave or be driven from it."[3]

The military crisis of 1864 forced white men on the home front to choose between fighting for the larger causes of Southern nationalism and state defense or caring for their families at home. Rejecting defeat as an outcome, Confederate loyalists from all social groups rallied to militia companies and defended their homes from invasion. Unwilling to risk their lives for the sake of the Confederacy or Georgia's defense, other men refused to join the loyal militia. They stayed home, banded together, and defended their families and neighborhoods from the loyal militia, county police patrols, and Confederate enrolling officers. Still others simply wanted to be left alone and waited out the war without taking part in any organized action.

In many respects, the military crisis revealed community fault lines similar to those that existed in 1861. Black belt neighborhoods along the river where the vote for secessionist delegates had exceeded 60 percent turned out loyal militiamen to defend Georgia in 1864. But in white belt neighborhoods where well over 60 percent of the votes had gone to cooperationist delegates in 1861, Union loyalties reasserted themselves. Many men eligible for militia service in such backwoods communities had been reluctant Confederates at best. Many of them now refused to muster with loyal militia companies and were considered deserters by Georgia and Confederate authorities. These divided loyalties were obvious to outsiders. As Lieutenant Colonel J. H. Hollinquist, a Confederate officer sent with his unit to sweep the lower river of deserters, wrote in early 1865: "The people in Pulaski and Telfair counties living on the river road are, generally speaking, true to our cause but those living in the back woods are, almost without exception, rank traiters."[4]

Governor Brown's initial appeal in 1864 did not call out men from fifty to sixty years of age and boys under seventeen largely because they were unfit to "endure hard service." But he did summon all "stout and able" men to rally to the state's defense. Both Confederate and state authorities invoked the Revolutionary language of "minute men" to encourage their service. Called on "to meet emergencies," the militiamen otherwise remained at home and continued to raise badly needed food crops. However, Brown had a job for the "old men" who stayed home when the minutemen took to the field. These paternalistic soldiers' fathers took down the names of all men who declined to enroll in the loyal militia, thus identifying the anti-Confederates to state authorities. When Sherman's army threatened Atlanta, however, Brown was forced to issue a cradle-to-grave call for the old men, too, as well as boys as young as sixteen. F. H. Bozeman, who had been a cadet at Georgia Military Academy in 1863, joined Company G, 5th Georgia Reserves, and was elected first lieutenant at age seventeen. A second unit of the 5th Georgia Reserves, Company I, was also organized in Pulaski County and W. P. Mobley elected captain. This urgent appeal to old men and boys was further evidence that the South was "growing desperate," as Bozeman put it. The Confederacy's policy of concentrating its manpower on the Virginia front, where almost fifty Georgia regiments were in service, failed to protect the vast Confederate interior. Sherman's army was now behind the lower river's Confederate soldiers, between them and their families, and leaving in its wake a wide path of devastation.[5]

The loyal militia was a collection of white men and boys not then in regular Confederate service. Swept into the fray by Sherman's invasion, they transcended class lines. Predictably, black belt neighborhoods in Pulaski, Telfair, and Wilcox Counties, where support for secession was strongest, turned out more men than white belt neighborhoods in Coffee and Irwin Counties. And again not surprisingly, the captains of loyal militia companies, such as Bozeman's captain, Charles E. Clark, were often planters or small slaveholders. In Wilcox County, for example, planters Samuel Fuller led Company G, 7th Regiment, Georgia Militia; Norman McDuffie led the Wilcox Home Guards; and George Reid led the Wilcox Grays. Across the river in Telfair County, Daniel F. McRae, a small planter and former state senator, led Company I, 7th Regiment, Georgia Militia. Described as a hard drinker and "quite dissipated" in 1860, McRae, like Samuel Fuller, had already seen Confederate service. Even in white belt counties militia officers such as Matt Ashley and Moses Peterson were either slaveholders or members of slaveowning families. Thus, slaveholding patriarchs (McDuffie was in his mid-fifties) did not dodge their obligation to lead plain folk into combat during the war's last desperate year.[6]

The men who entered loyal militia units ranged from plain folk to the lower river's largest planter, Charles Taylor, who at age fifty-four served "for about a month." The soldiers who joined I Company, 7th Regiment, in 1864 provide some insight into who comprised the loyal militia along the lower river. At least forty men and boys enrolled in this company from Telfair County, which had given unionist John Bell and cooperationists narrow majorities in 1860 and 1861. Despite its Whig and antisecession traditions, the new recruits were from virtually every neighborhood in the county, including black belt China Hill, Copeland, Jacksonville, and Lumber City, and white belt Cobbville and Sugar Creek.[7]

Among the members of Company I were a merchant, small planter, and former state senator; several yeoman slaveholders; prosperous plain folk; poor whites; and men previously exempt from Confederate service, including a miller and an overseer. The most prosperous soldiers exceeded the county's average household wealth of $3,608 per white family. Greene Brewer, an accomplished fiddler and two-bale cotton farmer, was one of them. He owned five slaves and property valued at $5,550, compared with the state average of $6,240. Some of the men, such as farmer and small slaveholder Stephen Boney, owned enough slaves to push their total wealth beyond both county and state averages. Boney claimed $10,000 in total wealth in 1860, making him an affluent slaveholding yeoman. Two of the company's youngest members, Henry Dopson and Charles Campbell, still lived at home with their parents, who were well-off farmers and slaveholders. At the opposite end of the social scale were men such as Perry Browning and Archibald McMillan. Independent but slaveless plain folk, they possessed total assets between $1,400 and $1,900, far below state and local averages, but not low enough to fall into the category of poor whites. Like regular Confederate soldiers, the dependents of slaveless plain folk serving on the Georgia front faced the greatest hardships at home. Nonslaveholder Thomas Laslie left his widowed mother Nancy on a fifty-acre corn farm; her name was soon added to the county's list of indigent soldiers' families.[8]

The militiamen's previous wartime experiences were as varied as their backgrounds. Greene Brewer had no history of direct military service, but the conflict shattered his household. Tragically, his youngest son Arthur, only fifteen when the war began, was killed while serving in the Confederate army. Two of Brewer's sons-in-law died of disease. His oldest son William joined James Humphreys's company in 1862, was captured at Gettysburg, and languished in a Yankee prison. On the other hand, Stephen Boney's family was relatively unscathed, largely because his three sons were too young to serve. The only member of Boney's household who volunteered to fight in the county's two regular Confederate infantry companies was his poor white farm laborer, John Shaw. Shaw also signed up with Humphreys's company and rose in the ranks to second sergeant before receiving a disability discharge early in 1864. Militiaman Thomas Laslie was in his early twenties when he joined Humphreys's company; eight weeks later he hired Spencer Brantley as his substitute so that he could remain at home until 1864, when he followed McRae's company into the field.[9]

McRae's rag-tag militia company bore little resemblance to the infantry units that optimistically left for Virginia in 1861. Of the militia that gathered at Macon in the fall of 1864 from Lovejoy Station, Howell Cobb wrote: "It is very amusing to see the men from Macon . . . who have never been in service a day before in their lives." They arrived in thin clothing without tents and in many cases without blankets or overcoats. Cobb observed that the "weather has been very hard on our new troops & the militia." McRae's force constituted what one planter called "a company of doublebarrel men," armed with old shotguns, flintlock muskets, and ordinary rifles.[10]

McRae's company of loyal militiamen is evidence that Confederate ideology and Southern nationalism were not entirely dead during the summer and fall of 1864. Given plain folk fears that white servitude awaited them in defeat, Southern independence was still worth the struggle. Thus, nonslaveholding plain folk fought alongside slaveholders in 1864 not because they desired to protect another man's human property, but because they themselves did not wish to be subjugated to the victorious Yankees. The interrelationship between planter leadership and plain folk deference, while not intact, had not yet dissolved.[11]

Then there was the matter of personal honor. In a world defined by rural neighborhoods, it mattered what other people thought and said about you and your family. A family's name and reputation were often the most valued possession of plain folk. White people who acted "right" in the community's eyes were honorable, regardless of their social class. To refuse to turn out for militia service when "able-bodied" was dishonorable behavior among secessionists. Loyal Confederate households thus established an intergenerational tradition of service and sacrifice that continued throughout the war, sending sons, soldiers' fathers, and ultimately grandfathers into combat, first into the Confederate army and later into the state militia. When death became the ultimate household sacrifice, survivors became even more determined to uphold the cause so their kinsmen would not have died in vain. By the time Miles Burnham left his parents near Hopewell Church to join McRae's company, for example, brother Thomas had been killed at Malvern Hill; before the war was over brothers James and Jack would die, too. No one questioned the commitment of the Burnham family to fight the Yankees well into the summer of 1864. Confederate loyalists exhibited a hardened resolve to continue the struggle. As Captain Samuel Fuller wrote Governor Brown following his company's service in the defense of Atlanta, "We done honor to ourselves."[12]

Another factor that motivated Confederate loyalists was their concern about protecting their women, children, and property. The governor repeatedly exploited plain folk fears in this regard. As he declared to the militia in September 1864, Atlanta's fall would leave "interior points" open to Sherman's army and put "many of your homes and loved ones within his lines and expose the homes of others to the ravages of his raids." Plain folk were aware of the 1863 burning of Darien, a favorite coastal market town, by "Yankee-negro forces." This "crowning act of wanton vandalism on Georgia soil," as one Macon newspaper editor described it, reduced the village to "one plain of ashes and blackened chimneys." As refugees from northern Georgia, Atlanta, and the coast sought a safe haven in the wiregrass country, their presence fulfilled Brown's prophecy that defeated Georgians would become "wanderers in destitution and beggary."[13]

On September 10, Brown detached militiamen from the Army of Tennessee and furloughed them en masse for thirty days. Atlanta had fallen, and the governor believed that it was time to send the soldiers home to put their "houses in order and provide as best you can for the future wants of those dependent upon you." Now that sugarcane was ready for harvest and syrup-making season was approaching, it was time for the "minute men" to go home and work their crops. It may "soon again" be necessary, Brown warned, to recall the militia.[14]

Brown also furloughed the militia to keep it out of General John Hood's Army of Tennessee. On August 30 Brown had received a letter from Secretary of War James Seddon requisitioning ten thousand Georgia militiamen for Confederate service. Fearful of an attack on lower Georgia, the governor was determined to keep the militia in Georgia under his control. In response to Seddon's letter, he chastised President Jefferson Davis for not sending reinforcements to Georgia's defense and demanded that Davis permit "all the sons of Georgia" in Confederate service "to return to their own State, and, within her own limits, to rally around her glorious flag." His refusal to release the militia to prolonged Confederate service after Atlanta's fall signaled to loyal militiamen and to local Confederates at the front that state and local loyalties were now more important than the larger, national cause. What was the point of defending the Confederate frontier if the Southern interior was under Yankee control?[15]

With Sherman's forces on the march across Georgia, Brown recalled the militia during the second week in October. Except for Captain Ruel Anderson's Pulaski County battery of light artillery and Joe Wheeler's cavalry, there were few if any regular Confederate forces to reinforce the state militiamen. They were on their own. As militia general Gustavus Smith recalled: "So far as I knew, or had reason to believe, mine was the only force, except the cavalry, that was likely to be brought into the field to oppose Sherman's march through the State."[16]

*Griswoldville*

By the time of the militia's recall early in October 1864, Company I consisted of a small band of men committed to home defense and each other. The militiamen of Company I and others like them formed the last levy of Confederate loyalists the lower river neighborhoods could muster and the final sacrifice of households still committed to fighting. The men were not entirely green. Some of the Telfair militiamen had been promoted for gallantry during the Atlanta campaign. These included cotton farmer and small slaveholder Stephen Boney (from second lieutenant to captain) and Thomas J. McDuffie (from private to first lieutenant). McRae was placed in command of a brigade. The veterans of the Atlanta campaign were joined in camp at Macon by new men so old and unfit that they were considered capable of "light duty"—that is, manning the city's defensive works—but incapable of marching very far. Aware that Sherman was on the move, General Howell Cobb believed that he would attack soon; "My opinion is that Macon is the point," he wrote on November 16.[17]

On November 19 the militia crossed the Ocmulgee River and took up defensive positions east of the city to await the attack. About ten miles east of Macon on the Central of Georgia Railroad stood the industrial village of Griswoldville. Established by Samuel Griswold, a Connecticut-born Yankee, the place boasted a large cotton gin, a candle factory, a soap factory, a shoe-blacking factory, and a pistol factory that manufactured the Griswold Navy Colt revolver for the Confederacy. Formerly the Duncan farm, Griswoldville and environs had fallen short of their agricultural promise. Fields once tilled by farmhands were covered in scrub pine. On November 21 Joe Wheeler's Confederate cavalry skirmished with approaching Union cavalry at both Clinton and Griswoldville. When the Yankees burned Griswoldville, the militiamen saw the smoke on the horizon.[18]

Unfortunately, Major McRae's men and others from the lower river in the 5th and 7th Regiments had become part of a larger movement of militia ordered from Macon toward Augusta once Sherman's actions near Macon were deemed "a feint." Believing that the Yankees were strong enough to attack Macon, General Richard Taylor, who had assumed command of the city's defenses, ordered militia general Smith to recall his troops from their position near Griswoldville. But word reached the militiamen too late. A light snow fell as they walked behind Brigadier General Pleasant Phillips, who had assumed command for the march to Augusta. Phillips was directed to move the men toward Griswoldville and "not to engage the enemy, but, if pressed to fall back to the fortifications of East Macon; or, if necessary, toward the south" into middle Georgia's woodlands. It was about noon on November 22 when the militia's four-hour march over hilly terrain ended approximately one mile west of Griswoldville. Convinced that he outnumbered the Yankee cavalry,

Phillips ordered the militiamen to follow the enemy until it was clear of Griswoldville. After they had marched about one mile down the railroad track, small arms fire began as the force drove back the Yankee skirmish line.[19]

Unknown to General Phillips, a brigade of seasoned Yankees protected Sherman's right wing from harassment by Wheeler's cavalry. These veterans took up defensive positions about a mile and a half east of Griswoldville and just south of the railroad tracks. The spot was described as "a strong position" along the crest of a ridge. The Yankees quickly threw up "temporary works of rails and logs." Battle-hardened and highly motivated, many of the Union soldiers had been fighting in the South since 1861 and 1862. They were so committed to defeating the Confederacy that half of them had reenlisted in their units in 1864. They now put two pieces of field artillery in the center of the line, their flanks protected by low swampy ground. From this defensive position, the Yankees looked west toward Griswoldville and across Little Sandy Creek, which more or less paralleled the Federal line at a distance of 50 to 100 yards. As one Union officer later observed: "We had a nice open field without even a fence on it, full 600 yards wide in our front."[20]

In the woods along the opposite side of the field, Phillips organized the militia for an all-out frontal assault. Ruel Anderson's Confederate artillery battery was placed just north of the railroad to rake the Federal line. At about 2:30 P.M. the attack signal was given. A surprised Union officer recorded that "a fine line of Johnnies pushed out of the woods" and crossed "the open field in three compact lines." According to Phillips's battle plan, the militia would run to the Little Sandy Creek bottom, find shelter and regroup, and charge up the hill in a coordinated attack supported by Anderson's artillery. Major McRae and Captain Boney led Company I across the fallow field. Behind them ran old farmers like Greene Brewer and boys like Henry Dopson.[21]

The Yankees thought that they "had a sure thing" and originally intended to let the militia charge "up close to us" before firing, a Union officer wrote, but there were so many men "rapidly running" toward them that they changed plans. The Yankee artillery cut loose soon after the militia left the tree line. Some of the men and boys began to fall among the scrub oaks and pine saplings. As the oncoming lines moved within rifle range, the enemy fire became "so terrible" that "many of his number were stretched upon the plain" before they reached the creek bottom. "One after another their lines crumbled to pieces," Union officer Charles W. Wills recalled.[22]

The initial assault was badly bungled. Rather than striking in one coordinated wave, the militia, like untrained regular troops early in the war, attacked piecemeal and were cut down by concentrated enemy fire. In the creek bottom, confusion reigned as a "terrific fire" poured into the disorganized militiamen who made it that far. One brigade became separated from the main assault by a deep ravine and was unable to link up with the rest of the troops. Militiamen held in a reserve brigade fired by mistake on their comrades in their front. Officers attempted to restore order and continue the attack. Remarkably, about half a dozen uncoordinated charges were made up the hill toward the Union breastworks. The seasoned Yankees turned them back with Spencer repeating rifles and artillery fire. The fighting, which lasted from midafternoon until sunset, "nearly exhausted" the Yankees' ammunition, but their line held.[23]

As darkness fell, the Yankees sent out a skirmish line to follow up their victory. They counted fifty-one dead militiamen before they marched on toward Irwinton. The lower river's militia companies took their share of the casualties. Three soldiers in McRae's company were killed. Two of them—Lieutenant John Powell and Lieutenant Thomas McDuffie—were leading their men into combat. The third was John McLean, a miller previously exempt from Confederate conscription. He left a wife and five daughters at home. Major McRae, Captain Boney, and Privates J. H. Lowery and James Lindsey were wounded, Lindsey so severely that he was disabled. Among the Pulaski County men killed was former store clerk Augustus McPhail. His body, like those of his dead comrades, was left on the field among the cries of the wounded by the retreating militia.[24]

What Sherman's hardened veterans found as darkness fell on the battlefield was difficult for even seasoned fighters to describe. Men and boys lay on the ground where they dropped. As Charles Wills wrote: "I was never so affected at the sight of wounded and dead before. . . . Old grey-haired and weakly looking men and little boys not over 15 years old, lay dead or writhing in pain . . . I hope we will never have to shoot at such men again." What seemed to bother him most about the Confederate casualties—what made him "pity" them—was their apparent familial and intergenerational nature: boys who had not yet begun to shave, laying beside men who could be their fathers and uncles, intermingled with the bodies of grandfatherly patriarchs. Yankee repeating rifles and artillery had cut down three generations of plain folk, most of them dressed in civilian clothes. They were now stretched before Wills, twisted and grotesquely postured by death, mute evidence that after three and one-half years of hard combat, some plain folk were still willing to fight.[25]

Looking back on the carnage at Griswoldville, men used different words to give it meaning. Militia general Gustavus Smith described it as "an unfortunate accident" that should have been avoided. According to his estimate, about 20 percent of his troops were casualties, including the fifty-one killed and almost five hundred wounded. One Union officer described it as a "terrible slaughter," while another preferred the words "fearful execution." Why were the militiamen willing to attack across the open field? In part, it was a clear understanding of what would happen to their homes and families if they did not take a stand. Images of refugees fleeing southward from Atlanta to Macon joined in their collective memory the torching of Darien by U.S. Colored Troops. Fresher still in their minds was their march through the smoking ruins of Griswoldville earlier that day in a landscape so similar to their homes'—"The country is very barren and thinly settled, Soil is Sandy and timber mostly fine"—that it could have been any neighborhood along the lower river.[26]

Clearly, the Yankees threatened the loyal militia's families, homes, and property. Sherman's army seemed unstoppable. It was a destructive firestorm within the Confederacy, proof that Jefferson Davis was unable to protect the interior's civilians in exchange for sending their men into the army, as Confederate leaders had promised. Company I, 7th Georgia Militia—its men dressed in coarse homespun and poorly equipped—was the best Telfair County had to offer in the waning months of 1864. Hard-drinking Daniel McRae may have been dissipated, old John "Horse Creek" Wooten was doubtless past his prime, and young Henry Dopson should have never shouldered a rifle, but they were human reminders of the effect of the hard war on ordinary people deep within the Confederacy. The ragged militia charged across the open field at Griswoldville in "heroic style," wrote one Union officer who witnessed the carnage, but the lessons of this village were unmistakable. Sherman's men normally confronted women and children as it marched to the sea, but when they met the home-front defenders at Griswoldville a humiliating "execution" followed. Further military action was futile. It was time to "stop the murdering of the human family by such a wholesale way."[27]

### We Have Lost the Hope

The fight at Griswoldville changed the meaning of the war for white people on the home front. Before the battle the war was somewhere else. Soldiers and supplies, both badly needed at home, had left to support the Confederate cause in Virginia or northern Georgia. Griswoldville brought soldiers' fathers and sons face-to-face with the carnage of modern warfare. Within weeks of the battle, community patriarchs along the lower river took actions reflecting that they were no longer concerned about the fate of the Confederacy or, for that matter, Georgia as a whole. Although they may have still hoped for some form of Southern independence, the soldiers' fathers were determined to avoid "utter ruin" by preserving the resources needed to rebuild postwar society on the neighborhood and county levels.[28]

About four weeks after Griswoldville, the Pulaski County Inferior Court voted to keep Confederate tax-in-kind corn at home and distribute it to needy soldiers' families instead of forwarding it to the front. This decision of the leading secessionist county signaled the reemergence of localism rather than Southern nationalism as a guiding principle three months before Appomattox. Within days, Major McRae reported tongue-in-cheek a skirmish with over one thousand Union soldiers and two pieces of artillery: "The Yankees won at the Ohooppey last evening." It was one of his last encounters with Union soldiers. He then proposed to planter Woodson Willcox, who was in charge of the county's police force, that scouts keep an eye on the Yankees. McRae seemed opposed to having his men "goe off," a possible reference to the Georgia militia and reserves then fighting in South Carolina, where morale was low. The officers of the 5th Georgia Reserves had demanded that their commander, John B. Cumming, resign. Cumming charged that the men "disgrace themselves" by refusing to fight outside of Georgia, had plotted against him, and used "language that the government have no right to hold them" in South Carolina. About 130 men deserted but were brought back to camp. All of the officers of Pulaski County's Company I were arrested, including Captain Mobley, Lieutenant J. L. Willcox, and Lieutenant G. W. Hendrick; Ensign Shelton was singled out for "making the remark that the men done right" to protest. The charges against F. H. Bozeman and several other members of Company G were dropped when they asked to have their names removed from the list of officers calling for Cumming's resignation.[29]

January 1865 marked a watershed in local sentiment. Griswoldville and Sherman's subsequent actions left inhabitants of the piney woods feeling confused, powerless, and uncertain. Increasingly, they concluded that the war had accomplished "but little," further military action was meaningless, and a negotiated peace offered the best prospects for the future. On January 14 a committee of seven concerned citizens met at Abbeville, in Wilcox County, to draft resolutions directing the state legislature and Governor Brown "to take some steps to compromise terms of peace." Although the document stated that the committee members were "willing to fight if it would do any good," they believed that further military action will never "settle this war." The resolutions reviewed the county's unflinching support of the war, to which "the bloody battlefields of the Old Dominion can well testify to, from the number of brave vetron soldiers whose bones are there bleeching." It went on to point out that local conditions were now "growing worse every day." Women and children faced starvation because their slaves were working "but very little," and few white men remained at home to farm. "We are sorofully tired of this most cruel, bloody war, having no hope that it will be settled until the people take it in hand themselves."[30]

The antiwar tenor of the resolutions was all the more remarkable because Wilcox County had been a secessionist and Southern rights stronghold in 1861 when, as the statement noted, so many men "hurried off to the bloody field." Moreover, peacemaking leaders included former Confederate soldiers, militia captains, and planters like Samuel Fuller and unionist George Reid. But times had changed. In a county that had barely met levels of self-sufficiency in corn before the war, the burdens created by four years of mobilization and food production had reached the point where "starvation is certainly close at hand." The county had nothing left to give to the Confederate cause "without we do it with men over fifty-five years of age." The war had to end "before the whole white male population is butchered up by the deadly missles of shell, ball, etc." The soldiers' fathers, who had ruled the home front in the interests of the state and Confederate nation, now declared their county untouchable to outsiders. As the Abbeville Resolutions warned Governor Brown and the General Assembly: "We are not disposed to be run over by raiding parties and stripped of all our provisions and left to starve in the land." The men left at home would "organize . . . into a company for local defence" and protect their families and homes until an "honorable" peace ended the war.[31]

On the same day that the resolutions were passed, anti-Confederate "rabble" invaded the village of Irwinville about twenty miles south of Abbeville. Led by well-known unionist Willis Bone, "fifty six deserters marched up to the Court House four deep in a line well armed." A loyal militia captain in neighboring Worth County described the meeting that followed as a "regular Lincoln demonstration." The anti-Confederates resolved "to return to the Union," thus symbolically seceding from the Confederacy, and expressed "incendiary sentiments." When a Confederate patriot and secessionist militia officer "remonstrated" with Bone, Bone "knocked him down with his musket, giving three cheers for Abe Lincoln, in which he was joined by the whole rabble." A Confederate enrolling officer and another Southern nationalist were forced to "decamp to save their lives."[32]

Sensing their power, the anti-Confederates took over the backwoods village. As the *Albany Patriot* editor put it: "Every man who was known to favor our cause was driven from his home, and threatened with instant death if he should return." Another Confederate wrote: "They beat Severely evry man who expressed loyal sentiment and it was with difficulty their lives were saved." The unionist resolution, the pro-Lincoln cheers, and the death threats to Southern patriots all openly challenged the authority and legitimacy of the Confederacy and the loyal militia, which was powerless "to do anything with them." Contempt for the Confederate cause previously expressed inside homes or at secret Union meetings now spilled over into the streets of the county seat. Unless such "open defiance of the Government" was put down quickly, the Confederate editor predicted, Georgia's wiregrass country "will have to be surrendered to them."[33]

The *Albany Patriot* did not exaggerate the threat to Confederate loyalists in the piney woods. In early 1865 the unionist hijacking of the *Governor Troup*, a steamboat used to collect the Confederate tax-in-kind provisions along the Ocmulgee River, only emboldened anti-Confederates. By the spring Colonel Duncan Clinch, whose 4th Georgia Cavalry patrolled the wiregrass range south of the Altamaha and Ocmulgee Rivers, reported that many cow counties were now solidly in anti-Confederate hands. According to Clinch, "almost the entire population" of Appling, Coffee, and surrounding counties was out "in full force" and openly defied Confederate authority. Such disloyal Southerners "banded together" to resist incursions by Confederate patrols and enrolling officers. The colonel added: "I know they effect aid from the enemy. They are determined to drive me out of the country."[34]

Clinch suggested that the enemy had an arsenal of weapons. On one occasion counting only seventeen firearms in the camp, he and his men were badly outgunned. The results could be disastrous. On April 4, 1865, one of his smaller units led by a Captain Crosby was "cut to pieces by the Deserters, and his company killed wounded and taken prisoners." Clinch called for reinforcements and an early offensive against the anti-Confederates, possibly attacking them in the "rear" through Coffee County. He felt that "any demonstration will have a favorable effect, and the sooner it be done the better."

The lower Ocmulgee River was now an internal Confederate frontier. Territory north of the river generally remained in Southern hands, while that south of the river was a no-man's-land, controlled by anti-Confederates of various stripes.[35]

The Abbeville Resolutions, the anti-Confederate takeover of Irwinville, and the attacks on Colonel Clinch's men remind us that the lower river was never a united community. In 1861 its voters had been evenly divided for and against secession. They were still divided in 1865. In some backwoods neighborhoods, as many as three-quarters of the voters opposed secession. Despite early enthusiasm for the cause, the Confederacy's inability to protect Georgia's home front from Yankee invasion and the slaughter at Griswoldville disheartened former loyalists such as those at Abbeville and emboldened anti-Confederates like those at Irwinville. By early 1865 the loyal militia had been humbled by the Yankees and their authority as soldiers' fathers put down. Anti-Confederates responded to the new situation in different ways, depending on the character of their neighborhood. In neighborhoods where the loyal militia was strong, they remained quiet. Bone's men banded together, struck out against a government they considered oppressive, and seceded from the Confederacy in a neighborhood where the loyal militia was weak. Himself perilously close to poor white in economic terms, deserter William "Bill" Wall attacked secessionists with words. He called loyalists "Confederate trash" who were willing to sell their neighbors into "bondage" for the Southern cause.[36]

For anti-Confederates such as Willis Bone and Bill Wall, resistance was as much a matter of honor as it was for the loyal militiamen who, in Samuel Fuller's words, claimed to have "done honor to ourselves" by fighting the Yankees. To "return to the Union" of their ancestors was in their eyes an honorable act. The signers of the Abbeville Resolutions, including Fuller, wanted an "honorable" end to the war without more fighting and dying. Loyalty to family and neighborhood was in each case a higher duty than loyalty to the failing Confederate nation. This disaffection did not develop overnight. It was based on an ethos that made desertion and draft dodging acceptable behavior in white belt neighborhoods where unionist sentiment had prevailed in 1861. Whether they covertly harbored deserters and draft dodgers or overtly took over the courthouse, men revealed their sentiments in neighborhoods that formed the human context for anti-Confederate activity. For die-hard and unconditional unionists like Willis Bone, their dissent was political and ideological in nature, but for others, including once loyal Confederates such as Fuller at Abbeville, war weariness and the central government's inability to effectively wage war made them hungry for an end to the "bloody war."[37]

Loyalties on the home front were fashioned by a complex web of family, kinship, and neighborhood political tradition. A closer look at the "rabble"—deserters, disaffected Confederates, and unionists—who supported Bone's secession offers some insight into a Confederate alter ego. Although such men defy easy categorization, their communities were white belt and claimed a higher-than-average number of plain folk farmers who engaged in cotton production without slave labor. Moreover, their leaders were much less likely to be planters or slaveholders than those of secessionist militiamen, but they were not necessarily poor whites. Bone lived in Irwin County near the Alapaha River and operated a corn mill. He claimed a total wealth of almost $3,000 in 1860, and, as a miller, he was heavily involved in barter and trade in his neighborhood. Seaborn Jones, a prosperous yeoman farmer and slaveholder of the Trippville neighborhood in eastern Pulaski County, owned eight slaves. He was listed as both a captain and a first lieutenant of the 387th Militia District and subsequently was identified as harboring anti-Confederate sentiments, though less demonstrative than Bone. Although Bone and Jones were far from the planter elite, they were clearly upwardly mobile middle-class Southerners when the war started.[38]

According to the *Albany Patriot*, "a large number of deserters" joined Willis Bone's takeover of Irwinville. Deserters are often associated with the piney woods, particularly south of the Ocmulgee River. Desertion from the lower river's regular Confederate infantry companies, however, was low. This was particularly true for companies belonging to the Army of Northern Virginia. Based on company rosters, the rate of desertion averaged 5.5 percent for 530 lower river men who served in the 49th Georgia. The rate was even lower (less than 3 percent) among the white belt Irwin County Volunteers and comparable to the 2.5 percent found in four infantry companies from black belt Greene County, Georgia. Obviously "PLAIN TALKER" was wrong when he identified the real deserter early in 1865 as the front-line Confederate soldier who went home and "persuaded others" to shirk their duty to "cover his own disgrace."[39]

Who were the lower river's deserters? When viewed from the inside out, citizens in traditionally unionist neighborhoods, not the Confederate soldier-turned-deserter, shaped a climate of opinion that not only tolerated "real" desertion by front-line troops but even encouraged draft evasion and desertion among men who were eligible for militia service. Such men, particularly in the backwoods, represented the majority opinion in their communities when the loyal militia took to the field and left their families at home. When enrolling officers or regular Confederate units made an appearance in their neighborhoods in force, the deserters took to the woods and swamps, but when Confederate loyalists were vulnerable, as they were at Irwinville, they were attacked.[40]

Several factors influenced plain folk notions about desertion. In nineteenth-century America there was no large peacetime standing army and militia laws were not strictly enforced. Individual relations with the military were more informal than after the turn of the century. Plain folk believed that their leaders at all levels—from district militia captains to generals—were accessible. Shortly after conscription became law early in 1862, G. M. McRae, an ensign from Telfair's backwoods Sugar Creek militia district, asked Georgia's adjutant general if his officer's commission exempted him from conscription. Expecting to be excused, he declared: "I am badly situated at the present time to leave for the war." Citizen soldiers such as McRae were provincial in orientation and outlook, putting local and family needs before those of the state and nation. Militia companies became closely identified with the militia districts and neighborhoods that surrounded their muster grounds. In peacetime, such localism posed no threat to broader regional or national affiliations and reinforced prevailing notions of race, class, gender, and egalitarianism among the white men who shared in the militia company's camaraderie.[41]

Conscription changed the meaning of military service. Previously, service in the militia, even in the Confederate army during the war's first year, was voluntary and of relatively short duration. Conscription made service compulsory for a three-year period, sent draftees to the units that needed them most, and barred them from voting for company-grade officers. The law's provisions for substitute hiring and a subsequent "twenty nigger" exemption for planters (later lowered to fifteen) smacked of favoritism for the planter elite. Many Georgians, including Governor Brown, considered the draft unnecessary and unconstitutional. Moreover, conscription undermined Brown's efforts to create a state army officered by his appointees, a type of service preferred over Confederate service by some local men. That Confederate conscription was both upheld by the Georgia Supreme Court and declared void by a joint committee of the state legislature further eroded its legitimacy in the minds of anti-Confederates who were inclined to avoid military service.[42]

Most of the "real" deserters, then, were not former Confederate soldiers but anti-Confederate, militia-eligible men. As individuals, they avoided service on the Georgia front by using every available excuse—disability, sickness, hardship, civic office—or openly defied state and Confederate authorities. In time, groups of men as well as individuals ignored the call to service and banded together, particularly during the war's final year. In August 1864, for example, Dennis Paulk, a Coffee County militia lieutenant and small slaveholder, admitted to Governor Brown that "a good many of the militia of my county have Deserted." Four months later slaveholder George D. Willcox wrote from neighboring Irwin County: "It seems impossible to get the militia reserve out of my District." Even as Sherman's army plundered its way across Georgia, much of the Irwin County militia did not muster. Willcox advised the state adjutant general to send a Confederate reserve cavalry company from Macon to round them up. "I know of no other plan to get them off, as I have tride every [thing]." It was evident that such men defied secessionist militia leaders like Paulk and Willcox and that the governor considered them deserters. In July 1864, with Atlanta under siege, Brown wrote to J. C. C. Blackburn. Noting that the crops in southern Georgia were now "laid by," he called every available man to the Georgia front. It was now time for those in "more comfortable, secure, and profitable positions" in the rear to step forward and join the loyal militia already in the field. Those who refused to turn out by July 20 would be arrested.[43]

Confederate loyalists knew who the deserters were and where they lived. Ironically, the deserters' influence and power increased whenever the loyal militia mobilized and left their families defenseless at home. In Pulaski County, the backwoods Trippville neighborhood became associated with deserters and anti-Confederate sentiment in the loyalist mind. Its men earned a reputation among Confederate patriots as "malcontents" and "skulkers" who were inclined toward "hiding in the woods" rather than fighting Yankees. Some of them were do-nothings who refused to be drafted or mustered into militia service. On the eve of Confederate conscription in March 1862, approximately eighty men were carried on the Trippville district militia's muster roll. Despite the draft threat, only six joined Seaborn Manning's Pulaski Greys early that month. A minority within an overwhelmingly secessionist county, the Trippville militia resembled an anti-Confederate home guard by 1864 and functioned to protect its neighborhood from incursions by pro-Confederate enrolling officers and the county sheriff.[44]

In examining deserters' refusal to fight the Yankees as well as their ability to shape public opinion, it is important to consider the militia's makeup by 1864. As the Confederate army repeatedly increased its age limit to meet the never-ending demand for manpower (the limit reached fifty early in 1864), the average age of the men at home increased as well. Indeed, in Georgia all white males from sixteen to sixty were eventually "expected at the Front." Left at home, however, were civil officers and members of county police companies, theoretically formed by exempt men between fifty and sixty. Since the police companies were literally and symbolically a collection of Confederate soldiers' fathers and grandfathers, generation rather than class is a more significant factor in Confederate disaffection and deserter resistance. One Telfair County resident stated as much when he asked the state adjutant general's office if militiamen over forty-five years old could stay home during the fall of 1864 and avoid fighting Sherman's army. Clearly annoyed, an aide-de-camp cynically wrote back that Governor Brown believed that "they could do much more good for the next 30 to 60 days in the field helping rid the State of our invaders." He closed his message with the admonition, "none must be left behind."[45]

White belt neighborhoods like Irwinville were not the only communities where the militia was reluctant to turn out during the summer of 1864. When George Willcox complained that he could not get the militia out of his district, he described the situation in Irwin County's Fourth District, the nearest the county had to a plantation neighborhood. In black belt Pulaski County during the summer of 1864, the state adjutant general's office leveled charges that inferior court justices made unauthorized exemptions to militia service by assigning militia-eligible men to the county police company. County police companies became hiding places for men under fifty, and later under fifty-five, who avoided militia service when older exempt males were available for police service. The adjutant's office ordered the justices to "see to it that they do not receive protection under an order *unauthorized and annulled*." Men who sought such "protection" had scant loyalty to the Confederate nation. It is little wonder white belt militia districts with a tradition of antisecession sentiment were reluctant to send their patriarchs to the front.[46]

Both at home and in Virginia, the fall of Atlanta and Sherman's march through Georgia had profound consequences that shaped the climate of public opinion. Militia deserters like those described by Paulk and Willcox as well as skulkers such as those at Trippville were convinced that the Southern cause was finished well before Griswoldville and the gloomy winter that followed. On the Georgia and Virginia fronts, local Confederate soldiers followed events in Georgia with a growing sense of apprehension. Conditions at home had deteriorated steadily in a material sense, but now the Yankees were loose in the Deep South and their own neighborhoods were divided into loyal and disloyal militia camps.

It was in this context of an increasingly destabilized home front that some soldiers in local Confederate infantry companies in Virginia began to leave their units. This practice peaked in 1864 and early 1865. Although not one deserter was listed on the roster of the Coffee County Guards, 10 percent of its men took "French leave"; slightly more than half of this ten percent left the Virginia front in 1864 and 1865. Crop failures, food shortages, speculation, and profiteering worked tremendous hardships locally. Letters from home reported high prices for livestock, the scarcity of hogs in the woods, and the need for women and hired labor to plow the fields. Kin also wrote about the divisions on the home front. From Wilcox County late in 1863, one soldier's father sent news of "some of the speculaters and enroleing officers and all these big men which ar hiding themselves behind some little offices for there is too many of them hear for the god of our country." A disillusioned member of Company G, 10th Confederate Cavalry, writing from an encampment near Atlanta in the spring of 1864, declared: "Tell them old cecesers that I have but little faith in the gloryous case and if they dont like it tel them to kiss _____ [.] . . . All of th secessers up hear have left ther fire sides and hav gone down South in Dixie But shit they l be no Dixie land nor Southern confederacy eather much longer." Warren Ward, whose father died at the front, later explained that "many of our soldiers who were at home on furloughs, were not able to return to their commands" because Sherman's invasion of the Carolinas had cut them off from Virginia. He admitted, however, that some of them "had lost heart and come home to stay, let the consequences be what they may."[47]

That the chaos within Georgia was partly responsible for such absences, including soldiers' "anxiety" over providing food, shelter, and clothing for their families, is reflected by the pattern in James Humphreys's old company of the 49th Georgia. Of the 9 percent of all men reported absent, every one departed between June 1864 and March 1865 at the peak of the crisis at home. Half of these men later maintained that they were on authorized "sick furlough" or a "furlough of indulgence." Private John Randolph Dowdy was carried on the roll as absent without permission, although his pension application stated that he was given a sick furlough of twenty-five days in March 1865. More than half of the troops on furloughs, including Dowdy, claimed that they had attempted to rejoin the company before the war ended. Twenty-two-year-old First Lieutenant Thomas Jefferson Smith was in the same boat with Dowdy in February 1865. Years later his pension application noted that he was on a "furlough of indulgence" and attempted "to rejoin command" as the war ended. Smith had reached Charlotte, North Carolina, at the time of the surrender.[48]

During this time loyal soldiers' families also needed protection from raids by deserters. Although deep within the Confederate interior, wiregrass Georgia was not clearly under Confederate control. In many respects, the landscape resembled a no-man's-land. Confederate loyalists controlled larger towns such as Hawkinsville, as well as the more accessible river road neighborhoods, while the isolated backwoods became contested ground. In neighborhoods like Irwinville, Confederate families were vulnerable to intimidation or attack by unionists, deserter bands, and occasionally runaway slaves. Continuing to live a normal life became impossible. County courts did not meet, mobility was restricted by marauding deserters, and a reign of fear set in among soldiers' families. Sarah Hilliard Ward, the widow of Private John Ward of the Coffee County Guards, was so terrified of attack that on one occasion she slept with a hatchet beneath her pillow. In light of these conditions, some soldiers may well have returned home to protect their families from emboldened anti-Confederates, in essence deserting a front-line war with the Yankees to face another threat within the Confederacy's deteriorating interior.[49]

This situation seems to have been particularly true in parts of Telfair County. Unlike the traditional unionist strongholds in backwoods Coffee and Irwin Counties, which were largely in anti-Confederate hands by mid-1864 if not earlier, Telfair's backwoods remained contested territory. Confederate loyalists, especially along the river road, were determined to keep their side of the Ocmulgee under control. The homes of anti-Confederates and unionists were subjected to search-and-seizure sweeps conducted by pro-Confederate county police in order to disarm deserters and others. Loyalists feared an anti-Confederate uprising. In the fall of 1864, planter Woodson Willcox and a Telfair County police company searched for "guns or other destructive weapons" in the homes of deserters and "laggards" as well as in the cabins of "negroes."[50]

The invasion of private households by the county police or Confederate cavalry patrols was deeply resented by anti-Confederates, who continued to exert their authority. In late 1864 conditions deteriorated to such an extent that an expedition of regular Confederate mounted artillery was sent to round up militia deserters and put down anti-Confederate bands, probably in response to appeals from loyalists for help. Commanded by Lieutenant Colonel J. H. Hollinquist, a young West Pointer, the expedition left Macon in mid-January to conduct operations along the lower river. Hollinquist depended on what he considered reliable information from "Scouts and citizens" along the road below Hawkinsville, where he reported on January 15, 1865, the capture of four deserters, three from Wheeler's cavalry. The fourth deserter, from the "Virginia army," was "persuaded to give me necessary information."[51]

As they prepared to cross the Ocmulgee into Pulaski and Telfair Counties and sweep the backwoods, Hollinquist's men faced the same weather conditions that slowed Sherman's march into South Carolina. Torrential rains made creeks and rivers impassable. Moreover, they traveled across a landscape where many citizens had given up hope of winning the war or openly defied Confederate authority. Based on the information he collected, Hollinquist planned to spend most of his time "scouring the country and picking up all deserters and stragglers on the eastern side of the river." His major target was Gum Swamp, a densely wooded area that ran through the backwoods of Pulaski and Telfair. Unable to penetrate the flooded swamps and reach the small islands where the deserters hid out, Hollinquist devised a strategy to draw the men from the woods. When sweeps turned up guns and horses in suspicious places, they were "taken as a means of compelling their [the deserters'] surrender, in order that the property might be returned to their families." In other words, disarmed anti-Confederate families without the means to defend themselves were as vulnerable to attack as loyal families who used the occasion to settle old scores.[52]

But deserters were difficult to corner and rarely surrendered. As Sherman's soldiers discovered in South Carolina, Hollinquist's cavalrymen rarely found their quarry. Instead, women and children stayed at home while their men disappeared into the woods. In one humorous incident, a homely plain folk wife unable to account for her husband's whereabouts emphasized his poverty instead, declaring that he had "nothin' in the world but one old hog." The cavalrymen broke out in laughter despite themselves.[53]

Hollinquist was aware that some deserters were determined to "fight us to the last." They felt no need to surrender to protect their families because entire backwoods neighborhoods were now controlled by "rank traiters." Even in contested Telfair County he reported that John Brown, one of the "ringleaders among the deserters," was recently elected justice of the inferior court, "and he is the most notorious traiter in this county, and expresses his treasonable sentiments on all occasions." Beyond the occasional capture of individual deserters moving between their homes and their camps, what Hollinquist discovered were "regularly organized bodies of deserters." Two of these bands used the small islands of Gum Swamp as their sanctuaries. Invariably, whenever the young colonel closed in on their camps, the deserters moved deeper into the swamp because of "accurate information they had regarding his movements." In addition to intelligence provided by deserters' families and their own mounted scouts, who would "ride a horse to death to give information to the others," the deserters communicated "by means of rockets and blowing of horns." They also took care to carry all canoes and boats deeper into the swamp once the alarm was sounded, making it impossible for the dismounted cavalrymen to catch up with them in waist-deep water. When the Confederates did reach an abandoned camp, they found "a quantity of leather, wool and tools of every description," indications that some form of domestic economy continued even in deserters' quarters.[54]

By late January 1865 Hollinquist was convinced that he had broken "anything like an organization" in Gum Swamp, but most of the deserters escaped and "crossed over into the counties on the west side of the Ocmulgee river." There they joined comrades in Appling and Coffee Counties, creating even larger bands. Had the Confederate cavalry not been recalled to Macon, Hollinquist believed that his men would have given the deserters there "a trial of those fighting qualities of which they boasted so loudly."[55]

The forest west of the river had become a part of Georgia's deserter and draft evader country as early as 1862 in the aftermath of conscription. By early 1865 the area was in open revolt. In early September 1864 the state adjutant general's office, in response to complaints from loyal Confederates, had directed Colonel Carey W. Styles, an aide-de-camp whose district included parts of the lower river region, to do something about the fifty to seventy-five men "subject to your late call" for militia who "have not responded." These individuals continued to employ every ruse to dodge military service. Some claimed they had served at the front but had "returned almost immediately & say they are relieved or discharged"; others declared exemptions due to their rank as militia officers when they were "in no service whatsoever." Still others were accused of having "put in" substitutes when both they and the substitutes were at home.[56]

The "gentleman of high standing" who reported the militia deserters was one of Coffee County's nonslaveholding plain folk, W. B. Overstreet. His charges were so serious that the adjutant general's office planned to forward his letter to the Coffee County Inferior Court. There the justices were to convene a court of inquiry and investigate the deserter problem using as evidence a list of offenders supplied by Overstreet and "other good citizens," namely Confederate patriots. Overstreet's gravest accusation, however, was leveled at Colonel Styles himself. His "agents" allegedly exempted "rich men" from Confederate service "on the payment of money . . . whilst poor men are sent to the front." The most glaring example of this practice reportedly was when men who had been called up left their neighborhood and walked to the nearest Savannah and Gulf Railroad station, only to return "home again" with exemptions in their hands. Charges that "those men got out by paying money to some person here" so "rich men" could stay at home while "poor men" fought the war openly challenged the legitimacy of Confederate and state authority. Patriots like Overstreet feared the consequences.[57]

The voices of "notorious" anti-Confederates such as John Brown are often difficult to recover. Bill Wall of Coffee County, however, was one of the disaffected Confederates that Hollinquist hoped to pursue west of the river. His wartime experience gives us some insight into desertion and anti-Confederate sentiment in a white belt neighborhood. Thirty-nine years old when the war began, Wall earned a living teaching school. Although educated, his economic status placed him among the plain folk's poorer households, his total wealth reaching only $485 in 1859. Wall cultivated a mere three acres of land, apparently without the benefit of a horse or mule; he grew forty bushels of corn and tended a few hogs. Only land ownership raised him above the level of a tenant farmer. Unlike the young men who hurried to join local infantry companies in 1861, Wall waited a year and then volunteered on the eve of Confederate conscription in March 1862, when the Coffee County Guards were organized. When his company joined the 50th Georgia and Wall was shipped to the front, approximately 60 percent of the military-aged men in Coffee County were already in service.[58]

At some point Wall returned to Coffee County and never rejoined his company. Evidently, he spent the remainder of the war in the same neighborhood he left in 1862, a backwoods community that was known for harboring deserters. Confederate loyalists, some of whom bought patriotic covers and sewed them onto their quilts, feared for their safety. Neighbors complained that their property was being stolen. Livestock routinely disappeared, and barns and smokehouses were pilfered. Wall was linked to the deserters by Benajah Pearson, a small planter whose place was situated near the backwoods community of Red Bluff. Pearson was a perfect target for deserters. As county treasurer, he symbolized local authority. His family was privileged by slave-holding and had plenty to eat, while backwoods soldiers' wives and families went hungry. Deserters doubtless reasoned that Pearson could afford to lose some livestock and corn on land that had produced 1,000 bushels of corn, 1,000 pounds of rice, and 4 bales of cotton in 1859.[59]

Bill Wall was one of the men Pearson accused of stealing his property. Apparently, Pearson's charges led to threats against him by the deserters, including the symbolic act of digging his grave. Wall took up his pen and wrote a poem—his answer to the planter's accusations. In the poem the former schoolteacher acknowledged that deserters had stolen Pearson's livestock, potatoes, and "your hoss and your plows." But he could not stop the thievery even if he tried. And he certainly would not identify the deserters, claiming that such an act would be his death sentence: "If I, these men betray and they were all taken away, And they did not in the battlefield fall, They would come back and kill 'Old Man Bill Wall.' "[60]

The poem continued: "I would rather take the lash than betray them for Confederate trash." It was this fear that also kept some Confederate patriots from naming the deserters in their own neighborhoods. The circle of kinship and friendship that included deserters such as Wall made it difficult for Confederate and local authorities to take them into custody. In early January 1865 a provost officer in Albany wrote that the enrolling officers in Berrien and Irwin Counties "have been run out of those counties by *deserters* and *Bushwackers*." And as early as 1862, Sheriff John A. Spivey had informed Governor Brown about the deserter problem in Coffee County. It was "hard to get hold of them," Spivey explained, because they were "harbored by Some of the Citizens." The number of deserters grew with each passing year, and Spivey depended on the votes of these same "Citizens" at election time.[61]

Sorting out deserters from those authorized to be at home was no easy task. With men constantly traveling to and from the front, others finding refuge as exempt and protected, and still others simply hiding out, it was difficult to tell who had been properly discharged from Confederate or state service. Concerning such men, a frustrated Confederate loyalist from Coffee County wrote: "The community here say they do not know whether it is so or not, as none of us have ever seen their discharges." But which "community," loyal or disloyal, was it? Given the potential for overwhelming anti-Confederate violence at home when the loyal militia was in the field, how many Southern patriots were willing to challenge a man's personal honor by asking to see his discharge? Zean Kirkland spent the war fighting with the Coffee County Guards and lived to tell about it, sitting out the last days of the struggle on wounded furlough. His brother, Manning Kirkland, lost his life on the home front when he was "killed by the deserters about the close of the war."[62]

As pervasive as anti-Confederate sentiment was in the no-man's-land south of the Ocmulgee River, patriots still controlled secessionist neighborhoods upriver, where an alternative narrative to anti-Confederate control unfolded during the war's final months. In Pulaski County, for example, Confederate stalwarts such as Norman McDuffie professed an undying loyalty to the cause and a commitment to a virtuous Confederate economy only weeks before Appomattox. Shortly after unionists captured the *Governor Troup*, McDuffie and "fellow citizens" at Hawkinsville took a stand that seemingly defied Confederate authority yet upheld local notions of what was just and right under "the laws of the State of Georgia, and the Confederate States." This incident involved the steamboat *Comet*, loaded down with two hundred bales of cotton "designed for traffic with the enemy," as McDuffie put it. The vessel's captain, former company commander Orran Horne, and a party "composed of gentlemen well known as speculators and blockade runners" planned to take the *Comet* to Doctortown and ship the cotton to Savannah, where it would be sold "to the Yankees." As captain of a loyal militia company, McDuffie and his men were "all determined to prevent this traffic on this river" and seized the steamer at Hawkinsville.[63]

McDuffie's men released the boat, cargo, and crew on condition that Horne "pledged his honor not to carry his boat below with a load of cotton for the Yankees," and only after McDuffie received a letter from Major General Howell Cobb admitting that the boat's officers were "acting under . . . orders." McDuffie was incredulous that an officer with Cobb's "bright and honorable" record was involved and refused to let the matter rest. He challenged Cobb's authority to permit such traffic and argued that it was "the duty of all good citizens" to prevent "trade in cotton or other articles with the Yankees." At issue for McDuffie and other Confederate loyalists was the maintenance of a moral Confederate economy even in the throes of national defeat. The *Comet*'s seizure was a loyal effort to "nip in the bud . . . illegal traffic with our enemies." If allowed to go unchecked, such trade would "render utterly worthless our currency, stimulate a desire already sufficiently strong for green backs & gold," and ultimately undermine "the firm and steadfast of our people, and demoralize the whole country." McDuffie concluded: "The true men of this section are determined that the Ocmulgee River shall not be used for an illegal trade with the enemies of our country, and they care very little whether the effort is made by high officials or the lowest characters in the land."[64]

About two months after his anti-Confederate band invaded Irwinville and the county's unionists took Irwin out of the Confederacy, unconditional unionist Willis Bone was publicly executed. Despite the deep neighborhood rifts exacerbated by the war, Bone's hanging indicated that citizens in Irwin County were as hungry for an end to the local killing as those at Abbeville had been for the slaughter to stop on the battlefields.

Although Bone's neighborhood was in the backwoods, many of its families had paid a high human price in the name of the Confederacy. And although they were tired of fighting, Bone's unconditional Unionism, his harassment of patriot households, and his overbearing subjugation of Irwinville were hard to take not only for his secessionist neighbors, but also for those who were essentially neutral. Bone crossed the line in April 1865, when he murdered an elderly soldier's father named John "Jack" Walker. Although they were unable to come to terms on the war and its outcome, most of the neighborhood's residents—Confederate patriots and passive unionists alike—agreed that such lawlessness had to stop and that Willis Bone should be brought to justice. They then formed a regulator band led by unionist and Primitive Baptist minister Jacob Young.[65]

Jack Walker could not have been more unlike Willis Bone. His father was among the county's earliest settlers, and Walker had frequently served as a juror and estate appraiser. By 1860 he was the head of one of the largest households along the Alapaha River in western Irwin County. It consisted of twelve people, including nine children, his wife Sabra Clements Walker, and Sabra's seventy-four-year-old mother Mary Clements. Through marriage, Walker was part of the local kinship network. A yeoman farmer and non-slaveholder, he worked about one hundred acres, growing corn and sweet potatoes; like many of his neighbors, he was also heavily involved in raising hogs and sheep. And like almost two-thirds of the farmers along the river, Walker grew some cotton for market, his family picking three bales in 1859.[66]

Willis Bone, on the other hand, was an outsider with no local kinship ties. Although the Alapaha area had been settled for more than a generation by 1860, there was room in the remote backwoods for newcomers. Bone moved into the neighborhood during the 1850s from Taylor County on the Georgia cotton belt. He began buying up unimproved land. Like the plain folk in the backwoods of Wilcox County, newcomers such as Bone recognized the cotton-growing potential of white belt land. By 1859 Bone was by far the largest cotton producer in his neighborhood, reporting fourteen bales to the census taker.[67]

Shunning livestock herding and self-sufficient farming for cotton growing, Bone the outsider differed from his neighbors in another important way. His approximately one thousand acres boasted a small natural lake called "Bone's Pond." On its bank he built a corn mill. On Wednesdays farmers went to Bone to mill their corn. He took a miller's toll, feeding his family on corn grown by his neighbors. It is possible that Bone's mill, like others along the lower river, also carded wool and ginned cotton on a toll basis. Perhaps this explains how he became a leading cotton producer without slave labor. In any event, Bone represented a different entrepreneurial model: he made a livelihood without the help of slaves, the open range, and local kinship networks, and he was more dependent on trade and white tenant labor. He turned Bone's Pond into what Abbot Hall Brisbane had envisioned for wiregrass Georgia a generation earlier—a white man's workshop independent of slavery.[68]

The secession crisis divided Irwinville just as it did other communities along the lower river. It forced families to reconsider their identities in terms of national, regional, state, and local loyalties. Willis Bone and Jacob Young were outspoken unionists. Young was elected one of the county's cooperationist delegates to the secession convention, where he remained antisecessionist to the end. Manassah Henderson, also a cooperationist delegate, switched his vote in favor of secession once he saw the writing on the wall at Milledgeville. Despite the community's white belt character and antisecession majority, the organization of two infantry companies during the war's first year affected many families. Jack Walker's son Abraham joined the Irwin Volunteers along with John and Bryant Smith and Silas Townsend. R. W. Clements became one of the company's officers. By the spring of 1865 Abraham Walker had died from bayonet wounds inflicted by a Yankee prison guard. Silas Townsend lost his life at Cedar Run, Virginia, and John Smith was wounded at Gettysburg. Private Bryant Smith had deserted in February 1865. In poor health, R. W. Clements returned home and joined Company H, Fourth Georgia (Clinch's) Cavalry.[69]

Within this community of growing wartime sacrifice, Willis Bone, now about forty-one, avoided Confederate service. Meanwhile, because of its remote location the Alapaha became a haven for deserters, runaway slaves, and escaped Yankee prisoners of war. Bone was suspected of harboring such men and using them to work his land. When two escaped Yankee prisoners stole two horses from secessionist Manassah Henderson, "everybody" felt that Bone was somehow responsible.[70]

It was in the context of Confederate patriots and anti-Confederates vying for neighborhood control that Jack Walker disappeared in April 1865. He left home to hunt deer and tend his hogs that ranged near Bone's Pond. Walker recognized a runaway slave named Toney who was working on Bone's land. Despite his age—Walker was about fifty-five—he tried to capture Toney. During the struggle, Bone arrived and shot Walker. Bone and Toney then buried him near the millpond and stuffed his shoes and hat into a hollow log.[71]

The disappearance of a community patriarch led to a search of Bone's property by men in the neighborhood, including some Confederate veterans. This group, later described as "the best people of the county," soon organized a regulator band to clear out Bone's Pond and restore law and order. Some of the regulators may well have been Confederate soldiers who returned home to protect their families from Bone's men. What they found on Bone's ground—evidence of a struggle, blood on a fence—led them to seize Bone. He refused to talk. The regulators then apprehended his son, Zachary Taylor Bone, about sixteen years old, and threatened to "hang the whole crowd," including Zachary, his mother, and his siblings if the boy did not "tell all he knew about it." With the specter of himself and his family swinging from a tree, Zachary allegedly stated that his father shot Walker and then "hit him on the head with his gun until he thought him dead." With Toney's help they buried the body and Toney disappeared. The search party quickly found Walker. According to local lore, the men were horrified by evidence that he had been "buried alive as his hands had worked upward through the mud and blood had come to the surface." Moreover, they were frustrated in their efforts to wash Walker's body in the pond and prepare it for decent burial because "the skin would burst and come apart."[72]

Unwilling to wait for the local court to resume session, the outraged regulators "organized a court of justice." Perhaps to add legitimacy to their proceedings, they selected Jacob Young, the Primitive Baptist lay preacher and former unionist delegate to the secession convention, as its "chairman or judge." Bone was "promptly" convicted and sentenced to hang. Scaffolding was constructed beneath a large tree. According to local tradition, the wife of one of Bone's neighbors provided the rope, which she had woven to use as a cotton bale tie. Walker's son Sam climbed the tree and dropped the rope over a limb. The last words of Bone's gibbet speech were supposedly: "Take warning from me and don't come to what I have." After his execution, Sarah Bone wrapped her husband's body in a sheet and buried him. The regulators told the members of Bone's family to settle their affairs, dispose of their property, and leave the county.[73]

The households in the vicinity of Bone's Pond, where the regulators themselves resided, included members of virtually every home-front group but planters. Among the regulators, unionist Jacob Young symbolized the legitimacy of county government and church authority. Deserters like Private Bryant Smith reflected the disaffected Confederate soldiers. At the opposite end of the spectrum were secessionists like Manassah Henderson and Confederate patriots like R. W. Clements, later pronounced "a thorough unreconstructed rebel." Between these extremes were people who merely sought neutrality and an end to the discord. Whether they were small masters or nonslaveholders, Primitive Baptists or Masons, loyalists or unionists, most of them agreed that Willis Bone, the murderer and defender of Yankees and runaways, deserved to die, both for his crime and as a precondition for the neighborhood's postwar healing. Thus, they took the first steps toward reconciliation of the divided white community when its leading nonviolent unionists passed judgment on its foremost violent unionist, Willis Bone.[74]

The war's final year found the lower river communities divided as never before. Along the river valley and in the plantation districts some Confederate loyalists still held out hope that their bid for Southern nationalism would become reality. But Sherman's campaign in Georgia exacerbated the divisions that existed at home. Answering Governor Brown's call, loyal militiamen fought on the Georgia front in 1864. After the battle at Griswoldville, however, many loyalists lost heart and resolved that continued fighting would settle nothing. Their only hope was for a negotiated peace. Anti-Confederates were emboldened by the departure of the loyal militia, which left them firmly in charge of their own neighborhoods. After the loyal militia's humbling at Griswoldville, they openly challenged Confederate and state authority. Attempts to break up bands of deserters in the backwoods were unsuccessful largely because too many citizens sympathized with their plight. The Abbeville Resolutions and the unionist invasion of Irwinville revealed that soldiers' fathers were ready to end the Confederate war before it concluded on the Virginia front. The execution of Willis Bone by regulators suggests that many prior identities—Confederate, unionist, deserter—had been set aside in a desperate attempt to stop the killing and restore order.[75]

"'members when they captured Jeff Davis," former slave Martha Everette recalled two generations later. As a thirteen-year-old on James Lathrop's plantation in the spring of 1865, Martha and other slave children were in the yard when in the distance "we heard th' drums jest a-beatin'." The overseer's wife refused to let the children leave the plantation yard to see the procession of Yankee soldiers and the captured Davis party as it passed along the river road through Pulaski County. "'Course we didn't know what had happened then," Everette remembered, "but later we heard that they'd got Jeff Davis."[1]

The Confederacy's president was captured on May 10, 1865, in the Irwinville neighborhood not long after unionist Willis Bone's hanging. Coincidentally, Jacob Young, the "judge" at his tribunal, chose the same morning to invite neighbors over to shear sheep. Some of Young's guests were Confederate veterans who had just returned home. Most of them brought along rifles and planned to hunt deer after the shearing was done. Their rifles were stacked against Young's yard fence. Earlier that morning the men had heard gunfire, the sounds of two Yankee cavalry units mistakenly shooting at each other as they captured Davis, but "no one knew what it meant." As the men stood talking in Young's yard, they were startled when two foraging

Union cavalrymen rode up and eyed the corncribs and smokehouse. They explained that wagons would soon arrive to haul off Young's provisions to feed Yankee soldiers and their horses. Tense moments followed. Young declared that "his family as well as quite a few widows and orphan children he was assisting, would suffer" if the food were taken. The cavalrymen "kept their eyes on the men and guns" as they departed. The Yankee forage wagons never arrived.[2]

Instead, the Union cavalrymen took Jefferson Davis and the other prisoners up the river road toward Macon. The ambulance that carried the Davis family gradually left the piney woods behind and entered the cotton belt as it reached Hawkinsville, where placards offered a reward for Davis's capture. Blacks and whites watched the Confederacy's funeral procession move through the countryside. Along the way, Davis passed countless homes of plain folk still in mourning for their Confederate dead and within shouting distance of Harriette and Seaborn Manning's graves. Spring was in full bloom; honeysuckle and wisteria partially disguised a landscape blighted by four years of warfare. But the two Yankee cavalrymen who had ridden into Jacob Young's yard on the morning of Davis's capture saw signs of the desolation. The unionist minister's home had become a refuge for the widows and orphans of dead Confederates. He fed them from his crib and smokehouse.[3]

The Confederate veterans in Young's farmyard were lucky. Unlike their dead comrades, they survived and came home. But how they came home is significant to our understanding of their postwar lives. Unlike Union soldiers, who returned to a victorious North with its legacies of emancipation and preservation of the Union, Confederates encountered a defeated South with its legacies of mourning, poverty, and thwarted national ambitions. Union soldiers mustered out as companies and regiments. Confederates arrived individually or in small groups. F. H. Bozeman and Jim Johnson expected "to tramp" the final twenty miles to Hawkinsville but were lucky enough to catch a wagon ride. There was no victory parade. While Union veterans looked to the future with hope and optimism, Confederate veterans were weighted down by the uncertainty of life in a postwar world "shadowed and darkened by great sorrow."[4]

And what they found at home was different from the Old South memories they had carried through the years of hard fighting. The war had literally deconstructed home as they knew it. It had killed hundreds of young white men, disabled many others, and reconfigured households and neighborhoods. Only three of the eleven men in the Gibbs family of Wilcox County survived Confederate service. The war also freed the area's enslaved African Americans, one-third of its people. This demographic revolution created a new social reality, the

The backwoods site of Jefferson Davis's capture on the outskirts of Irwinville. (Courtesy of Georgia Archives)

one glimpsed at Jacob Young's farm. Hundreds of women and nearly a thousand children were listed as soldiers' dependents. Many of them received government corn along with the freedpeople. Household after household had been impoverished. Former Confederate officer R. W. Clements was more fortunate than many: he came back to twenty head of scruffy "piney-woods cattle" and $100 worth of poor land. Even in black belt neighborhoods where people hoped cotton would restore their fortunes, prosperity proved elusive. Thirteen years after Appomattox, a Pulaski County farmer asked his neighbors if they were any better off than in 1865. Pointing to "a multitude of broken farmers" and "comfortless homes," he pessimistically concluded that "the sunlight of prosperity" still failed to shine on his people.[5]

The war devastated the home front in psychological as well as material ways. Beneath the fallow fields and broken homes stretched a darker emotional landscape that provided a context for postwar life. The secessionist dream of a separate political identity was gone. When the son of one secessionist reached home, he found that his "poor father" was "crushed at our defeat . . . he asked if Lee and Johnston had really surrendered. I told him, yes. He said no more." Feelings of anger, guilt, and loss shadowed Confederate veterans and their families for years and caused some to question their own self-worth. The war was a test of manhood. Local soldiers had fought because they believed that they could protect their families and homes from the Yankees. These men knew they had failed both on the battlefront and the home front. Despite all the deaths, all the sacrifices, they had been powerless to hold the Yankees at bay. The survivors were living symbols of this defeat. Publicly, they acknowledged that the war was over and they had to get on with their lives. Privately, they doubted their ability to deal with the changed world at home, where shrinking economic opportunities made life even harder.[6]

Scores of limbless veterans epitomized the physical and psychological damage to Southern manhood. A soldier in the 8th Georgia put it this way: "It was all over but the empty sleeves and wooden legs." A steady stream of amputees entered county courthouses and filled out applications for artificial limbs. Charles McCall arrived at the Wilcox County ordinary's office in 1867. For over two years he had fought with the Pulaski Greys before being severely wounded in Virginia. Surgeons cut off his leg. But McCall was not interested in the artificial limb that Georgia now offered its veterans. What he wanted was "the value of an artificial leg in money," an option open to amputees like himself. His application explained that "the nature of the wound" and the "condition of the stump" rendered an artificial leg of little "service." McCall took the badly needed money rather than the state-issued leg.[7]

Although the Lost Cause objectification of Confederate veterans rendered them whole, the immediate postwar reality was messy. If disabilities such as McCall's were serious enough, veterans became less than full men in their own eyes and in those of family members. Joseph Rhodes of the State Rights Guards was wounded through the knee during the Seven Days campaign. After returning to the front, he was captured at Petersburg and sent to Point Lookout prison, where his body was wracked by diarrhea prior to his release in June 1865. These experiences exhausted Rhodes physically and emotionally. His wife Amanda later wrote: "He suffered from his wound and Bowels, never was able to work, always sick . . . lingered and died from the wound and Diarrhea." Being an "invalid up to his death," as Amanda described her husband, Joseph returned home a physically broken man.[8]

To be a "cripple" in the postwar rural South was to become a burden on the household. "Never has been able to plow or do manual labor" was a description that fit many disabled veterans, much to their discomfort. Yet the ability to do farmwork and produce what was required to make a family economically independent was central to the plain folk sense of masculinity and personal honor. If veterans were to resume their rightful place as heads of households and regain their masculinity, they must restore the antebellum home place and fortunes as they remembered them.[9]

At the core of a man's self-worth in wiregrass Georgia was a healthy sense of personal domain—all that he owned and controlled as the master of his household. Confidence in his own physical qualities and abilities to perform manual labor formed the center of this concept, then extended outward from self to family and personal property, including homestead, valued household objects, land and livestock. These were the things that meant most to yeoman farmers and linked them to country people of similar background, class, and race. Maintaining self-esteem based on self-sufficiency was not easy, even for commercial men like Northern-born warehouse owner Simon Merritt. His demise came quickly as postwar debts and lawsuits against him piled up. "Struggling to make money" in December 1866, the aging former militiaman was declared insolvent eighteen months later.[10]

Few examples of the loss of self-worth were as dramatic or as tragic as that of plain folk veteran James Fraser. His experiences reminded neighbors how former Confederate soldiers privately struggled with the war's inner consequences—anger, depression, and violence—and how their actions could disrupt postwar life. Private Fraser had joined Captain Ryan's Pulaski Volunteers during the excitement and enthusiasm of the war's first weeks. A year after the 8th Georgia was bloodied at First Manassas, his regiment attempted to break the Union line and capture a Yankee battery at Garnett's farm. The "disastrous" assault on the afternoon of June 28, 1862, cost his regiment thirteen killed and sixty-three wounded. Fraser was so badly shot up that his right leg was amputated "below the knee joint." Discharged, he spent the remainder of the war at home unable to plow or do other manual labor in a community desperate for agricultural workers. In 1866 he indicated that his sole means of support was teaching school.[11]

Emotionally troubled by his physical injuries, Fraser, according to neighbors, believed that "he had a right to the sympathies of the people." Thus, he found meaning for his physical loss in entitlement in much the same way that soldiers' wives thought they were entitled to protection and support at home while their husbands served at the front. Such sympathies were not always forthcoming during the hardscrabble postwar years. A decade after Appomattox, Fraser was described as an intensely angry and violent man who "abused" others over the "slightest" affronts and differences. Nevertheless, he managed to find a wife, Eliza Crenshaw, and took in her children from a prior marriage. "He has not led a very enviable life since the war," wrote one who knew him in 1875; indeed, Fraser's belief that the community owed him something "led him astray in many instances."[12]

Although the precise nature of his transgressions is unclear, the court of public opinion judged that Fraser's honor and reputation had been badly damaged. Soon after the war, he moved to Hayneville in neighboring Houston County, a physical relocation that symbolized his emotional estrangement from his old community. There, Fraser was first accused of mistreating his stepchildren, whose mother had died and left them in his care. After the children found refuge in the home of Dr. Joseph Dunwoody, a relative of the children's mother, Fraser was charged with killing him. Years after the shooting stopped, then, the Civil War claimed additional casualties.[13]

The war's emotional casualties were not limited to men with physical losses and psychological problems, however. Many veterans returned home to lead quiet if desperate lives and continued to farm. A few, such as ex-Confederate officer Samuel Fuller, organized local chapters of the Patrons of Husbandry in which their wives participated. But all who had witnessed the horrific carnage of war brought these memories home. Men like James Fraser reflected the worst that happened when a veteran's sense of personal domain was so badly damaged—amputated limbs, economic hardship, loss and alienation of family and neighborhood—that he was unable to function honorably in the community.[14]

The connection between a private sense of self-worth and its public manifestations was not lost on the community. If the war and its consequences damaged the character and reputation of individuals, it could do the same for entire neighborhoods. In 1870, for example, a Pulaski County grand jury reported that it found little "public pride" among the citizens or the county officers they had elected. They had been humbled by the war. The community's morality and reputation, its collective sense of decency, were called into question. The editor of the *Hawkinsville Dispatch* was outraged to discover that "*white*" men" violated "all sense of propriety and rules of modesty" by bathing naked on Sunday morning in full view of the Hawkinsville ferry. Communal bathing in creeks and rivers had been common among soldiers at the front, but now "ladies cannot cross the river to attend church, without being insulted by this indecency." Women were the most exalted symbols of home, family, and virtue. How could Southern women rehabilitate their men and honor their dead in a community whose pride and decency had come into question?[15]

What observers perceived as emotional and moral manifestations of waning self-worth were reflected in a blighted landscape where "a good and safe bridge" was not to be found and roads were in "awful condition." A dozen years after Appomattox a traveler through the once wealthy western part of Pulaski County wrote: "It was painful to note the signs of un-prosperous times on most of the plantations. . . . Fields are washed and poor, fences decayed, gates down, and buildings generally in a deplorable condition." Like the veterans themselves, the war prematurely aged the landscape. Plain folk did not blame each other for the poverty at the end of the secession road they narrowly voted to take. They blamed the war. Men and women alike were united in their bitterness toward Yankees who killed and maimed their men and boys and left them to a squalid existence on equal footing with former slaves seemingly free to do what they pleased.[16]

### The "Republic of Irwin"

"Few Negroes, and every one almost a producer" was the way one person described white belt Irwin County in 1875. The man was asked to give a credit rating for Byrd Fussell, a small farmer and former slaveholder. Fussell opened a general store at Irwinville in 1868, and the credit company needed an update on his standing in the community. "Don't know much about him," the reporter confessed, "but all those Irwin Co. men are good almost without exception, there is not a county in the state in better condition financially." What he meant was that the county's white men, almost all self-sufficient plain folk, were "good" for their financial obligations, such as they were. Thus, the reputation of a county known for self-sufficient white farmers, sound financial condition, and "Few Negroes" was available to all local white men, including Byrd Fussell.[17]

Unlike blighted Pulaski County and the Georgia cotton belt, which became increasingly preoccupied with the transition from slave to free labor, recovering prewar levels of cotton production, and securing Northern credit and Western provisions, postwar Irwin County avoided the crop lien trap. "Irwin is right side up; out of debt; money in her Treasury," an observer proudly wrote in 1874 as the nation slid deeper into depression. It was as if the lower river's white belt population, temporarily united with its black belt neighbors for much of the war, had reestablished the traditional antebellum boundaries blurred by mobilization and wartime sacrifice in the name of postwar recovery. Like Willis Bone's anti-Confederates, piney woods white folk "seceded" from the cotton South and reassumed their local identities as independent self-working farmers. Although Lost Cause leaders often defined the region in terms of its morality and religion, plain folk practiced their own version of cultural nationalism based on antebellum concepts of a moral economy.[18]

Recorded ten years after the war, such images of independence belie stories of hardship that shaped the character of white belt neighborhoods. Unlike Georgia's urban areas, which recovered relatively quickly, backwoods neighborhoods followed a longer path to recovery, one made all the more difficult by wartime manpower losses and lingering poverty. In the summer of 1866, for example, many soldiers' households in Telfair County remained on lists of needy families whose dependence on state assistance for corn in many cases dated back to 1863. Moreover, some former slaveholding households that managed to stay off wartime indigent rolls because of their access to slave labor found themselves joining nonslaveholding plain folk on the corn list. The name of Mary Dopson, the widow of slaveholder Alexander Dopson, appeared on the July 1866 Telfair "list for corn for the needy familys." Identified on the same list were soldiers' wives and widows such as Catherine Anderson, a nonslaveholding poor white who had been receiving corn for over three years, and Pamela Brantley. Pamela, who lost her husband Thomas in 1863 during Lee's invasion of Pennsylvania, had four children to feed on a farm that had claimed only twenty improved acres in 1859. Thus the war's cost in casualties and its consequences in economic terms had a leveling and unifying effect on the households of white belt plain folk and small masters thrown into the world of the "needy."[19]

Also worse for wear were the wiregrass counties south of the river, although the forest often hid the harsher realities. In 1867 an Irwin grand jury reported that the county was out of debt and recommended "a very small tax for school purposes." But the jurors admitted that "our people are so reduced financially" that they were "at a loss to know what to say" about their ability to pay the tax. Impoverished citizens could only do one thing at a time on the road to recovery. Feeding the people came first. True, roads and bridges were still in poor condition in May 1868, but farm labor normally sent to repair roads was badly needed for planting food crops. The grand jurors therefore postponed roadwork until "the farmers can lay by their crops," noting that "we think it imprudent to take them from their fields." Two years earlier, the grand jury had concluded that "there is sufficient provisions to avoid suffering among the people," but crop failures in 1869 once again reduced the margins of self-sufficiency. A writer from Wilcox County observed that conditions there had "completely blasted the hopes of all farmers."[20]

How could postwar white belt neighborhoods restore some measure of prosperity? Would their communities become the antebellum backwoods reborn, or would they move, as some neighborhoods had in the 1850s, toward a growing reliance on cotton? Part of the answer lies in the actions of white people during the last months of the war to avoid "utter ruin." At Abbeville, Irwinville, and Gum Swamp, plain folk took collective steps to isolate their neighborhoods from the "cruel" war. Localism triumphed over nationalism as community leaders withdrew support for the Confederacy and drew boundaries around a restricted rural world that they intended to protect from raids and lawlessness with volunteer "local defence" companies. These plain folk then attempted to restore a collective sense of self-worth by returning to the yeoman model of self-sufficiency. In time, this path to economic recovery was in the local vernacular expressed by references to the "Republic of Irwin." The origin of this phrase is unclear, but it was grounded in part in the area's pride in the economic independence and freedom of action dramatically illustrated by the unionist takeover of Irwinville early in 1865.[21]

Just as war itself democratized the region by including women and children, rich and poor, slave and free in its mobilization, death and mourning, and household sacrifice, so too was the revival of postwar rural neighbor-hoods a people's crusade. But in this imagined republic the residents who mattered were the Irwin County credit reporter's white "producers." Accord-ing to another account, such plain folk were "free and independent, and do as they please." That language—economic independence and freedom of action—was essentially Jeffersonian republicanism applied in succession to the secession crisis, the Confederate cause, and the plain folk's postwar hopes for an antebellum piney woods status quo. After all, Joseph E. Brown had warned repeatedly that a Yankee victory meant nothing less than unmanly submission and enslavement for common white people followed by their loss of honor, property, and rights. For backwoods Confederate veterans, a retreat into a largely white world of limited market involvement seemed to be the best way to escape the governor's prediction.[22]

To some extent, the challenges of postwar life required that people set aside their differences as much as possible to deal with community challenges. Grand juries and county courts between 1866 and 1870 were composed of an odd assortment of alleged deserters, Confederate veterans, draft dodgers, loyal and disloyal militiamen, wartime exemption holders, and old-time unionists. It might have seemed odd to Oliver Cook, formerly a planter and captain of the Irwin County Volunteers, that the grand jury he led as foreman in 1866 included Jehu Fletcher Sr., a man who tried to avoid conscription by sending his own son to the front, but such was the state of postwar society. Collectively, such juries and courts made recommendations for badly needed county im-provements, including a new courthouse and jail, better bridges and roads, and increased support for the school fund.[23]

Although the Republic of Irwin referred to a geographic place, in time it was expanded in the popular imagination to mean backwoods neighborhoods characterized by frontier-stage economic independence, regardless of county. Such plain folk notions incorporated the wartime cult of self-sacrifice for a higher cause, but now Confederate nationalism was replaced by antebellum-style Jeffersonian republicanism and denunciations of commercial agricul-ture. In the spring of 1873 the *Albany Central City* described how plain folk in Irwin and neighboring counties turned their backs on cotton production, black labor, and tenancy and became "more independent, pecuniarily, every year." Indeed, by rejecting the alternative black belt pathway to economic recovery and its financial risks in the cotton market, plain folk had become more prosperous than at any time "since the close of the war." In this way, the disciplined veteran's household could withstand economic domination by Northern creditors, Western grain dealers, and local merchants.[24]

The sentiments expressed by the Republic of Irwin were in many respects a plain folk critique of the crop lien system then emerging in the older plantation districts. This critique was filtered through the selective wartime memories of veterans and their families, particularly where cotton planting and slavery were concerned. Among its basic precepts was white land ownership over tenancy, white family labor over black hirelings, and the production of food crops over cotton growing. Living on a household's "ready means," or those resources found on the home place or in the woods, was a maxim of the plain folk's creed. Confederate veterans who had failed to protect their families during the war could regain their honor by providing for them now. And just as the Confederate cause had in many respects resembled a religious crusade, so too did the plain folk cause for self-sufficiency. "Economy" and "industry" became bywords of the New South creed, but these had been Primitive Baptist watchwords long before. An 1847 gathering of local elders, for instance, had declared that economy and industry were "favorable traits in the christian character." In some congregations one could not be "innocent" and at the same time willingly go into debt merely in pursuit of material gain. Such "sins" reflected a lack of true economy, self-control, and virtue, especially when so many dead soldiers' widows and orphans suffered from the lack of necessities.[25]

Land ownership was the critical "ready means." In the antebellum piney woods, as much as 70 percent of nonslaveholding plain folk owned land. But death and wartime disabilities had left fewer white men to farm. In many households, the acreage under cultivation declined during and immediately after the war. Newspaper editors, however, repeatedly described how self-sufficient plain folk grew more food, often on less land, than before the war by concentrating on the production of crops for home consumption rather than for market. According to one account, one acre of poor "piney woods" land in 1873 produced 25 bushels of corn, 350 pounds of fodder, and 2,500 pounds of "good hay." Some farmers grew 30 to 175 bushels of corn per acre, although in an ordinary season 25 was average. It was unnecessary, wrote an observer, "to cultivate the whole of creation to make a little crib of corn or half a dozen bags of cotton." Furthermore, land not farmed or fenced continued to form an extensive open range for livestock. By combining cattle herding and food crop production, plain folk produced self-sufficiencies on small tracts and avoided one trap of the cotton culture—renting land for shares or for cash.[26]

In many respects, who worked the land was as important to plain folk as who owned it. The use of predominantly white family labor was another sign of the yeomanry's continued rural communalism and its rejection of the antebellum cotton and black labor nexus. Plain folk households traditionally produced most of what they consumed, but the postwar emphasis on white labor reflected both the rising cost of postemancipation black labor and the negative memories of wartime dependence by soldiers' families on slave-grown food. Eating food produced by white family labor reestablished traditional boundaries between prewar black and white belt neighborhoods, borders that had been blurred by wartime mobilization, death, and food shortages.[27]

Rejecting black labor even when it was unavailable or unaffordable became white belt declarations of independence from the wartime dependence on slave-grown food. It was a type of communal posturing that united plain folk families not only where field work was concerned, but also in the domestic sphere. As one observer noted of Telfair County in 1874, the "ladies are doing more of their own work, cooking, milking, etc., thus showing themselves independent of negro help." Admittedly, domestic independence from black female labor was in large measure a result of African American women withdrawing from field work and "keeping house" for their own families at the insistence of black men. But among white "ladies" previously accustomed to such help, the decline in black female labor took place within the context of plain folk notions that stressed a domestic economy dependent on white household labor. Thus, the plain folk creed provided a race-conscious rationalization for the decline of black domestic labor, one that crossed class lines and fit white belt perceptions of a restored economic order.[28]

Cotton failed to win the South the diplomatic recognition that it had desperately sought during the Civil War and, despite initially high postwar prices, the prosperity needed to expand economic opportunities for its entire people. Although it made significant inroads in the backwoods during the late antebellum period, the idea of cotton as a first crop, one commanding the primary resources of farmers and one bound for market, had not taken hold. As in the antebellum years, most plain folk continued to raise a little cotton for home consumption in the immediate postwar years. But cotton production for market was considered the bane of these independent-minded citizens. From House Creek in Wilcox County in 1873, one anticotton resident wrote that Southern farmers had "ceased to be a free and independent people"; he placed the blame squarely on "King Cotton," which was rapidly "driving farmers to ruin."[29]

Rather than planting cotton first, postwar plain folk grew corn, peas, potatoes, sugarcane, and oats, and raised cows, hogs, and sheep in an effort to make their households largely self-sufficient in food. Local newspapers repeatedly printed success stories deemed worthy of emulation. In 1873 Manassah Henderson, the former sheriff and secession convention delegate from Irwin County, raised five hundred bushels of corn and two bales of cotton with one horse. Although Henderson dabbled in cotton, there was a clear distinction between his crop mix and those of black belt planters. The way he grew cotton was the important lesson. Rather than buy bacon, corn, and guano from merchants and then mortgage his cotton crop "to pay for it," Henderson raised hogs and corn, produced a small amount of cotton, and walked away from its sale with "clear cash in his pocket," a safety-first course followed by many farmers in his county.[30]

The white belt neighborhoods where many Confederate veterans were born and lived out their lives thus offered the best hope for success through a mix of farming and herding. Impoverished by the war, plain folk were convinced that the restoration of communal honor and a moral economy depended on their own withdrawal from the market as much as practicable. It was impossible, they reasoned, to regain a sense of self-worth while indebted to the Westerners and Northerners who supplied the postwar South with grain and credit. Such a relationship smacked of economic bondage and regional submission to the victors. As one unreconstructed observer wrote to the *Hawkinsville Dispatch* in 1873, "We say, tear up the Western railroads, stop communication with the Yankees, and 'let us starve and go naked,' or be an independent people." Such jeremiads expressed the widespread belief among plain folk that postwar materialism based on outside credit led to greater Southern degredation.[31]

The defining moment in the debate between white and black belt pathways to economic recovery arrived with the panic of 1873, which in the eyes of many plain folk revealed the folly of the crop lien system. Like much of the South, the lower river was already impoverished by the war. The present depression only deepened the hole for those already in debt to merchants and other creditors, who held a property right to farmers' crops as security for loans. A public discourse unfolded on the pages of local newspapers as both editors and their correspondents argued the merits and shortcomings of expanding cotton production or plain folk–style retrenchment, which was not an invention of Bourbon politicians but rather a reflection of the sentiments of plain folk veterans.[32]

The collapse of lines of credit in 1873 convinced plain folk that their non-participation in the crop lien system was the correct course to follow. Merchants advanced cotton farmers supplies against future crops, while the merchants themselves used the crop as collateral to secure the Northern credit required to stock their stores. This was little more than speculating on cotton futures with borrowed money. When the panic of 1873 caused the price of cotton to plummet, planters withheld their crops in the hope that the price would soon rise. That left the merchants stuck in the middle. In "A Last Appeal to Planters" signed by twenty-six Hawkinsville creditors and merchants, the middlemen in the cotton economy offered planters fifteen cents per pound "on your drafts and accounts" due November 1. The "monetary crisis" was beyond their control, they confessed, because Yankee creditors threatened to foreclose on all merchant drafts not paid at maturity. We "hope and beg," the Hawkinsville merchants implored, that the cotton crop would be delivered to their stores and warehouses.[33]

Two days after the merchants' plea appeared in the newspaper, "Ocmulgee" penned a letter to the editor supporting the cotton farmers' case for withholding cotton from the market. Fifteen cents per pound "won't pay him out," wrote "Ocmulgee," who declared that he would not recover his own investment in labor, fertilizer, and supplies at that price. He recalled that Northern speculators had been responsible for the same situation in the late 1850s. "Ocmulgee" suggested cutting "Wall Street" out of the equation altogether in favor of direct trade with Liverpool, a familiar antebellum- and secession-era refrain of Southern free traders. "Holding the crop," he suggested, was a time-honored way for farmers to bargain for better prices and preserve a sense of independence of action, although they were now under the gun to honor their contracts and deliver the cotton on time.[34]

Backwoods plain folk watched this economic crisis and its planter-merchant clash unfold from the relative security of their small farms and reflected on its meaning. It was not lost on them that the farther south one traveled from black belt Pulaski County into the lower counties, the more self-sufficient and secure white households became. The Republic of Irwin ideal seemed immune to the economic chaos brought down on Dixie by greedy Yankee creditors and speculators, money-hungry town merchants, and indebted cotton farmers. Shortly after the depression began, the Wilcox tax collector reported that farmers in his county grew sixty-two bushels of corn per year for every bale of cotton. But downriver in Irwin County, the ratio was just over one hundred bushels of corn per bale. Moreover, planting additional food crops such as sweet potatoes (Irwin produced four times as many sweet potatoes as Wilcox) was largely responsible for the reputation of Irwin's people as "the most thrifty and independent in Georgia."[35]

In light of their willingness to avoid large-scale cotton growing and the conspicuous consumption it engendered, self-sufficient yeoman farmers had little sympathy for those who took the black belt road to indebtedness and ruin. Pulaski County cotton farmers like John Taylor, who sought shelter under the homestead law in "self defense," had simply made poor choices and sold themselves into white servitude. Announcing "To the Public" that he was good for his debts, itself a humbling experience, Taylor needed protection under the law even before the depression hit. For "while money is as scarce as it is now," he informed his neighbors, he would not realize one-half the value of his farm after foreclosure and a sheriff's sale. It was one thing to have fought the war and lost, plain folk argued, but it was another thing entirely for Confederate veterans such as Taylor to survive the conflict, fall into the crop lien trap, and lose their home—the symbol of so much fighting and dying—while chasing cotton dollars. There were economic and moral connections between Confederate sacrifice and plain folk independence that the crop lien system severed by its necessary submission to Yankee creditors and the "bondage" of indebtedness that followed. John Taylor's family was now as unprotected in the marketplace as it had been when he went to the Virginia front.[36]

Growing food crops with white labor on family-owned land was the plain folk's way of upholding an alternative to Victorian mass production and consumption and its regional manifestation—the cotton culture. Moreover, plain folk anti-Yankee rhetoric, race consciousness, and war memories shaped something akin to a collective Southern white nationalism. Rejecting the cotton economy was critical if the war's sacrifices were to be honored through the preservation of the home place—all that was left for many Confederate veterans. Cotton farmers like John Taylor and merchants such as those at Hawkinsville quickly found themselves owing someone else money and losing their independence, one of the goals of secession and the war, in the bargain.[37]

This is not to say that Confederate veterans with some means and reputation, notably ex-officers such as John Pate, failed to get ahead by dealing goods to cotton farmers. Trading on his prewar status as a storekeeper and small planter and on his war record as a company-grade and regimental officer in the 49th Georgia, Major Pate paid cash for his stock of dry goods and took in as much as $7,000 in trade by the close of 1866. Described as a "popular & reliable" Hawkinsville businessman who commanded "a large share of trade," he held his own in good times and bad. Even after the depression deepened, Pate managed to prosper, an observer reporting in 1878 that his company's financial condition was "better than it has been at any time here. Hear of no trouble at all." But Pate was far luckier than his planter and secessionist neighbor Cornelius Bozeman, with whom he briefly operated a cotton warehouse after the war. Unlike Pate, Bozeman, a soldiers' father and home-front patriarch, became deeply involved in postwar cotton speculation and was "completely used up" by the spring of 1875.[38]

Even in white belt counties, some unfortunate men learned the hard lessons that came with living on borrowed money. Matthew Kirkland, for example, ran a successful store in Coffee County during the antebellum period and did well prior to the panic of 1873. At the time he was known as a "reliable and worthy" man who "stands well" in the community. As the depression wore on, however, Kirkland's business reputation slipped despite the fact that he owned considerable land and livestock, the traditional ways to wealth. It was noted that although he was still considered "an experienced and safe" businessman, he was "somewhat involved owing to crediting but has come out all right." This was an overly optimistic forecast. By the summer of 1878 Kirkland was "badly behind" on payments to three Savannah creditors for his store stock. Moreover, he "refuses to pay them anything," a local man declared. The once solid and reliable Kirkland was now considered "unreliable," and the only property he could call his own was nonbusiness-related assets "covered" by a homestead exemption. Now "very much embarrassed & regarded as utterly insolvent," the storekeeper was sued by his creditors and declared "virtually broke & on the verge of failure." Ten months later Matthew Kirkland closed up shop.[39]

If gentlemen of high standing such as Bozeman and Kirkland fell victim to the whims of the marketplace, what chance did the plain folk have? Better to retreat into the safety of the Republic of Irwin ideal, to live in self-sufficiency and republican simplicity, than to become the victim of a fickle cotton market. After all, theirs was a rural world where thrifty, hardworking individuals like Reason Paulk grew 120 bushels of sweet potatoes on one acre of land. It was a world that prided itself on self-sufficiency and the continuity of people in place. In 1873 Jacob Paulk Sr., a former Irwin County small planter, harvested his fifty-first crop on the same ground, himself still "stout and firm" and his thirty-year-old mule "Old Beck" as up for another year in the fields as her seventy-eight-year-old owner.[40]

Plain folk cries for household self-sufficiency and personal accountability had political as well as economic implications. The homestead provision of the new state constitution of 1868 drew the most fire. Although Republicans in northern Georgia and the plantation counties viewed the provision as class legislation that protected indebted small farmers and freedpeople and supported the measure, radical Governor Rufus Bullock received little support in wiregrass counties such as Irwin. The yeomanry drew clear distinctions between homestead exemptions that truly protected needy rural families from those that provided shelter for risk-taking cotton farmers and overextended merchants. "No man should be allowed to homestead on ten head of mules, five hundred acres of land, a crib of corn, even if his cotton will not pay him out," declared the *Hawkinsville Dispatch* one year after the depression began. "We are opposed to lien laws, usury laws, homestead laws, and all other laws that benefit one man and injure another," the newspaper wrote, noting that lien laws favored merchants and guano dealers and "placed the farmers completely in the power of venders of fertilizers and retailers of corn and bacon at ruinous prices." Such views were widely held among the plain folk. The General Assembly, now removed to more distant Atlanta against plain folk wishes, flexed its political muscle and created legal shelters that encouraged small farmers to risk planting cotton on credit. But as farmers like John Taylor realized too late, the crop lien system was the pathway to ruin.[41]

Moreover, in white belt neighborhoods there were often faith-based reasons for plain folk denunciations of homestead, lien, and usury laws. Indeed, using homestead laws as a "means of sustaining life," even for the "helpless and dependent families of improvident unfortunate debtors," was antithetical to Primitive Baptist religious doctrine. Primitive antihomesteaders believed that borrowers were the submissive servants of lenders and their independence and reputations suffered in the bargain, as Matthew Kirkland learned the hard way. "Taking the homestead," as invoking the exemption was called, was a breach of financial contract and a violation of their notions of integrity. Moreover, it displayed a lack of faith in God's ability to care for His chosen flock as biblically promised. Men who "take shelter from troublesome but honest debts under its protection" were brought before the church conference to explain their actions. If the elders could not reach a judgment, a committee from a neighboring church was called in to render a verdict, which could include excommunication.[42]

The Republic of Irwin ideal gave meaning and order to the plain folk's wartime suffering. Their postwar struggle for economic independence required the same sacrifices as the fight for Southern independence. And it included a place for women. For just as the virtuous soldier's wife kept the home fires burning during the war, her busy hands would help see the postwar household through the exertions ahead. One local newspaper painted a moving word picture of such a plain folk family. Emerging from the forest rode "the independent and honest owner of a one-horse cart" with his "cleanly" dressed wife seated amid country produce and "choice table supplies." These models of republican simplicity and virtue entered the market on their own terms, trading surplus farm produce for the few items they could not make at home. Such self-sufficiency was, an observer declared, "like the cloud of Elijah . . . the ONLY HOPE of this section of the State." Such was the plain folk exemplar.[43]

A key word in the plain folk critique of the crop lien path to postwar recovery was "appearances," but appearances clearly at odds with that of the humble farming couple. To common Confederate veterans and their families, those who suffered most from wartime privation, appearances meant a hollow outward show of wealth. Conspicuous consumption among antebellum planters had became more evident during the 1850s in black belt neighborhoods; it was reflected in the Greek revival architecture of planter churches and houses, better education for their children, robust evangelicalism, and homes filled with Victorian furnishings. Such conspicuous consumption distanced planters from plain folk, who understood that elite appearances were based on access to slave labor. This unflattering image of planter privilege did not improve during the war as soldiers' families became more dependent on slave-grown food sold at government rates. It was this world of cotton, black labor, and Northern credit that postwar planters attempted to revive and expand under a "new order" with troubling implications for plain folk.[44]

Emblematic of the new order were black families settled on small tracts of less than fifty acres. They grew cotton on shares for white landlords and made possible planterly "appearances." Although small cotton farmers such as veteran John Taylor lost their land because of cotton farming on credit, antebellum planters exhibited an uncanny ability to keep their land even during the economic chaos that followed the war. Major John Pate and Captain Ruel Anderson, another antebellum master and ex-Confederate officer, were among Pulaski County's leading cotton planters at the time of the 1873 panic. Examples of planters who negotiated with former slaves to create what amounted to landless black plain folk, the level to which John Taylor slipped, were not hard to find, nor were their lessons lost on white plain folk. Lovett Harrell, described as one of Pulaski's "most thorough and practical planters," had divided his old plantation into "small farms . . . cultivated by his former slaves on their own account." The freed slaves were "doing well." Such descriptions of small farmers working on their own account and doing well had traditionally been applied to the white yeomanry, not to blacks who in slavery belonged to a laboring mudsill defined by their skin color.[45]

True, there were limits to the prosperity enjoyed by such African Americans. Plain folk chuckled at the fate of Zeno Powell, a "colored planter" whose failed business left $100 in liabilities and assets described as "one old blind mule, a bob tail coon dog and a frying pan." But the free labor system created for Powell and many others by freed slaves, planters, and their creditors had frightening implications for plain folk notions of self-sufficiency. Indeed, the model farm and household for ex-slaves such as Powell was the white yeoman's small estate. If former slaves could be elevated to a status resembling that of white plain folk, then Confederate veterans and their families could be lowered to Powell's—the mudsill in a crop lien world. It was a warning that Governor Brown repeatedly returned to during the secession crisis and the Civil War to stir up the yeomanry. Emancipation blurred the boundaries between the privileges and rights of black and white men, threatening to make them all submissive hewers of wood.[46]

In 1866 Anaca Phillips gave her affidavit to the Freedmen's Bureau agent at Hawkinsville while he was investigating an incident between Epson Phillips, a former slave, and Exum Phillips, one of Pulaski County's leading planters. Anaca testified that she overheard an argument between Exum Phillips and his hired hand Epson when Epson returned from Macon to the Phillips plantation. When the planter questioned his absence, Epson said "that he was as free a man as he [Exum] was." The planter then asked: "If I should strike you would you desire to strike me?" Epson said yes and repeated, "I am as free as you are." The white man responded: "If you are as free as I am your freedom will not do you much good." When Epson announced that he was going to Macon again, the planter entered his house, got his gun, and followed him down the road. The verbal sparring between freedpeople and their former masters symbolized their search for new identities as slaves without masters and masters without slaves. Epson knew that freedom meant he could go where he pleased. Exum, who had owned almost fifty slaves only a year earlier, recognized that emancipation had devalued both his authority and his sense of self-worth.[47]

As one Union officer observed along the Ocmulgee River in the summer of 1865: "I find that the negro much sooner understands and more readily accepts his status than does the former master . . . the greatest trouble being in convincing the planter that he is no longer slave-holder, and can no longer whip and chase with bloodhounds freemen he once called chattel property." Whatever increased tolerance Southerners may have shown toward slaves who supported the Confederate cause out of military necessity was quickly lost in defeat.[48]

The good news of emancipation usually reached slaves in the familiar voice of owners and overseers. In cases where Yankee soldiers directed masters to call their slaves together and free them, the master submitted and his or her authority was immediately diminished. Caroline Malloy learned of the new order when her mistress Fanny Brown "came to her and told her that she was free and had to work for no one unless she was paid for it." Martha Everette, a slave of James Lathrop, remembered: "When th' war wuz over th' overseers tole us we wuz free an' could go whar we pleased." One child remembered the emancipated slaves singing "I Am Glad Salvation Is Free for Us All." As Sara Crocker recalled, "The slaves were glad to be freed and many of the women began to sing songs of praise." Owning their own labor and enjoying a freedom of motion beyond their master's supervision were the immediate fruits of emancipation enjoyed by formerly enslaved African Americans in the summer of 1865.[49]

For white planters, however, the ideal postwar agricultural laborer was a dutiful, pliant worker who toiled for years on the same estate without causing trouble. Rejecting the reality that confronted them in the person of ex-slaves like Epson Phillips, they created the perfect worker in their imaginations. "A Model Freedman" became a postwar version of the antebellum "trusty," a faithful but liberated "Uncle Tom." In 1877 the *Hawkinsville Dispatch* believed that it had found such a freedman in Richmond Phillips. Phillips had worked diligently on the property of Madison Snell, an antebellum small planter, for nine years. During that time he had not "neglected his duty a day" or traveled to town a single time, perhaps more an indication of the extent of his dependence on his employer for food, shelter, and clothing than of his willingness to stay put. Isolated on his employer's cotton plantation, Phillips took care of Snell's crops and livestock. His service was characterized by one word—"faithfulness."[50]

Perhaps the newspaper's editor publicized the example of Richmond Phillips because of its exceptional nature and its potential as an exemplar for freedpeople. But the world of postwar social relationships was not a stable place, as former master Exum Phillips learned. Ex-slaves freely traveled the landscape in search of kinfolk, more favorable living arrangements, and the best working conditions. They sought to be as independent of planter supervision as plain folk sought to be independent of the cotton marketplace. Writing to the editor of the *Georgia Weekly Telegraph* from Hawkinsville early in 1866, "Orion" noted that few white farmers and planters had actually succeeded in keeping "according to contract, the freemen whom he has employed." Black workers were a fluid group of people who moved from place to place, "pretending to desire employment." As a result, "Orion" predicted that the 1866 cotton crop would amount to only one-third of the last prewar crop at best "even if the freedmen work."[51]

What most blacks wanted was what most white plain folk possessed before the war—freedom from supervision, land of their own, and access to the open range. Their failure to achieve these fundamental symbols of freedom was reflected by the almost routine violence that marked the end of yet another failed contract between white employers and freed slaves. In a familiar postwar scenario, freedman Henry Whitaker was ordered off the plantation of his employer in 1868 in a dispute over wages and rations. Whitaker complained to the Freedmen's Bureau agent at Hawkinsville that his landlord "threatened to shoot him" if he "did not deliver up the goods" he drew. Whitaker sought to have his contract annulled because he now had "no peace on the place."[52]

Like the Confederate veterans who returned home, freed slaves sought to shape their own sense of self-worth in a world where, as one Yankee officer put it, the "revolution is so complete, the change so radical, that it seems impossible for them [whites] to comprehend it." Nevertheless, ex-slaves sought a place of peace where they could create a personal domain that extended outward to include their family and property. With the exception of the black town elite, most often represented by former free persons of color at places such as Hawkinsville, most African Americans did not own land. Isolated in the countryside like Richmond Phillips and cut off from the legal and political centers of power, they were surrounded by whites of all classes who clung to "a hope that something will yet turn up which will give them at least a life lease of slavery."[53]

Given the institution's legacy of brutality, racism, sexual abuse, stereotyping, and violence, developing a sense of self-worth was no easy task for former slaves. Under slavery, African Americans had been denied the customs and laws that protected them from violation by whites. Indeed, their bodies, labor, and time, their productive and reproductive capacities, all belonged to white masters. Once freedom came, ex-masters were reluctant to see their former property enjoy the action and language that expressed their liberation. Although beatings and killings were frequently reported to Freedmen's Bureau agents, the daily layering of insults, slights, and stereotypes debilitated the human spirit. The character of African Americans was routinely assaulted both verbally and in the press: two freedmen fighting before church services were "yaller sassy niggers"; the lower river's most prominent black highwayman—Mingo Baker—was little more than a "Wild African"; preacher Daniel Harris, accused of looting another freedman's smokehouse, was a "ginger cake mulatto"; and the stolen cow last seen crossing Big Creek was "in charge of a tall, black negro." Whether community leaders or thieves, freed slaves were repeatedly tarred with the same racist brush.[54]

Within this chaotic and hostile environment, former slaves created networks of security through stronger family ties. Ironically, white plain folk and blacks both entered the postwar years with broken or incomplete families. For some freedpeople, the foundation of their postwar households began with preexisting antebellum families. Slaves' conjugal unions had had no legal protection and were recognized by their masters only so long as it was convenient for the operation of farms and plantations and maintained morale. After the war, however, many black couples formally legalized their preexisting relationship. As Easter Reed explained, she had been "keepin' comp'ny" with another slave owned by her master Alfred Burnham, "so when they were freed, they married." On the other hand, Arthur Colson did not marry until 1869, after about a year of courtship in which he competed with "many other beaux" for the hand of his wife.[55]

Others attempted to reunite broken families, a process that accelerated as white masters such as Seaborn Manning died during the war. Reuniting families represented a strong emotional quest for many freedpeople. Sallie Manning bought a small house in town and saved enough money to return to Virginia to find "her people," but it took over ten years before she could make the trip. In 1877 she traveled to her old home to "view the scenes of her early days and mingle with those she knew" more than thirty years after she had been sold into Georgia. It was a bittersweet journey. "Nobody peared to know me," she recalled, learning that her old master was dead. However, little "missus," now a grown woman, fondly remembered "Mammy Sally." She also found her first husband, since remarried, though not her son by him. "But my boy—I'se never seen him yit. Da say he went to 'Orleans." Sallie returned to Hawkinsville satisfied that "I'se seen de old country and de folks." For some slaves, new family relationships were necessary because old kinship ties had been lost. Caroline Malloy had been given to one of her master's daughters as a wedding present when she was "a very small child." Although told she belonged to a slave family of fifteen, Caroline had "no recollection of any members of her family" because of their separation during her infancy.[56]

By the late 1860s freedmen like William Stokes, a Pulaski County farm laborer, had created though marriage and childbirth the clearly defined nuclear family that characterized the antebellum era. Fifty years of age in 1870, Stokes had married Martha, who was fifteen years younger than him. Five years after the war, their household consisted of five children ranging from one to fourteen years of age. Four of the five children had been born into slavery, either to them as a couple or to one or both through prior unions. Like their father, fourteen-year-old Woodley and twelve-year-old Clara worked as farm laborers. The Freedmen's Bureau regarded husbands like Stokes as heads of households and held them responsible for making labor contracts for all family members, thus reinforcing traditional white views of the family as a patriarchal institution.[57]

It was in the fields that former masters and former slaves negotiated the new terms of free labor. Ex-slaveowners sought to continue the master's prerogatives into the postwar years, often with violent results. Freedman Silas Walters "ran a couple of white men out of their field" with a singletree. During the following year he was shot in the stomach after repeatedly attacking a white man with a hoe. Walters may have worked in "their field," but there were stark boundaries between white supervision and black sense of self-worth that, when crossed, were violently resisted by blacks.[58]

Nowhere was the determination to escape white male domination and construct black male dominion more clearly demonstrated than in regards to black women. Slave women worked as field hands alongside slave men, a fact that set them apart from elite white women, but which gave them much in common with the wives of plain folk, particularly during the Civil War when white manpower dwindled. In the postwar years, however, black men, motivated in part by memories of the sexual abuse of slave women, tried to spare their women from field work to avoid white male supervision and sexual exploitation. It became a mark of manly honor and pride for a freedman such as William Stokes to list his wife's occupation as "keeps house" under his own roof. Black women also viewed domesticity in terms of greater control over their own lives, rather than merely acquiescing to the wishes of their husbands. Stokes's wife Martha cooked, cleaned house, washed clothes, sewed, and cared for sons Charles, Andrew, and Samuel, all under the age of ten, while William and his older children Woodley and Clara worked in the fields. Thus black women were, to some extent, removed from the marketplace and created a labor shortage that benefited the negotiating position of black men.[59]

The desire of black men and women to extend the Victorian cult of domesticity to black females, to reshape their roles in the postwar world within rural household space rather than in cotton fields, was widespread in the South. Black preachers and politicians espoused their cause. An 1869 Colored Labor Convention at Macon, one that found Hawkinsville's Reverend Robert Anderson opening the third day's session with a prayer, took up the issue of black women and agricultural labor. Citing the "teachings" of both the Bible and nature as authority, the convention condemned "females performing field labor of the same kind and quantity as that performed by men." In the interest of "improved and hardy posterity," the delegates called for a gendered division of labor where field work was concerned, beseeching black men to "take their wives and daughters from the drudgery and exposure of plantation toil as soon as it is in their power to do so." Freedom and manhood demanded that black men liberate black women from the vestiges of plantation slavery and its legacy of exploitation by white men.[60]

Husbands such as William Stokes thus saw domestic work as a form of protection for women and children, particularly young girls. The desire to instill the major elements of the cult of domesticity in black girls led to working arrangements that ironically placed them outside black households and beyond the supervision of black parents. In what became a frequent arrangement, the thirteen-year-old daughter of former slave Agnes Anderson was contracted out by freedman Henry Patton, her stepfather and the head of his household, as domestic help in merchant Simon Merritt's Hawkinsville home. In early 1867 Agnes's daughter went to work for the Merritts in exchange "for the board and clothing of said girl only." Instead of being paid wages, her parents desired that she "learn to cook, wash, & do other necessary work about the house correctly" because the child possessed no skills beyond those of a field hand. Presumably this arrangement would teach her the domestic arts, train her as a domestic servant for hire, and prepare her to be a wife and homemaker.[61]

This form of apprenticeship, however, was fraught with possibilities for abuse and misunderstanding. Henry Patton later sought remuneration for his stepdaughter's work for the Merritts despite their previous agreement. He claimed that "you [Simon Merritt] refuse to make any settlement for her time." Similar cases were brought before the Freedman's Bureau agent at Hawkinsville. In 1868 ex-slave Judith McGriff accused her daughter's white employer of refusing to "give her her Freedom." Ellen Phillips, who agreed to hire out her daughter Nancy Mims in exchange for "victuals & clothes," complained that Mims was not given "one cent" by her white employer, who had moved to Macon County. Phillips now feared that he "will take her daughter North with him."[62]

Like African American men, black women sought the meaning of freedom in the postemancipation South. They shared the sense of powerlessness that slaves felt regardless of gender. The Freedmen's Bureau recognized black men as heads of households, and freedmen voted and even held political office—all rights that freedwomen did not possess. Black women did not unquestioningly exchange submission to white men for black male authority. The evidence of their unwillingness to blindly yield to black patriarchy surfaced repeatedly in court records and in the Freedmen's Bureau office. In 1875, for example, Jim Cowart and his wife went before the mayor's court at Hawkinsville "for not living together as man and wife should live." Cowart's wife "wanted to wear the breeches, and because Jim objected, she proceeded to give him a genteel flogging." When Mary Proctor was caught by her husband in a "bad act" with a white steamboat captain, she continued to see him despite her husband's protests. Their marriage ended in divorce.[63]

All too often, however, physical abuse was the result of such disputes, as black women repeatedly experienced violence or abandonment at the hands of black men. In 1868 Amanda Willcox charged that her husband Thomas Rountree left her and their children and took up with another woman. Moreover, Rountree and the other woman had beaten and otherwise mistreated her. Willcox also complained that the children "is his," that she was unable to support them, and that Rountree had not come home, although the Freedmen's Bureau agent had ordered him to return to his "lawful wife." Lavania Williams, on the other hand, discovered to her horror that her husband had "pawned articles" to pay his jail fees and court costs. She learned this only after his death when a white creditor hauled away her bed clothes, clothing, and furniture. Missouri Johnson complained that freedman Abraham Dennis threw sticks at her and drove her off a plantation "by violence." He refused to allow her to "to go home but threatens to kill her." After the Freedmen's Bureau ruled against Dennis and fined him $7.50, Pulaski County's white superior court announced that "these trials and cases are out [of] the Bureaus jurisdiction" and directed that the money be returned to Dennis.[64]

As these cases indicate, black families accumulated material possessions, including beds and bedding, clothing, and furniture, in addition to the belongings they brought out of slavery. These items were a part of their personal domain and gave them a sense of self-worth. Therefore, their loss represented a serious setback. In 1868 Charles Taylor, Pulaski County's largest antebellum planter, went to the house of Lauria Williams and "did seize by force" many of her possessions to settle a debt of her husband's. Taylor hauled away 3 bedsteads and mattresses, 7 chairs, a dining table, 140 pounds of pork, and a horse. At day's end she did not have a bed to sleep on.[65]

In places such as Hawkinsville, the property often included real estate, especially if the African Americans were merchants or skilled workers. Black-owned land was the key to escaping white supervision. It formed the core of any lasting sense of household dominion and stability among the emerging black plain folk, just as it was for white plain folk, but for most it proved illusive. By the mid-1870s, however, Adam and Marshall McGehee, two of Hawkinsville's most prominent African Americans, owned more property than many white plain folk. Adam ran a general store and Marshall was a carpenter. Each man owned an estimated $1,200 in real estate; Adam also claimed $600 stock in trade and $150 in cash. The ownership of land and personal property had a direct bearing on how African Americans viewed themselves and on how whites viewed them. It was noted in 1875, for example, that Buck Matthews, the owner of a general store at Hawkinsville, "owns a house & lot" and was considered "a good steady Negroe."[66]

In new railroad towns like Cochran, located in eastern Pulaski County on the Macon and Brunswick line, risk-taking blacks moved their families from agricultural settings and created new lives for themselves. By 1870 Richard Childs, a "wood-workman," owned $400 in real estate and lived in his own home with his wife Emma and four children. Jonathan F. Daily, whose employment was listed as "Section hand on R R," owned no land but claimed $500 in personal property five years after the war ended. His wife Martha kept house and his son Jonathan Jr. worked as a farm laborer. Together, they diversified the household income by combining agricultural and railroad labor.[67]

Although some black families took risks by uprooting themselves and moving to town, the majority remained mired in the countryside. To some extent, the power of place and the conservative nature of agricultural life exerted an influence over former slaves, just as it did over white plain folk. Both groups tended to farm the fields and hunt the woodlands they knew best. As former slave Arthur Colson later said: "I 'members that plantation better'n any place on this earth." That memory included the restrictions of the pass system, a kindly but paternalistic master, food rations, and patrollers. Freedom forced Colson to choose between the world beyond the plantation and the only "home" he knew. Ultimately, the negative reminders of slavery were not powerful enough to drive him away. After working for his former master for about a year after emancipation, his mother "hired him to another white man living in the same community." But Colson "went back to his own home after a few months and remained with his master for many years." He recalled that "most of the slaves remained with him for several years." Doubtless some stayed because they became bogged down in the crop lien system, but as Colson's experience indicates, others chose to stay in a familiar and paternalistic place rather than strike out across an increasingly violent landscape.[68]

Arthur Colson's story does not suggest that postwar plantation life, with its bitter memories of agricultural bondage, was better than freedom narratives that unfolded elsewhere. But it does imply that in an impoverished and violent landscape of "misery and want," antebellum familiarity with place and people held a powerful sway over some freedpeople. Easter Reed continued to work on Alfred Burnham's farm for about two years before moving to a nearby plantation; afterward she "would often go back to visit her 'white fokes' and help . . . with their work." Paternalism, despite its debilitating dependencies, was better than the vigilante justice meted out by the faceless gangs of white men who roamed the roads and woods. Plantations could mean safety in terms of black people living together, as well as the knowledge that some white landlords, especially antebellum "white fokes" with familiar faces and temperaments, still held paternalistic attitudes toward their former slaves.[69]

In 1870 Catherine Williamson, at age fifty, continued to run her deceased husband's plantation that was striking in the continuity of its labor force. Antebellum field hands Alex, Jack, Jim, and Sam—all in their prime in the mid-1850s—were still working there five years after emancipation, as were former slave women Hannah, Nancy, and Rose. Like their white landlord, they were country people who worked the land, but now as freedpeople they lived in clearly discernible and legal households. Alex and Rose, for instance, had nine children under the age of eighteen, five of them born into slavery and four into freedom. What they shared with others who lived on the Williamson place, and elsewhere for that matter, was no property of record. Landownership, so critical to a sense of self-worth among white plain folk, was largely missing among rural blacks such as those who remained on the Williamson plantation.[70]

This was certainly true of William Stokes, who owned no real or personal property despite five years of hard work as a free man. Nine years after emancipation, he finally purchased an ox for $25 and seed for corn, cotton, and vegetables. Virtually everyone in his family worked on land owned by someone else. Although his wife Martha listed her occupation as "keeps house," she guided the draft animal as it opened the cotton beds. Their eleven-year-old daughter dropped in the seed, and two sons aged nine and twelve pulled a plow behind them while the "old man" carefully guided it along to cover the seed. In 1874 the Stokes family produced five "heavy bales" of cotton, one hundred bushels of corn, and enough potatoes and peas to feed themselves. After hiring himself out to hoe, pick cotton, and "run the farm" of his landlord, Stokes finished the year with $15 "over in cash," better than many tenants and sharecroppers. His was the fate that many white plain folk feared would become the war's final legacy for them if the crop lien system were to expand unchecked.[71]

Indeed, a tenant of planter Robert Anderson Sr. produced in one year 10½ bales of cotton, 214 bushels of corn, 75 bushels of potatoes, and 5 stacks of fodder with a single plow horse. By all accounts he was a model freedman in Anderson's eyes, a hard and steady worker helped by a family of cotton choppers and pickers. But the black tenant bought a horse on credit for $180, and his year's supply of provisions and guano, along with his rent, which was half the cotton crop, left him $50 short "of paying out." There were clear trade-offs, then, for the familiarity and relative safety of postwar plantations. Their owners demanded that every able-bodied laborer, regardless of age or gender, work the fields for long hours and for little reward. Compared to freedmen who took the risk of relocating in town, the reward for agricultural labor was almost always something short "of paying out."[72]

The families of both Confederate veterans and former enslaved African

Americans struggled to make ends meet in a war-impoverished region during the postwar years. Ex-Confederates and ex-slaves struggled to build a personal domain that gave them a sense of self-worth. Both groups had been beaten down: Confederates on the battlefield and home front by the war and slaves by institutionalized racial slavery. Enslaved African Americans had been the traditional benchmarks by which white plain folk measured their economic, political, and social standing. Their elevated sense of self-worth was dependent on the degraded condition imposed on blacks as white people's property, but that was changing.[73]

E arly in January 1871 planters and plain folk put on one of Hawkinsville's largest public rituals: a mock funeral procession that put Reconstruction to rest. Walking slowly at the head of the line was a band playing a funeral dirge, followed by a dray. Sitting on the dray was a large black coffin. Suspended from the coffin's foot was a carpetbag, "the last relic of the departed sinner." Pulling the coffin toward the town limits was a ponderous mule named "Old Logan," his step "firm and proud." A large crowd of emotional followers who nonetheless shed no tears brought up the rear. Altogether it was, according to the editor of the *Hawkinsville Dispatch*, a "never-to-be-forgotten occasion" summed up with a pronouncement befitting a coroner: "The deceased came to his death at the hands of his foe—Honesty and Integrity—known as the Democracy."[1]

One week later the *Dispatch*'s editor offered proof of the extent to which Radicalism had been vanquished from the lower river. In a recent election voters in Coffee, Irwin, and Telfair Counties had "covered themselves in glory." Of the 1,386 ballots cast, only 13 Radical votes were counted. It was a matter of honor that "not a Radical in the county" was printed next to the returns for Coffee and Irwin, the core of the "Republic of Irwin" territory. In language reminiscent of a battlefield salute, the editor declared: "We lift our hat . . . to the gallant Democracy of the wire grass region." Defeated on the battlefield, Confederate veterans came home, won the violent struggle for home rule, and erased one of the major political consequences of Union victory—the black vote. The significance of plain folk votes transcended their own local contests, for the huge white majorities in the wiregrass region offset black votes in Georgia's cotton belt.[2]

The mock funeral was one of many public and private rituals that collectively reflected plain folk rejection of Radicalism. Southern nationalism on a more modest scale outlived the Confederacy's death in a region where localism remained strong. It was resurrected in a postwar political culture that embraced secessionists' desires for white liberty and regional identity along with traditional plain folk notions of white supremacy, public virtue, and religion. The mock funeral's symbolism was not lost on soldiers' families. Ironically, there was no body in the coffin Old Logan hauled off at the end of the rites. Many of their brothers, fathers, and sons were lost in a war that ended in defeat. Preserving the vote for white men while denying it for freedmen validated their Confederate dead.[3]

More important to whites, however, was the knowledge that what they had truly buried was a political doctrine that espoused social and political equality for blacks. The Confederacy had fought a bloody war in defense of slavery. As one local veteran put it years later, the war was about slavery and little else. Keeping blacks in their place in the social hierarchy was central to plain folk ideology. Their brand of racism bordered on Negrophobia. They had little use for the paternalist-conservative form of racism put forth by New South elites who were dependent on black labor, because that combination expanded postwar economic development into the piney woods. Radical ideals also threatened the plain folk's conservative notions of how society was structured and who should participate in its governance as full citizens. The Union soldiers' sacrifices, the Yankees' victory parades, and emancipation's political consequences were all ceremoniously hauled off and buried on that day in early January 1871.[4]

Reconstruction is often described as a violent and conservative white reaction to Radical goals of black social and political equality based on seemingly instinctive forces of racism and anti-Radicalism. In this scenario, white people's racism largely explains the outbursts of "arbitrary violence" aimed at freedpeople and their white Republicans allies. But racism and violence were not new to the postwar South. These evils had made slavery possible. Moreover, if racism and anti-Radicalism were adequate historical explanations for such postwar violence, then it would have taken place on a similar scale elsewhere, just as antebellum antiabolitionist mob violence had known no geographic boundaries.[5]

What was unique to the South was the Confederate defeat and postwar efforts by Republicans to displace a tenacious Southern patriarchy using the votes of emancipated slaves organized into their own paramilitary units. The plain folk reaction resembled "a traditional folk movement aimed at upholding the white community's moral standards." Whites used violence to call into question the very legitimacy of Reconstruction, for a government that failed to protect its citizens from freedmen, carpetbaggers, and scalawags was no government at all. This was a lesson former Confederates learned the hard way as they had watched Yankees undermine the Confederacy's legitimacy by exposing its civilians to the hard war. Just as the North waged war on civilians, so too did the plain folk wage a campaign of political terrorism against the foremost human symbols of Yankee victory—freedpeople.[6]

But some "legitimizing notion," to use E. P. Thompson's words, informed white participants that the "outrages" they committed were community-sanctioned defenses of traditional white beliefs of what a good society should look like. Thus, "outrages," a word used by Radicals to describe the beatings and killings meted out to freedmen and white Republicans, was equally employed in the discourse of Southern whites. They used the term to describe what they considered an equally offensive act committed by a victorious North against Southern white notions of what was right and proper in civil society, namely, advancement of the black vote. Rather than arbitrary or random violence, white popular reaction against Radicalism had clear objectives. Foremost among these was the protection of a white patriarchy now assumed by the veterans themselves. This struggle took place within the context of what white people considered appropriate behavior of voters and political parties in a moral society.[7]

The plain folk's moral economy was deeply rooted in their assumptions of what constituted a legitimate body politic. To their way of thinking, honest and economically independent white freeholders were the bedrock of any country republican government. On the eve of the Civil War, Georgia had been one of the most democratic states in the Lower South. Property qualifications for voting were dropped, although voters were expected to pay taxes required by the state constitution. Most white males of the voting age of twenty-one or older were carried on voter lists, and a sense of white egalitarianism prevailed. Such people were judged, in the words of Governor Joseph

Brown, to be "competent for self-government." Positive feelings of self-worth were reinforced among white males by membership in a restricted body politic that excluded women and blacks. Only white men who exhibited "virtue and intelligence" deserved to vote in a culture shaped by concepts of male honor and masculinity. Thus, on the county level, the consent of the governed depended on the votes of a few dozen white men on the election district level and a few hundred men on the county level. Moreover, political tradition held that it was the right and duty of these white men—indeed, their moral obligation—to remove an oppressive government by any means necessary, including insurrection.[8]

Plain folk also had firm ideas about what a Radical overthrow of local government would mean, namely, the degradation of white civil society. Because only honest, intelligent, and virtuous white male freeholders deserved to vote, plain folk believed that former slaves, whom they regarded as innately inferior and morally bankrupt, were unfit for self-government. In fact, according to Joseph Brown, history illumined that "a republican government can only be maintained upon the basis of domestic slavery." To define "the term people to include the whole people and to permit every class, white and black indiscriminately, to exercise political rights," Brown argued, was setting a course for social chaos similar to France in the wake of the French Revolution.[9]

Fighting and losing the Civil War necessarily imposed a certain measure of moral degradation on the plain folk, as their landscape reflected, but to allow white government to be destroyed by Radicals further eroded their concepts of honor, masculinity, and self-worth. After all, Radicals proposed to replace Southern paternalism with a Northern version that viewed white Southerners as wayward children deserving punishment and incapable of self-government without military occupation. The threat of losing home rule united white men of varied backgrounds—secessionist, Confederate, anti-Confederate, and unionist—in a new struggle between localism and nationalism. These men belonged to the voluntary local defense companies that first protected the home front in the war's waning months and then practiced vigilantism to restore postwar order.[10]

In 1865 and 1866, however, it was political business as usual in Georgia, where voting was limited to free white men. The political culture was still based on networks of white families and neighborhood party tradition, although wartime deaths had thinned out the voters. The white patriarchy continued to rule the county courts, and plain folk returned men with proven leadership qualities to the General Assembly, including their former Confederate officers.

These men shared a unique worldview shaped by their wartime experiences and their postwar status as defeated Confederate veterans. In Pulaski County, veterans and their kin sent Charles Kibbee, former captain of the Georgia Rangers, to the state legislature. Downriver Oliver Cook, a former planter and a lieutenant colonel in the 49th Georgia Regiment, was reelected to the General Assembly in unionist Irwin County. And in Coffee County, an anti-Confederate stronghold early in 1865, Major John Spence, an infantry company commander and regimental officer in the 50th Georgia, won a seat in the state legislature a few years after Appomattox. As legislators, ex-Confederates passed laws that relegated freedmen to second-class citizenship.[11]

The year 1867 thus opened with conservative whites in control of the political landscape and the plain folk's political culture seemingly secure despite the Confederate defeat. Early in the year, however, Radical Republicans took control of Reconstruction and imposed martial law in much of the South. In Georgia, as a part of the Third Military District, military rule was restored, and the state returned to the status it had held when the Confederacy fell in 1865—a defeated military province. The Reconstruction Acts demanded that Georgia include freedmen in a new body politic and enroll freedmen on voter lists. Just over 100,000 whites and just under 100,000 blacks were enrolled in Georgia by federally appointed registrars. Within a single year Radicals created a new and divided political culture based on race, different memories of the past, and radically different visions of the future.[12]

In May 1867 African Americans in Georgia created their own Republican Party and launched a campaign to form local Grant Clubs and Union Leagues, the grassroots foundation of the state's new party. Although the formation of Republican clubs and the continued politicization of former slaves most commonly occurred in cities and towns under the protection of the Union army, such activities took place in rural areas as well. A "union Ligue" was established at Hawkinsville and Dykesboro in Pulaski and at Dublin in neighboring Laurens County, where George Linder served as president, although one member who was attacked by whites thought that Linder "leans altogether [toward] the whites & the whites is geting very contrary." Along the lower river, 3,635 black and white voters were enrolled that year. Fifty-four percent of them lived in Pulaski County, which was also home to the largest black population and the greatest number of local Confederate veterans. There, the registration of freedmen reached 1,131 voters compared to 839 whites, which potentially gave Radicals political control of the wealthiest and most populous county. Freedmen and Republicans had nothing to win by embracing the conservative leadership espoused by the white patriarchy. Their leaders instead preached a truly Radical doctrine that called for social and political equality for black men. Pulaski County thus became the major political battlefield.[13]

### The Language of Political Warfare

In July 1865 Major General J. H. Wilson issued his final orders to the officers and troops of his cavalry corps at Macon. Wilson stated that the men's "courage, zeal, and endurance" helped end "the rebellion," adding that such "noble impulses which have inspired you in the past will be a source of enduring honor in the future. Peace has her victories no less than war." Ironically, for Confederate veterans the same peace held out a final chance for victory. The campaign to preserve white patriarchy enabled defeated Confederate veterans not only to preserve their political heritage, but also to reclaim their traditional role as defenders of their families, a role undermined by the war. By protecting the plain folk's moral economy from the political and social degradation they saw in Radicalism, white men regained their traditional status as masters of their neighborhoods. Victory was possible in large measure because of the early withdrawal of Federal troops, who advised freedpeople to remain at home. As one former slave remembered, "The Yankees left . . . soon after the end of the war." Rural blacks were left virtually defenseless in isolated settlements. White men quickly carved out local areas that they collectively controlled through violence. In the process, they regained their sense of self-worth and their dominion over both households and neighborhoods.[14]

Both conservative and Radical camps depended on a war of words to mobilize their followers for the fight over political control of the lower river. For conservatives, the rhetoric drew heavily on images of the plain folk's moral economy and their emphasis on honesty, honor, and integrity. These values, they believed, were threatened by Radical-inspired black supremacy. On the other hand, plain folk were convinced that their way of life represented the final bastion of country republican simplicity and virtue and the best pathway into the future. Even before Congress unveiled Radical Reconstruction early in 1867, George P. Woods, editor of the conservative *Hawksinville Dispatch*, noted in "The New Year" edition that the times were very "discouraging." The first complete year of postemancipation life had been a "black record" filled with "broken vows, ruined futures, blasted characters, blighted hopes, crushed joys."[15]

Honesty and truth, according to Woods, were the first casualties of peacetime. "What men once scorned to do," he wrote, "they now excuse and practice." These practices included farming on credit and dodging past-due obligations. This was nothing new in a plantation economy, but the times threatened to spread such shortcomings throughout society and into the plain folk economy. Moreover, cattle rustling, which was widespread during the war as deserter bands raided the countryside, persisted and was largely blamed on freedmen. It would take a "noble, manly resolve" to redeem a society so "demoralized." To succeed, veterans and their families must "return to the old beaten paths of our fathers, the paths of strict industry which led them to honor, prosperity and happiness." By embracing the "cardinal principles" of an earlier era and reconstructing their households inside out the self-sufficient lifestyle of the past could be restored. The editor implied that former slaves must continue to work as landless, second-class citizens in the dominant white culture, where communal expectations were shaped by a selective white memory of the past.[16]

In his first editorial of 1868, Woods summed up the opinions of most plain folk: The "prosperity, honor and happiness of the whole people" hung in the balance in a dominant Yankee nation where the Southern states were essentially conquered territories. His definition of the "whole people" did not include recently freed African Americans. Memory rather than law shaped the status of black people in the white mind. True, the freedpeople were no longer slaves, but precisely what defined their role in the postwar South? Were they truly citizens in a state that refused to ratify the Fourteenth Amendment? Certainly not, thought Woods. Setting aside the verdicts of the Civil War and Reconstruction, Woods's memory traveled back in time to a more comfortable and pleasant place in the legal definition of black people—the *Dred Scott* decision. "That this is a white man's Government—that the negro is not a citizen, and as such, has no rights," Wood's wrote, was the correct and prevailing opinion among most whites. The coming year would tell whether the Dred Scott decision would be upheld by Southern white men or overturned by freedmen and their white Republican allies in the postwar fight for political control of the lower river.[17]

Conservative whites reacted quickly to the Republican Party's mobilization of black voters. In December 1867 delegates from sixty counties met at Macon and united in Democratic opposition to Radicalism. The Macon convention called for each county to organize a Committee of Seven (the so-called county central committee) to rally local white opposition to Reconstruction and the formation of Republican clubs. The delegates then pronounced Radical Reconstruction "a crime" and went home to organize.[18]

Along the lower river, Democrats called meetings to endorse the Macon convention's resolutions and set up the machinery of counterrevolution. In Pulaski County, a meeting was held on Christmas Eve at Hawkinsville. The language of the resolutions adopted at this gathering reflected the bitterness of local whites about the Reconstruction Acts, which they denounced as the "vindictive and partisan" designs of an illegitimate Radical Congress. Reconstruction violated the plain folk's democratic ideal because it "is not of the people," meaning that the governed—white male voters—had not consented to Reconstruction. Moreover, its goals violated plain folk notions of race, white supremacy, and polity. The Radicals' illegal designs were "leading to the supremacy of the negro race, the destruction of free government, the peace of society, and volative of the dignity and character of representative institutions." The resolutions endorsed at this meeting provided an ordering of the veterans' experiences and added meaning to their wartime sacrifice in the name of white supremacy and home rule.[19]

Plain folk's concepts of honesty, integrity, and morality were central to their critique of Reconstruction and provided a context for discussions of corruption in places high and low. Conservatives delighted in publicizing dishonesty and waste among black and white Republicans, for they called into question the very legitimacy of Reconstruction. Thus, freedman John Gainer, a Republican "street politician" and "bucksnorter" with a reputation for "active partisanship," was described as a "chicken lifter" and watch thief. Such a black political leader, George Woods implied, was unfit to vote. Referring to the Civil Rights bill sponsored by U.S. Senator Charles Sumner, Woods declared it an "outrageous measure." Sumner's grand scheme was designed to bring disgrace and humiliation on the Southern people; he added that "ignorance and immorality are the common heritage of the African race."[20]

The language of Radical politics, like that of conservative whites, was emotionally charged by memories of slavery, war, and emancipation. The Civil War had largely pitted white Northerners against white Southerners in an interregional military contest decided on the front lines and the home front. Postwar politics in the Lower South generally pitted Southern whites against blacks in a struggle for political control that began on the county level. But the images and rhetoric used by both sides were similar. The Radical campaign for black "independence" and "rights" employed two words etched into the memory of white Southerners during the secession crisis and their own war for "freedom." Elections became contests of which memory—Confederate or Radical—would be legitimized in the court of public opinion.

Although Radicalism was dead along the lower river by the early 1870s, no one knew what the outcome would be in the late 1860s. Only in the fall of 1875, when the voting strength of Republicans in Pulaski County had plummeted from 1,131 in 1868 to virtually zero did the editor of the *Hawkinsville Dispatch* write: "We do not blame any colored man for wanting his rights, nor do we believe that any just dealing white man will ever attempt to deprive him of them." By that time, however, the vote as the major symbol of black citizenship and manhood had been stolen.[21]

The language of Radical politics kept the raw images of white defeat and black freedom in the plain folk's mind. The Republican Party effectively employed the popular rhetoric of emancipation, black masculinity, and Union patriotism to rally black voters, and it painted former slaveholders and Confederate veterans as the enemies of freedom and liberty. Most plain folk found these references offensive. After taking over the Radical *American Union*'s editorial duties in 1867, J. Clarke Swayze, a former Freedmen's Bureau agent, immediately played up memories of slavery and the war to move freedmen to political action. Urging black males to register, he advised them to "pay no attention to the advice of men who were formerly your masters, and now Rebels against the government that gave you liberty."[22]

The act of voting was thus the defiant expression of freedom in the face of threats and warnings from reactionary whites. "Don't let the men who fought to keep you in slavery, now keep you there by prevailing on you not to register," Swayze warned, for this only presented former masters "a chance to make you more abject slaves than ever." Union victory and a benevolent Yankee government gave former slaves their freedom, the most precious gift imaginable, but if freedmen failed to register and vote, the argument went, they would become "little better than a slave, and cannot exercise the right placed in your hands by Congress." Former slaves, then, owed it to the Yankee dead to vote or their emancipationist memory would be lost. Henry M. Turner, a black political leader and Republican club organizer who spoke at Hawkinsville, was convinced that the Civil War was caused by white America's failure to live up to the equality vision of the Declaration of Independence. God punished white Southerners with military defeat for keeping blacks in bondage. Voting, Turner argued, was a "solemn duty" that every African American man "owes to himself, his family and his country, to maintain his manhood and his right of citizenship."[23]

As Turner's words reveal, voting was an expression of black manhood as well as emancipation and patriotic duty. Just as white men joined the Confederate army and fought to protect their new nation and their families from harm, black men must now vote in the postwar fight to preserve their freedom and protect the rights of their families. Indeed, a sense of black self-worth centered on the vote in a society that had denied them land and economic independence. "You are freemen now," Sawyze wrote in 1869. "Stand up, then, and assert your independence." Not voting rendered freedmen "unfit to enjoy the boon of Liberty," the *American Union* warned in 1867, marking them as something less than full men. The only "plain solution is that it would return them all to their former masters as slaves."[24]

Black males could become free men and patriots only if they enlisted in the Republican political army and exercised their right to vote. By joining Grant Clubs and Union Leagues organized by Turner and local men such as freedman Mathew Arnold, freedmen supported and defended their new country with votes. They could, in short, become patriots and political soldiers themselves. It was not a campaign for the weak-hearted, but a brutal battle between "loyal men" and "violent rebels," as the *American Union* described the two camps. Voting Republican brought freedmen into the Northern victory culture, with its emancipation and Union memories, a "boon" most ex-Confederates bitterly resented and rejected out of hand.[25]

Ultimately the vote became a contested symbol of manhood between freedmen and whites in a violent campaign of white political terrorism emotionally charged by memory and race. Radicals organized on the neighborhood level, both as a source of political expression and for personal protection, and armed themselves. Early in 1869 the editor of the *American Union* advised freedmen: "Make no loud boasts or threats and then show the white feather. ORGANIZE! . . . Do nothing rash. But, as there is no law for Republicans in Georgia, *defend yourselves* against the assaults and impositions of rebels. Show them that you are no longer the pliant tools of servitude they have always regarded you." Grant Clubs were formed, and black men drilled and marched in preparation for the expected white assault on their rights. At times, much to the consternation of whites, freedmen marched "in armed force" at Hawkinsville and raised fears that an insurrectionary "outbreak was imminent."[26]

Confrontations between whites and freedmen over Radical politics and the black vote, however, were the most visible signs of the two major outcomes of black emancipation and white defeat. In the early postwar years the struggle over voting was far more important on the local level than issues like black ownership of land. Acts of political terrorism followed a pattern. Small gangs of white men, many of them Confederate veterans, would attack a single black voter, often a Republican club organizer. Former soldiers and their families could accept free black families scratching out an existence as tenants on white men's land, but watching them politically organize and cast ballots was another matter entirely. As a consequence of the Confederate defeat, landless black men with no war record had gained the freedom and the rights of white freeholders. The anger of former Confederates was directed toward these black men in an effort to circumscribe politically the meaning of emancipation. Since most black voters lived in Pulaski County, the battle lines were drawn along the traditional borderland between cotton planting and piney woods districts.

In light of repeated acts of white terrorism, it is not surprising that freedmen came to view political power less in terms of what it could bring them in future economic rewards, such as land, and more in how the vote could provide what they needed to survive in the violent postwar era—protection. African Americans clearly understood the importance of using their franchise to elect men they believed were willing to protect them on every level. Writing in the spring of 1869, "A Colored Baptist" denounced former slaveholders as "our most bitter political opponents," noting: "They have tried as moral and religious men to keep us from voting, by which means we could protect ourselves, in making choice of those who would protect us." Cautioning against associating with whites either in church or at the polls, he sarcastically concluded: "These good people have killed us and put their sons up to doing the same because we tried to peaceably get our rights."[27]

Republican leaders such as J. Clarke Swayze were careful to distinguish between rank-and-file Confederate veterans and the planter elite, who in Radical eyes were responsible for secession and the war. In an attempt to exploit class differences and recruit plain folk into the Republican ranks, Swayze withheld harsh criticism of legitimate "Rebels," or men who backed up their secessionist rhetoric by risking their lives at the front. But he roundly condemned the "home-warriors" as hypocrites. Such men talked loudly of disunion and war and urged others to enlist when the fight began, but they personally remained at home and exploited the soldiers' wives and children. Moreover, the masters of slaves "assumed all the respectability in the country and based it upon the fact that they owned 'niggers and mules.' " Thus, former slaveholders, not plain folk veterans, were the freedmen's "most bitter political opponents."[28]

Radical attempts to drive a wedge between local whites based on class interests failed. Despite their wartime differences on the home front, whites united to fight what they perceived as a greater threat posed by Radicalism. Although defeated on the battlefield, plain folk were determined to win the political war and with violence if necessary. As the editor of the *Hawkinsville Dispatch* warned freedmen in an editorial entitled "The Trouble with Negroes," the lower river's white men "are old soldiers, possessing a thorough knowledge of all the arts of war." Former soldiers not only brought home this "knowledge" of military tactics, but also turned to their wartime leaders to symbolically lead and legitimize their campaign in a virtually seamless transition of power from battlefront to home front.[29]

Who took part in the popular action to defend the plain folk's moral economy? Although contemporary accounts frequently pointed to the plain folk themselves, whites of all classes participated in the organized campaign of intimidation and violence to defeat Radicalism. In 1871 "XX," in a letter to the Radical *American Union,* challenged the popular assumption that the "better class" of white men was not involved in political terrorism. The writer believed that Ku Klux Klansmen "have got control" of all the county courts and jails, where civil officers looked the other way and refused to bring white terrorists to justice. Along the lower river, the "better class" of white men played conspicuous roles in the violent campaign to preserve the traditional moral economy and patriarchy, one in which their own paternalism and authority figured prominently. Conservative white men of high social standing formed the symbolic core of a counterrevolutionary movement that drew on virtually every meaningful tradition—Confederate memory, paternalism, racism, religion, ritual, and secessionism—to remind plain folk that violence against blacks and Republicans was legitimate and fulfilled the white community's expectations.[30]

One has only to look at the members of Pulaski County's Committee of Seven, or the central committee that implemented the conservative agenda of the Democratic convention held at Macon, to see how men of high standing and Confederate background embodied plain folk notions of moral economy in the postwar era. Confederate memory was only the latest and most powerful thread in a traditional tapestry that included ideals of honor, paternalism, and sacrifice. A Democratic candidate waved the "bloody shirt" in 1873, when he declared during a speech in Coffee County that he had lived off red oak tree bark and shoestrings for three weeks while soldiering in Tennessee. Poking fun at the politician's efforts to make political hay from his Confederate record, a newspaper editor wrote that his claim had about as much merit as the candidate who declared he "fit, bled, and died" for the "Cause." Though voters found humor in the mutual negotiations for votes based on Confederate service, the significance of a good war record in the political arena was no laughing matter. Honorable service was a reflection of masculinity and individual willingness to defend traditional customs and rights regardless of the personal risks involved. Holding up such characteristics for all to see was much more than a nostalgic postwar trip into Confederate memory, for the same traits were needed in the here and now to defeat Radicalism.[31]

The meeting that organized the Committee of Seven was presided over by former slaveholders and secessionists and Confederate officers. Among them were Norman McDuffie, one of the lower river's largest planters, and Batts Mitchell, a small slaveholder. Both men had actively supported the Confederacy. McDuffie led a home guard unit, and Mitchell was captain of Company F, 22nd Battalion, a State Guards cavalry unit mustered into service in 1863. Such men represented the same conservative planters and town professionals who had spearheaded the secession and war mobilization movements in 1861. Their influence and power helped create a new quasi-military association of white men determined to defend their traditional place in the region's hierarchical society.[32]

It was no accident that the Committee of Seven included four more combat veterans, three of them former officers and two of these (Washington Grice and Charles Kibbee) lieutenant colonels of infantry regiments. As regimental officers, they assumed the paternalistic role of father to large groups of young men and boys–turned citizen soldiers. This also was true of Orran Horne, the antebellum banker, small slaveholder, Mexican War veteran, and militia officer who had served as the county's drillmaster during mobilization. A captain of the Georgia Rangers, Horne was an authority figure whose reputation, like Grice's and Kibbee's, rose during the war. Both Grice and Kibbee were antebellum lawyers drawn from a town professional class of higher social standing than the majority of their soldiers. As officers, they knew the men and their kin, heard their complaints about no pay and poor food, and considered their requests for furloughs and disability discharges. They did their best to make sure that their troops were as healthy, well equipped, and well trained as possible. Just as soldiers' fathers continued to fill the role of patriarch on the home front, officers like Grice, Horne, and Kibbee were symbolic soldiers' fathers in the field. When the war ended, they became the new patriarchs at home.[33]

But it was leadership by example that meant the most to the plain folk fighting with Grice and Kibbee. The citizen soldiers admired and trusted officers who had risked their lives and did what they asked of their men. Kibbee's meteoric rise to the rank of lieutenant colonel was due to the "valor and skill" he had demonstrated for over three years as captain of the Georgia Rangers after Horne departed. Moreover, he stuck by his comrades and their cause when his Northern parents objected to his Confederate service and "never forgave him for aiding the South." Although Grice did not move to Hawkinsville until 1866, his reputation as a hard fighter in Thomas's brigade of A. P. Hill's corps, which included the 49th Georgia, was well known in the wiregrass country by the war's end. Many veterans considered Grice the coolest, bravest officer they had seen under fire. For these reasons—bravery, common community bonds, kind treatment, and trust—veterans depended on their wartime officers for postwar leadership and reciprocated the officers' wartime concern for them by electing them to political office after the war. Both Horne and Kibbee, for example, were elected mayor of Hawkinsville shortly after the war, and Kibbee served continuous terms as a state senator from the Fourteenth District between 1871 and 1876.[34]

The Reverend George McCall was another influential member of the Committee of Seven. As minister of the planter-dominated evangelical Evergreen Baptist Church at Longstreet, he had traveled to Hawkinsville in 1861 to deliver the farewell address to the Pulaski Volunteers on the Methodist church grounds. He also commanded a unit of reserve cavalry. McCall's presence lent church authority and legitimacy to the committee's campaign to overturn Reconstruction's "unconstitutional" designs to destroy "free government," just as evangelical religion played a critical role in the Confederacy's cause. In 1865 McCall replaced former unionist James Williamson in the pulpit at Hawkinsville Baptist Church.[35]

A "man of means" was the way one contemporary in 1872 described Cornelius Bozeman, another member of the Committee of Seven. Despite losing property that included thirty slaves, the planter was doing "all right" as a warehouse owner and cotton speculator before the panic of 1873. An archsecessionist of the lower river, Bozeman had received more votes to the secession convention than any other local candidate. Almost fifty when the committee was formed, the paternalistic Bozeman enjoyed an enviable antebellum record as justice of the inferior court and county sheriff. Moreover, his family distinguished itself in the war effort. Cornelius Bozeman Jr. joined the Georgia Rangers, and son Frank served as a first lieutenant in the 5th Georgia Reserves. The old patriarch never seemed to recover from the Confederacy's defeat.[36]

The political Committee of Seven met in town, but its influence reached into every rural militia district. It was there that small paramilitary outfits of white men attacked prominent black and white Republicans in a violent campaign to destroy the foundations of Radicalism on the neighborhood level. In Pulaski County, members of well-known families were publicly identified as participants in the terrorism, including Norman McDuffie. A former state senator and captain of a Wilcox County militia company, McDuffie physically and verbally abused Republican voters at the polls in 1868. His violent outbursts visually linked the nighttime actions of the Ku Klux Klan to one of the community's foremost leaders. The participation of paternalists like McDuffie in attacks on Radicals further legitimized plain folk violence against freedmen in the countryside.[37]

Sanders Coalson, a member of another prestigious family, was charged with the murder of Wilbur Mason and became the target of a proclamation issued by Governor Rufus Bullock in January 1870. A long-standing disagreement between Coalson and Mason became so heated over some "high words" that a shooting on sight "was expected between the parties." The incident was regretted in the community, "where Mr. C. stood well." In 1861 Coalson had dropped out of Emory and Henry College at age sixteen, joined the Confederate army, and served until the war ended. In any previous decade, Coalson would have looked forward to a promising political future in a society dominated by white men who wielded absolute control over blacks and enjoyed the deference of the yeomanry. Instead, Radical Reconstruction now reshaped his world and sharply circumscribed his realm of authority, placing freedmen on equal footing with whites regardless of their status in the community. That freedmen organized themselves in paramilitary fashion was an affront to white authority. It was this Radical "outrage" against traditional white male privilege that justified white violence by men like Coalson and McDuffie and plain folk of lesser standing in the eyes of the white community.[38]

Such members of "the respectability," as one local Radical called them tongue-in-cheek, were joined by plain folk in the campaign to eliminate black self-rule. Despite the best efforts of Radical newspapers like the *American Union* to appeal to the class interests of veterans—yeomen should no longer be "the willing tools of Slaveocrats" or the cannon fodder in "rich men's wars, in which the poor men must do the fighting and dying"—plain folk overwhelmingly remained loyal to the Southern position in the postwar fight. Men with family names such as Gaskins, Graham, Lott, Luke, Pool, Rogers, and Taylor were publicly identified with attacks on freedmen, Republicans, and Federal officials. Such "political rowdies" and "violent rebels" filled out the ranks of local Democratic clubs. Their vigilantism made it unsafe for freedmen and white Republicans to travel alone in the countryside; some Radicals were assaulted in towns and villages under the cover of darkness.[39]

Race consciousness played a critical role in plain folk rejection of Radicalism and the Republican Party, just as it had in their motivation for supporting secession and war. But unlike Joseph Brown's northern Georgia, a low slaveholding region that opposed secession in 1861 and saw significant numbers of yeomen joining postwar Republican clubs, few lower river plain folk became Republicans. Despite its reputation as a barren and low slaveholding region, slavery was more deeply entrenched here than in upcountry Georgia. White men judged their self-worth and social status based on the condition of black men they saw on a daily basis. Plain folk were unwilling to embrace a biracial paramilitary coalition that advanced black political rights at their expense, just as expansion of the crop lien system threatened the economic independence of white yeomen. To join Republican clubs filled with freedmen put whites on an equal footing with black men, who would outnumber and outvote them within the clubs.[40]

Looking back on the paramilitary fight to reclaim Pulaski County's countryside from Radicalism, one conservative wrote in 1874 that even in the darkest days of Reconstruction most white men "stood by their colors." There were a few exceptions. He identified "several white men (perhaps twenty-five or more) who voted the Radical ticket at Trippville." Situated near the headwaters of Gum Swamp in eastern Pulaski, Trippville was a rough-and-tumble backwoods neighborhood with a reputation for "fist and skull" combat. It was a low slaveholding area inhabited by the yeomanry and led during the Civil War by Seaborn Jones, the captain of his militia district, a slaveholder, and one of the neighborhood's more prosperous farmers. Gum Swamp was the major target of the Confederate expedition early in 1865 to break up deserter bands. Indeed, evidence suggests that in addition to Republican and Democratic paramilitary clubs, white unionist bands continued to operate as neighborhood regulators. In the summer of 1869 John Brown, the notorious anti-Confederate in Telfair County, was charged with the murder of Joseph Rollins.

Described as "rather assuming in manners," Brown led a band of five "young men and boys" in an attack on neighbors "whom they considered dishonest."[41]

To explain Trippville as a Radical aberration, the writer linked the neighborhood's pro-Republican leanings to another memory—its anti-Confederate past. Of the white Republicans at Trippville, he wrote: "These men are malcontents. They were skulkers in the late war. When their neighbors were fighting the battles of their country, these men were hiding in the woods." Their refusal to join white conservatives in the fight against postwar Radicalism should not be surprising, since these "disaffected renegades" refused to stand by the Confederacy in its darkest hours. "Shall we place Seabe [Seaborn] Jones with this class?" The writer was reluctant to do so. Jones was a community leader, a former master and militia officer, as well as "a man of too much good head sense." However, if Jones, "like Ephriam, . . . is still joined to his idols, we must let him alone that the ____ devil may claim his dues." Clearly, Jones's role as a militia leader before and during the war played a part in the organization of white Republicans into a platoon-sized group to defend their political stand. There is, however, no indication that the Trippville Republican Club included African Americans.[42]

Seaborn Jones and the Trippville Republicans were not the only white men to join a Radical coalition and be demonized by conservatives. Some white Republicans leaders were described as anti-Confederate commercial and professional men who made their living off the hardworking yeomanry or newcomers who settled in railroad towns. Plain folk distrusted both groups and considered them outsiders, postwar replacements for dangerous paramilitary leaders such as Willis Bone. At Hawkinsville, William D. King and Seaborn F. Salter were leading Republicans. Both men served as the town's federally appointed postmaster during the late 1860s. In 1860 King, a Massachusetts native, was employed as a machinist in Houston County; Salter resided in Wilkinson County and ten years later gave his occupation as physician, although a detractor described him as merely "a pill and eye-water doctor." Like King, Virgil Perry lived in neighboring Houston County in 1860. A merchant, he joined King and Salter in the county's inner circle of local white Radicals. Like his Radical colleagues, Frank B. Green moved to a railroad town, possibly also from Houston County, where he hung out his lawyer's shingle at Cochran. In recommending him as a notary public and justice of the peace for the Trippville district to Governor Rufus Bullock, one of his acquaintances described Green as "a warm supporter of Reconstruction." Although by the end of Reconstruction King was a middle-class gunsmith and jeweler, the others were struggling professionals. In 1870 Perry and Salter rented houses and owned little personal property (Perry claiming assets of $150 and Salter, of $500). It is doubtful that there were scarcely more than fifty white Republicans in Pulaski County, including the yeomanry at Trippville.[43]

### Ritual and Violence

Of course, the major participants in the Republican camp were freedmen, who accounted for perhaps as many as 95 percent of Pulaski's Radicals. They were the main targets of white political terrorism. Three developments helped plain folk win their counterrevolutionary conquest to defeat the Radical "sinner" and restore "honesty" and "integrity" to local politics. First, emancipation and the demise of white paternalism devalued the lives of freedmen. No longer the property of white masters, African Americans were more vulnerable to attack by whites. Indeed, the Confederate cause and the death of black men were linked in the white mind before the war ended. Nine years after Appomattox the *Hawkinsville Dispatch* reminded its readers that a Wilcox County white man, sentenced to prison for murdering a slave, was released from jail "on a promise to service in the Confederate army." The devaluation of black life continued into the postwar years, with the conservative *Macon Daily Telegraph* warning in June 1865 that problems were certain to arise from the "sudden termination of the long existing patriarchal relation" between masters and slaves. It was a prophetic statement. In 1874 an aged freedman named Bill Johnson was found dead on the plantation of James Jelks, a veteran of the Pulaski Volunteers. In need of medical care, a feeble Johnson tried to walk off the Jelks place but was too weak and died in the woods. He was so emaciated that "not enough flesh was left on his body to make it offensive." A coroner's inquest concluded that Johnson died from "want and attention."[44]

Although Republicans hoped to permanently break the power of planters by organizing freedmen into Union League clubs and marching them to the polls to elect candidates, Federal power extended only so far into the countryside. It never seemed to reach far enough to stop the onslaught of ritualized violence that came with darkness once freedmen began to vote. Though one Union officer recommended that two hundred to three hundred cavalrymen be stationed at Hawkinsville during the summer of 1865, they did not stay long. Reporting from Pulaski County early in 1866, a conservative white citizen wrote: "Thanks to a kind Providence, I can write you that we have no military guards and garrisons nearer than Macon; and we are happy to see a change for the better." The removal of Union soldiers inevitably left freedmen in the hands of conservative whites.[45]

In the summer of 1868, as violence began to increase in southern Georgia, General George G. Meade, military commander of Georgia, Alabama, and Florida, issued General Order No. 108, which led to the further withdrawal of Federal troops from central Georgia. To lessen military interference in civil matters and to reduce the number of personnel in the field, the order instructed the commanders of military subdistricts to concentrate their infantry and cavalry companies at key urban areas. The nearest Yankee garrisons became Atlanta and Savannah, and the violent results were felt immediately. At the height of political violence that year, the *American Union*'s editor wrote that as long as the "enforcing power" of the U.S. Army and the Freedmen's Bureau remained in place, blacks had a chance to defend their rights. By late summer of 1868, he lamented, both Union troops and the bureau's agents had been "practically withdrawn, and the poor, ignorant, defenceless negro is left to the tender mercies of the men who hate him because he is free." Reconstruction died night by night, year after year, in a ruthless campaign of political terrorism waged on the Republican clubs by ex-Confederates and their allies.[46]

Civil authorities did little or nothing to protect Republicans, regardless of color, from the abuse heaped on them by whites, nor did they arrest their assailants. Town police and county sheriffs considered Radicalism a threat to their own authority; moreover, they depended on plain folk votes. It was partly due to the inaction of civil authorities that Seaborn Salter, Pulaski's Radical state representative, sought the creation of a state police force to defend freedmen and Republicans. At issue was the state's unwillingness to protect the national authority represented by Radical Reconstruction from assault by the localism represented by the plain folk's conservative counterattacks. It did not help the Republican cause that Confederate veteran John Hendley, formerly captain of Company G, 10th Georgia Cavalry, served as the sheriff of Pulaski County when the violence peaked in the summer of 1868.[47]

Cases illustrating the unwillingness of local authorities to protect freedmen from white political terrorism were numerous. On the night of February 14, 1871, Anderson Hobbs, a Pulaski freedman, was attacked in his cabin by an armed squad of about six white men. Hobbs's arm was shattered by one of several gun blasts. The men left Hobbs with the threat that "if he was seen in Pulaski county the next day he would be killed." Although Hobbs recognized three of the "Ku-Klux" assailants—Bob Pool, Tom Pool, and John Taylor—he refused to report the incident to the sheriff for fear of being killed. The *American Union* asked: "When will the present stock of sneaking, cowardly, midnight assassins give way to law and order?" In the absence of local law enforcement officers who were willing to defend the rights of freedmen, the editor called for executive action and an amendment to the Enforcement Act giving Federal courts jurisdiction in such cases. "It is frequently the case," the editor continued, "that there are no Justices of the Peace who will issue a warrant for a negro, while in others they dare not do it for fear of violence or proscription from their neighbors." The following April Congress enacted the Ku Klux Klan Act of 1871, which provided that crimes such as the one against Hobbs were punishable under Federal law.[48]

Such local violence did not result in full-scale deadly white attacks on black voters as in the 1868 Camilla riot in southwestern Georgia, but the course of political intimidation charted by conservative whites was effective nonetheless. It began with threats. These could be indirect, such as the report circulated by Laurens Hill planter Joseph M. White that "the Kuklux passed my place one night by moonshine, and scared my wife with their white horses and disguised riders." The Klan's appearance often indicated activity by Republican Party organizers. That White's letter was printed in the *Hawkinsville Dispatch* was a not-so-subtle reminder to freedmen that mounted white bands controlled the countryside parading as the ghosts of Confederate soldiers. Attending Union League meetings could be dangerous. Or the threats could be more direct and personal. A miniature coffin was left at the door of a freedman shortly after the presidential election of 1868 with the warning: "This is for Tardy Peas . . . he can live or die just as he chooses," signed "K. K. Klan." And when freedman Wherry Massey organized a Republican club in 1868, local Democrats warned that he would be killed if he continued recruiting members. On his way to Macon to see if his "rights" could be protected, a squad of six white men boarded his train with pistols drawn. Massey was removed and marched to McRae's store, where twenty armed men made "severe threats" against his life. More fortunate than many Radical organizers, Massey merely was warned never to attempt to organize another Republican club and was released.[49]

Wrecking, or destroying the property of freedmen and white Republicans, took organized intimidation a step further. It struck at the material and social foundations of the black community by denying freedmen their most valued personal possessions, including bedding, clothing, food, and shelter. Although barn burning and livestock poisoning were often associated with white "scoundrel" attacks on the property of the wealthy, raids of property were directed at freedmen and Radicals as well. In some cases the wreckings were legally sanctioned repossessions of property, but the disruption of black households by whites was demoralizing just the same. Early in 1868 Charles Taylor, formerly the lower river's largest slaveholder, arrived at the home of widow Lavinia Williams "with a note said to be from Lavinia's husband and then & there . . . did seize by force" much of her personal property. Weeks later John Carroll took what was left, including Lavinia's "bed clothes," furniture, and a suit that belonged to her deceased husband. In this way the symbolic erosion of black property was made public for all to see.[50]

In most cases, wreckings, though considered legitimate acts by whites, had no legal justification. In the fall of 1868 a Confederate widow literally pulled the floor out from under a freedman's family then residing in a schoolhouse. During the school term, the widow had loaned the teacher planks to floor the cabin. Once the term was over, the well-meaning teacher allowed a freedman and his family to temporarily move into the schoolhouse. The widow was outraged by the schoolteacher's action. She entered the cabin and hauled off her planks, symbolically returning the black family to the mudsills. Her actions reflected the determination of plain folk, including women, to defend their ascendancy over blacks, no matter how tenuous. This wrecking was filled with meaning for both the widow and the white community. In her fight with the schoolteacher, a newspaper observed, the widow "handled him like a big puss cat sporting with the mouse." Her neighbors were "so much pleased with the widow's prowess and chivalry" that they took up a small collection for her. By defending family property and the memory of her dead Confederate husband, she was thought to reclaim her family's honor.[51]

Yet the destruction and repossession of property paled in comparison to the ritual violence that plain folk meted out to Republicans regardless of color. Repeatedly, stonings were used to intimidate and injure them. Shortly after the news of President Ulysses S. Grant's election in 1868 reached Hawkinsville, Seaborn F. Salter, the town's leading Radical and General Assembly member, placed lamps in his windows "fronting the public street" to celebrate the Republican victory. Two hours later a party of three men wrecked the house "with rocks, one of which entered the room where my family were sitting, and came very near striking my little daughter, which must have proved fatal if it had. This was purely on political grounds." Despite cries for help, only one man came to the family's assistance, "although plenty of others were in hearing." Salter soon moved away.[52]

When freedman John Caldwell inadvertently attended a church service in 1869 with flour on his face "after working in that article," thus artificially lightening his color, whites in the congregation were incensed. Although Caldwell removed the flour after it was called to his attention, several parishioners "assailed" him with stones after the service. He could have been killed, according to one witness, had it not been for "timely interference." Although his attackers were not arrested, Caldwell was bound over to the Hawkinsville City Council after Allen Cole, a member of the church, swore out a warrant for his arrest for disturbing the peace. For his injuries, the freedman was fined twelve dollars and "the town authorities sent him to jail for sixty days."[53]

White Republicans and Federal officers were also the targets of stonings. In a widely publicized incident in Coffee County in 1873, two of the community's white men stoned postmaster J. W. Barber, who like Seaborn Salter was a Federal appointee. The attack and the reactions of both the white community and Federal authorities plainly reflected the divided political culture of the postemancipation South. Federal officials accused Simon Gaskins and Jesse Lott of attempted mail robbery when they threw rocks and pieces of iron at Barber. The two men denied the charge. Rather, they insisted, the attack was of a "personal nature." Barber's superior, an Internal Revenue Service agent in Brooks County, ordered the case turned over to Federal authorities in Savannah rather than be handled by the state. But the legal strategy backfired. Outraged plain folk defended the alleged assailants as "persons of good character in the county" and branded Barber an "unprincipled scoundrel." Is it any wonder, a newspaper editor asked, that "Federal laws are so obnoxious to our people when such outrages and persecutions are perpetrated by those appointed to administer them?" Thus, in the cases of John Caldwell and J. W. Barber, the targets of stoning became the perpetrators of "outrages" against traditional white notions of moral conduct and either spent time in jail or were ostracized.[54]

Beatings, on the other hand, brought plain folk closer to their victims. Batterings with sticks became the anti-Radical's version of a Preston Brooks–style caning. At times, stick beatings were combined with stonings; such was the fate of John Caldwell at the hands of fellow churchgoers. In an incident noteworthy for its links to paternalistic authority and the legitimization of violence by "Ku-Klux democrats," former planter, state senator, and militia officer Norman McDuffie drove a Republican from the polls at Hawkinsville "with a stick, for presuming to vote in this county, and be a resident of another county." The powerful image of the aging, paternalistic planter taking up a stick and violently defending the moral economy of the community against Radicalism was not lost on plain folk.[55]

By the end of 1869 political terrorism had left "many stations vacant" among the "loyal men." During the previous year many freedmen who had voted for the Radical ticket were taken from their homes by squads of whites and beaten "nearly to death," wrote the Freedmen's Bureau agent at Hawkinsville. Two men attacked the blacksmith shop of Dean Whitfield and broke his arm after he refused "to abandon a political club." The gun-wielding assailants, who threatened to kill him if he complained to authorities, chased Whitfield to a friend's house. But more than wreckings, stonings, and beatings, guns quickly became the weapon of choice among violent ex-Confederates and their allies. William King, Hawkinsville's Republican postmaster, was the subject of a mock funeral and J. W. Barber and Seaborn Salter were stoned, but white Republicans were rarely brought into the sights of firearms. Freedmen were generally the targets of violence involving firearms but, like their white allies, were singled out for their prominent roles as Radical leaders. Union League and Grant Club leaders, schoolteachers, and Republican election organizers were identified and attacked, usually under the cover of darkness, by small squads of white men.[56]

In the fall of 1867 an African American schoolteacher named Cole was shot in Hawkinsville. The man who attacked him was identified as M. D. McDuffie, whose family was associated with die-hard secessionists and unapologetic Confederates. Cole was shot in the dark "without sufficient cause or provocation," according to E. A. Pollock, the Freedmen's Bureau agent at Hawkinsville. Pollock believed it his "duty" to inform Captain N. Sellers Hill, the subassistant commissioner at Macon, that "no steps as yet have been taken to bring him to justice." Schoolhouses, like churches and private homes, were important centers of organization and communication for the Union League. Although it is uncertain that Cole was engaged in such activities, his role as an educator and communicator within the black community made him a marked man. A warrant was sworn out for McDuffie's arrest, but it was not served by Sheriff John A. Hendley, former captain of Company G, 10th Confederate Cavalry, because "Cole & McDuffie have settled it between themselves."[57]

Similar incidents increased during the height of anti-Radical violence in 1868, when whites themselves were fearful of retaliation by organized groups of black men who used "violent language, the threats and almost nightly assembling of armed negroes for drill." Freedmen believed that they were authorized to conduct the drills in defense of their rights by statements made by Jefferson Long, of Macon, the state's only black congressman during Reconstruction. Amid rumors and counterrumors, African Americans interpreted Long's authorization to also mean they had the blessing of Governor Rufus Bullock, or perhaps the state's Radical Executive Committee.[58]

Fears of organized black insurrection were symptomatic of the deeper desire of plain folk to keep freedpeople in their place. As the Freedmen's Bureau agent at Hawkinsville wrote Erastus A. Ware, the agency's superintendent of education, "the whites it seems are hostile to the blacks & will not do anything towards the advancement of the col'd race." To the plain folk's way of thinking, the elevation of blacks only resulted in their own decline on the social scale. The vote was the common white man's badge of equal citizenship and masculinity among gentlemen of standing and wealth. They were loath to share this traditional privilege bestowed by their color and gender with black men. Anyone associated with communicating the Radical doctrine was vulnerable to attack.[59]

Arnold Mathews, described as "a Republican of Pulaski County," was only one of many black men who learned the high price of voting for the party of Lincoln. Like many other black Republicans, he was "called out" to answer for his actions. As president of the Grant Club at Dykesboro, a station on the Macon and Brunswick Railroad, Mathews voted for Ulysses S. Grant in 1868 and publicly advised other freedmen to do so. Literate and motivated to politically organize the African Americans in his neighborhood, Mathews emerged as one of the most prominent black leaders in the eastern part of his county. For this reason alone, he became a target of political terrorism.[60]

According to his affidavit, Mathews was lying on the floor in front of his fireplace reading the Bible on the night of December 1, 1868. At about nine or ten o'clock he was called to his front door by a voice he recognized. Newspapers had arrived on the train, the voice announced. Would Arnold come out and read them aloud to the freedmen gathered in his yard? One of the duties of a literate club president was to educate members who could not read or write regarding the politics and rituals of their clubs. It was through the voice of men such as Mathews that rumor and information spread among the rank and file. As he walked toward the door, Mathews "saw the muzzle of a gun" poke through an old "auger hole." Before he could react, the muzzle and several other weapons fired and hit him with lead and splinters in the face, right wrist, and left leg. "Murder," he screamed, as several neighbors came to his aid, but not before the "disguised party" that "called him out" escaped.[61]

The extent to which paternalistic figures in the community acquiesced to or even took part in such violence is revealed in this attack on Mathews. One of his five assailants was identified as Shadrack Graham, a justice of the peace and a former Confederate soldier. Graham quickly disappeared. His status as a public official, however, legitimized ritual violence against black and white Republicans in plain folk's eyes. Officers of the law not only looked the other way, thus meeting plain folk expectations of favoritism and approval, but they also occasionally participated in the terrorism. The Mathews incident, according to the *American Union*, illustrated the fraudulent nature of claims by Georgia Democratic Party newspapers that the presidential election of 1868 was a calm one. As one correspondent remarked: "Lawlessness seems to be on the increase; . . . officers will not execute papers put in their hands to arrest friends who are perpetrating crime."[62]

The best example of how communities played a powerful role in the legitimation of paramilitary action against black Republicans was the murder of Joshua Williams in Irwin County. Portrayed as an "irrepressible Radical" by the conservative press, Williams was a prominent advocate of the Republican cause in Irwin during 1867 and early 1868. In all likelihood he was a Republican club leader in the white belt county, which explains why he was considered "in bad odor" among "respectable" whites. In June 1868 "a gang of white men" attacked Williams at an "untimely hour" on Saturday night. In keeping with ritual, the white men called him out of his house. In "defense of his own premises," Williams "ordered them to leave." When the men refused, he set his dog on them. Enraged by this insult, one member of the gang shot the dog and threatened to shoot Williams. But the freedman "shot and killed" the white man and his brother, who "seemed disposed to fight it out." Williams immediately went to the Freedmen's Bureau officer in his district and turned himself in. He admitted that he had killed the white men in self-defense and stated, "Let justice be done him."[63]

The two brothers Joshua Williams killed were David and William Luke. Like most white families in the county, the Lukes were nonslaveholding plain folk. Nine members of their extended family had served in local Confederate companies, four alone in the Irwin Volunteers. As their neighbors, the Lukes fought, sacrificed, and died during the war. Meanwhile, slaves such as Joshua Williams had remained in the relative safety of the Confederate interior, where they were fed and clothed by masters and their labor grew the crops that fed the master's family and slaves, as well as hungry soldiers' families. The white neighborhood's response to the killing of the Luke brothers was in part shaped by its memory of the war and its costs.[64]

Although Williams was willing to leave his fate to "justice" when he surrendered to the Freedmen's Bureau, whites immediately reacted to the death of their friends at the hands of a former slave. Whatever sense of paternalism that had protected Williams in slavery was now gone. In all likelihood his white neighbors knew that the attack on Williams was not a random instance of racist violence, but rather an act of political terrorism in response to his prominent role as a Radical leader in recent local elections. Thus, the raid on his house was on one level part of a larger campaign to defend white self-rule and supremacy in a white belt county where blacks could not possibly return a majority of votes. After all, the franchise was a symbol of freedom and manhood. The Lukes and their neighbors decided that it was time to "clear him out" because Williams, a black man, presumed to be their equal. Members of the Luke clan arrived at his house after dark under the pretext of searching for stolen property, formerly the prerogative of masters, patrollers, and the wartime county police force. But Williams stood his ground. The white men were taken aback by his determination to defend the sanctity of his home and his demand that they produce "any authority" to search his home.[65]

A reward for Williams's capture was immediately offered, and the manhunt began. Even as a Freedmen's Bureau agent turned Williams over to Irwin's civil authorities, another black man was hunted down and shot in a case of mistaken identity. The county was as frightened of uncontrolled black men as it had been of the mixed-race labor force of A. H. Brisbane's antebellum railroad, which threatened its social equilibrium in the 1840s. It was ill prepared to protect Joshua Williams until his trial. The fate that awaited him was apparent to a Freedmen's Bureau agent upriver at Hawkinsville. Hearing of the incident, he wrote: "I understand he will be taken to Irwin Co & there he will be at the mercy of the relatives of deceased as the freedman is unable to employ a lawyer. This case should be looked into."[66]

It was already too late. Williams was taken to a primitive log jail and dropped through a trap door into its lower-level dungeon. He was "fastened" to a wall, and there he remained, depending on the account, from one day to "a few." During the night the jail was set on fire. The log jail blazed away near the center of Irwinville and within sight of the Masonic lodge, a few residences, and the village store. According to the *American Union*, the building and Williams were consumed by the flames "without a single effort to rescue the prisoner from the horrid death of burning!" The next day his "ashes and bones were gathered and were buried in the old cemetery." The murder of Joshua Williams announced that the piney woods country would not tolerate attempts by black men to protect their rights even when they did not pose a political threat.[67]

Radicals blamed Williams's death on the "devilish prejudices" of white people, but wartime memories now provided a powerful emotional context for diametrically opposed causes—a Lost Cause and an emancipation cause. Their own understanding of the Civil War's meaning prompted the Lukes and their white neighbors to attack Williams. Williams's newly gained freedoms—the vote, a home, property—threatened their sense of a fragile domain and, perhaps more significant, potentially rendered the Confederate cause meaningless. From their point of view, Williams could gain these valued symbols of freedom and manhood only by violating the memory of dead Confederate soldiers. In their minds, soldiers defended their homes and families to preserve their own freedom and independence, to prevent their own slavelike subjugation by Yankees.

With his dog, gun, home, yard, vote, and willingness to challenge white authority, Joshua Williams symbolized black advancement in the postwar world, the boon freedmen received because of the Confederate defeat. Now he was his own man, willing to challenge the antebellum white male prerogative to govern without question all dependents—including women, children, and other African Americans. He confirmed the plain folk's worst antebellum fears of freed blacks settling in the wiregrass. But Williams's new freedom carried with it enormous risks. He was now vulnerable to physical harm at the hands of whites, particularly if his actions challenged their notions of the Republic of Irwin as a white man's country where Confederate veterans and their families aimed to preserve prewar economic self-sufficiency and white supremacy. Thus, the postwar equivalent of the slave patrol—a gang of armed white men from the neighborhood—arrived at Williams's gate that fateful night to enforce the older memory of Joshua the slave as opposed to the new reality of Joshua the freed man.

Ironically, the social revolution of the postwar South found both the Luke brothers and Joshua Williams struggling to redefine their identities and find self-worth in a changed world. For white men, this process of redefinition unfolded within the context of the Confederate defeat with its sense of death, loss, and sacrifice. For former slaves like Williams, it was a complicated and dangerous redefinition of self shaped by old memories of slavery and new memories of emancipation and freedom, but unfolding within a dominant white culture, one emotionally charged by anger, defeat, fear, and resentment of the war's consequences.[68]

The violence and instability engendered by postwar emancipation, the transition to a free labor economy, the paramilitary political struggle, and the expansion of cotton production, railroad construction, and forest industries were overwhelming. Some people gave up on the land. Between 1868 and 1877 a significant emigration movement gained momentum among both whites and blacks. Although economic considerations played a significant role in decisions to leave the lower river behind, especially as the depression deepened after 1873, emigration was also a political act, especially among blacks who sought to realize the full blessings of freedom in some other place. Similar patterns characterized the black and white experiences. Prospecting parties visited the Promised Land, reports returned to excite prospective emigrants, and parties were organized and left. The local press predicted disaster for those who moved away.[69]

The white emigrants were described in two words: "Texas rovers." Even before the panic of 1873, plain folk joined "the crowd" headed for eastern Texas. In Wilcox County, James Griffin resigned as sheriff and left with Daniel Eubanks in a prospecting party. Eubanks reported back early in 1873. The land was more productive but more expensive than along the lower river; farm laborers received first-rate wages, but clerks and others seeking lucrative positions in town would be disappointed. His mixed report did not stop the emigration. From Smith County, Texas, John K. Partin wrote: "I meet daily many old Georgians." In time, families with such names as Barron, Burch, Eubanks, Gordon, Griffin, Hendley, Holland, McDuffie, Partin, Smith, Wilkinson, and Williams all prospected in Texas or moved there. In the spring of 1873 the *Hawkinsville Dispatch* reported that it had subscribers in Brazos, Caldwell, Colorado, Upshur, Fort Bend, Smith, and Titus Counties. Most of the emigrants settled in counties east of Dallas or west of Houston. From Montgomery County in 1875, G. W. Barron related that he was "well pleased with this country." The land was higher than back home, but it would make more corn in a year than four years in Telfair County. He also noted that the area north of Houston was good cattle range with plenty of wild game, thus describing a landscape capable of supporting plain folk accustomed to the piney woods.[70]

In the spring of 1875 the *Hawkinsville Dispatch* waged a campaign of words intended to cure the "Texas fever." Editor George Woods declared that the "curse of Reuben seems to rest upon the people." In January his paper reported that about seventy people had left Coffee County for Texas in a "funeral procession." Woods was determined to stop the exodus. According to him, emigration destabilized the South and caused people to neglect their farms, a trend that had increased since the war. Indebtedness and the instability of local land titles brought on by the arrival of timber companies were often given as reasons for plain folk emigration, but, Woods argued, "God turned Adam out of the garden under far more gloomy circumstances." Aware that many emigrants were Confederate veterans, he employed Lost Cause rhetoric to keep them at home: "Stand by your plows like Stonewall Jackson did to his guns at Bull Run, amid gloom, dismay, and death." E. A. Burch, however, did not give up. In 1877 he pronounced Falls County a "wonderful" country, where land titles were not in dispute and the chief crops were cotton and corn.[71]

The emigration of African Americans from the lower river was in all likelihood even greater. Freedmen left the area singly or in small groups in search of family members or better living conditions, but organized parties began to move out as white violence increased. In 1868 an "Exodus of Freedmen" was reported at Hawkinsville shortly after their 1867 contracts expired. One observer described the departure of a group "on the lookout for the blessings of freedom" in these words: "Such a tumble of bundles, dragging of boxes, packing away of cackling chickens, crying babies and whining puppies."[72]

The most publicized emigration was to Liberia between 1872 and 1874. Sponsored by the American Colonization Society (ACS), this movement was centered in Hawkinsville's active African American churches, which became the gathering places for freedmen from Pulaski County and beyond. In September 1870 an estimated 2,500 to 3,000 people attended the Colored Baptist Association's meeting held in the town's churches and courthouse, where "not a case of misbehavior occurred." A year later Henry McNeal Turner addressed a similar gathering at the black Methodist church, where all African American congregations attended "The Colored People's Camp Meeting." At least one white minister was traveling with the "sable divinities." In November 1872 William Coppinger of the ACS met with a number of freedmen at their schoolhouse in Hawkinsville. Coppinger brought along samples of products from Liberia and, according to a conservative white who did not approve of his presence in the area, "pictured to them in glowing language the advantages of emigrating to Liberia" under the auspices of the ACS.[73]

On November 5, 1872, an advance party of about thirty emigrants under the leadership of the Reverend John Adams left Hawkinsville for Savannah, where they boarded a steamer. Among the Hawkinsville men were Lloyd Fountain, Joseph Folsom, Henry Lucius, John McBurrows, George Rawls, and

Charles Smythers. Emily Burch, described as "the enthusiastic negress," also joined the party. In her early thirties, Emily left behind her husband Joseph, a sixty-two-year-old shoemaker, and several children. According to one account, she "jumped up and slapped her hands together, and thanked her God that she was going where there was no poor white trash." But no doubt a missionary impulse fueled the emigrationist sentiments of many members of Adams's prospecting party. They hoped to "fulfill the doctrine preached to the colored people that the Almighty intended they should return to Africa—the home of their fathers—and aid in the civilization of their country, as spoken of in Scripture." Unable to create a stable community on the lower river, they hoped to help the less privileged members of their race in Africa.[74]

Generally speaking, the Hawkinsville emigrants tended to be better educated than most rural blacks. Reverend Adams was a well-versed leader in the eyes of his followers. John McBurrows was a steamboat pilot, "a sensible, intelligent colored man, possessed of hard practical sense," although he lacked a formal education. Emily Burch had resided in the household of a skilled craftsman. Based on the information allegedly provided by William Coppinger, the Hawkinsville group expected to find a thriving colony in Liberia that would offer plenty of economic opportunities. They were disappointed. Within a year or two, many of them wanted to return home. Henry Lucius, a farm laborer who had taken his wife and daughter along, returned in 1874 with "no good report to make of Liberia." The climate was hostile, and many emigrants could only find work making palm oil. Despite Coppinger's so-called assurances, McBurrows found no steamboats to pilot there. He had lost a child before the steamer left New York for Liberia and returned so bitterly let down that he traveled through Georgia warning blacks of the "Grand Swindle."[75]

Conservative whites delighted in recounting the woes of black emigrants, just as they attempted to discourage plain folk from leaving the region. When Esau Harden, "a well-known colored carpenter," died in Macon on his way to Arkansas in 1874, his story was offered as a cautionary tale. Esau chose Arkansas as his new home because he had heard that Radicals still ruled there, but he had lost his life trying to reach the place. The emigrants to Liberia lost capital, land, and family members as well. It must have given the old secessionists and ex-Confederates some satisfaction to find their former slaves humbly asking them for the price of the return passage from Liberia to Georgia. It restored their sense of authority and power if only for a while. Leading secessionist Cornelius Bozeman paid the passage for Henry Lucius and his family to return to Savannah, but Emily Burch was still seeking the money "to come home." She wrote Confederate veteran J. J. Jelks: "Me and my daughter Fanny will satisfy you in labor, let it be long or short." John McBurrows asserted that emigration to Liberia had left him "penniless" and stolen the fruits of his freedom—about $700 in property. Emily Burch was willing to hire out herself and her child to return to a place she had dreamed of escaping.[76]

Unable or unwilling to leave the lower river and believing that the worst of the paramilitary violence was over, some freedmen turned in desperation to biracial cooperation with white Democrats. Others gave up. When Joe Collier was called on to vote with Democrats, he asked if there weren't enough "white folks to settle the matter." But as early as the fall of 1868, one white man wrote from Hawkinsville: "Our clubs are being filled with Democratic freedmen." Doubtless the relentless violence that the terror squads meted out on black voters had something to do with the trend. After the paramilitary campaign of 1868, there were few "open Radicals" in Pulaski County. One optimistic observer concluded that the freedmen "are beginning to open their eyes, and to see who their real friends are." Voting for paternalistic whites for offices such as sheriff was the best alternative left to freedmen to secure their basic rights. By the mid-1870s that tactic gave blacks a sense of political power acknowledged by some whites. From Telfair County, a white voter wrote: "It seems that Africans hold the balance of power here at the ballot box."[77]

Centers of black political power survived the late 1860s and grew stronger in rural communities such as Telfair County, where blacks worked in the forest industry. But despite the spirit of biracial cooperation that seemed to characterize the mid-1870s following the white's paramilitary victory in 1871, differences of opinion based on very different memories of the past continued to surface. These rifts became readily apparent when the lower river counties selected delegates to the constitutional convention of 1877, a retrenchment effort to dismantle the Radical-inspired constitution of 1868, which had strong support in the piney woods and northern Georgia. Former Confederate officers like Ruel Anderson, remembered by one militiaman "as one of the best officers," were entrusted to roll back the tide of corruption, extravagance, and liberalism seen by conservative whites in the 1868 document.[78]

Of all the issues debated at country crossroads and county seat courthouses—including biennial legislation, corporate taxation, a new homestead law, and the restriction of state aid for economic development—none so clearly drew a line between the memories of blacks and whites as the measure to return the state capital to Milledgeville. "This question is causing more discussion than the new constitution or homesteads," wrote George Woods of the *Hawkinsville Dispatch*. Among former slaves the boon of freedom, protection, and political power emanated from Atlanta. It was from Atlanta that the Republican Party sent Grant Club and Union League organizers into the lower river region. And it was to Atlanta that the state's African American legislators went to represent freedmen.[79]

The lower river's plain folk, on the other hand, considered Atlanta as illegitimate as Radical Reconstruction itself. It was not selected by "*the people as their Capital*" and therefore did not reflect the consent of the governed. Instead, wrote "Wiregrass," Atlanta was the "offspring of radicalism and corruption" and the "work of military satraps, carpet baggers and scalawags." If Atlanta represented the emancipationist memory of freedmen, then the city symbolized Confederate defeat and Yankee military rule among the "sturdy yeomanry." Milledgeville, by contrast, was the capital of Old South memory. Situated near the center of Georgia with state government buildings already in place, it was also favored by plain folk in purely economic and practical terms. Local whites were confident that the constitution of 1877 would be ratified and the capital returned to Milledgeville.[80]

The conservative counterrevolution embodied in the constitution of 1877 ensured that one-party rule and white supremacy would prevail in Georgia, but the plain folk's dream of moving the seat of state government from Atlanta failed. Although 76 percent of the lower river's ballots were cast in favor of the capital's removal to Milledgeville, the measure was defeated statewide. Whites blamed black voters. Indeed, the largest anti-Milledgeville votes were cast at Hawkinsville and in areas where the railroad construction and forest industries were most important. These were the new centers of the African American community. One disappointed conservative, who mistakenly believed that freedmen would not care where the capital was located, wrote that hundreds of pro-Atlanta tickets had been "secretly distributed to them." However, African Americans were convinced that if "they voted against Atlanta they would vote away their rights and violate the Constitution of the United States." The disappointed conservative, along with many other whites, underestimated the power of emancipationist symbols among freedmen.[81]

For Confederate veterans, the paramilitary victory to preserve white patriarchy, which was largely over by 1871, was sealed in the constitution of 1877. As George Woods wrote in 1877, the "colored line is broken, and the rank and file of the Radical party is scattered." The formerly powerful "negro party," which had been "cemented by Union leagues and led by scalawags and carpetbaggers," ceased to exist as a political threat. Old soldiers' fathers such as

Norman McDuffie were involved at every level of the campaign to rid the lower river of Radicalism, and so were the soldiers themselves. In 1870 James Boothe replaced the Radical Seaborn Salter as Pulaski County's representative in the state legislature. His election symbolized the shifting tide. A farmer and former slaveholder, Boothe had served as an officer in the 10th Georgia Cavalry. With blacks and white Republicans eliminated through terrorism from meaningful political participation, Boothe was easily elected by the same deferential plain folk who made him a Confederate officer. After the defeat of the Republicans, the state's leading conservative politicians debated "Who Saved Georgia?" Though each claimed credit, one newspaper editor accurately believed that victory belonged to "the grand army of voters . . . merely soldiers paroled." Many of them had never stopped fighting.[82]

**A**few weeks after the mock funeral procession buried Radicalism at Hawkinsville, John K. Whaley, the lower river's storied frontiersman, went home to die. His Rip van Winkle–like appearance ended almost fifteen years of solitude on the fringes of the Okefenokee Swamp. Now that he was in his mid-seventies, the days when he could draw a bead on a coon's eye by the light of a pine knot had long passed. Nevertheless, Whaley's identity as the quintessential woodsman prompted a notice in the *Hawkinsville Dispatch*, which referred to his prowess as a hunter and his earlier flight from the hubbub of the cotton frontier. He lived for three more years among his Pulaski County kinfolk before he quietly passed away in the spring of 1874.[1]

The world that Whaley discovered at his homecoming was entirely different from the one he had left in the late 1850s for better hunting grounds on the Georgia-Florida border. Thousands of plain folk cut from his cloth fought for the Confederate cause, and hundreds died to save their families and homes from the Yankee invasion and the feared consequences of their own defeat—black emancipation and migration into the forest. The war added another layer to the area's collective memory that often measured people by the stand their family took. In 1874 Archibald Campbell of Telfair

County died at age eighty-one. He was memorialized as a "great patriot" who lost four sons in the "Confederate War." Thousands of local African Americans were now free citizens of the United States. Each year more arrived to work on railroads and in sawmills and turpentine distilleries. Households and neighborhoods had been reconfigured by the war, emancipation, and economic development. Rural industrialization spawned railroad lines, towns, county seats, and even a county that did not exist when Whaley left. A single conservative Democratic Party had replaced a vibrant antebellum two-party political system. But some things had not changed. Cotton was still the major cash crop; it had not only rebounded in the black belt neighborhoods but also expanded into the backwoods in the wake of postwar deforestation. Most people—black and white—still farmed for a living. But increasingly blacks and whites found themselves working land owned by someone else. A white patriarchy still ruled local government and promised to defend white male privilege and keep the piney woods a white person's country, even as New South industrialization replaced a landscape of longleaf pine forest and wiregrass range with sawmills and cotton fields.[2]

Attorney and former colonel Thomas Dawson, a Democratic Party insider and a New South booster, could not have been more different from John Whaley. The old frontiersman's identity was wedded to the natural landscape and its bounty until he died. Dawson's identity, on the other hand, experienced a drastic transformation after the war. In 1861, in Pulaski County, he and Ruel Anderson had raised Dawson's Battery of Georgia Light Artillery, a unit led by Anderson after Dawson's resignation during the bloody campaigns in Tennessee and northern Georgia. Attached to the state militia in 1864 from the Army of Tennessee, the battery was pushed across Georgia from Chickamauga to Savannah by the Union army. By the early 1870s, however, the war seemed remote in Dawson's memory. Indeed, the Confederate identity that had urged him to lead men to fight the Yankees in a desperate struggle for Southern independence was replaced in defeat by the identity of a New South advocate and reconciliationist who was willing to turn over Whaley's woods to the victors. Dawson now believed that impoverished plain folk could prosper only if they embraced the new economy symbolized by the new railroads, sawmills, and boomtowns chiefly financed by Northern capital investment.[3]

Perhaps for this reason Dawson was chosen in 1873 to accept the gift of a new county courthouse from William E. Dodge, a powerful New York capitalist-politician and the lower river's leading Yankee investor. Dawson stepped to the podium and led the pageant of New South industrialization and sectional reconciliation as a crowd listened on the courthouse grounds. His words reveal that he had redefined the region in his imagination as well as his personal identity. Ironically, Dawson described the land that his Confederate comrades had fought and died to protect as a "desert or darkling wilderness" that the Yankee industrialist "found" largely unoccupied and untamed. Referring to the locals in his audience, the ex-Confederate officer thanked Dodge for "the civilization you have brought amongst them" in their "wild, unimproved country." Dawson then turned to the future and played the role of New South seer. "I can almost see with a prophet's eye in the not far distance a garden . . . that will be an ornament to your bounty, that will fill your eye and heart with pleasure for the success of the grand and noble work undertaken by you."[4]

The courthouse gift and dedication hailed by Dawson as a new beginning for the region resembled a ritual of dispossession. He verbally emptied the piney woods of its people and their culture when he described the forest as a featureless "desert" seemingly devoid of the families and neighborhoods that had occupied the area for two generations. In Dawson's opinion, the "unimproved" nature of the plain folk's "wild" landscape justified Dodge's "grand and noble work," Dawson's metaphor for deforestation. Dodge's gift of the frame courthouse sealed the transaction. Naming played a critical role in the process of reidentification. The 1873 dedication took place at Eastman, a new town named for William Pitt Eastman, a New Hampshire native who arrived in 1866 and engaged in land speculation along with Dodge. Not coincidentally, Eastman was the county seat of Dodge County, created in 1870 by Georgia's Reconstruction legislature, largely from portions of backwoods Pulaski and Telfair Counties. The land spreading for miles beyond the town was now part of Dodge County, and within its boundaries stretched much of the timberland Dodge claimed.[5]

A former Republican congressman and three-time president of the New York Chamber of Commerce, William Dodge was the partner of a corporate giant called Phelps, Dodge, and Company. Dodge and his associates, including Eastman, purchased dubious titles to 300,000 acres of white belt pineland east of the Ocmulgee River and formed the Georgia Land and Lumber Company (GL&LC), incorporated in New York. The Georgia legislature funded the extension of the Macon and Brunswick Railroad through the heart of the company's claim. The creation of Dodge County and the town of Eastman, as well as the removal of Telfair County's courthouse to McRae, reflected a fundamental realignment of economic and political power from the lower

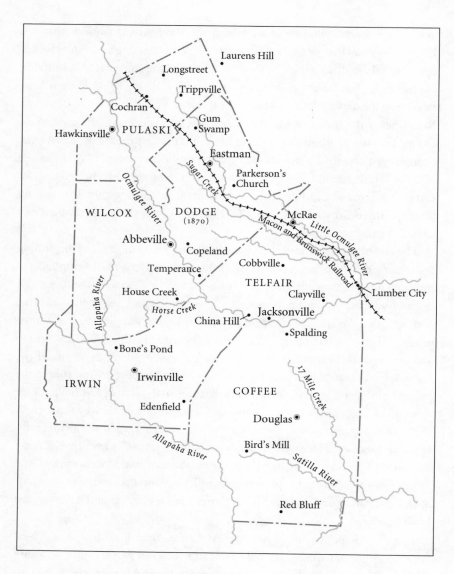

The lower Ocmulgee River region in 1871. Railroad
construction and the creation of Dodge County situated
county seats east of the river into backwoods neighborhoods,
where support for secession was low in 1861 and anti-
Confederate sentiment was high in 1865.

river's black belt neighborhoods to the railroad, where the GL&LC was gearing up for deforestation on a massive scale. To the railroad towns flocked locals and newcomers determined to cash in on the timber boom. Caught in the scramble for quick riches were the backwoods and rural families that plain folk Confederates had fought and died to defend. Although the new county honored Dodge's name and was largely carved from white belt neighborhoods in eastern Pulaski and Telfair Counties, Dodge represented much that the plain folk loathed, including corporate power and wartime profit, an evangelical impulse for reform, Republican Party affiliation, and the victorious and wealthy North.[6]

The plain folk's paramilitary fight ended in the defeat of Radicalism, but it was only a partial victory. Their violence and votes helped perpetuate white patriarchy along the lower river, just as their ballots aided secession and war. But the question of which white men ruled at home lingered as new political and economic realities reshaped the area's identity. Increasingly, key economic and political decisions affecting the plain folk's lives were being made in places far from their neighborhoods and counties. Many of the consequences of a Yankee victory that Governor Joseph E. Brown had predicted during the secession crisis and the Civil War were coming true, particularly the loss of real property and a political voice. By the early 1870s a new economic and political landscape had emerged in the white belt east of the river, one that lent credence to Brown's warning that defeated Confederates would become "slaves to Northern avarice and Northern insolence."[7]

That Dodge County even existed reflected the declining political clout of plain folk. In the antebellum period the backwoods yeomanry had flexed their political muscle and located the county seats of Douglas and Irwinville far from the Ocmulgee River and planter power. But the creation of Dodge County in 1870, and the similarly timed removal of Telfair's county seat from Jacksonville to a white belt neighborhood named McRae, indicated that new boundaries and seats of power were being moved across the political landscape without the consent of the governed. Along the lower river the old white patriarchy was also losing political control, not because of the war but because of collaborations between New South boosters, Northern industrialists, and real estate speculators who delivered the wealth of the region—its longleaf pine forest—into the hands of William Dodge and his company in deals struck in places like New York and Atlanta.

The old white patriarchy did not let this power grab pass without protest. In 1872 the aging Baptist preacher-farmer and old-time unionist James Williamson, along with almost one hundred men from southern and western Telfair County, petitioned the General Assembly to repeal the removal of their courthouse from Jacksonville to McRae. The citizens, the petition declared, had had no opportunity to "express their wishes" on the removal, the courthouse's relocation was "neather in the Center of population or wealth," and the "right[s]" of voters to voice their opinions "were not respected." Similar complaints were heard in Pulaski County, which lost most of its eastern white belt neighborhoods when Dodge County was created by the Reconstruction legislature the day after it voted to move Telfair's courthouse. At a public meeting held at the Hawkinsville Courthouse in August 1870, Orran Horne and Charles Kibbee, both former Confederate officers, drew up a communication declaring that "few, if any, of the citizens of said [backwoods] districts are in favor of being detached . . . to the new county proposed."[8]

Lost on Colonel Dawson, or perhaps ignored by him, was a tremendous irony. The plain folk's poverty was largely the result of the war, which claimed so many of their men and drove their families into indigence. Now a Yankee corporation that had profited during the war promised to rescue Confederate veterans from their economic straits by dispossessing them of their land. What further proof of "Northern avarice and Northern insolence" was needed? some plain folk wondered. The GL&LC, a corporate subsidiary of Phelps, Dodge, unleashed the industrial machine in nature's "garden," the thousands of square miles of virgin longleaf pine forest and open range that stretched eastward from the Ocmulgee. The "grand and noble work" that Dawson lauded in his speech was in reality the destruction of the forest. The garden was "blooming with its fragrance," but the odor was resin and sawdust. The new town of Eastman symbolized the dramatic change that New South industrialization quickly brought to once quiet and isolated plain folk neighborhoods. The clatter of saw and shingle mills rose from crude sheds, tree stumps littered the town site, and streets were formed by several feet of packed sawdust topped off by a layer of dirt. The new economic model of industrialization based on railroad construction and the forest industry emerged so quickly that it was likened to "magic change." *Hawkinsville Dispatch* editor George Woods was "astonished" at how quickly Eastman had "suddenly sprung up." He described its rapid growth as "something a little miraculous." John Whaley would have agreed.[9]

Antebellum railroad promoter and land speculator Abbot Hall Brisbane would have envied GL&LC's success. Yet the New South industrialization that astonished plain folk was neither miraculous nor sudden. In reality, the courthouse dedication at Eastman was the capstone of an eight-year collaboration between Yankee capitalists and land speculators, the state's Reconstruction General Assembly, the Macon and Brunswick Railroad, and a few local boosters to establish a Northern-controlled lumber empire in southern Georgia. In Colonel Dawson's mind, this was the "grand and noble" part of William Dodge's work.[10]

Dawson's speech implied something akin to consensus, a characteristic the plain folk did not possess during the secession crisis or on the wartime home front. Although the fight against Radicalism united most plain folk whose traditional status was threatened by emancipation and postwar economic development, the consensus was another product of Dawson's imagination. In fact, a chaotic world of sectional bitterness and local competition existed beneath Dawson's wishful veneer of reconciliation, one that signified a countryside undergoing change so radical that it rivaled the social and political consequences of emancipation. That revolution pitted whites against blacks in the struggle for self-worth, but the New South fight played off whites against whites, whites against blacks, and plain folk against each other in a struggle for the diminishing natural resources—lands, pine trees, ranges, and waterways—central to their economic independence and identity.

If the pageant of industrial progress could happen at Eastman, plain folk concluded, it could happen anywhere. The site of the new county seat was an unlikely location for an industrial community. Eastman popped up on the Macon and Brunswick Railroad in the middle of a vast open range near the center of the lumber company's land claims. For miles the railroad followed an antebellum cart path that ran along a sandy ridgeline roughly ten to twenty miles from the Ocmulgee's rich bottomland. It was a white belt area sparsely populated by plain folk often cultivating on less than fifty acres. From such remote and hardscrabble places families with names such as Davis, Harrell, Kinchen, Lee, and Livingston had sent men and boys into the Confederate army to fight and die. It was to this type of rural place that many Confederate veterans returned and hoped to rebuild their lives. But as one local critic of Dodge's timber company warned, these neighborhoods would be turned into "ashes before the wheels of progress." Postwar industrial progress rather than Sherman's army would ultimately claim their homes.[11]

It is within this context of Confederate defeat and sacrifice that plain folk reaction to Republicanism and New South industrialization can best be understood. The Northern timber men, their critics charged, were carpetbaggers and "sharpers" who founded "the little Yankee town" called Eastman.

To the plain folk's way of thinking, these men took advantage of defeated Southerners. Land speculator William Pitt Eastman had arrived immediately after the war, when "every-thing was in confusion," and put together a dubious title to 300,000 acres of pineland, which he in turn sold to a lumber company. The plain folk's occupation and ownership of the land—which in one case included "the oldest homestead in this section, where titles have been transmitted from father to son"—were obstacles to deforestation. Their dispossession through costly and lengthy legal action that most plain folk could ill afford was a necessary first step before Dodge's "grand and noble work" could begin.[12]

The language of plain folk's reaction to rural industrialization, like that of their Republic of Irwin ideal and their political campaign against Radicalism, was shaped in part by Confederate memory. Yankees, one unreconstructed writer complained in a metaphor sure to strike raw nerves, had come "to this section to make war upon the peaceful owners of these lands." The Northern lumber company violated wartime Confederate sacrifice by "insulting . . . widows and crippled soldiers" by taking their land from them. Confederate defeat and emancipation were two clear verdicts of the Civil War, but even in defeat veterans believed that they could return home and redeem themselves through productive lives on their own land. Now a Yankee lumber company, one that sought to destroy the foundation of their rural neighborhoods, was waging a new "war" of dishonest dispossession on the plain folk. John Wesley Griffin, a land speculator associated with the GL&LC, was accused of removing county records from the Telfair Courthouse and returning them with "many Erasures [changes] and such like made on the Books." The list of land lots claimed by the timber corporation ran for column after column in local newspapers and displaced wartime casualty lists as the bearer of bad news. Among those who appeared to answer the company's claim to his land was Daniel McRanie Sr. He had lived on the same tract since 1834. The patriarch found a suit lodged against him in 1872 as he entered his early seventies, almost a decade after he lost two of his four sons in the war. When after two years of litigation a local court upheld McRanie's right to five of the seven land lots in question, GL&LC lawyers moved for a new trial. It was a common tactic to force plain folk to settle out of court by turning over half of their property to the timber company rather than see it eaten up in lawyer's fees.[13]

Almost a generation after Appomattox, in the spring of 1895, a posse of federal marshals surrounded a house in Telfair County. They had hunted

Lucius Williams for twenty-five days and discovered that he had taken refuge in the river swamp near his son's home. They waited. Formerly captain of the Telfair Volunteers, the nonslaveholding yeoman farmer had joined James Humphreys's company in 1862 as a lieutenant. He was elected captain by his men in February 1864 and led them in the trench fighting around Petersburg. In the desperate waning days of the Confederacy, Williams and fellow officers of the 49th Georgia petitioned their superiors to let them recruit slaves at home to fight beside them in the trenches. The officers wrote that they had "freely" discussed this plan with their enlisted men, "who almost unanimously agree to it." In peacetime they had worked beside black men in the fields "and did not consider it disgraceful" and "certainly will not look upon it in any other light at this time, when an end so glorious as our independence is to be achieved." Captured a week before Lee's surrender at Appomattox, Lucius Williams spent almost three months in a prisoner of war camp at Johnson's Island, Ohio. After his release, he returned home to farm. In the 1870s he, like so many other plain folk, found some of his land lots listed among those claimed by the GL&LC.[14]

Since the war, Williams had changed. "Old man Williams," as he was called, was an angry, embittered, and sometimes violent veteran. Now sixty-one years old, he was wanted in U.S. District Court on charges of conspiracy to murder John C. Forsyth, a GL&LC agent killed by an assassin. A man who once "stood as fair as any man in Telfair County," Williams was now involved in the messy business of forging deeds to pineland claimed by the lumber company, both to defend plain folk land against the timber company and to gain access to timberland for himself and others. The possibility that he could stand shoulder-to-shoulder with a black man against a common enemy, as he had proposed in 1865, had long since passed for him and most ex-Confederates as racial violence increased in the postwar years. Indicted for killing a black timber cutter employed by the GL&LC, Williams was considered an "outlaw" by federal authorities but not by his neighbors. A previous attempt to bring him before the court in December 1894 failed when the federal posse that had captured him was ambushed by "an armed mob" of plain folk and "compelled to surrender their prisoner or lose their own lives." Unreconstructed until the end, Williams openly challenged federal authorities. He told a friend that the court was "prejudiced against him," that he would "kill his ownself" before surrendering, and that "he would fight until he died."[15]

The federal posse finally cornered Williams as he napped after lunch on the porch of his son's house. He had covered his face with a newspaper and dozed off while the women cleared the table. The posse watched. When ordered to surrender by a federal marshal, Williams refused. In the exchange of gunfire that followed, Williams was hit five times, at least once in the back. The doctor who examined him recorded that one shot glanced off his forehead, another hit near his jaw, and three more entered his body, any one of which "would have produced death." The survivor of such storied Civil War battles as Fredericksburg, Gettysburg, and the Seven Days lingered into the next day surrounded by his sons. "My liver is shot all to pieces," the old veteran told them. "They have killed me."[16]

Lucius Williams's fate was violent in the extreme. But throughout the postwar years, acts of violence large and small signaled the destruction of the forest and the disintegration of the plain folk's world. In the spring of 1878, four years after Colonel Dawson's speech at Eastman, Anson Dodge routinely wrote to one of his agents from a Telfair County lumber camp: "Nothing of interest." Nothing could have been further from the truth. The lumber company's engrossment of 300,000 acres of timberland increasingly destabilized the open range as railroading, timber cutting, and naval stores widened out. Traditional hunting grounds and "sheep ranges" were altered in subtle ways perhaps not evident to Anson Dodge but inescapable to plain folk dependent on the grazing lands. The growth of sawmills and turpentine stills at Dodge's camps drove up land prices to the point where "poor people" no longer had access to the woods. Deforestation created new boundaries in the forest between virgin and cut-out stands of timber, with devastating economic and social implications for the yeomanry.[17]

In southern Telfair County, for example, sheep were stolen, driven across the river, and sold in Coffee County, where the open range remained largely undisturbed. Confederate veterans and their families were often caught up in such range disputes, which pitted one neighborhood against another, either as victims of rustling or as homes of the rustlers themselves. In the summer of 1878 Jesse Bennett, formerly a third sergeant of the Coffee County Guards, was implicated in sheep stealing. The ex-Confederate had supposedly bought sheep stolen north of the river and driven them to the Coffee side. Telfair sheep men accused Bennett of complicity in the thefts and demanded that he help recover and sort out the sheep, or they would "deal with him." In actions reminiscent of clashes between deserter bands and Confederates, regulators, or paramilitary political groups, the Telfair men armed themselves and crossed the river. They stopped at the Coffee County farm of Thomas C. Pate and, having invaded their neighboring county, adopted a resolution demanding that Coffee's citizens help recover the stolen sheep and pledge to no longer purchase livestock crossed at the river. Their local pride wounded, the residents of Coffee charged that the Telfair sheep men had acted in a "hasty" and "uncalled for" manner. Citizens south of the river would always "be ready to respond and aid in hunting out offenders of the law," they declared, but without "the invasion of our county by armed bands and companies of men, armed as though hostilities were at hand and this were not a peaceable land." The images and memories of war—invasions by armed companies of men— were employed to describe a new postwar fight for survival on the shrinking open range.[18]

Within a twenty-year period, plain folk were forced to confront one of their greatest fears. The forest that shaped their antebellum identity was growing smaller. The secession crisis and the war had engendered a measure of artificial unity that had at its core the defense of family, home, and property. Piney woods men had volunteered to fight the Yankees at rates comparable to the inhabitants of other regions in Georgia and had assumed Confederate identities. They died of disease and wounds at frightening rates. The soldiers and their families at home possessed the will to fight well into 1864, but the home front, stripped of much of its agricultural manpower, disintegrated from within under the pressure of the "hard war." After Sherman's march and the fight at Griswoldville, even staunch Confederates at home doubted that more fighting would settle anything. Thus they began to redirect their energies from support for the Confederacy to the preservation of their neighborhoods and the human and material resources needed to rebuild them. In early 1865 Confederate cavalry, deserter bands, and regulators competed for control of the countryside. Patriarchs organized defense companies to protect a world of ever-constricting boundaries that ranged in size from counties to neighborhoods to, in the case of Lucius Williams, a hideout in the river swamp. After successfully uniting to purge the countryside of Radical Republicanism during a paramilitary reign of terror, New South economics and politics divided former Confederates into the New South camp of men such as Colonel Dawson and the reactionary and violent camp of men like Lucius Williams. As rangeland disappeared, cotton production expanded, and white tenancy increased. Former governor Joseph Brown's warning that a Yankee victory meant submission and ruin for white plain folk seemed to have come true.

# NOTES

*Abbreviations*

AGIC  Adjutant General's Incoming Correspondence, Record Group
22-2-17, Georgia Department of Archives and History, Atlanta

AGLB  Adjutant General's Letter Books, Georgia Department of Archives
and History, Atlanta

AS  Rawick, George P., gen. ed. *The American Slave: A Composite
Autobiography*. 19 vols., 12 vols. in supplement. Westport, Conn.:
Greenwood Publishing Co., 1977. *AS* citations take the following
form: volume number(part number):page number.

BRFAL  Records of the Bureau of Refugees, Freedmen, and Abandoned
Lands, National Archives, Washington, D.C.

CRSG  Allen D. Candler, comp., *The Confederate Records of the State of
Georgia*. 6 vols. Atlanta: State Printer, 1909–11.

CWM-GDAH  Civil War Miscellany, Personal Papers, Georgia Department of
Archives and History, Atlanta

DAR-H  Daughters of the American Revolution, Hawkinsville Chapter

*Dispatch*  *Hawkinsville Dispatch*

GDAH  Georgia Department of Archives and History, Atlanta

GHS  Georgia Historical Society, Savannah

GIC-GDAH  Governor's Incoming Correspondence, Georgia Department of
Archives and History, Atlanta

JPL  Jacksonville Public Library, Jacksonville, Florida

MC  Manuscript Census, National Archives, Washington, D.C.

*Messenger*  *Georgia Journal and Messenger*

*Morning News*  *Savannah Daily Morning News*

NA-A  National Archives, Atlanta Branch

NA-W  National Archives, Washington, D.C.

OR  U.S. Government, *The War of the Rebellion: A Compilation of the
Official Records of the Union and Confederate Armies*. 70 vols.
Washington, D.C.: Government Printing Office, 1902. *OR*
citations take the following form: volume number(part number,
where applicable):page number. All volumes cited throughout
notes are from series 1.

PCC  Pulaski County Courthouse, Hawkinsville, Georgia

| PCIC Minutes | Pulaski County Inferior Court Minutes, Georgia Department of Archives and History, Atlanta |
| --- | --- |
| *Recorder* | *Milledgeville Southern Recorder* |
| RG | Record Group |
| SHC | Southern Historical Collection, University of North Carolina, Chapel Hill |
| TCIC Minutes | Telfair County Inferior Court Minutes, Georgia Department of Archives and History, Atlanta |
| UGA | Hargrett Rare Book and Manuscript Library, University of Georgia, Athens |
| *Union Recorder* | *Milledgeville Union Recorder* |

*Prologue*

1 *Confederate Veteran* 5, no. 2 (February 1897): 81; Henderson, *Roster*, 5:279, 287.

2 Henderson, *Roster*, 1:963, 967–68.

3 Gallagher, *Confederate War*, 3–4; Berry, *All That Makes a Man*, 9–10. On class conflict and internal dissension as causes for the Confederate defeat, see Williams, Williams, and Carlson, *Plain Folk*, 1–7, and Escott, *After Secession*, chap. 4. Richard Beringer et al. (*Why the South Lost*, 4–34) maintain that a loss of Southern will was the primary cause of defeat.

4 Owsley, *Plain Folk*, 7–8; Magdol and Wakelyn, *Southern Common People*, xi–xii; McCurry, *Masters of Small Worlds*, 48–51.

5 McCurry, *Masters of Small Worlds*, 49–51, 107; Owsley, *Plain Folk*, 7–8, 142–43; Boles, "Revisiting the Plain Folk," ix–x. A useful classification of occupations for 1860 and 1870 based on census samples appears in Ash, *Middle Tennessee Society Transformed*, app. B, 264–67. For occupations of plain folk living in Hawkinsville, see U.S. Census, 1860, Ga., Pulaski County, Population, 1–8, MC.

6 U.S. Census Office, *Eighth Census*, Population, 58–60, and Agriculture, 226–27; Kulikoff, "Transition to Capitalism," 140–44; Ash, *When the Yankees Came*, 3–5.

7 J. William Harris, *Plain Folk and Gentry*, 2–7; Fredrickson, *Black Image*, 58–64, 130–34, 145–46; Link, *Roots of Secession*, 178–79, 213–15; Degler, *The Other South*, 14–17; Kolchin, *American Slavery*, 180–82; Rable, *Confederate Republic*, 55–56.

8 Kulikoff, "Transition to Capitalism," 126–32. For corn production and consumption patterns in Georgia, see Hilliard, *Hog Meat*, 157–61.

9 Bond, "Herders, Farmers"; Hahn, *Southern Populism*, 60–63; U.S. Census Office, *Eighth Census*, Agriculture, 226–27; J. William Harris, *Plain Folk and Gentry*, 5–7.

10 U.S. Census Office, *Eighth Census*, Agriculture, 226–27; U.S. Census, 1860, Ga., Pulaski County Slave Schedule, 26–27, MC; Kenzer, *Kinship and Neighborhood*, 10–11. Arthur Colson, in *AS* 3(1):218, described his master's Pulaski County plantation home as "only a good common log house."

11 U.S. Department of the Interior, *Cotton Production*, 47–50; Wetherington, *New South*, 1–6. Today the antebellum study area would include, in addition to these five counties, parts of Atkinson, Ben Hill, Bleckley, Dodge, Jeff Davis, Tift, and Turner Counties.

12  For secessionist fears and plain folk in Georgia, see Carey, *Parties, Slavery*, 250; Michael P. Johnson, *Patriarchal Republic*, 46–52; and J. William Harris, *Plain Folk and Gentry*, 6–7.

13  Harper, "Agriculture in Lower Georgia," 115; Doyon and Hodler, "Secessionist Sentiment," 333–38 (59 percent of the wiregrass delegates were secessionists); Weitz, *Higher Duty*, 30; Bohannon, "They Had Determined to Root Us Out," 100–101.

14  McPherson, *For Cause*, 23–26; U.S. Census, 1860, Ga., Pulaski County Population Schedule, 3, MC; Whites, *Crisis in Gender*, 108.

15  For different views, see Faust, *Mothers of Invention*, 30–32, and Williams, *Rich Man's War*, 1–7.

16  Michael P. Johnson, *Patriarchal Republic*, 46–52; Fredrickson, *Black Image*, 58–64, 130–34, 145–46; Doyon and Hodler, "Secessionist Sentiment," 333. On racial fear in the Upper South, see Link, *Roots of Secession*, 178–79, 213–15.


*Chapter 1*

1  *Dispatch*, February 16, 1871, May 14, 1874.

2  Bartram, *Travels*, 363; Ethridge, *Creek Country*, 28, 33–34, 209, 222, 236; U.S. Department of the Interior, *Cotton Production*, 46–50; *Dispatch*, February 16, 1871, May 14, 1874. On frontier society along the upper Ocmulgee River, see Reidy, *From Slavery to Agrarian Capitalism*, chap. 1.

3  U.S. War Department, "Survey of the Ocmulgee River," 25–29; *Morning News*, March 10, 1860; John Malloy to "Dear Brother," February 9, 1843, Duncan Malloy Papers, SHC.

4  J. William Harris, *Plain Folk and Gentry*, 6–7; Brisbane, "Detailed Report," 21; Hahn, *Southern Populism*, 10, 50; Owsley, *Plain Folk*, 134–35; Freehling, *South vs. the South*, 20–23; Ash, *When the Yankees Came*, 2–4; *Savannah Republican*, June 18, 1861.

5  U.S. Bureau of Soils, *Survey of Dodge County*, 233; Bartram, *Travels*, 68, 307; Freehling, *South vs. the South*, 19–21.

6  Kenzer, *Kinship and Neighborhood*, 10–11; Wallace Leigh Harris, *Pulaski and Bleckley Counties*, 1:72–73, 86.

7  Dearborn to "My dear Children," October 22, 1836, JPL; Brisbane, "Detailed Report," 26; Cobb, *Dodge County*, 216; McWhiney, *Cracker Culture*, 51–52; U.S. Census Office, *Eighth Census, Population*, 72–73, and *Agriculture*, 226–27. For a description of the "lower" counties, see "A Ramble in the Low Country," *Dispatch*, April 5, 1873.

8  Harper, "Agriculture in Lower Georgia," 115; Wallace Leigh Harris, *Pulaski and Bleckley Counties*, 1:72–73; U.S. Census Office, *Eighth Census, Population*, 72–73; Reidy, *From Slavery to Agrarian Capitalism*, 20–21; *Brunswick Advertiser and Appeal*, September 26, 1885.

9  U.S. Census Office, *Ninth Census, Population*, 349, and *Eighth Census, Agriculture*, 196; Clements, *Irwin County*, 193; Wallace Leigh Harris, *Pulaski and Bleckley Counties*, 1:560; Owsley, *Plain Folk*, 154–57; U.S. Census, 1860, Ga., Coffee County Agriculture Schedule, 11, MC; Harper, "Agriculture in Lower Georgia," 115.

10  U.S. Census, 1860, Ga., Telfair County Population Schedule, 20, and Agriculture Schedule, 67, MC.

11  Faust, *Mothers of Invention*, 31–32; McCurry, *Masters of Small Worlds*, 81–85; Dearborn to "My dear Children," October 22, 1836, JPL.

12  *Recorder*, October 28, 1862; *Dispatch*, December 19, 1878; Hilliard, *Hog Meat*, 98–99, 137–38, 150–58; U.S. Census, 1860, Ga., Telfair County Agriculture Schedule, 73, and Pulaski County Agriculture Schedule, 17, MC; *Statistics of the United States in 1860*, 4:341; U.S. Census Office, *Eighth Census, Agriculture*, 26–27; Herring, *Saturday Night Sketches*, 58–64; "Appraisement of the Estate of Henry Bohannon Late of Pulaski County, Decs'd," in "Inventory, Appraisals, and Sales, 1851 to 1858," Pulaski County, 149–52, and "Inventory and Appraisement of the Estate of Thully Williamson, Deceased," Office of Probate Judge, Pulaski County, 254–57, Probate Records, PCC.

13  Ash, *When the Yankees Came*, 3–5; U.S. Census Office, *Eighth Census, Agriculture*, 26–27, and *Population*, 72–73; U.S. Department of the Interior, *Cotton Production*, 50 (quotation). For a similar situation in Augusta's hinterland, see J. William Harris, *Plain Folk and Gentry*, 31–32. The 1859 corn production-consumption ratios—with 1.00 meeting self-sufficiency—were Pulaski, 1.72; Telfair, 1.07; and Wilcox 0.92. For determining self-sufficiency in corn, see Hilliard, *Hog Meat*, 158.

14  Dearborn to "My dear Children," October 22, 1836, JPL (first quotation); U.S. Census, 1860, Ga., Irwin County Agriculture Schedule, 7–8, MC; *Dispatch*, August 2, September 6, 1877, November 14, 21, 1878; *AS* 3(1):239 (second quotation, Martha Everette), 221 (Arthur Colson); Herring, *Saturday Night Sketches*, 35–38; U.S. Census Office, *Eighth Census, Agriculture*, 29; Hilliard, *Hog Meat*, 61.

15  Julia Floyd Smith, *Slavery and Rice Culture*, 36–38; U.S. Census Office, *Seventh Census . . . Appendix*, 379, and *Eighth Census, Agriculture*, 23–27; Dearborn to "My dear Children," October 22, 1836, JPL.

16  White, *Statistics*, 540; U.S. Census, 1860, Ga., Coffee County Agriculture Schedule, 1, 11–12, 21, Wilcox County Agriculture Schedule, 1, and Pulaski County Agriculture Schedule, 15, MC; *Dispatch*, June 3, 1875; Hilliard, *Hog Meat*, 39, 50–51; Ward, *Coffee County*, 40–60; McRae and McMillan Store Ledger, 1854–56, 4, 12, Laurens County Historical Society. See also McCurry, *Masters of Small Worlds*, 65–66, and Joyner, *Down by the Riverside*, 96–97. George Walker's plantation at Longstreet produced four hundred bushels of wheat in 1859, and many upriver yeomen grew small crops of the grain.

17  U.S. Census, 1860, Ga., Telfair County Agriculture Schedule, 73, MC; U.S. Census Office, *Eighth Census, Agriculture*, 196; McCurry, *Masters of Small Worlds*, 63–65. On increasing yeoman involvement in cotton production on Georgia's piedmont in the 1850s, see J. William Harris, *Plain Folk and Gentry*, 31–32; Bond, "Herders, Farmers," 86–99; and Bryant, *How Curious a Land*, 19–20.

18  U.S. Census, 1860, Ga., Wilcox County Agriculture Schedule, 9, and Pulaski County Agriculture Schedule, 17, MC; Nathaniel Gibbs to "Dear Wife," March 25, 1863, UGA. For plantation belt comparisons, see J. William Harris, *Plain Folk and Gentry*, 31–32.

19  *Pulaski Times*, quoted in *Union Recorder*, October 5, 1858; U.S. Department of the Interior, *Cotton Production*, 48–50.

20  U.S. Department of the Interior, *Cotton Production*, 48–50; U.S. Census, 1860, Ga., Wilcox County Agriculture Schedule, 3, MC. David Williams (*Rich Man's War*, 7) minimizes the significance of yeoman involvement in cotton production and slaveholding in a more fertile region of Georgia. Of the Chattahoochee Valley, he notes: "Only the

planters . . . and their families benefited significantly from an economic system based on cotton and slavery."

21  U.S. Census, 1860, Ga., Telfair County Slave Schedule, 56, and Agriculture Schedule, 71, MC; Hall, *Travels*, 3:279; *AS* 4(2):503 (Easter Reed).

22  U.S. Census Office, *Eighth Census, Agriculture*, 226–27; U.S. Census, 1860, Ga., Coffee County Slave Schedule, 2, MC; Hundley, *Social Relations*, 195–98; Ward, *Coffee County*, 76 (Hargraves). For a glimpse of a yeoman master and a cotton farmer and the scarcity of manuscript sources documenting their lives, see J. William Harris, "Portrait of a Small Slaveholder."

23  U.S. Census, 1860, Ga., Irwin County Agriculture Schedule, 7–9, Coffee County Agriculture Schedule, 11, and Pulaski County Agriculture Schedule, 17, MC; Clements, *Irwin County*, 194; U.S. Census Office, *Eighth Census, Population*, 72. On the sex and age of yeoman slaveholders, see McCurry, *Masters of Small Worlds*, 48–51.

24  Kolchin, *American Slavery*, 180–81; Clements, *Irwin County*, 515–16; U.S. Census, 1860, Ga., Coffee County Slave Schedule, 2, MC; Hahn, *Southern Populism*, 89–90. Although the percentage of slaveowning households along the lower river was slightly more than that for the South generally in 1860 (26 percent), it was well below the 56 percent found on the cotton belt in Greene County, Ga. See Bryant, *How Curious a Land*, 23.

25  Cobb, *Dodge County*, 216; U.S. Census Office, *Eighth Census, Agriculture*, 226–27; John Malloy to "Dear Brother," February 9, 1843, Duncan Malloy Papers, SHC. For a description of celebrations like the Fourth of July, see *AS* 3(1):238 (Martha Everette).

26  U.S. Census Office, *Eighth Census, Statistics*, 4:298, 341; John Malloy to "Dear Brother," February 9, 1843, Duncan Malloy Papers, SHC.

27  C. M. Bozeman to Mr. Butts, August 19, 1830, File II, box 15, GDAH; Reidy, *From Slavery to Agrarian Capitalism*, 31–35; Wallace Leigh Harris, *Pulaski and Bleckley Counties*, 1:72–73, 2:1006–27; U.S. Department of the Interior, *Cotton Production*, 41; Sherwood, *Gazetteer*, 194; U.S. Census Office, *Ninth Census*, 1:349–50.

28  For the wealth of Manning's household, see the will of Harriette J. Manning, Will Book B, 113–15, and Tax Digest, 1857, entry for "S. M. Manning," both in Pulaski County Superior Court, PCC; DAR-H, *History of Pulaski County*, 441; U.S. Census, 1860, Ga., Pulaski County Slave Schedule, 10, and Agriculture Schedule, 15, MC.

29  U.S. Census, 1860, Ga., Pulaski County Agriculture Schedule, 15, and Slave Schedule, 37–44, MC; Hahn, *Southern Populism*, 45–49; Wallace Leigh Harris, *Pulaski and Bleckley Counties*, 1:264; Bryant, *How Curious a Land*, 22–25.

30  John Malloy to "Dear Brother," February 9, 1843, Duncan Malloy Papers, SHC; U.S. Census Office, *Eighth Census, Agriculture*, 226–27; U.S. Census, 1860, Ga., Coffee County Slave Schedule, 3–7, and Agriculture Schedule, 1–3, MC.

31  U.S. Census, 1860, Ga., Coffee County Agriculture Schedule, 1. and Slave Schedule, 3–7, MC; U.S. Census Office, *Eighth Census, Population*, 72, and *Ninth Census, Population*, 101; Bryant, *How Curious a Land*, 24.

32  Bartley, *Modern Georgia*, 16–21; U.S. Census, 1860, Ga., Telfair County Agriculture Schedule, 5, 9, MC; Julia Floyd Smith, *Slavery and Rice Culture*, 6–7.

33  Harper, "Agriculture in Lower Georgia," 115; McWhiney, *Cracker Culture*, 51–79; Owsley,

*Plain Folk*, 44–45, 157; Richardson, *Lights and Shadows*, 26 (circuit rider); U.S. Census Office, *Eighth Census, Agriculture*, 26–27. On Indian use of the range, see Ethridge, *Creek Country*, 162–66.

34  *Dispatch*, June 21, 1877 (quotation); Hahn, *Southern Populism*, 60–63; U.S. Census, 1860, Ga., Coffee County Agriculture Schedule, 1, MC; Hummel, *Emancipating Slaves*, 48–49.

35  U.S. Census Office, *Eighth Census, Agriculture*, 27; U.S. Census, 1860, Ga., Coffee County Agriculture Schedule, 1, MC; McRae and McMillan Store Ledger, 1854–55, 10–11, 163, Laurens County Historical Society; J. C. Wilkes, "Wilkes Family Recollections," 5, GDAH.

36  Hahn, *Southern Populism*, 59–53; *Georgia Acts, 1855–56*, 411–12 (quotation), *1859*, 297, *1860*, 164, *1866*, 39; Schama, *Landscape and Memory*, 139.

37  J. C. Wilkes, "Wilkes Family Recollections," 7, GDAH; Ward, *Coffee County*, 316–17; U.S. Census, 1860, Ga., Wilcox County Population Schedule, 5, and Telfair County Population Schedule, 1, MC; *Recorder*, July 12, 1853; *Georgia Acts, 1857*, 250; John G. Muan to W. W. Paine, February 8, 1856, box 2, folder 25, Paine Papers, GHS.

38  DAR-H, *History of Pulaski County*, 432–33; Wallace Leigh Harris, *Pulaski and Bleckley Counties*, 1:259; U.S. Census Office, *Eighth Census, Agriculture*, 226–27.

39  Kolchin, *American Slavery*, 96; Bailum Sparrow to L. Lieberman, April 11, 1868, BRFAL; *Dispatch*, June 21, 1877. For slave "speculators" in Bibb County, see the statement of Alice Battle in *AS* 3(1):39.

40  Kolchin, *American Slavery*, 103–4. U.S. Census Office, *Eighth Census, Agriculture*, 226–27; Blassingame, *Slave Community*, 259–60; Reidy, *From Slavery to Agrarian Capitalism*, 36–37. In *AS* 4(2), see the statements of Sarah Nance (71), Sarah Virgil (626), and Easter Reed (526).

41  *AS* 3(1):219 (Arthur Colson); "Inventory and Appraisal of the Estate of Thully Williamson," 254–57, Office of Probate Judge Pulaski County, Probate Records, PCC; Clements, *Irwin County*, 193; U.S. Census Office, *Eighth Census, Population*, 68–69.

42  U.S. Census Office, *Eighth Census, Population*, 66–68; McCurry, *Masters of Small Worlds*, 48–51; U.S. Census, 1860, Ga., Irwin County Slave Schedule, 1, and Agriculture Schedule, 1, MC.

43  *Statistics of the United States in 1860*, 4:341; U.S. Census Office, *Eighth Census, Agriculture*, 226–27; Wallace Leigh Harris, *Pulaski and Bleckley Counties*, 2:1006–27; "Inventory and Appraisement of the Estate of Isaac Johnson, Deceased," 364–65, Office of Probate Judge, Pulaski County, Probate Records, PCC. David Williams (*Rich Man's War*, 7) dismisses the unifying potential of small slaveholding.

44  Ash, *When the Yankees Came*, 2–7; *CRSG* 2:121 (Brown).

45  McCurry, *Masters of Small Worlds*, 6–8; *Minutes of the Primitive Baptist Pulaski Association*, . . . *1847*, 5–6; Rose, *Victorian America*, 70–71.

46  McCurry, *Masters of Small Worlds*, 58–61, 86–88; *Minutes of the Primitive Baptist Pulaski Association*, . . . *1847*, 6.

47  U.S. Census, 1860, Ga., Telfair County Population Schedule, 23, MC; Rable, *Civil Wars*, 1–2; Ash, *When the Yankees Came*, 86–88; Rose, *Victorian America*, 70–71.

48  U.S. Census, 1860, Ga., Telfair County Slave Schedule, 49–59, MC; Charlotte E. Taylor to "My Beloved Husband," April 13, 1849, in Stevens, *Family Letters*, 219; Clinton, *Plantation Mistress*, 18, 29–33. For a transcription of Daniel's will, see Cobb, *Dodge County*, 216–17.

49  Ash, *When the Yankees Came*, 4–6; Hubbs, *Guarding Greensboro*, 25–27.

50  Cobb, *Dodge County*, 183–85 (transcript of Parkerson's church minutes and its 1855 membership roll); *Statistics of the United States in 1860*, 4:365–70; Wyatt-Brown, *Southern Culture*, 106–13; McCurry, *Masters of Small Worlds*, 159; Clements, *Irwin County*, 75; Crowley, *Primitive Baptists*, 19.

51  *Statistics of the United States in 1860*, 4:365–70; McCurry, *Masters of Small Worlds*, 140, 146; Chalker, *Pioneer Days*, 58–59, 63–64; Wallace Leigh Harris, *Pulaski and Bleckley Counties*, 1:365, 2:1019–20; Richardson, *Lights and Shadows*, 9–10, 26–27; Crowley, *Primitive Baptists*, 19.

52  U.S. Census, Ga., 1850, Pulaski County Population Schedule, 246–48, and 1860 Agriculture Schedule, 17, MC; Joiner, *Pioneer Families*, 1:2–3.

53  Cobb, *Dodge County*, 184–85; Clements, *Irwin County*, 454–57, 466–69, 510; Bode, "A Common Sphere," 775–809. The best discussion of plain folk in such congregations in the Deep South is McCurry, *Masters of Small Worlds*, chap. 5.

54  U.S. Census, 1860, Ga., Irwin County Slave Schedule, 1–4, MC. For church membership lists, see Clements, *Irwin County*, 456–57, 466–69, 510.

55  Clements, *Irwin County*, 468; Crowley, *Primitive Baptists*, 58, 65–67; Wyatt-Brown, *Southern Culture*, 114–15.

56  *Minutes of the Primitive Baptist Pulaski Association, . . . 1847*, 6; Wyatt-Brown, "Antimission Movement," 502–3, and *Southern Culture*, 116–17; George G. Smith, *History of Georgia Methodism*, 264 (second quotation); Richardson, *Lights and Shadows*, 26–27 (third quotation); Bode, "Evangelical Communities in Middle Georgia," 711–48; Olmsted, *Seaboard Slave States*, 454–55. See also "Circular Letter" in *Primitive Pulaski Association, 1872*, 1.

57  Richardson, *Lights and Shadows*, 10. For Walker's wealth, see Pulaski County Superior Court, Tax Digest, 1857, PCC, and U.S. Census, 1860, Ga., Pulaski County Population Schedule, 82, and Slave Schedule, 39–40, MC.

58  *Christian Index*, April 26, 1855; *AS* 3(1):238 (Martha Everette), 4(1):412 (Caroline Malloy), 4(1):505 (Reed); Clements, *Irwin County*, 466–68; Wallace Leigh Harris, *Pulaski and Bleckley Counties*, 1:365.

59  Clements, *Irwin County*, 466–67; *Primitive Pulaski Association, 1872*, 1; Crowley, *Primitive Baptists*, 58, 65–67.

60  Clements, *Irwin County*, 485; McCurry, *Masters of Small Worlds*, 136–47; Crowley, *Primitive Baptists*, 58, 65–67; *Christian Index*, February 20, 1861 (quotation).

61  *Christian Index*, April 26, 1855; "Pulaski" to Editor, *Messenger*, April 28, 1858.

62  *Messenger*, February 9, 1859; Wallace Leigh Harris, *Pulaski and Bleckley Counties*, 1:275 (quotation); R. G. Dun and Co., GA26, 137, Harvard University; Hubbs, *Guarding Greensboro*, 25–30.

63  Hahn, *Southern Populism*, 34–39; Thompson, "Moral Economy," 90–93; Wetherington, *New South*, 50; Hubbs, *Guarding Greensboro*, 25–30.

64  Brisbane, "Detailed Report," 21–22; Clements, *Irwin County*, 415–19.

65  Brisbane, "Detailed Report," 22–25.

66  Ibid., 22–25, 27; Clements, *Irwin County*, 415–19.

67  Brisbane, "Detailed Report," 28–29.

68  Ibid., 24–27; Clements, *Irwin County*, 24–27, 417–18.

69 Brisbane, "Detailed Report," 24–27 (first quotation); Clements, *Irwin County*, 415–19; "Old Brisbane Road," in *Valdosta Times*, October 19, 1895 (second quotation); Hahn, *Southern Populism*, 34–37.

70 *CRSG* 3:429; Brisbane, "Detailed Report," 26; *Savannah Republican*, June 18, 1861; Harper, "Agriculture in Lower Georgia," 109–14; U.S. Census Office, *Ninth Census, Population by Counties*, 22; Kennett, *Marching through Georgia*, 35–36.

71 Harper, "Agriculture in Lower Georgia," 111–15. See also "Visit to Hawkinsville," in *Messenger*, April 25, 1860.


*Chapter 2*

1 *Recorder*, December 4, 18, 25, 1860; Wooster, *People in Power*, 11–12; Hahn, *Southern Populism*, 98–99, 114–15; McCurry, *Masters of Small Worlds*, 242; U.S. Census Office, *Eighth Census, Population*, 58–61; *Messenger*, February 1, 1860; Michael P. Johnson, *Patriarchal Republic*, 46–52, and "New Look," 259–75.

2 Doyon and Hodler, "Secessionist Sentiment," 327, 333; Michael P. Johnson, "New Look," 268–71; *Recorder*, December 18, 1860; Barney, "Resisting the Republicans," 76–77; Freehling and Simpson, *Secession Debated*, 13, 24. On regionalism in Virginia, see Link, *Roots of Secession*, 63–64. On white men's liberty and slavery, see Carey, *Parties, Slavery*.

3 Murrell, "Union Father, Rebel Son," 361–63; U.S. Census, 1860, Ga., Telfair County Population Schedule, 5–6, and Slave Schedule, 49, MC; *Union Recorder*, April 6, 1852; *Recorder*, June 22, 1847; Clements, *Irwin County*, 159, 161 (quotation); Christopher J. Olsen, *Political Culture*, 121–22.

4 Owsley, *Plain Folk*, 133–34; Christopher J. Olsen, *Political Culture*, 25–27, 122–23; Hahn, *Southern Populism*, 94–95; McCurry, *Masters of Small Worlds*, 256–59; Ash, *When the Yankees Came*, 3–5.

5 Wallace Leigh Harris, *Pulaski and Bleckley Counties*, 1:90–91, 96, 102; U.S. Census, 1860, Ga., Pulaski County Slave Schedule, 1–46, Irwin County Slave Schedule, 1–4, MC; Wooster, *People in Power*, 41; Hahn, *Southern Populism*, 94–95. For a biographical sketch of one plain folk politician, see "Rowan Pafford," File II, box 109, GDAH; Clements, *Irwin County*, 43–47.

6 Hahn, *Southern Populism*, 92–95; Wooster, *People in Power*, 65–67; Ash, *When the Yankees Came*, 2–5; Clements, *Irwin County*, 42; U.S. Census, 1860, Ga., Irwin County Slave Schedule, 1–4, and Coffee County Slave Schedule, 1–9, MC; Ward, *Coffee County*, 322–23.

7 U.S. Census Office, *Eighth Census, Population*, 58–59; U.S. Census, 1860, Ga., Irwin County Slave Schedule, 1–4, MC; Christopher J. Olsen, *Political Culture*, 122–25.

8 Christopher J. Olsen, *Political Culture*, 104–5, 131.

9 Ash, *When the Yankees Came*, 4–5; Clements, *Irwin County*, 43–47, 509–10; Ward, *Coffee County*, 323; Christopher J. Olsen, *Political Culture*, 104–5.

10 Frank, *With Ballot and Bayonet*, 1–2; Ward, *Coffee County*, 260–64; Cobb, *Dodge County*, 163–64, 192–93; Chalker, *Pioneer Days*, 51, 182–83.

11 Kenzer, *Kinship and Neighborhood*, 10–11; Frank, *With Ballot and Bayonet*, 2–6; Wooster, *People in Power*, 65–66; Clements, *Irwin County*, 91; McCurry, *Masters of Small Worlds*, 265–75; Wallace Leigh Harris, *Pulaski and Bleckley Counties*, 1:63–64, 95.

12  Paine to Crawford, July 14, 1845, File II, box 109, GDAH; *Union Recorder*, April 20, 1847; *Recorder*, June 22, 1847.

13  U.S. Census, 1860, Ga., Telfair County Slave Schedule, 51–56, and Agriculture Schedule, 71, MC; R. G. Dun and Co., GA36, 123, Harvard University; Cobb, *Dodge County*, 248–50.

14  Cobb, *Dodge County*, 212–13, 248–49; Christopher J. Olsen, *Political Culture*, 10–11.

15  Doyon and Hodler, "Secessionist Sentiment," 338–39; Coulter, *Georgia*, 240–44; Hahn, *Southern Populism*, 99–101; Phillips, *Whig Party*, 104–27; Burnham, *Presidential Ballots*, 346–54, 358.

16  *Recorder*, August 7, 1860; U.S. Census, 1860, Ga., Telfair County Population Schedule, 4, Slave Schedule, 49, and Agriculture Schedule, 63, MC.

17  Crowley, *Primitive Baptists*, 35–40, 56–57, 89–90; Clements, *Irwin County*, 454–69; McCurry, *Masters of Small Worlds*, 169, 171–79, 256–62; Wyatt-Brown, *Southern Culture*, 153–56; Heyrman, *Southern Cross*, 151–52.

18  Wyatt-Brown, *Southern Culture*, 106–16, 133–35; Crowley, *Primitive Baptists*, 35–47, 95, 142; Pleasant Primitive Baptist Church Minutes, 1857–96, 4, microfilm drawer 199, box 65, GDAH.

19  McCurry, *Masters of Small Worlds*, 160–64, 169; Crowley, *Primitive Baptists*, 89–92 (quotations, 90–92).

20  Burnham, *Presidential Ballots*, 346–54, 358; Wooster, *People in Power*, 42–44; Phillips, *Georgia and State Rights*, 97, 104–8; Hahn, *Southern Populism*, 99–101. On the Whigs, see Holt, *Rise and Fall*.

21  *Recorder*, June 22, 1847; Christopher J. Olsen, *Political Culture*, 13–14; *Memoirs of Georgia*, 598; Cobb, *Dodge County*, 199–201; Ward, *Coffee County*, 260–64; U.S. Census, 1860, Ga., Coffee County Slave Schedule, 3–7, MC.

22  *Recorder*, June 22, 1847; *Messenger*, August 6, 1856; U.S. Census, 1860, Ga., Telfair County Population Schedule, 21, Slave Schedule, 51–52, and Agriculture Schedule, 67, MC; Paine to Governor Geo. Crawford, July 14, 1845, File II, box 109, GDAH.

23  Christopher J. Olsen, *Political Culture*, 5–6.

24  Bartley, *Modern Georgia*, 28; Ash, *When the Yankees Came*, 4–8; *Fifth Annual Report of the . . . Savannah Cotton Exchange, . . . 1877*, 5.

25  *Recorder*, November 11, 1851; Doherty, "Union Nationalism"; Reidy, *From Slavery to Agrarian Capitalism*, 86–89; J. William Harris, *Plain Folk and Gentry*, 125–27.

26  *Recorder*, November 5, 1850; Reidy, *From Slavery to Agrarian Capitalism*, 87–88; Freehling, *South vs. the South*, 30–31; Doherty, "Union Nationalism," 19–38.

27  R. G. Dun and Co., GA36, 123, Harvard University; *Journal of the State Convention, . . . 1850*, 1–14; Doherty, "Union Nationalism," 19–38.

28  *Journal of the State Convention, . . . 1850*, 14–15, 18, 31–32 (quotations); Coulter, *Georgia*, 309–10; Michael P. Johnson, *Patriarchal Republic*, 35–36.

29  Doherty, "Union Nationalism," 19–38; Reidy, *From Slavery to Agrarian Capitalism*, 88–89; Michael P. Johnson, *Patriarchal Republic*, 92–93.

30  *Recorder*, November 11, 1851; Doyon and Hodler, "Secessionist Sentiment," 338–41; Coulter, *Georgia*, 309–10.

31  Hahn, *Southern Populism*, 105–10; Freehling, *South vs. the South*, 22–23; Ash, *When the Yankees Came*, 4–5.

32 J. William Harris, *Plain Folk and Gentry*, 125–28; *Messenger*, July 8, 1857, June 15, 1859; Burnham, *Presidential Ballots*, 346–54, 358; Trowell, "Douglas before Memory," 4; Coulter, *Georgia*, 311–12; Eaton, *History of the Old South*, 477–79; Wallace Leigh Harris, *Pulaski and Bleckley Counties*, 1:91, 609–10.

33 Christopher J. Olsen, *Political Culture*, 150–56; *Recorder*, August 25, 1857; U.S. Census, 1860, Ga., Telfair County Slave Schedule, 49–50, 57, and Pulaski County Slave Schedule, 1–4, 9–11, 27–28, MC; *Messenger*, July 8, 1857, September 15, 1858, June 15, 1859; R. G. Dun and Co., GA21, 138, Harvard University.

34 Hettle, "Ambiguous Democrat," 582–83; Hahn, *Southern Populism*, 111–16.

35 Hettle, "Ambiguous Democrat," 582–84; Burnham, *Presidential Ballots*, 346–54, 358.

36 *Messenger*, August 6, 1856; Clements, *Irwin County*, 43–47, 454–78; Hubbs, *Guarding Greensboro*, 30–32; U.S. Census, 1860, Ga., Telfair County Slave Schedule, 53, MC.

37 Collins, "Joseph E. Brown," 216–25; Kennett, *Marching through Georgia*, 16–18.

38 Collins, "Joseph E. Brown," 197–98; Hahn, *Southern Populism*, 102–4.

39 Collins, "Joseph E. Brown," 216–17; Hahn, *Southern Populism*, 34–39; *Testimony . . . upon the Condition of the Macon and Brunswick Railroad*, 10.

40 *Messenger*, February 9, 1859, February 13, 1861; *Recorder*, June 30, 1857; Wooster, "Georgia Legislature of 1860," text and app.; Mrs. James W. Campbell to W. W. Paine, March 14, 1860, Paine Papers, GHS; Collins, "Joseph E. Brown," 216–17.

41 Collins, "Joseph E. Brown," 216–17; Brown to W. W. Paine, March 25, 1859, Brown Papers, typescript, 435, UGA.

42 Reidy, *From Slavery to Agrarian Capitalism*, 28–29; *Messenger*, April 14, May 5, 1858; Miller and Genevose, *Plantation, Town*, 241; Mohr, *Threshold of Freedom*, 10–11.

43 Freehling and Simpson, *Secession Debated*, 40 (Toombs); S. D. Fuller to Governor Brown, August 17, 1864, box 30, GIC-GDAH; McCurry, *Masters of Small Worlds*, 47–52; Clements, *Irwin County*, 505.

44 *Messenger*, July 14, 1858 (Brown); Mohr, *Threshold of Freedom*, xviii–xxi.

45 Reidy, *From Slavery to Agrarian Capitalism*, 22–24; Kolchin, *American Slavery*, 79, 96–97; McCurry, *Masters of Small Worlds*, 48–52; *Southern Citizen*, quoted in *Messenger*, February 16, 1859, December 22, 29, 1858, March 21, 1860; *Recorder*, June 22, 1847; *Telfair Enterprise*, October 31, 1907; Ward, *Coffee County*, 259. On the incident, see Wells, *Slave Ship Wanderer*.

46 *Messenger*, November 2, 1859 (quotation), April 4, 1860; F. J. B. Brown to Governor Brown, April 23, 1860, box 21, GIC-GDAH; McCurry, *Masters of Small Worlds*, 259; Link, *Roots of Secession*, 179–82.

47 Barney, "Resisting the Republicans," 72, 76–77; Hettle, "Ambiguous Democrat," 582–85; Hahn, *Southern Populism*, 105–6.

48 Mohr, *Threshold of Freedom*, 20–27; Hill, *Joseph E. Brown*, 11–12; CRSG 3:429, 431; Hahn, *Southern Populism*, 107; S. D. Fuller to Brown, August 17, 1864, box 30, GIC-GDAH.

49 Bond, *Political Culture*, 2–3, 81–82; Wyatt-Brown, *Southern Culture*, 208–9.

50 R. N. Taylor to [Charlotte Taylor], n.d. [May 1849?], in Stevens, *Family Letters*, 266–67.

51 *Union Recorder*, August 7, 1860 (quotations); Michael P. Johnson, *Patriarchal Republic*, 10–15.

52  U.S. Census, 1860, Ga., Telfair County Population Schedule, 19, Slave Schedule, 52, and Agriculture Schedule, 67, MC; Cobb, *Dodge County*, 248–50.

53  *Union Recorder*, August 7, 1860; U.S. Census, 1860, Ga., Telfair County Population Schedule, 18–19, 23, 33, Slave Schedule, 49, 51–52, 55, and Agriculture Schedule, 69, MC; Murrell, "Union Father, Rebel Son," 360–62; *Recorder*, October 9, 1860.

54  Michael P. Johnson, *Patriarchal Republic*, 11–13.

55  Burnham, *Presidential Ballots*, 338, 346, 354, 358, 362; Michael P. Johnson, *Patriarchal Republic*, 11–17; Phillips, *Georgia and State Rights*, 204–6; Doyon and Hodler, "Secessionist Sentiment," 333–38; *Union Recorder*, August 7, 1860.

56  Freehling and Simpson, *Secession Debated*, 155; Burnham, *Presidential Ballots*, 338, 346, 354, 358, 362; Phillips, *Georgia and State Rights*, 184–92; Michael P. Johnson, *Patriarchal Republic*, 65–66.

57  Michael P. Johnson, *Patriarchal Republic*, 17; *CRSG* 1:123–24 (quotation); Coulter, *Georgia*, 318; Wooster, "Georgia Secession Convention," 21–22.

58  Collins, "Joseph E. Brown," 190–93; Hahn, *Southern Populism*, 115; Wyatt-Brown, *Southern Culture*, 106–8; Hettle, "Ambiguous Democrat," 579–80.

59  Barney, "Resisting the Republicans," 75–83; *Recorder*, November 27, 1860; Freehling, *South vs. the South*, 37–39.

60  *Recorder*, December 4, 25, 1860.

61  Ibid., December 18, 1860.

62  *Recorder*, December 11, 1860; Michael P. Johnson, *Patriarchal Republic*, 52–53; Inscoe, *Mountain Masters*, 224–26.

63  Michael P. Johnson, *Patriarchal Republic*, 28–49; Bond, *Political Culture*, 2–3, 114; *CRSG* 1:123–24; Freehling, *South vs. the South*, 38–39; Christopher J. Olsen, *Political Culture*, 188–89.

64  Michael P. Johnson, "New Look," 268–71: U.S. Census Office, *Eighth Census, Agriculture*, 226–27; Doyon and Hodler, "Secessionist Sentiment," 327, 333.

65  *Recorder*, December 4, 1860; Wooster, "Georgia Secession Convention," app. I; Michael P. Johnson, *Patriarchal Republic*, 63–78, and "New Look," 268–70; U.S. Census Office, *Eighth Census, Agriculture*, 226–27.

66  Michael P. Johnson, "New Look," 268–70; Wooster, "Georgia Secession Convention," app. I.

67  U.S. Census, 1860, Ga., Pulaski County Slave Schedule, 15–16, and Wilcox County Agriculture Schedule, 5, MC; Wallace Leigh Harris, *Pulaski and Bleckley Counties*, 1:96; R. G. Dun and Co., GA8, 3, Harvard University (quotation); Ward, *Coffee County*, 136.

68  Michael P. Johnson, "New Look," 268–70; *Messenger*, July 8, 15, 1857; Wooster, "Georgia Secession Convention," 35–36.

69  U.S. Census, 1860, Ga., Wilcox County Population Schedule, 42, and Agriculture Schedule, 13, MC; Clements, *Irwin County*, 47, 457; McDonald and Lawson, *Passing of the Pines*, 26.

70  U.S. Census, 1860, Ga., Telfair County Slave Schedule, 58, MC; "Rowan Pafford," File II, box 109, GDAH; Wooster, "Georgia Secession Convention," app. I.

71  *Union Recorder*, May 5, 1857; Clements, *Irwin County*, 454–69; McCurry, *Masters of Small Worlds*, 169, 256–62; Wyatt-Brown, *Southern Culture*, 153–56.

72  Michael P. Johnson, "New Look," 56, 268–71.

73  Doyon and Hodler, "Secessionist Sentiment," 338–41; Michael P. Johnson, "New Look," 268–70; Wooster, "Georgia Secession Convention," app. I; Phillips, *Georgia and State Rights*, map preceding p. 205; U.S. Census, 1860, Ga., Wilcox County Population Schedule, 41, MC; Amnesty Papers, pardon applications of Charles Taylor and Smith Turner, M1003, reels 8 and 9, NA-W; McDonald and Lawson, *Passing of the Pines*, 26; Clements, *Irwin County*, 43.

74  Michael P. Johnson, "New Look," 270; Wooster, "Georgia Secession Convention," app. I.

75  Michael P. Johnson, "New Look," 270; Wooster, "Georgia Secession Convention," app. I; *Union Recorder*, May 5, 1857; U.S. Census, 1860, Ga., Irwin County Slave Schedule, 3–4, and Agriculture Schedule, 9, MC; R. G. Dun and Co., GA18, 2, Harvard University; Clements, *Irwin County*, 41, 159, 208, 461.

76  Doyon and Hodler, "Secessionist Sentiment," 338–39; McCurry, *Masters of Small Worlds*, 288–92; Wallace Leigh Harris, *Pulaski and Bleckley Counties*, 1:185; Clements, *Irwin County*, 461; Michael P. Johnson, "New Look," 270.

77  Michael P. Johnson, *Patriarchal Republic*, 67–68; *Recorder*, December 18, 1860.

78  *Messenger*, January 23, 1861; Wooster, "Georgia Secession Convention," app. I; Clements, *Irwin County*, 77.

79  *CRSG* 1:218 (first quotation); *Messenger*, January 23, 1861 (second quotation); Wooster, "Georgia Secession Convention," app. I; Michael P. Johnson, *Patriarchal Republic*, 112–13.

80  Michael P. Johnson, *Patriarchal Republic*, 114–17; Stephens, *Constitutional View*, 313–14; Coulter, *Georgia*, 320–21; John N. M. McRae to S. H. Latimer, January 25, 1861, Latimer Papers, Duke University.

81  Wooster, "Georgia Secession Convention," 39–40; Michael P. Johnson, *Patriarchal Republic*, 120–21; U.S. Census, 1860, Ga., Irwin County Agriculture Schedule, 7, and Slave Schedule, 3, MC.

82  Michael P. Johnson, *Patriarchal Republic*, 118–20; *Messenger*, January 30, 1861; Paine to "Dear Governor," March 13, 1861, box 42, GIC-GDAH.


*Chapter 3*

1  Frank, *With Ballot and Bayonet*, 18, 57–58; Wallace Leigh Harris, *Pulaski and Bleckley Counties*, 1:128–36 (family names in the company); U.S. Census, 1860, Ga., Pulaski County Population Schedule, 4, and Slave Schedule, 23–24, MC; Michael P. Johnson, "New Look," 268–70; Thomas, *Confederate Nation*, 3–4, 8–9; Wilkinson and Woodworth, *Scythe of Fire*, 19–21. The best description of the unit's organization and life is D. G. Fleming's "Historical Sketch of the Pulaski Volunteers, Company G, 8th Georgia Regiment," in *Dispatch*, July 10, 17, 24, 31, and August 7, 1879.

2  Fleming, "Sketch of the Pulaski Volunteers," *Dispatch*, July 10, 1879 (quotation); Wallace Leigh Harris, *Pulaski and Bleckley Counties*, 1:268–69.

3  Whites, *Crisis in Gender*, 30–33, 36–38; Richard, *Busy Hands*, 28–29; Gallagher, *Confederate War*, 3–5, 28–29; McPherson, *For Cause*, 12; *CRSG* 1:125 (quotation).

4  U.S. Census, 1860, Ga., Pulaski County Slave Schedule, 23–24, MC; Donald, Baker, and Holt, *Civil War*, 33; *CRSG* 2:189; Mitchell, *Vacant Chair*, 21–23; Whites, *Crisis in Gender*, 33.

5  Whites, *Crisis in Gender*, 36–38; Richard, *Busy Hands*, 13–14, 19; Donald, Baker, and Holt, *Civil War*, 33–35; Fleming, "Sketch of the Pulaski Volunteers," *Dispatch*, July 10, 1879.

6  Brown's "Message to Senate and House," November 6, 1861, *CRSG* 2:124–25; McPherson, *For Cause*, 12–13, 20–21, 106–7; Frank, *With Ballot and Bayonet*, 13–15; P. H. Coffee to H. C. Wayne, March 4, 1862, AGIC, box 6, GDAH.

7  Brown's "Message to Senate and House," November 6, 1861, *CRSG* 2:124–25; *Recorder*, August 21, 1860; Fredrickson, *Black Image*, 43–51; *Messenger*, February 20, 1861; Reidy, *From Slavery to Agrarian Capitalism*, 54, 266; E. A. Nisbet, "To the Planters of Middle Georgia," in *Messenger*, May 29, 1861 (last quotation); Wyatt-Brown, *Southern Culture*, 50–52; Bozeman, "Reminiscences," private collection.

8  *CRSG* 2:33; Frank, *With Ballot and Bayonet*, 8–9; Brown, "To the People of Georgia," *Messenger*, June 5, 1861.

9  Wyatt-Brown, *Southern Culture*, 32–39; Coulter, *Georgia*, 322–23; McPherson, *For Cause*, 21, 104–6; *CRSG* 2:28; Paine to Brown, March 13, 1861, box 42, GIC-GDAH.

10  Paine to Brown, March 13, 1861 (box 42), and Bussey and Studstill to Brown, July 21, 1863 (box 4), GIC-GDAH; Bryan, *Confederate Georgia*, 22; Henderson, *Roster*, 1:963–72, 2:45–51, 52–58, 817–24, 1071–82, 3:620–28, 5:210–18, 235–53, 279–88, 303–12, and 6:203–8, lists all CSA infantry companies from the area. Wallace Leigh Harris, *Pulaski and Bleckley Counties*, 1:125–27, lists additional cavalry companies and an artillery company from Pulaski County. This rate of mobilization is comparable to that of black belt Greene County, Ga. See Bryant, *How Curious a Land*, 83, 210, n. 34; J. William Harris, *Plain Folk and Gentry*, 198–99; and U.S. Census Office, *Eighth Census, Population*, 58–61. The estimate is based on white males between the ages of 10 and 50, while discounting half of those between 10 and 14 (i.e., 10- and 11-year-olds) as being too young to serve between 1861 and 1865. The percentage for the first year of the war increases if only those males between 18 and 40 are counted and those too young or old are discounted for the initial volunteering in 1861 and early 1862. In this case, Coffee, Irwin, and Wilcox led with about 89, 83, and 78 percent, respectively, of the men between 18 and 40 joining; Pulaski and Telfair followed with 73 and 68 percent, respectively. Interestingly, these percentages generally reflect the popularity of Breckinridge and the Southern Democrats in 1860, with the old-line Whig county of Telfair coming in last. The high percentages for Coffee and Irwin suggest one reason why both counties turned out few men in 1864 and tolerated desertion: there were few men left to muster with the militias.

11  Paine to Crawford, July 14, 1845, File II, box 109, GDAH; J. W. A. Sanford to Brown, *Recorder*, October 16, 1861.

12  *Messenger*, May 1, June 5, 1861.

13  Henderson, *Roster*, 1:963–72, 2:45–58, 817–24, 1071–82, 3:620–28, 5:210–18, 235–53, 279–88, 303–12, 6:203–8; U.S. Census Office, *Eighth Census, Population*, 58–61; McDuffie to Davis, June 20, 1861, box 36, GIC-GDAH.

14  *Messenger*, May 1, June 5, August 21, 1861; Bryan, *Confederate Georgia*, 18; Coulter, *Georgia*, 329; Michael P. Johnson, "New Look," 268–70; DAR-H, *History of Pulaski County*, 302; Wallace Leigh Harris, *Pulaski and Bleckley Counties*, 1:125; U.S. Census Office, *Eighth Census, Population*, 58–61; McDonald and Lawson, *Passing of the Pines*, 26; Ward, *Coffee*

*County*, 127, 221; Ashley to Brown, August 26, 1861, Adjutant General's Muster Rolls, A-C, box 1, GDAH.

15 Fleming, "Sketch of the Pulaski Volunteers," *Dispatch*, July 10, 1879; Wallace Leigh Harris, *Pulaski County and Bleckley Counties*, 1:145; U.S. Census, 1860, Ga., Pulaski County Slave Schedule, 1, MC. According to Fleming, the "relatives in both companies were expecting to be kept near each other," but once in Virginia the Pulaski Volunteers were assigned to the 8th Regiment and the Georgia Rangers to the 10th Regiment.

16 Fleming, "Sketch of the Pulaski Volunteers," *Dispatch*, July 10, 1879.

17 McCleod, "Reminiscence," microfilm drawer 282, box 33, CWM-GDAH; Hugh McCartney to "Secretary of War," June 10, 1863, Letters Received, NA-W; Mann, *Telfair County*, 116–21; U.S. Census, 1860, Ga., Telfair County Slave Schedule, 49–50, MC; Wooster, "Georgia Legislature of 1860," app.

18 McRae to Brown, May 26, 1861, File II, box 90, GDAH. See also C. M. Bozeman to Brown, June 17, 1861, box 24, GIC-GDAH.

19 R. Pafford and L. W. H. Pittman to Secretary of War, November 7, 1863, Letters Received, NA-W; U.S. Census, 1860, Ga., Telfair County Population Schedule, 6, and Slave Schedule, 49–50, MC; Mann, *Telfair County*, 122.

20 U.S. Census, 1860, Ga., Telfair County Population Schedule, 21, and Slave Schedule, 49–59, MC; Henderson, *Roster*, 2:817–24; *Statistics of the United States in 1860*, 4:341; U.S. Census Office, *Eighth Census, Agriculture*, 226–27; J. William Harris, *Plain Folk and Gentry*, 142–43.

21 U.S. Census, 1860, Ga., Telfair County Population Schedule, 11–12, 23, MC; Henderson, *Roster*, 2:817–24.

22 Henderson, *Roster*, 5:235–44, 3:602; U.S. Census, 1860, Ga., Wilcox County Population Schedule, 1, MC; Paine to "Dear General," April 15, 1861, AGIC, box 20, GDAH; Robertson, *Soldiers*, 25–26.

23 Robertson, *Soldiers*, 25–26; Henderson, *Roster*, 5:241, 243, 3:602; U.S. Census, 1860, Ga., Wilcox County Population Schedule, 1, MC; Fleming, "Sketch of the Pulaski Volunteers," *Dispatch*, July 10, 1879; Wallace Leigh Harris, *Pulaski and Bleckley Counties*, 1:268–69.

24 Robertson, *Soldiers*, 26; *Messenger*, May 29, 1861.

25 U.S. Census, 1860, Ga., Telfair County Population Schedule, 23, and Coffee County Agriculture Schedule, 19, MC; Paine to George Crawford, May 23, 1846, File II, box 109, GDAH; Ward, *Coffee County*, 128–30; Henderson, *Roster*, 5:214; *CRSG* 2:102 (Brown); Mitchell, "Confederate Loyalties," 97–98.

26 U.S. Census, 1860, Ga., Pulaski County Population Schedule, 1–8, MC; *Messenger*, June 5, 1861; Ash, *When the Yankees Came*, 7–8; Wallace Leigh Harris, *Pulaski and Bleckley Counties*, 1:128–35.

27 Henderson, *Roster*, 5:235–44; McPherson, *What They Fought For*, 15; U.S. Census, 1860, Ga., Pulaski County Population Schedule, 6, and Slave Schedule, 2, MC; Wallace Leigh Harris, *Pulaski and Bleckley Counties*, 1:129.

28 Jordan, *Black Confederates*, 187–91; Robertson, *Soldiers*, 30; U.S. Census, 1860, Ga., Pulaski County Slave Schedule, 1, MC; *Messenger*, June 5, 1861; *Union Recorder*, April 2, 1861.

29 Robertson, *Soldiers*, 21; Bryant, *How Curious a Land*, 86; Mitchell, *Vacant Chair*, 21–23; Kennett, *Marching through Georgia*, 53–57; Mann, *Telfair County*, 81; Studstill to "Dear

Father, Mother & Sisters," March 23, 1862, microfilm drawer 283, box 41, CWM-GDAH; *Savannah Republican*, May 8, 1861; Gallagher, *Confederate War*, 58–59; McPherson, *For Cause*, 82–87.

30   Wallace Leigh Harris, *Pulaski and Bleckley Counties*, 1:559; U.S. Census, 1860, Ga., Pulaski County Slave Schedule, 1, 23–24, MC.

31   U.S. Census, 1860, Ga., Wilcox County Population Schedule, 1, Pulaski County Slave Schedule, 1, 10–12, 23–24, and Telfair County Slave Schedule, 51, MC; Henderson, *Roster*, 1:963, 2:45, 52, 3:620–28, 5:210–18, 235–53, 279–88, 303–12, 6:203–8; Wallace Leigh Harris, *Pulaski and Bleckley Counties*, 1:128–42; Clements, *Irwin County*, 117–21, 196–97.

32   Clements, *Irwin County*, 85, 114, 206, 476; U.S. Census, 1860, Ga., Wilcox County Agriculture Schedule, 14, MC. The analysis of company officers is based on Henderson, *Roster*—for page numbers, see the previous note.

33   Frank, *With Ballot and Bayonet*, 110–22; McPherson, *For Cause*, 54–55.

34   Wallace Leigh Harris, *Pulaski and Bleckley Counties*, 1:126; *Recorder*, June 30, August 18, 1857; Inscoe, *Mountain Masters*, 65–66.

35   Henderson, *Roster*, 1:963–64, 2:817–18, 5:210, 235, 244, 279, 303; *CRSG* 2:115–18 (Brown). Based on a comparison of officers listed in the published rosters and occupations given in U.S. Census, 1860, Ga., Pulaski County Population Schedule, 1–8, MC, this pattern was particularly strong at Hawkinsville.

36   Henderson, *Roster*, 3:620; *CRSG* 2:115–18; Michael P. Johnson, *Patriarchal Republic*, 73–75; R. G. Dun and Co., GA26, 138, Harvard University; Donald, Baker, and Holt, *Civil War*, 75; McPherson, *For Cause*, 12–13; W. W. Paine to "Dear Governor," March 13, 1861 (box 42) (local attorney to governor), and James K. Hilliard to Joseph Brown, May 5, 1862 (box 34), GIC-GDAH; *Morning News*, June 18, 1861; Trowell, "Douglas before Memory," 5–6.

37   Frank, *With Ballot and Bayonet*, 8–12, 121–23, 140–41; Burnham, *Presidential Ballots*, 354–55; Coulter, *Georgia*, 316; U.S. Census, 1860, Ga., Telfair County Population Schedule, 18, and Wilcox County Population Schedule, 1, MC; *Union Recorder*, August 7, 1860; Henderson, *Roster*, 5:244; Michael P. Johnson, "New Look," 270.

38   McPherson, *For Cause*, 16–21; Henderson, *Roster*, 5:210–18, 235–53, 279–88, 303–12; U.S. Census Office, *Eighth Census, Population*, 58–61; *CRSG* 2:191; C. W. Styles, "To the Men of Southern Georgia," in Confederate Imprints, reel 83, no. 2548.

39   *CRSG* 2:191–92, 208–11; Bryant, *How Curious a Land*, 83–84; Frank, *With Ballot and Bayonet*, 8–10.

40   Wallace Leigh Harris, *Pulaski and Bleckley Counties*, 1:136–43 (quotation, 143); Henderson, *Roster*, 5:235, 244, 279; McDonald and Lawson, *Passing of the Pines*, 26; Clements, *Irwin County*, 47; Bryant, *How Curious a Land*, 83; U.S. Census, 1860, Ga., Pulaski County Slave Schedule, 1, Telfair County Population Schedule, 18, and Wilcox County Population Schedule, 1, MC. Four of the five new companies (the Irwin Volunteers as Company F, the Pulaski Greys as Company K, the Telfair Volunteers as Company B, and the State Rights Guards of Wilcox County as Company E) were mustered into Confederate service in the 49th Georgia Regiment. Collectively, they represented the largest concentration of infantrymen from the lower river in a single Confederate regiment. The fifth company, the Coffee County Guards, was organized at the same time and became

Company C, 50th Georgia Regiment. In addition to Manning, the original officers of the Pulaski Greys included slaveholding merchants John H. Pate and Henry Whitfield.

41  Henderson, *Roster*, 5:289–90, 303; U.S. Census, 1860, Ga., Coffee County Slave Schedule, 3–4, and Agriculture Schedule, 1, MC; *Recorder*, November 5, 1850. For a description of William Manning's plantation, see "Early Days in South Georgia," *Atlanta Constitution*, May 20, 1895.

42  Thomas, *Confederate Nation*, 6–7; Henderson, *Roster*, 5:279–88; U.S. Census, 1860, Ga., Telfair County Slave Schedule, 51, Pulaski County Slave Schedule, 10, and Coffee County Slave Schedule, 3–4, MC; McDonald and Lawson, *Passing of the Pines*, 26; *CRSG* 2:192; Whites, *Crisis in Gender*, 36–40; Williams, *Rich Man's War*, 4–5, 98–103. For a different view of planter involvement, see Fred Arthur Bailey, *Class*, 86, 104.

43  U.S. Census, 1860, Ga., Telfair County Population Schedule, 32, Slave Schedule, 55, Agriculture Schedule, 69, and Pulaski County Population Schedule, 3–4, MC; Wallace Leigh Harris, *Pulaski and Bleckley Counties*, 1:143; Henderson, *Roster*, 5:279; Humphreys to Brown, September 19, 1861, box 14, GIC-GDAH; Cobb, *Dodge County*, 226.

44  Henderson, *Roster*, 5:287; Humphreys to Brown, September 19, 1861, box 14, GIC-GDAH.

45  McCurry, *Masters of Small Worlds*, 265–67; Humphreys to Brown, September 19, 1861, box 14, GIC-GDAH; Henderson, *Roster*, 5:210; U.S. Census, 1860, Ga., Telfair County Slave Schedule, 51, 52, 55, MC.

46  Fleming, "Sketch of the Pulaski Volunteers," *Dispatch*, July 10, 1879 (Horne); Richard, *Busy Hands*, 87–88.

47  Richard, *Busy Hands*, 88–89; Cobb, *Dodge County*, 226; Frank, *With Ballot and Bayonet*, 57–58.

48  Fleming, "Sketch of the Pulaski Volunteers," *Dispatch*, July 10, 1879; Mann, *Telfair County*, 85; *AS* 4(1):416 (Caroline Malloy), 4:508 (Easter Reed); Henderson, *Roster*, 2:817; Ward, *Coffee County*, 262–63.

49  *CRSG* 2:124–25; Speech of Luke Campbell, in Mann, *Telfair County*, 86; Fleming, "Sketch of the Pulaski Volunteers," *Dispatch*, July 10, 1879. See also Whites, *Crisis in Gender*, 22–23.

50  *Messenger*, July 10, 1861; Speech of Luke Campbell, in Mann, *Telfair County*, 85. See also Mitchell, *Vacant Chair*, xii–xiii, and Whites, *Crisis in Gender*, 36.

51  Mitchell, *Vacant Chair*, 4–8; Whites, *Crisis in Gender*, 38; Speech of Luke Campbell, in Mann, *Telfair County*, 85.

52  *Morning News*, June 18, 1861, quoted in Trowell, "Douglas before Memory," 5–6 (Spivey); Ward, *Coffee County*, 118.

53  Wyatt-Brown, *Southern Culture*, 34–35. See *Recorder*—e.g.,October 1, 1861—which regularly carried such lists.

54  Wyatt-Brown, *Southern Culture*, 34–35; Whites, *Crisis in Gender*, 40; *Recorder*, October 1, 1861; Mann, *Telfair County*, 85–86 (first quotation); *Savannah Republican*, June 18, 1861 (second quotation).

55  Speech of Luke Campbell, in Mann, *Telfair County*, 85–87.

56  Christopher J. Olsen, *Political Culture*, 49; Speech of Luke Campbell, in Mann, *Telfair County*, 85–87 (quotations); Fleming, "Sketch of the Pulaski Volunteers," *Dispatch*, July 10, 1879; Wyatt-Brown, *Southern Culture*, 145–46.

57  Speech of Luke Campbell, in Mann, *Telfair County*, 86.

58  *Dispatch*, October 18, 1877 (quotation); Richard, *Busy Hands*, 180–81; McCurry, *Masters of Small Worlds*, 77–78, 252–58.

59  *Messenger*, June 5, July 10, 1861, October 7, 1863.

60  Rose, *Victorian America*, 172–79; *Messenger*, July 10, 1861, June 8, 1864; DAR-H, *History of Pulaski County*, 134; Whites, *Crisis in Gender*, 32–34, 46–47; Richard, *Busy Hands*, 8, 27.

61  *Messenger*, August 28, October 30, 1861; *Recorder*, June 18, 1861.

62  Faust, *Mothers of Invention*, 5, 47–49 (quotations, 48, 47); Bartley, *Modern Georgia*, 20–21; McCurry, *Masters of Small Worlds*, 72–77.

63  Rose, *Victorian America*, 179–80; McCurry, *Masters of Small Worlds*, 72–78; U.S. Census Office, *Seventh Census*, xxiv (quotation), 383–84, and *Eighth Census, Agriculture*, 25, 29; Faust, *Mothers of Invention*, 45.

64  Ward, *Coffee County*, 185; Clements, *Irwin County*, 213; Richard, *Busy Hands*, 22–23; McRae and McMillan Store Ledger, 14–15, 22, 76, 87.

65  Faust, *Mothers of Invention*, 47–48; AS 4(2):415 (Caroline Malloy), 4:504 and 507 (Easter Reed).

66  Whites, *Crisis in Gender*, 86–87; Humphreys to Brown, September 9, 1861, box 14, GIC-GDAH; *Messenger*, October 30, 1861.

67  Coffee to Brown, December 14, 1861, box 6, GIC-GDAH; McCurry, *Masters of Small Worlds*, 72–78; Pulaski County Superior Court, April 1864, Minute Book E, 73–74, GDAH.

68  N. M. McDuffie to Howell Cobb, March 25, 1865, Cobb Papers, UGA.

69  Fahs, *Imagined Civil War*, 121–28, 311; Weitz, *Higher Duty*, 30–31; Whites, *Crisis in Gender*, 32–36; Frank, *With Ballot and Bayonet*, 10–11; *Savannah Republican*, May 8, 1861.


*Chapter 4*

1  D. G. Fleming, "Historical Sketch of the Pulaski Volunteers, Company G, 8th Georgia Regiment," in *Dispatch*, July 17, 1879; Wallace Leigh Harris, *Pulaski and Bleckley Counties*, 1:145 (quotation); McPherson, *Battle Cry*, 326–27; Christopher J. Olsen, *Political Culture*, 97; Brooks, "Soldiering in Hood's Texas Brigade," 536–37; Michael P. Johnson, *Patriarchal Republic*, 169.

2  Wallace Leigh Harris, *Pulaski and Bleckley Counties*, 1:128, 145; Robertson, *Stonewall Jackson*, 242, 245; Johnson and Buel, *Battles and Leaders*, 1:195–97; Robertson, *Soldiers*, 21; McPherson, *Battle Cry*, 308–10, 317. The estimated strength of the Army of the Shenandoah, which included several artillery batteries, was a little over 8,000 men. On the 8th Georgia, see Wilkinson and Woodworth, *Scythe of Fire*, 25–29, 60–101.

3  Wallace Leigh Harris, *Pulaski and Bleckley Counties*, 1:145. See also "The Eighth Georgia Regiment in the Battle at Stone Bridge," *Richmond Dispatch*, July 29, 1861, in *Recorder*, August 6, 1861.

4  William C. Davis, *Bull Run*, 139; Johnson and Buel, *Battles and Leaders*, 1:196–205; McPherson, *Battle Cry*, 339–41; *Recorder*, August 6, 1861.

5  William C. Davis, *Bull Run*, 176–78; McPherson, *Battle Cry*, 340; Mann, *Telfair County*, 85; Robertson, *Stonewall Jackson*, 253, 257–60; Johnson and Buel, *Battles and Leaders*, 1:205.

6  JoAnna M. McDonald, *First Battle of Manassas*, 50.

7  Ibid., 50, 66–69, 71; Johnson and Buel, *Battles and Leaders*, 1:207 (Beauregard); *Recorder*, August 6, 1861.

8  *Recorder*, August 6, 1861 (quotation); JoAnna M. McDonald, *First Battle of Manassas*, 72; Johnson and Buel, *Battles and Leaders*, 1:207.

9  *Recorder*, August 6, 1861.

10 Johnson and Buel, *Battles and Leaders*, 1:207–10; McPherson, *Battle Cry*, 341–42 (quotations, 342); Robertson, *Stonewall Jackson*, 264–66.

11 Robertson, *Stonewall Jackson*, 266–67; JoAnna M. McDonald, *First Battle of Manassas*, 72.

12 JoAnna M. McDonald, *First Battle of Manassas*, 72; Johnson and Buel, *Battles and Leaders*, 1:195; *Messenger*, August 7, 1861; *Recorder*, August 6, 1861; Fleming, "Sketch of the Pulaski Volunteers," *Dispatch*, July 24, 1879.

13 *Recorder*, August 6, 1861; Wilkinson and Woodworth, *Scythe of Fire*, 93–94. See also Zettler, *War Stories*, 62–63.

14 Wallace Leigh Harris, *Pulaski and Bleckley Counties*, 1:128–36; Fleming, "Sketch of the Pulaski Volunteers," *Dispatch*, July 24, 1879; U.S. Census, 1860, Ga., Pulaski County Population Schedule, 4, MC.

15 *Messenger*, August 21, 1861; McPherson, *For Cause*, 62–63.

16 Smith Diary, February 20, 1864, GDAH; A. R. Taylor to "Dear Sister," January 6, 1863, R. N. Taylor Papers, Washington Memorial Library, Macon; Wallace Leigh Harris, *Pulaski and Bleckley Counties*, 1:126–27; U.S. Census, 1860, Ga., Telfair County Slave Schedule, 57, MC; Clements, *Irwin County*, 196–99; McDuffie to Brown, June 20, 1861, box 36, GIC-GDAH; *Messenger*, August 7, 21, 1861; Henderson, *Roster*, 1:45–51, 2:817–24, 1071–82, 3:620–28; DAR-H, *History of Pulaski County*, 331; Donald, Baker, and Holt, *Civil War*, 184–85.

17 Smith Diary, March 23, 1864, GDAH. On the toll taken by disease in the 8th Georgia, see Wilkinson and Woodworth, *Scythe of Fire*, 102–3, 113–15.

18 "The Morning Report of the 20th Ga. Regt., Gen. Early's Brigade, Col. John R. Cumming, Commanding," Eldridge Collection, box 13, Huntington Library; Henderson, *Roster*, 2:817–24.

19 Wallace Leigh Harris, *Pulaski and Bleckley Counties*, 1:128–36; Barker to "Dear Wife," June 12, 1862, in McDonald and Lawson, *Passing of the Pines*, 266.

20 Robertson, *Soldiers*, 145–47; Donald, Baker, and Holt, *Civil War*, 239, 371.

21 McPherson, *Battle Cry*, 319; Wallace Leigh Harris, *Pulaski and Bleckley Counties*, 1:129; Wiley, *Johnny Reb*, 245–46; Barker to "Dear Wife," June 12, 1862, and Daniel Smith to "Dear Wife," May 16, 1864, both in McDonald and Lawson, *Passing of the Pines*, 266–67; William H. Smith Diary, March 1864, GDAH.

22 Robertson, *Soldiers*, 155; Henderson, *Roster*, 5:285; Pate to Brown, December 31, 1862, box 42, GIC-GDAH.

23 *Messenger*, August 21, 1861; Henderson, *Roster*, 5:287; [Unknown] to "Dear Bill," June 16, 1861, Latimer Papers, Duke University.

24 Robertson, *Soldiers*, 75–77; Fisher Diary, January 21, 30, 1862, GDAH.

25 Henderson, *Roster*, 5:210–18, 235–53.

26  Wiley, *Johnny Reb*, 250–51; Fleming, "Sketch of the Pulaski Volunteers," *Dispatch*, July 17, 1879; Henderson, *Roster*, 5:238, 244, 247, 308; Clements, *Irwin County*, 114, 127–28 (R. W. Clements to Jehu Fletcher, May 16, 1862); Humphreys to Governor Brown, September 19, 1861, box 14, GIC-GDAH.

27  Stafford Thigpen to "Dear Father and Mother," May 25, 1862, Kirkland Collection, GDAH; Henderson, *Roster*, 5:236, 3:626.

28  Wiley, *Johnny Reb*, 254–58; Clements, *Irwin County*, 128; *Christian Index*, February 23, 1865; Henderson, *Roster*, 5:210, 235–44.

29  Robertson, *Soldiers*, 150; Henderson, *Roster*, 5:236–40, 246, 248.

30  Clements, *Irwin County*, 127–28; T. E. Lee to "Dear Wife," July 26, 1862, Lee Letters, UGA; Studstill to "Dear Father, Mother & Sisters," March 23, 1862, and Williams to "Dear Uncle," May 7, 1863, CWM-GDAH. See also Henderson, *Roster*, 5:218.

31  Roberts to "Dear Cousins, Unkle & Aunt," June 7, 1863, microfilm drawer 283, box 38, CWM-GDAH; Henderson, *Roster*, 5:244–53, 303–12; McPherson, *Battle Cry*, 464–67, 470.

32  J. William Harris, *Plain Folk and Gentry*, 148–53; Escott, *After Secession*, 63–64, 80–88; McPherson, *Battle Cry*, 430–32; Robertson, *Soldiers*, 37–40; Williams, *Rich Man's War*, 129–32; Thomas, *Confederate Nation*, 152–55.

33  *CRSG* 2:187–93; McPherson, *Battle Cry*, 432; Thomas, *Confederate Nation*, 155.

34  J. William Harris, *Plain Folk and Gentry*, 148–53; Beringer et al., *Why the South Lost*, 449–53; Paine to Brown, March 13, 1861, box 42, GIC-GDAH.

35  J. William Harris, *Plain Folk and Gentry*, 148–52; Williams, *Rich Man's War*, 129–35; Coulter, *Georgia*, 330; Paine to Brown, March 13, 1861, box 42, GIC-GDAH; McPherson, *Battle Cry*, 430–31; Thomas, *Confederate Nation*, 152–53.

36  Humphreys to Brown, September 19, 1861, box 14, GIC-GDAH; Henderson, *Roster*, 5:210–18; C. W. Styles, "To the Men of Southern Georgia," in Confederate Imprints, reel 83, no. 2548.

37  W. B. Overstreet to Brown, April 26, 1862 (box 42), and H. T. Bussey and William Studstill to Brown, July 21, 1863 (box 4), GIC-GDAH.

38  George P. Woods, editor, *Dispatch*, December 21, 1876 (story of draft dodger); Daniel M. McRae to Brown, December 30, 1863, box 39, GIC-GDAH; L. H. Briscoe to Driden, February 9, 1863, no. 13, AGLB.

39  PCIC Minutes, November 28, December 3, 1864.

40  Briscoe to Newbern, November 19, 1863, no. 20, 256, AGLB, and Henry C. Wayne to Lieutenant Colonel Charles J. Harris, May 26, 1863, no. 15, 463, AGLB.

41  PCIC Minutes, May 30, 1864. On objections to exemptions among men in the 8th Georgia, see Wilkinson and Woodworth, *Scythe of Fire*, 267–68.

42  McPhail to Brown, July 25, 1864, April 9, 1865, box 39, GIC-GDAH. McPhail joined the Pulaski Greys in March 1862. Of his service, the roster states "Fate unknown." Henderson, *Roster*, 5:284.

43  McPhail to Brown, July 25, 1864, April 9, 1865, box 39, GIC-GDAH; L. H. Briscoe to Young, July 14, 1863, no. 16, 389, AGLB.

44  McPhail to Brown, April 9, 1865, box 39, GIC-GDAH; Escott, *After Secession*, 117–19, 144–46; Thomas, *Confederate Nation*, 152–53; McPherson, *Battle Cry*, 431, and *For Cause*, 90–

98, 102–3; Williams, *Rich Man's War*, 129; Henderson, *Roster*, 5:210–18, 235–53, 279–88. On substitute hiring in Greene County, see Bryant, *How Curious a Land*, 84–85.

45 Henderson, *Roster*, 5:245, 249, 252, 285; U.S. Census, 1860, Ga., Irwin County Slave Schedule, 1–4, and Pulaski County Population Schedule, 84, MC; Clements, *Irwin County* 493; Wallace Leigh Harris, *Pulaski and Bleckley Counties*, 1:131; DAR-H, *History of Pulaski County*, 330–31; Carruthers to Governor Brown, July 22, 1862, box 5, GIC-GDAH.

46 Clements to Fletcher, May 16, 1862, in Clements, *Irwin County*, 128; Carruthers to Brown, July 12, 1862, box 5, GIC-GDAH.

47 Clements to Fletcher, in Clements, *Irwin County*, 127–28; Henderson, *Roster*, 5:246.

48 Clements to Fletcher, May 16, 1862, in Clements, *Irwin County*, 127–28. On the resentment of officers, see Fred Arthur Bailey, *Class*, 86, 104, and Williams, *Rich Man's War*, 121–22.

49 Frank, *With Ballot and Bayonet*, 11; Williams, *Rich Man's War*, 1–4; McPherson, *For Cause*, 12–13, 55–58, 101, 108–10, 114; Wallace Leigh Harris, *Pulaski and Bleckley Counties*, 1:128–36; Henderson, *Roster*, 1:963–72, 2:52–58, 3:620–28, 5:210–18, 235–53, 279–88, 303–12; Robertson, *Soldiers*, 12–13; Gallagher, *Confederate War*, 24–26, 46–47; C. W. Styles, "To the Men of Southern Georgia," in Confederate Imprints, reel 83, no. 2548.

50 Henderson, *Roster*, 5:210–18, 235–53, 279–88, 303–12.

51 Ibid., 5:279–87; U.S. Census, 1860, Ga., Pulaski County Population Schedule, 2, MC.

52 McPherson, *For Cause*, 56–57; U.S. Census, 1860, Ga., Telfair County Population Schedule, 32, MC; Robertson, *Soldiers*, 21; Henderson, *Roster*, 5:244; Clements, *Irwin County*, 127–28.

53 Lee to "Dear Wife," July 26, 1862, Lee Letters, UGA; McPherson, *For Cause*, 53–54, 58–60; Brooks, "Soldiering in Hood's Texas Brigade," 542–43; Kennett, *Marching through Georgia*, 56–59; Henderson, *Roster*, 2:817, 5:210, 283; *Recorder*, August 26, 1862; Mann, *Telfair County*, 109–10.

54 Henderson, *Roster*, 5:210, 218; U.S. Census, 1860, Ga., Telfair County Agriculture Schedule, 73, and Population Schedule, 32, MC.

55 Henderson, *Roster*, 5:210, 218; U.S. Census, 1860, Ga., Telfair County Agriculture Schedule, 73, and Population Schedule, 32, MC; McPherson, *For Cause*, 56; Henderson, *Roster*, 2:818, 5:210, 218.

56 Henderson, *Roster*, 5:235–36; McDonald and Lawson, *Passing of the Pines*, 26; U.S. Census, 1860, Ga., Telfair County Slave Schedule, 49–59, MC.

57 Henderson, *Roster*, 5:280, 288; U.S. Census, 1860, Ga., Pulaski County Slave Schedule, 5, MC; Frank, *With Ballot and Bayonet*, 121–22.

58 Smith to W. E. Graham, August 8, 1863, in Mann, *Telfair County*, 71; Lee to "My Dear Wife," July 8, 1863, Lee Letters, UGA.

59 Lee to "My Dear Wife," July 8, 1863, Lee Letters, UGA; E. B. Barrett to Bro. Boykin, January 12, 1863, *Christian Index* 42, no. 4, January 26, 1863; Smith to W. E. Graham, August 8, 1863, in Mann, *Telfair County*, 71; McPherson, *Battle Cry*, 664–65; U.S. Census, 1860, Ga., Telfair County Population Schedule, 20, MC.

60 Faust, "Christian Soldiers," 73–83; Berry, *All That Makes a Man*, 91–94; McPherson, *For Cause*, 62–71; Wilkinson and Woodworth, *Scythe of Fire*, 104–5, 208–9; Lee to "My Dear Wife," July 8, 1863, Lee Letters, UGA.

61  Faust, "Christian Soldiers," 73–83; Robertson, *Hill*, 6–7; DAR-H, *History of Pulaski County*, 301–3.

62  Warren to Bro. Boykin, *Christian Index*, February 23, July 31, 1863; Wyatt-Brown, *Southern Culture*, 174, 206–7; Robertson, *Soldiers*, 172–78.

63  Wiley, *Johnny Reb*, 174–75; Wyatt-Brown, *Southern Culture*, 206–7; *Christian Index*, February 2, 1862.

64  Sears, *Chancellorsville*, 442; Hyman to "Dear Bro. Boykin," *Christian Index*, July 6, 1863.

65  Henderson, *Roster*, 5:244–53; Clements, *Irwin County*, 495; *Christian Index*, June 15, 1863.

66  Faust, "Christian Soldiers," 71–72; Wiley, *Johnny Reb*, 180–81; Hyman to "Dear Bro. Boykin," *Christian Index*, April 30, July 6, 1863.

67  *Christian Index*, February 2, 1863; Barrett to Bro. Boykin, *Christian Index*, January 26, 1863.

68  Fisher Diary, June 28, 1863, GDAH; Barrett to "Dear Bro. Boykin," *Christian Index*, January 26 and November 6, 1863 (quotations); Smith Diary, August 13, 1864, GDAH.

69  Faust, "Christian Soldiers," 75–76; *Christian Index*, May 25, 1863 (William Smith, W. M. McDuffie), February 23, 1865; *Confederate Baptist*, quoted in *Christian Index*, September 25, 1863 (draft dodgers); Beringer et al., *Why the South Lost*, 83–90.

70  Henderson, *Roster*, 5:281, 283; Lee to "Dear Wife," July 8, 26, 1863, Lee Letters, UGA.

71  Henderson, *Roster*, 5:235–44; Gallagher, *Confederate War*, 29; OR 46(2):1315–17.

72  Henderson, *Roster*, 5:235–44; McPherson, *For Cause*, 85–89; CRSG 2:107 (quotation).

73  Warren to "My dear little Son," November 14, 1861, and "To the Church at Friendship," November 17, 1864, in McDonald and Lawson, *Passing of the Pines*, 29; McPherson, *For Cause*, 90–95.

74  Smith to Kirkland, June 12, 1864, Kirkland Collection, folder 7, GDAH; Gallagher, *Confederate War*, 59, 65; Blair, *Virginia's Private War*, 131–33; Grimsley and Simpson, *Collapse of the Confederacy*, 1–2; N. M. McDuffie to Howell Cobb, March 24, 1865, Cobb Papers, UGA.

75  Berry, *All That Makes a Man*, 20–21, 111–13; McPherson, *For Cause*, 90–95, 131–38; Lee to "Most Kind & Affectionate Wife," July 31, 1862, and Lee to "Dear Wife," July 26, 1862, July 26, 1863, Lee Letters, UGA; McDonald and Lawson, *Passing of the Pines*, 266–68.

76  Berry, *All That Makes a Man*, 9–12; Barker to "Dear Wife," June 12, 1862, in McDonald and Lawson, *Passing of the Pines*, 266–67 (quotation, 267); Henderson, *Roster*, 5:236; Frank, *With Ballot and Bayonet*, 9, 57.

*Chapter 5*

1  "HOMESPUN" to Editor, *Recorder*, February 21, 1865. See also Gallagher, *Confederate War*, 3–5, 12, and Whites, *Crisis in Gender*, 132–33. On the South's ever-growing need for soldiers, see Luraghi, *Rise and Fall*, 140–41.

2  "HOMESPUN" to Editor, *Recorder*, February 21, 1865.

3  Ibid.; Clinton, *Tara Revisited*, 57–58; McCurry, "Soldier's Wife," 20–21; Richard, *Busy Hands*, 94–95; Whites, *Crisis in Gender*, 32–33; Kerber, *Women of the Republic*, 200, 210.

4  Faust, *Mothers of Invention*, 30–35 (quotation, 31). On slaveholding along the upper

Ocmulgee, see Reidy, *From Slavery to Agrarian Capitalism*, app., 249–51; U.S. Census Office, *Eighth Census, Population*, 60–72.

5 Faust, *Mothers of Invention*, 30–33.

6 Coulter, *Georgia*, 331; Wooster, *People in Power*, 95. Bozeman ("Reminiscences," private collection) estimated that Pulaski County alone sent 1,500 "men and boys" into Confederate and state units during the war. On regional rates of mobilization, see Gallagher, *Confederate War*, 27–29.

7 Henderson, *Roster*, 1:963–72; Wallace Leigh Harris, *Pulaski and Bleckley Counties*, 1:130–31, 134.

8 Faust, *Mothers of Invention*, 30–35; Rose, *Victorian America*, 70–71; Wyatt-Brown, *Southern Honor*, 164–73; McCurry, *Masters of Small Worlds*, 194–96, and "Soldier's Wife," 20–21; Frank, *With Ballot and Bayonet*, 13–14; Baker, *Affairs of Party*, 29–70.

9 U.S. Census, 1860, Ga., Telfair County Population Schedule, 21, and Slave Schedule, 51, 53, MC; Mann, *Telfair County*, 79–80; Henderson, *Roster*, 2:818–19, 822, 5:213; Rable, "Despair, Hope, and Delusion," 131–37.

10 Speech of Luke Campbell, in Mann, *Telfair County*, 85–86; McCurry, "Soldier's Wife," 20–21.

11 Gibbs to "Dear Wife," March 25, 1863, Gibbs Letters, UGA; Smith to "Dear Friend," August 8, 1863, in Mann, *Telfair County*, 71.

12 Wooster, *People in Power*, 66; PCIC Minutes, January 12, 1865. In Telfair County, the inferior court established a tax of 200 percent of the state tax rate to "be levied for the purpose of Supplying the Telfair Volunteers with winter clothing and Shoes." TCIC Minutes, September 1861.

13 Pulaski County Superior Court, Tax Digest, 1857, PCC; Wallace Leigh Harris, *Pulaski and Bleckley Counties*, 1:96; Henderson, *Roster*, 1:46; McCurry, "Soldier's Wife," 21.

14 PCIC Minutes, August 14, 1865; McCurry, "Soldier's Wife," 22, and " 'Brothers' War?,' " 11.

15 Irwin County Inferior Court Minutes, September 1861, microfilm drawer 99, box 69, GDAH; U.S. Census, 1860, Ga., Irwin County Slave Schedule, 2, 4, MC; TCIC Minutes, March 5, 1862; McCurry, " 'Brothers' War?,' " 11–12.

16 TCIC Minutes, July 1864; PCIC Minutes, July 28, 1864; U.S. Census, 1860, Ga., Telfair County Slave Schedule, 51, MC.

17 U.S. Census, 1860, Ga., Pulaski County Population Schedule, 8, and Slave Schedule, 16–18, MC; Pulaski County Superior Court, Tax Digest, 1857, PCC; U.S. Census, 1860, Ga., Irwin County Slave Schedule, 1–4, MC; Wooster, *People in Power*, 95; Ward, *Coffee County*, 323; PCIC Minutes, July 28, 1864; Clements, *Irwin County*, 201. For a different interpretation, see Williams, Williams, and Carlson, *Plain Folk*, 100.

18 PCIC Minutes, September 1863.

19 Fahs, *Imagined Civil War*, 121–28; *CRSG* 2:117; McCurry, " 'Brothers' War?,' " 10–11; Whites, *Crisis in Gender*, 26–27.

20 U.S. Census Office, *Eighth Census, Population*, 60–61. On the status of women, see McCurry, " 'Brothers' War?,' " 18–19; Varon, *We Mean to Be Counted*, 50–51, 80–83; Lebsock, *Free Women of Petersburg*, chap. 2.

21 *CRSG* 2:284, 470, and 472 (Brown); C. W. Styles, "To the Men of Southern Georgia," in Confederate Imprints, reel 83, no. 2548.

22 "PLAIN TALKER" to Editor, *Recorder*, March 28, 1865; Overstreet to Brown, April 26, 1862, box 42, GIC-GDAH; C. W. Styles, "To the Men of Southern Georgia," in Confederate Imprints, reel 83, no. 2548; Berry, *All That Makes a Man*, 164–73.

23 McCurry "Soldier's Wife," 20–21; Blair, *Virginia's Private War*, 143–44.

24 *CRSG* 2:103, 105; Blair, *Virginia's Private War*, 94–95, 119–20; *Recorder*, March 18, 1862.

25 PCIC Minutes, 1846–67, July 1861, May, August 1862.

26 "Countryman" to *Thomasville Times*, quoted in *Recorder*, September 16, 1862.

27 *CRSG* 2:399; Clements, *Irwin County*, 204.

28 *CRSG* 2:403–6; *Statistics of the United States in 1860*, 4:341; Henderson, *Roster*, 5:235–44.

29 *CRSG* 2:403–5; *Statistics of the United States in 1860*, 4:341; PCIC Minutes, January 31, 1865.

30 Bryan, *Confederate Georgia*, 22; Ward, *Coffee County*, 127 (first quotation); Faust, *Mothers of Invention*, 30–32; Gallagher, *Confederate War*, 36–37, 106–7; Blair, *Virginia's Private War*, 85–87, 109–10; *Savannah Republican*, quoted in *Messenger*, April 10, 1861; *Recorder*, October 28, 1862 (last quotation).

31 "A List of Indigent Soldiers Families in Telfair Entitled to Thread, August 15, 1863," microfilm drawer 172, box 42, TCIC Minutes; U.S. Census, 1860, Ga., Telfair County Population Schedule, 11–23, and Slave Schedule, 51–54, MC; Whites, *Crisis in Gender*, 26–27.

32 U.S. Census, 1860, Ga., Telfair County Population Schedule, 19, and Agriculture Schedule, 67, MC; Hilliard, *Hog Meat*, 158 (self-sufficiency rate); Henderson, *Roster*, 2:821, 5:214.

33 Henderson, *Roster*, 5:214; *Messenger*, November 6, 1861; "A List of Indigent Soldiers Families in Telfair Entitled to Thread, August 15, 1863," microfilm drawer 172, box 42, TCIC Minutes; U.S. Census, 1860, Ga., Telfair County Slave Schedule, 53, MC.

34 Clements, *Irwin County*, 268; Henderson, *Roster*, 5:238–39; U.S. Census, 1860, Ga., Wilcox County Population Schedule, 34, and Agriculture Schedule, 9, MC; Bartley, *Modern Georgia*, 21, 30.

35 Gibbs to "Dear Wife," March 25, 1863, in McDonald and Lawson, *Passing of the Pines*, 30; U.S. Census, 1860, Ga., Wilcox County Population Schedule, 34, and Agriculture Schedule, 9, MC.

36 TCIC Minutes, July, 1864; Kenzer, "Uncertainty of Life," 113–16; Gross, " 'Good Angels,' " 133–37; McCurry, "Soldier's Wife," 23 (quotation).

37 *CRSG* 2:399–406; TCIC Minutes, April 1865; Henderson, *Roster*, 5:211; U.S. Census, 1860, Ga., Telfair County Population Schedule, 16, and Agriculture Schedule, 67, MC; Hilliard, *Hog Meat*, 157.

38 See Faust, *Mothers of Invention*, 30–35: U.S. Census Office, *Eighth Census, Agriculture*, 226–27, and *Statistics*, 4:341; Overstreet to Brown, April 26, 1862, box 42, GIC-GDAH.

39 U.S. Census Office, *Eighth Census, Population*, 66–67; Overstreet to Brown, April 26, 1862, box 42, GIC-GDAH. Male slaves who were fifteen and older in 1860 are considered adults for the years 1861–65. For views of the home front as a world of women and slaves, see Faust, *Mothers of Invention*, 30–35, and Williams, Williams, and Carlson, *Plain Folk*, 71–72.

40 U.S. Census Office, *Eighth Census, Population*, 59–60, and *Ninth Census, Population*, 106;

Faust, *Mothers of Invention*, 31 and 35 (quotations); Pulaski County Superior Court, Minute Book E, April 1864, 73–74, GDAH.

41 U.S. Census, 1860, Ga., Telfair County Population Schedule, 11–23, MC.

42 Henderson, *Roster*, 2:819, 821, 5:214: Coulter, *Georgia*, 330–31; U.S. Census, 1860, Ga., Telfair County Population Schedule, 19, and Slave Schedule, 53, MC; Mann, *Telfair County*, 80, 92, 103.

43 McCurry, "Soldier's Wife," 20–21; Fox-Genovese, *Plantation Household*, 60–64; U.S. Census, 1860, Ga., Telfair County Population Schedule, 21, MC.

44 U.S. Census, 1860, Ga., Telfair County Population Schedule, 20, and Agriculture Schedule, 67, MC.

45 U.S. Census, 1860, Ga., Telfair County, Population Schedule, 12, MC; Henderson, *Roster*, 5:210.

46 U.S. Census, 1860, Ga., Telfair County Population Schedule, 18, MC; Henderson, *Roster*, 2:817–24, 5:210–18; Fuller to Brown, August 17, 1864, box 30, GIC-GDAH.

47 U.S. Census, 1860, Ga., Telfair County Population Schedule, 11–23, and Slave Schedule, 51–52, MC; Faust, *Mothers of Invention*, 30.

48 U.S. Census Office, *Eighth Census, Population*, 73.

49 Henderson, *Roster*, 1:970; Petition of C. M. Bozeman and others to Governor Brown, PCIC Minutes, July 28, 1864; Petition of Hugh McCartney and others to Secretary of War, June 10, 1863, Letters Received, Confederate Secretary of War, reel 116, NA-W.

50 U.S. Census, 1860, Ga., Irwin County Slave Schedule, 1, MC.

51 Ash, *When the Yankees Came*, 151, 158–59; Barney, *Flawed Victory*, 121–22, 138–39; *AS* 3(1):241 (Martha Everette), 227 (Sara Crocker).

52 White to Hon. Geo. W. Randolph, September 8, 1862, in Berlin, *Freedom*, 699–700.

53 Reidy, *From Slavery to Agrarian Capitalism*, 113–17; "A Visit to Hawkinsville," *Messenger*, April 29, 1863.

54 *AS* 3(1):221; Faust, *Mothers of Invention*, 53–56, 79 (quotation), 256.

55 U.S. Census, 1860, Ga., Telfair County Population Schedule, 11–23, and Slave Schedule, 50–55, MC; Henderson, *Roster*, 2:820; *Messenger*, August 6, 1856.

56 U.S. Census, 1860, Ga., Telfair County Population Schedule 12, 18, 21, and Slave Schedule, 51, 53, MC; Mann, *Telfair County*, 88; "A List of Indigent Soldiers Families in Telfair County Entitled to Thread," August 15, 1865, microfilm drawer, 172, box 42, TCIC Minutes; Whites, *Crisis in Gender*, 26–27.

57 U.S. Census, 1860, Ga., Telfair County Population Schedule, 51–52, MC; Faust, *Mothers of Invention*, 53–54 (quotation, 54).

58 U.S. Bureau of Soils, *Survey of Dodge County*, 239; *Recorder*, October 28, 1862; *Pulaski Times*, quoted in *Union Recorder*, October 5, 1858; Escott, *After Secession*, 104–13.

59 Henderson, *Roster*, 5:238; Clinton, *Tara Revisited*, 112–14; U.S. Census, 1860, Ga., Telfair County Population Schedule, 19, 26, Slave Schedule, 52, 56, and Agriculture Schedule, 69, MC; Hilliard, *Hog Meat*, 157; *Messenger*, April 29, 1863.

60 U.S. Census, 1860, Ga., Telfair County Population Schedule, 36, Slave Schedule, 56, and Agriculture Schedule, 71, MC; Joiner, *Pioneer Families*, 1:20.

61 Payment vouchers for Norman McDuffie and others, in Letters Received, Confederate Secretary of War, Microfilm Publications, M346, NA-W; TCIC Minutes, March 5, 1862.

62  Berlin, "Did Confederate Women Lose the War?," 168–71; Luraghi, *Rise and Fall*, 84–85.

63  Ward, *Coffee County*, 90–91; Clements, *Irwin County*, 144; Thompson, "Moral Economy," 79, 90–94; *CRSG* 2:103–5 (Brown); Donald, Baker, and Holt, *Civil War*, 454, 459; Williams, *Rich Man's War*, 83–87; Escott, *After Secession*, 122–25, 139, 146–48.

64  *Messenger*, September 18, 1861, January 18, 1865, and J. M. W. to Editor, February 3, 1864; TCIC Minutes, March 5, 1862.

65  *Recorder*, February, 21, 1865; Coffee to Brown, December 14, 1861, box 6, GIC-GDAH; Henderson, *Roster*, 2:817, 819. Coffee's son John was elected captain of the Telfair Volunteers in October 1861; his son Joshua was a private in the same company. Blair, *Virginia's Private War*, 5, 118–19. For an emphasis on class conflict, see Williams, *Rich Man's War*, chap. 3, Williams, Williams, and Carlson, *Plain Folk*, 1–2, 100, and Fred Arthur Bailey, *Class*, 84, 104.

66  J. M. W. to Editor, *Messenger*, February 3, 1864.

67  Ibid.; Henderson, *Roster*, 2:817; Berlin, "Did Confederate Women Lose the War?," 169–71.

68  PCIC Minutes, January 31, 1865. On crop shortages in the Upper South, see Ayers, *In the Presence of Mine Enemies*, 333–35.

69  Wallace Leigh Harris, *Pulaski and Bleckley Counties*, 1:96; U.S. Census, 1860, Ga., Pulaski County Slave Schedule, 1, 4, 48, MC; McCurry, "Soldier's Wife," 15–17; Murrell, "Of Necessity," 84; Berlin, "Did Confederate Women Lose the War?," 169–73.

70  McCurry, "Soldier's Wife," 17–36; Clinton, *Tara Revisited*, 150–52; Caroline Conner and others, July 26, 1864, Petitions, box 3 (Q–W), GIC-GDAH; Murrell, "Of Necessity," 78–79.

71  Rable, *Civil Wars*, 15–16; Varon, *We Mean to Be Counted*, 138–62; Whites, *Crisis in Gender*, 26–27; U.S. Census, 1860, Ga., Pulaski County Slave Schedule, 3, and Agriculture Schedule, 1, MC; McRae to S. H. Latimer, January 25, 1861, Latimer Papers, Duke University.

72  Faust, *Mothers of Invention*, 211–14; McCurry, "Soldier's Wife," 17–20; Bennett's Wife to Brown, July 29, 1864, box, 2, GIC-GDAH.

73  Varon, *We Mean to Be Counted*, 50–53, 141–65; H. M. McLean and others, July 30, 1864 (box 3 [Q–W]), and Petition of "Citizens & Soldiers' Wives of Pulaski & Wilcox County," n.d. [May 1864?] (box 2 [H–P]), Petitions, GIC-GDAH; Murrell, "Of Necessity," 82–83.

74  Murrell, "Of Necessity," 88–89; Petition of "Citizens & Soldiers' Wives of Pulaski & Wilcox County" (box 2 [H–P]), and Petition of Caroline Conner and others, July 26, 1864 (box 3 [Q–W]), Petitions, GIC-GDAH; Ayers, *In the Presence of Mine Enemies*, 224–25, 244–45.

75  Petitions of Caroline Conner and others, July 26, 1864 (box 3 [Q–W]), H. M. McLean and others, July 30, 1864 (box 3 [Q–W]), and Mrs. Elizabeth Gray and others, October 10, 1864 (box 1 [A–G]), Petitions, GIC-GDAH.

76  Petitions of "Citizens & Soldiers' Wives of Pulaski & Wilcox County," n.d. [May 1864?] (box 2 [H–P]), and H. M. McLean and others (box 3 [Q–W]), Petitions, GIC-GDAH; Murrell, "Of Necessity," 78–79. On disaffection, see Anne J. Bailey, "Far Corner"; Escott, *After Secession*, 94–134; and Storey, *Loyalty and Loss*.

77  Petition of Caroline Conner and others, July 20, 1864, Petitions, box 3 (Q–W), GIC-GDAH; McCurry, "Soldier's Wife," 28–29.

78 Clements, *Irwin County*, 177, 206, 208, 497; U.S. Census, 1860, Ga., Irwin County Slave Schedule, 3, and Agriculture Schedule, 5, MC.

79 Clements, *Irwin County*, 117; Henderson, *Roster*, 5:244–45; James T. Branch petition, May 1864, Petitions, box 2 (H–P), GIC-GDAH.

80 James T. Branch petition, May 1864, Petitions, box 2 (H–P), GIC-GDAH; Clements, *Irwin County*, 496–501, 508–9; Berlin, "Did Confederate Women Lose the War?," 181–87.

81 James T. Branch petition, Petitions, May 1864, box 2 (H–P), GIC-GDAH; McCurry, "Soldier's Wife," 21; Murrell, "Of Necessity," 92–93; Berlin, "Did Confederate Women Lose the War?," 187–88.

82 Whites, *Crisis in Gender*, 5, 104–5; Murrell, "Of Necessity," 92–93; Berlin, "Did Confederate Women Lose the War?," 187–88.


*Chapter 6*

1 *AS* 4(2):502, 508 (Easter Reed).

2 Ibid.; U.S. Census, 1860, Ga., Telfair County Population Schedule, 36, and Slave Schedule, 56, MC; *Recorder*, February 21, 1865; Henderson, *Roster*, 2:819, 5:212; Joiner, *Pioneer Families*, 1:20.

3 Frank, *With Ballot and Bayonet*, 20–21; Faust, *Confederate Nationalism*, 19–21; Linderman, *Embattled Courage*, 20–23; Speech of Luke Campbell in Mann, *Telfair County*, 86–87; *CRSG*, 2:284 and 380–81 (Brown); Whites, *Crisis in Gender*, 106–7.

4 Blight, *Race and Reunion*, 1–5; Faust, "Civil War Soldier," 4; Barnabas Williamson to George Williamson, December 28, 1863, in McDonald and Lawson, *Passing of the Pines*, 267. For an interpretation that emphasizes class conflict and disunity in Georgia, see, e.g., Williams, *Rich Man's War*, 116–50, and Williams, Williams, and Carlson, *Plain Folk*, 91–96.

5 Varon, *We Mean to Be Counted*, 137–39, 153–68; Faust, "Civil War Soldier," 3–4; Whites, *Crisis in Gender*, 32–33; *Minutes of the Twenty-Fourth Annual Session of the Primitive Baptist Association, . . . 1863.*

6 Samuel Day Fuller File, CWM-GDAH; U.S. Census, 1860, Ga., Wilcox County Population Schedule, 1, MC.

7 Laderman, *Sacred Remains*, 24–26; Clements, *Irwin County*, 505; Charlotte Taylor to "My Dear Husband," April 12, 1849, R. N. Taylor Papers, Washington Memorial Library, Macon.

8 Ward, *Coffee County*, 93–94, 225–26; *AS* 3(1):220 (Arthur Colson); Charlotte Taylor to "My Dear Husband," August 14, 1849, R. N. Taylor Papers, Washington Memorial Library, Macon; Laderman, *Sacred Remains*, 27–29; Faust, "Civil War Soldier," 12–13; Arnold, "Expressions of Grief," 14–18.

9 Laderman, *Sacred Remains*, 27–37; Herring, *Saturday Night Sketches*, 44–50; Arnold, "Expressions of Grief," 25–29.

10 Laderman, *Sacred Remains*, 30–37; Herring, *Saturday Night Sketches*, 44–50; *Dispatch*, April 16, 1885 (McGriff); Ward, *Coffee County*, 225–26; Arnold, "Expressions of Grief," 35–38.

11 *Christian Index*, April 1, 1862 (quotations); Wallace Leigh Harris, *Pulaski and Bleckley*

*Counties*, 1:272; U.S. Census, 1860, Ga., Pulaski County Population Schedule, 78, and Slave Schedule, 37, MC; Laderman, *Sacred Remains*, 54–58; Arnold, "Expressions of Grief," 14–17.

12  *Morning News*, March 17, 31, 1860; *Milledgeville Southern Cultivator*, March 20, 1860.

13  *Milledgeville Southern Cultivator*, March 20, 1860; "Step Roberts to Dear Cousins, Unkle, & Aunt," June 7, 1863, CWM-GDAH; Henderson, *Roster*, 1:963–72; Faust, *Confederate Nationalism*, 3–5.

14  Stampp, *Peculiar Institution*, 30; U.S. Census, 1860, Ga., Telfair County Population Schedule, 11–23, and Slave Schedule, 51–55, MC; Henderson, *Roster*, 2:817–24, 5:210–18. For this interpretation applied to Georgia's Chattahoochee River Valley, see Williams, *Rich Man's War*. The proportion of plain folk from nonslaveholding families in the Jacksonville district is close to the 72 percent found in Texas and to the percentage of soldiers from such families in Hood's Texas Brigade. See Brooks, "Soldiering in Hood's Texas Brigade," 538–41.

15  U.S. Census, 1860, Ga., Telfair County Population Schedule, 11–23, and Slave Schedule, 51–55, MC; Henderson, *Roster*, 2:817–24, 5:210–18; Speech of Luke Campbell, in Mann, *Telfair County*, 85–86.

16  Speech of Luke Campbell, in Mann, *Telfair County*, 85–86 (quotations); U.S. Census, 1860, Ga., Telfair County Population Schedule, 19, and Slave Schedule, 53, MC; Henderson, *Roster*, 2:819; Faust, *Confederate Nationalism*, 69–71.

17  Frank, *With Ballot and Bayonet*, 21–22; *Recorder*, July 19, 1864 (Mason); Speech of Luke Campbell, in Mann, *Telfair County*, 85.

18  Speech of Luke Campbell, in Mann, *Telfair County*, 85; *Recorder*, July 19, 1864; McPherson, *For Cause*, 20–22; Barker to "Dear Wife," June 12, 1862, in McDonald and Lawson, *Passing of the Pines*, 266–67; Henderson, *Roster*, 5:236.

19  Frank, *With Ballot and Bayonet*, 26–28; *Christian Index*, February 23, 1865.

20  *Recorder*, July 19, 1864 (Mason), September 23, 1862 (Smith); Henderson, *Roster*, 2:49; Faust, "Christian Soldiers," 75–76; Frank, *With Ballot and Bayonet*, 21–22; J. M. Warren "To the Church at Friendship," November 17, 1864, in McDonald and Lawson, *Passing of the Pines*, 29.

21  *Recorder*, July 19, 1864; Rable, "Hearth, Home, and Family," 95–96.

22  *Recorder*, October 29, 1861, January 14, 1862; *Union Recorder*, August 4, 1863.

23  *Recorder*, July 19, 1864 (Mason); Whites, *Crisis in Gender*, 168; Henderson, *Roster*, 5:256, 3:622; Joiner, *Pioneer Families*, 1:2.

24  Wallace Leigh Harris, *Pulaski and Bleckley Counties*, 1:128; Pulaski County Superior Court, Will Book B, 95–96, PCC.

25  Laderman, *Sacred Remains*, 9–17, 101–4, 113–15; Fleming, "Sketch of the Pulaski Volunteers," *Dispatch*, July 24, 1879; Wallace Leigh Harris, *Pulaski and Bleckley Counties*, 1:96, 128–36; Thigpen to "Dear Father and Mother," May 25, 1862, Kirkland Collection, folder 9, GDAH; Smith to "Dear Wife," May 16, 1864, in McDonald and Lawson, *Passing of the Pines*, 267.

26  Robertson, *Soldiers*, 224–26; *Recorder*, July 19, 1864; Mann, *Telfair County*, 72; Henderson, *Roster*, 2:620–28; McPherson, *Battle Cry*, 665.

27 "Family Grave Yards," *Recorder*, October 29, 1861; Henderson, *Roster*, 5:214; Mann, *Telfair County*, 71; U.S. Census, 1860, Ga., Pulaski County Population Schedule, 4, MC.

28 Pulaski County Superior Court, Will Book B, 88–90, PCC; Wallace Leigh Harris, *Pulaski and Bleckley Counties*, 1:143; Henderson, *Roster*, 5:279. Sutherland (*Seasons of War*, 193–94) notes that rooting animals uncovered the bodies of hastily buried fatalities at Cedar Mountain.

29 Manning grave marker, Orange Hill Cemetery, Hawkinsville; Pulaski County Superior Court, Will Book B, 113–15, PCC; U.S. Census, 1860, Ga., Pulaski County Population Schedule, 8, MC; Whites, *Crisis in Gender*, 36.

30 PCIC Minutes, September 22, 1862; R. G. Dun and Co., GA26, 138, Harvard University; Henderson, *Roster*, 3:620, 628; Wallace Leigh Harris, *Pulaski and Bleckley Counties*, 1:126.

31 See, e.g., *Recorder*, October 28, 1862.

32 Pulaski County Superior Court, Will Book B, 75, 95–96, PCC.

33 Clements, *Irwin County*, 196–97; Henderson, *Roster*, 5:250.

34 Clements, *Irwin County*, 196–97. See, e.g., *Recorder*, October 28, 1862.

35 *Recorder*, October 28, 1862; AS 4(2):416 (Caroline Malloy); Pulaski County Superior Court, Will Book B, 88–90, 144–45, PCC.

36 Genevose, *Roll, Jordan, Roll*, 350–52; Henderson, *Roster*, 1:45; AS 3(1):221 (Arthur Colson).

37 AS 4(2):508 (Easter Reed); Blassingame, *Slave Community*, 109–14; Ward, *Coffee County*, 93–94.

38 See AS 3(1):240–41 (Martha Everette), 221 (Arthur Colson), 4(2):507 (Easter Reed), 415 (Caroline Malloy), 458 (Elsie Moreland).

39 Ward, *Coffee County*, 226; AS 4(2):507 (Easter Reed); Botkin, *Southern Folklore*, 641.

40 Henderson, *Roster*, 3:627, 5:251–52; Affidavit of Sarah Townsell (Townsend), Wilcox County Ordinary, Loose Records, microfilm drawer 187, box 31, GDAH; Clements, *Irwin County*, 196.

41 Cedar Creek Baptist Church Minutes, Wilcox County, 57, microfilm drawer 232, box 2, GDAH; McPherson, *Battle Cry*, 274–75.

42 Ward, *Coffee County*, 31–32, 153; Faust, *Confederate Nationalism*, 22–24; Wyatt-Brown, *Southern Culture*, 154–55; Miller, Stout, and Wilson, *Religion*, 6–13; Harvey, " 'Yankee Faith' and Southern Redemption," 167–70; McCurry, *Masters of Small Worlds*, 136–41; *Christian Index*, February 13, 1861 (first quotation), November 11, 1862 (second quotation).

43 Miller, Stout, and Wilson, *Religion*, 6–7; Mitchell, "Christian Soldiers?," 299–308; Speech of Luke Campbell in Mann, *Telfair County*, 87; Faust, *Confederate Nationalism*, 26–27.

44 Wyatt-Brown, *Southern Culture*, 133–34.

45 Crowley, *Primitive Baptists*, 19, 88–93; McDonald and Lawson, *Passing of the Pines*, 26; Clements, *Irwin County*, 457, 461–62; U.S. Census, 1860, Ga., Irwin County Slave Schedule, 3–4, MC; McCurry, *Masters of Small Worlds*, 136–41; Wyatt-Brown, *Southern Culture*, 133–34.

46 *Minutes of the Seventeenth Annual Session of the Primitive Baptist Pulaski Association, . . . 1855*, 7.

47  *Minutes of the Twenty-Fourth Annual Session of the Primitive Baptist Pulaski Association,* . . . *1863*, 6; *Minutes of the Twenty-Fifth Annual Session,* . . . *1864*, 7.

48  Clements, *Irwin County*, 454–59, 507; Henderson, *Roster*, 5:241; U.S. Census, 1860, Ga., Wilcox County Population Schedule, 42, MC; *Recorder*, August 4, 1863.

49  Henderson, *Roster*, 5:235, 241; Clements, *Irwin County*, 47, 454–59; *Minutes of the Twenty-Fourth Annual Session of the Primitive Baptist Pulaski Association,* . . . *1863*, 6.

50  Clements, *Irwin County*, 144, 459; McDonald and Lawson, *Passing of the Pines*, 26; *Minutes of the Seventeenth Annual Session of the Primitive Baptist Pulaski Association,* . . . *1855*, 7; Faust, "Christian Soldiers," 77–78.

## Chapter 7

1  Abbeville Resolutions, January 14, 1865 (first quotation), typescript, 1418, Brown Papers, UGA; Grimsley, *Hard Hand of War*, 2–4; *Messenger*, June 1 (quotations), July 20, 1864; Donald, Baker, and Holt, *Civil War*, 388–92; Thomas, *Confederate Nation*, 296–97; Jacqueline Glass Campbell, *When Sherman Marched North*, 5–6.

2  Abbeville Resolutions, January 14, 1865, typescript, 1416–18, Brown Papers, UGA; Jacqueline Glass Campbell, *When Sherman Marched North*, 10–11.

3  Seddon to Cobb, May 11, 1864, Cobb Papers, box 68, UGA; *OR* 52(2):673–74; Michael P. Johnson, *Patriarchal Republic*, 28–37.

4  J. H. Hollinquist to Major Lamar Cobb, January 23, 1865, Cobb-Erwin-Lamar Papers, box 3, UGA; Thomas, *Confederate Nation*, 294–99. For purposes of this discussion, I describe men rallying to secessionist-led militias as loyal due to their willingness to fight for Georgia and the Confederacy in state-authorized militia units; on the other hand, anti-Confederates are considered disloyal to the Confederacy because they did not fight in regular militia units. They are called "anti-Confederates," although being such did not necessarily mean a willingness to risk their lives for the Union. Stephen Ash (*When the Yankees Came*, 21–22, 95–96, 129–30) provides the best analysis of this subject. For votes for and against immediate secession, see Michael P. Johnson, "New Look," 268–70.

5  James A. Seddon to Howell Cobb, May 20, 1864, Cobb Papers, box 68, UGA; Coulter, *Georgia*, 330–31; PCIC Minutes, November 8, 1864; Blair, *Virginia's Private War*, 103–3; Bozeman, "Reminiscences," private collection; Jacqueline Glass Campbell, *When Sherman Marched North*, 5.

6  Civil War Unit Card Files, Telfair and Wilcox Counties, GDAH; R. G. Dun and Co., GA32, 182, Harvard University (McRae); Mann, *Telfair County*, 88; Wallace Leigh Harris, *Pulaski and Bleckley Counties*, 1:126–27; U.S. Census, 1860, Ga., Pulaski County Slave Schedule, 21; Clements, *Irwin County*, 212. On slaveholder reluctance to fight and resulting class resentment among the yeomanry, see Williams, Williams, and Carlson, *Plain Folk*, 21–22; on the persistence of antebellum elites and plain folk deference, see Ash, *Middle Tennessee Society Transformed*, 88.

7  Amnesty Papers, M1003, reel 8, NA (Taylor's service); Mann, *Telfair County*, 88–94 (includes brief biographical sketches for some of these men); Burnham, *Presidential Ballots*, 354.

8   U.S. Census Office, *Eighth Census*, 4:298, 341; U.S. Census, 1860, Ga., Telfair County Population Schedule, 1–21, Slave Schedule, 49–53, and Agriculture Schedule, 73, MC; Brooks, "Soldiering in Hood's Texas Brigade," 538; TCIC Minutes, July 1864, "Widows Having Son in Army"; Mann, *Telfair County*, 65–66.

9   Mann, *Telfair County*, 65–66, 88; Hummel, *Emancipating Slaves*, 227; U.S. Census, 1860, Ga., Telfair County Population Schedule, 5, and Slave Schedule, 21, 49, 53, MC; Henderson, *Roster*, 5:210–11, 214, 2:822.

10  Cobb to "My Dear Wife," November 3, 1864, Cobb Papers, box 69, UGA; J. M. White to R. R. Slappey, November 29, 1862, box 50, GIC-GDAH.

11  Gallagher, *Confederate War*, 17–32, 58; *OR* 3(2):673; Faust, *Confederate Nationalism*, 3–5.

12  Wyatt-Brown, *Southern Culture*, 89; Ash, *When the Yankees Came*, 3–8; McPherson, *For Cause*, 136–37; Gallagher, *Confederate War*, 56; Henderson, *Roster*, 5:212; Cobb, *Dodge County*, 210; Ward, *Coffee County*, 128, 142–43; Fuller to Brown, August 17, 1864, box 30, GIC-GDAH.

13  *OR* 52(2):673–74; *Macon Daily Telegraph*, June 30, 1863; 1860 Census, Telfair, 4–5, 14–15, 18–19; McPherson, *For Cause*, 95–98; Fuller to Brown, August, 17, 1864, box 30, GIC-GDAH.

14  *OR* 52(2):735–40.

15  Ibid.

16  Johnson and Buel, *Battles and Leaders*, 4:667.

17  Ibid., 4:335; Mann, *Telfair County*, 88–94; A. M. Rowland to Howell Cobb, November 17, 1864, and Cobb to "My Dear Wife," November 16, 1864, Cobb Papers, box 69, UGA.

18  McInvale, "Griswoldville," 121–24; *OR* 44(1):83.

19  Johnson and Buel, *Battles and Leaders*, 4:667; McInvale, "Griswoldville," 124–25; Mann, *Telfair County*, 88.

20  Woods, After-Action Report, *OR* 44(1):98 (first two quotations); Catterson, After-Action Report, *OR* 44(1):105; Donald, Baker, and Holt, *Civil War*, 386–89; Wills, quoted in McInvale, "Griswoldville," 126–27.

21  Wills, *Army Life*, 322–23 (Union officer); Wallace Leigh Harris, *Pulaski and Bleckley Counties*, 1:136–40; Henderson, *Roster*, 5:284.

22  McInvale, "Griswoldville," 126–27; Catterson, After-Action Report, *OR* 44(1):105; Wills, *Army Life*, 322–23.

23  McInvale, "Griswoldville," 126–28; Catterson, After-Action Report, *OR* 44(1):105; Willison, After-Action Report, *OR* 44(1):107 (quotations).

24  Mann, *Telfair County*, 88–95; Wallace Leigh Harris, *Pulaski and Bleckley Counties*, 1:140; Henderson, *Roster*, 5:284; U.S. Census, 1860, Ga., Pulaski County Population Schedule, 3, MC.

25  McInvale, "Griswoldville," 128; Grimsley, *Hard Hand of War*, 10–11; Wills, *Army Life*, 323–24; Jacqueline Glass Campbell, *When Sherman Marched North*, 10–12; Kennett, *Marching through Georgia*, 276, 321.

26  Johnson and Buel, *Battles and Leaders*, 4:667; Catterson, After-Action Report, *OR* 44(1):105 ("terrible slaughter"); Willison, After-Action Report, *OR* 44(1):107 ("fearful execution"); McInvale, "Griswoldville," 128–29; Woods, After-Action Report, *OR*

44(1):98; Grimsley, *Hard Hand of War*, 142–43; Donald, Baker, and Holt, *Civil War*, 389; James Leath, "A Journal of Movements & Incidents of the 3rd Brig., 4th Div., 15th A. C., during the March from Rome, to Savannah, Georgia, Commencing November 10, 1864 and Ending December 21, 1864," November 22–25, 1864, Huntington Library.

27  Donald, Baker, and Holt, *Civil War*, 391–93; Dyer, *Secret Yankees*, 183; Osterhaus, After-Action Report, *OR* 44(1):83; Abbeville Resolutions, January 14, 1865, typescript, 1418, Brown Papers, UGA.

28  Abbeville Resolutions, January 14, 1865, typescript, 1417–18, Brown Papers, UGA.

29  McRae to W. Willcox, January 6, 1865, N. McDuffie to Howell Cobb, January 8, 1865, and J. B. Cumming to Major Lamar Cobb, January 8, 1865, Cobb Papers, box 69, UGA; Bozeman, "Reminiscences," private collection. McDuffie's letter of January 8 forwarded McRae's message to Lamar Cobb.

30  Abbeville Resolutions, January 14, 1865, typescript, 1416–18, Brown Papers, UGA. On civilian confusion in South Carolina, see Jacqueline Glass Campbell, *When Sherman Marched North*, 10–11.

31  Abbeville Resolutions, January 14, 1865, typescript, 1416–18, Brown Papers, UGA.

32  *Albany Patriot*, quoted in *Messenger*, March 1, 1865; W. H. Harris to Howell Cobb, January 16, 1865, Cobb Papers, box 69, UGA.

33  *Albany Patriot*, quoted in *Messenger*, March 1, 1865; W. H. Harris to Howell Cobb, Cobb Papers, box 69, UGA.

34  Clinch to Major General Howell Cobb, April 4, 1865, Cobb Papers, UGA; *OR* 47(3):464–65; *Savannah Daily Herald*, June 2, 1865.

35  Ibid.; Carlson, "Loanly Runagee," 590, 597, 603; Inscoe and Kenzer, *Enemies of the Country*, 4–5; Williams, Williams, and Carlson, *Plain Folk*, 183–84. On the spatial dimensions of the occupied South, see Ash, *When the Yankees Came*, 76–78.

36  Williams, Williams, and Carlson, *Plain Folk*, 32; Ash, *When the Yankees Came*, 11; Inscoe and Kenzer, *Enemies of the Country*, 5–7, 55; Ward, *Coffee County*, 142 (Wall); Paine to Dear Governor, n.d., box 42, GIC-GDAH; Henderson, *Roster*, 5:289.

37  Sutherland, *Guerrillas, Unionists*, 5–6; Fuller to Governor Brown, August 17, 1864, box 30, GIC-GDAH; Abbeville Resolutions, January 14, 1865, typescript, 1416–18, Brown Papers, UGA.

38  U.S. Census, 1860, Ga., Irwin County Population Schedule, 22, and Pulaski County Slave Schedule, 33, MC; Sutherland, *Guerrillas, Unionists*, 3–6; Wallace Leigh Harris, *Pulaski and Bleckley Counties*, 1:127–28, 152–53. On Jones's loyalties, see *Dispatch*, October 1, 1874.

39  Weitz, *Higher Duty*, 88, 137; *Albany Patriot*, quoted in *Messenger*, March 1, 1865 (see, e.g., Carlson, "Loanly Runagee," 590–98); Henderson, *Roster*, 2:1073–74, 5:210–18, 235–53, 279–88; Bryant, *How Curious a Land*, 84–85; Lonn, *Desertion*, 19; Donald, Baker, and Holt, *Civil War*, 453; *Recorder*, March 28, 1865. On desertion from Company A, see clipping in "Unit File" for 61st Georgia Volunteer Infantry, microfilm drawer 283, box 59, CWM-GDAH. Wilkinson and Woodworth (*Scythe of Fire*, 302) note no desertion in Company G of the Eighth Georgia, whereas Henderson (*Roster*, 1:965, 967) mentions the desertion of Josiah Hudnell in 1863 and Samuel Buchanan in 1864.

40  *Recorder*, March 28, 1865; Lonn, *Desertion*, 19; Weitz, *Higher Duty*, 137; Carlson, "Loanly Runagee," 590–98.

41  Lonn, *Desertion*, 106–7; G. M. McRae to Henry C. Wayne, box 17, AGIC; Laver, "Social Role of the Militia," 777–90; Brooks, "Soldiering in Hood's Texas Brigade," 542–46; Wilkinson and Woodworth, *Scythe of Fire*, 19.

42  Coulter, *Georgia*, 330–31; Donald, Baker, and Holt, *Civil War*, 250–51; McPherson, *Battle Cry*, 429–32; Daniel F. McRae to Governor Brown, December 15, 1863, box 39, GIC-GDAH; U.S. Census, 1860, Ga., Telfair County Slave Schedule, 49, MC.

43  Clements, *Irwin County*, 43; Carlson, "Loanly Runagee," 590–92; Paulk to Governor Brown, August 5, 1864, box 42, GIC-GDAH; U.S. Census, 1860, Ga., Coffee County Slave Schedule, 1, MC; Willcox to General Wayne, December 9, 1864, AGIC; *Messenger*, July 20, 1864.

44  Cobb, *Dodge County*, 189; *Dispatch*, October 1, 1874; Carlson, "Loanly Runagee," 595–96, 598; U.S. Census, 1860, Ga., Pulaski County Slave Schedule, 33–34, MC; Wallace Leigh Harris, *Pulaski and Bleckley Counties*, 1:65, 152–53; Henderson, *Roster*, 5:279–87.

45  Coulter, *Georgia*, 331; U.S. Census, 1860, Ga., Irwin County Slave Schedule, 1–2, MC; Wooster, "Georgia Secession Convention," app. I; Sutherland, *Guerrillas, Unionists*, 6–7; E. N. Broyles to D. McRae, October 10, 1864, no. 26, 588, AGLB.

46  L. H. Briscoe to "Hon. Justices of the Inferior Court of the County of Pulaski," August 12, 1864, no. 25, 310, AGLB; Blair, *Virginia's Private War*, 57–58.

47  Weitz, *Higher Duty*, 1–6; James Pate to "Dear Sun," October 29, 1863, Jane Pate to "Dear Husband," July 19, 1864, and Bennett Pate to Unknown, May 25, 1864, Pate Family Letters, private collection; Donald, Baker, and Holt, *Civil War*, 453; Ward, *Coffee County*, 141.

48  Henderson, *Roster*, 5:210–18; *Albany Patriot*, quoted in *Messenger*, January 18, 1865; TCIC Minutes, July 1864; "Soldiers Wives," microfilm drawer 172, box 47, GDAH.

49  Ash, *When the Yankees Came*, 76–77, 103–7; Williams, Williams, and Carlson, *Plain Folk*, 168–76; Ward, *Coffee County*, 65, 128–29; *Albany Patriot*, quoted in *Messenger*, March 1, 1865.

50  E. N. Broyles to Woodson Willcox, September 29, 1864, no. 26, 438, AGLB.

51  *Macon Southern Confederacy*, February 5, 1865; Hollinquist to Lamar Cobb, January 15, 1865, Cobb-Erwin-Lamar Papers, box 3, UGA.

52  Jacqueline Glass Campbell, *When Sherman Marched North*, 5; E. N. Broyles to Woodson Willcox, September 29, 1864, no. 26, 438, AGLB; *Macon Southern Confederacy*, February 5, 1865; Hollinquist to Lamar Cobb, January 15, 1865, Cobb-Erwin-Lamar Papers, box 3, UGA.

53  Jacqueline Glass Campbell, *When Sherman Marched North*, 12–13; *Macon Southern Confederacy*, February 5, 1865.

54  Hollinquist to Lamar Cobb, January 25, 1865, Cobb-Erwin-Lamar Papers, box 3, UGA (quotations); *Macon Southern Confederacy*, February 5, 1865.

55  Hollinquist to Lamar Cobb, January 23, 1865, Cobb-Erwin-Lamar Papers, box 3, UGA; *Macon Southern Confederacy*, February 5, 1865.

56  Ben L. Yancey to Colonel Carey W. Styles, September 5, 1864, no. 26, 189–90, AGLB, and Yancey to W. B. Overstreet, September 17, 1864, no. 26, 275–76, AGLB. For an excellent discussion of draft evasion in southern Georgia, see Carlson, "Loanly Runagee," esp. 595–602.

57 Yancey to Styles, September 5, 1864, and Yancey to Overstreet, September 17, 1864, no. 26, 189–90, 275–76, AGLB.

58 U.S. Census, 1860, Ga., Coffee County Population Schedule, 519, 538, and Agriculture Schedule, 11, MC; Henderson, *Roster*, 5:311; U.S. Census Office, *Eighth Census, Population*, 58–59.

59 Henderson, *Roster*, 5:311; U.S. Census, 1860, Ga., Coffee County Slave Schedule, 1, and Agriculture Schedule, 11, MC; Ward, *Coffee County*, 147, 343–44.

60 "If it is my choice to stay at home" (first line of untitled poem) from Ward, *Coffee County*, 141–42.

61 Ward, *Coffee County*, 141–42; B. F. White to Lamar Cobb, January 6, 1865, Cobb Papers, box 69, UGA; Spivey to Brown, September 8, 1862, box 46, GIC-GDAH.

62 Henry C. Wayne to Major General McLaws, October 18, 1864, no. 27, 69, AGLB, and Ben L. Yancey to Colonel Carey W. Styles, September 5, 1864, no. 26, 189–90, AGLB; Henderson, *Roster*, 5:308; Ward, *Coffee County*, 64.

63 McDuffie to Major General Howell Cobb, March 25, 1865. See also "Syd" to "My Dear Uncle," January 21, 1865, in which authorization for bringing the steamer upriver by Asher Ayers and others was ostensibly for the purpose of transporting rosin and other supplies needed by the government and "the people." Both in Cobb Papers, box 69, UGA.

64 McDuffie to Major General Howell Cobb, March 25, 1865, Cobb Papers, box 69, UGA.

65 Clements, *Irwin County*, 133–38; Williams, Williams, and Carlson, *Plain Folk*, 183–84; Hyde, "Backcountry Justice," 228–29, 235–36, and *Pistols and Politics*.

66 Clements, *Irwin County*, 60–61, 87–89, 192, 196, 393; U.S. Census, 1860, Ga., Irwin County Agriculture Schedule, 7, and Population Schedule, MC.

67 U.S. Census, 1860, Ga., Irwin County Agriculture Schedule, 1, 7, MC.

68 Ibid., 7; Clements, *Irwin County*, 134–45.

69 Henderson, *Roster*, 5:244–53; Clements, *Irwin County*, 45, 114–15, 117–21; Carlson, "Loanly Runagee," 602–3.

70 Clements, *Irwin County*, 134–35. "Irwin County, Georgia, 1860 Census," typescript, 17, GHS, lists the households of Walker's neighbors.

71 Sutherland, *Guerrillas, Unionists*, 8; Clements, *Irwin County*, 135–36; "Irwin County, Georgia, 1860 Census," typescript, 17, GHS. Walker's household is 136; his age was given as fifty.

72 Sutherland, *Guerrillas, Unionists*, 11–12; Clements, *Irwin County*, 136–37. Almost certainly Toney would have been executed if found alive. Some people in the neighborhood believed that Bone killed the runaway to silence a potential witness. See Clements, *Irwin County*, 136–37.

73 Clements, *Irwin County*, 136–37. Bone's family returned to Taylor County, where it was listed in the census of 1870.

74 Sutherland, *Guerrillas, Unionists*, 8–10, 76–78; Ward, *Coffee County*, 141–43; Henderson, *Roster*, 5:250; Carlson, "Loanly Runagee," 602–3; Clements, *Irwin County*, 119–21, 143 ("a thorough unreconstructed rebel"); Inscoe and Kenzer, *Enemies of the Country*, 55.

75 Williams, *Rich Man's War*, 168–86.

## Chapter 8

1   *AS* 3(1):236, 242 (Martha Everette).

2   Clements, *Irwin County*, 143–44.

3   Ibid.; "A Reminiscence of Mr. George F. McLeod, Abbeville," in McDonald and Lawson, *Passing of the Pines*, 28.

4   Henderson, *Roster*, 5:235–44; Blight, *Race and Reunion*, 38–39, 76–78; Berry, *All That Makes a Man*, 9–10; *Dispatch*, August 29, 1878; Wilkinson and Woodworth, *Scythe of Fire*, 305–6; Bozeman, "Reminiscences," private collection.

5   *CRSG* 2:403–5; Reidy, *From Slavery to Agrarian Capitalism*, 136–37; Clements, *Irwin County*, 144–45; "Longstreet Granger" to Editor, *Dispatch*, August 29, 1878.

6   Bozeman, "Reminiscences," private collection (quotation); Berry, *All That Makes a Man*, 10–12, 193–96; Bryant, *How Curious a Land*, 112–13; Jacqueline Glass Campbell, *When Sherman Marched North*, 69–70; Wilkinson and Woodworth, *Scythe of Fire*, 299–302; Wilson, *Baptized in Blood*, 1–2.

7   Wilkinson and Woodworth, *Scythe of Fire* (first quotation, 305); C. S. McCall, Application for Artificial Limb, Wilcox County Ordinary, Loose Records, pt. 3, microfilm drawer 187, box 31, GDAH; Henderson, *Roster*, 3:626.

8   Affidavit of Amanda Rhodes, January 16, 1893, Wilcox County Ordinary, Loose Records, microfilm drawer 187, box 31, GDAH; Henderson, *Roster*, 5:241.

9   Joseph Durham, Application for Benefits, March 7, 1896, Wilcox County Ordinary, Loose Records, microfilm drawer 187, box 31, GDAH; Berry, *All That Makes a Man*, 10–12, 193–96; Wyatt-Brown, *Southern Culture*, 209–10, 293.

10  R. G. Dun and Co, GA26, 137, Harvard University; Ford, "Popular Ideology," 207.

11  *Dispatch*, January 7, 1875; Wilkinson and Woodworth, *Scythe of Fire*, 145; James Fraser, Application for Artificial Limbs, 1866–67, Pulaski County Ordinary, microfilm drawer 302, box 124, GDAH; Henderson, *Roster*, 1:966.

12  *Dispatch*, January 7, 1875 (quotations); Wallace Leigh Harris, *Pulaski and Bleckley Counties*, 2:734.

13  *Dispatch*, January 7, 1875; Wyatt-Brown, *Southern Honor*, 14.

14  *Dispatch*, January 22, April 9, 1874; Mitchell, "Confederate Loyalties," 102–3.

15  *Dispatch*, August 18, 1870; Jacqueline Glass Campbell, *When Sherman Marched North*, 105, 107; Wilson, *Baptized in Blood*, 46–47.

16  *Dispatch*, August 18, October 27, 1870, and January 4, 1877 (quotations); Mitchell, "Confederate Loyalties," 102–3; Paludan, *Victims*, 123; Jacqueline Glass Campbell, *When Sherman Marched North*, 108–10.

17  R. G. Dun and Co., GA18, 2, Harvard University; U.S. Census, 1860, Ga., Irwin County Slave Schedule, 2, MC.

18  *Dispatch*, July 28, 1874; Wilson, *Baptized in Blood*, 3, 7.

19  DeCredico, *Patriotism for Profit*, 115–33; "A List of Names Sent for Corn for the Needy Familys [*sic*] of Telfair County," July 1866, TCIC Minutes; U.S. Census, 1860, Ga., Telfair County Population Schedule, 16, and Slave Schedule, 51, MC; *CRSG* 2:403; Henderson, *Roster*, 5:211. For the transition from slave to free labor on the upper Ocmulgee, see Reidy, *From Slavery to Agrarian Capitalism*, chap. 6.

20  Clements, *Irwin County*, 92–94 (grand jury reports); *Dispatch*, September 30, 1869.

21  Abbeville Resolutions, January 14, 1865, typescript, 1416–18, Brown Papers, UGA. The phrase "Republic of Irwin" appears in *Dispatch*, July 24, 1873.

22  Fahs, *Imagined Civil War*, 311–12; *Dispatch*, July 24, 1873; *CRSG* 2:284.

23  J. B. Clements (*Irwin County*, 92–99, 127–28) lists the jurors for the period.

24  *Albany Central City*, quoted in *Dispatch*, May 15, July 24, 1873; Mitchell, "Confederate Loyalties," 103; Malone, "Piney Woods Farmers," 51–84; Wilson, *Baptized in Blood*, 23.

25  *Minutes of the Primitive Baptist Pulaski Association, . . . 1847*, 6; *Albany Central City*, quoted in *Dispatch*, May 15, 1873; Crowley, *Primitive Baptists*, 106–9.

26  Owsley, *Plain Folk*, 154–57; *Dispatch*, November 27, 1873, August 27, 1874.

27  Ash, *When the Yankees Came*, 4–5, 45–46; *Albany Central City*, quoted in *Dispatch*, May 15, 1873.

28  *Dispatch*, August 27, 1874.

29  Hubbard, *Burden of Confederate Diplomacy*, 25–26; "House Creek" to Editor, *Dispatch*, September 25, 1873.

30  J. J. H. to Editor, *Dispatch*, September 25, 1873; Wright, *Old South, New South*, 107.

31  *Dispatch*, October 30, 1873; Wright, *Old South, New South*, 107–11; Wilson, *Baptized in Blood*, 81–82.

32  Bartley, *Modern Georgia*, 34–35; Wright, *Old South, New South*, 110.

33  *Dispatch*, October 16, 1873.

34  "Ocmulgee" to Editor, *Dispatch*, October 30, 1873; Wright, *Old South, New South*, 113–14.

35  *Dispatch*, December 4, 1873.

36  *Dispatch*, February 1, 1872; Henderson, *Roster*, 3:628, 5:286; Wright, *Old South, New South*, 107–9.

37  Wilson, *Baptized in Blood*, 81–84.

38  Henderson, *Roster*, 5:279; R. G. Dun and Co., GA26, 132–33, 137, 145, Harvard University.

39  On such closures, including Kirkland's, see R. G. Dun and Co., GA26, 132–33, 137, 145, GA32, 183, and GA8, 5, Harvard University.

40  *Dispatch*, May 22, 1872, December 4, 1873.

41  Foner, *Reconstruction*, 326; Bartley, *Modern Georgia*, 60–62; *Dispatch*, December 24, 1874; Wright, *Old South, New South*, 110–11.

42  *Dispatch*, February 1, 1872, April 10, 1873, November 8, 1877; Crowley, *Primitive Baptists*, 106–8 (first quotation, 107); Wilson, *Baptized in Blood*, 81–84.

43  Wright, *Old South, New South*, 99–103, 113; *Dispatch*, May 15, 1873 (quotations).

44  *Dispatch*, December 18, 1873; Reidy, *From Slavery to Agrarian Capitalism*, 136–60.

45  *Dispatch*, December 18, 1873 (quotation); Wright, *Old South, New South*, 84.

46  *Dispatch*, November 18, 1875.

47  Affidavit of Anaca Phillips, March 14, 1866, Miscellaneous Records, Macon, 1865–68, box 22, BRFAL; Litwack, " 'Blues Falling Down,' " 110.

48  Ibid.; *OR* 49(2):1042; U.S. Census, 1860, Ga., Pulaski County Slave Schedule, 13–14, MC. On such tolerance, see Barney, *Flawed Victory*, 133.

49  *AS* 4(2):416 (Caroline Malloy), 3(1):242 (Martha Everette), 228 (Sara Crocker); Reidy, *From Slavery to Agrarian Capitalism*, 138–39; Flynn, *White Land*, 8–9.

50  *Dispatch*, June 21, 1877.

51 Kolchin, *American Slavery*, 218–19; "Orion" to Editor, *Georgia Weekly Telegraph*, April 9, 1866.

52 Freedman's Bureau Journal, Hawkinsville agency, Henry Whitaker vs. Leander Taylor, June 4, 1868, 54–55, BRFAL; *Dispatch*, July 24, 1873.

53 Ibid.; *OR* 49(2):1042.

54 *Dispatch*, March 19, July 23, 1874, July 15, 1875; Litwack, " 'Blues Falling Down,' " 116–17.

55 Foner, *Reconstruction*, 84–85; Kolchin, *American Slavery*, 220–21; *AS* 4(2):506 (Easter Reed), 3(1):220 (Arthur Colson).

56 *Dispatch*, June 21, 1877 (Sallie Manning); *AS* 4(2):410 (Caroline Malloy).

57 Kolchin, *American Slavery*, 220–37; U.S. Census, 1870, Ga., Pulaski County Population Schedule, 425, MC; Foner, *Reconstruction*, 87.

58 *Dispatch*, April 29, 1875.

59 U.S. Census, 1870, Ga., Pulaski County Population Schedule, 425, MC; Foner, *Reconstruction*, 84–85; Drago, *Black Politicians*, 104–5.

60 Foner, *Reconstruction*, 87; *American Union*, October 29, 1869.

61 Deposition of Hawkinsville agent, Agnes Anderson, February 27, 1868, BRFAL; Bryant, *How Curious a Land*, 106, 115.

62 L. Lieberman to Mr. McGriff, March 9, 1868, Letters Sent, 31, and Lieberman to Simon Merritt, February 24, 1868, 52–53, both in Freedmen's Bureau Journal, Hawkinsville Agent, 1868, BRFAL.

63 Foner, *Reconstruction*, 87; *Dispatch*, October 27, 1870, July 15, 1875 (quotations); Statement of Elbert Proctor, February 19, 1868, BRFAL.

64 Amanda Willcox to Agent, April 8, 1868, and Freedmen's Bureau Journal, Hawkinsville Agent, 1868, 42–43, 46–47, BRFAL.

65 Freedmen's Bureau Journal, Hawkinsville Agent, March 13, 1868, 38, BRFAL.

66 Pulaski County Tax Register, 1876–78, 3–13, GDAH; Foner, *Reconstruction*, 104–5; R. G. Dun and Co. GA26, 164, Harvard University (quotation); *Dispatch*, August 12, 1875, July 16, 1874.

67 U.S. Census, 1870, Ga., Pulaski County Population Schedule, 43, MC; Pulaski County Tax Register, 1876–78, 3, Pulaski County Courthouse.

68 *AS* 3(1):218–22 (Arthur Colson).

69 *AS* 4(2):508–9 (Easter Reed).

70 Inventory of the Estate of Thully Williamson, Office of Probate Judge, Probate Records, Pulaski County Courthouse; U.S. Census, 1870, Ga., Pulaski County Population Schedule, 17–18, MC.

71 "Occasional" to Editor, *Dispatch*, December 17, 1874; U.S. Census, 1870, Ga., Pulaski County Population Schedule, 425, MC; Flynn, *White Land*, 4–5.

72 "A Freedman's Crops," *Dispatch*, December 18, 1873.

73 Flynn, *White Land*, 4–5.


*Chapter 9*

1 *Dispatch*, January 7, 1871.

2 *Dispatch*, January 12, 1871; Perman, *Emancipation and Reconstruction*, 5; Litwack, *Been in*

*the Storm So Long*, 546–47. On the continued legacy of Confederate nationalism, see Doyle, *Nations Divided*, 10, 66.

3   *Dispatch*, January 7, 1871; Wilson, *Baptized in Blood*, 11–13.

4   Farrell, *Rituals and Riots*, 7–8; Bozeman, "Reminiscences," private collection; Wilson, *Baptized in Blood*, 100–102.

5   See Franklin, *The Militant South*, and, more recently, Reidy, *From Slavery to Agrarian Capitalism*, 139, 209–12 (quotation, 192). Steven Hahn (*Nation under Our Feet*, chap. 6) views the struggle as one of both black and white paramilitary politics.

6   Flynn, *White Land*, 31 (quotation); Foner, *Reconstruction*, 443; Faust, *Mothers of Invention*, 245–48; Wyatt-Brown, *Southern Culture*, 281–82, 293–94.

7   Richards, *Gentlemen of Property*, 5–6, 10–19, 44–46; Thompson, "Moral Economy," 76–79.

8   Wooster, *People in Power*, 12, 107–8; *CRSG* 2:118–19.

9   *CRSG* 2:118–19.

10   Ibid.; Wyatt-Brown, *Southern Culture*, 281; Flynn, *White Land*, 29–32. On the formation of local companies by both unionists and secessionists, see Bohannon, "They Had Determined to Root Us Out," 101–11.

11   Bartley, *Modern Georgia*, 47; Wallace Leigh Harris, *Pulaski and Bleckley Counties*, 1:126; Henderson, *Roster*, 5:244, 303; Clements, *Irwin County*, 47; Ward, *Coffee County*, 353.

12   Drago, *Black Politicians*, 30–31; Thompson, *Reconstruction in Georgia*, 171–72; Bartley, *Modern Georgia*, 48. On developments along the upper Ocmulgee, see Reidy, *From Slavery to Agrarian Capitalism*, chap. 7.

13   Drago, *Black Politicians*, 30–31; U.S. Congress, *Elections in Georgia*, 2–3; *American Union*, September 26, 1868; Bozeman, "Reminiscences," private collection; Joe Bown [Brown?] to General Lewis, December 5, 1867, Letters Received and Unentered, Macon, December 1865–October 1868, box 22, BRFAL.

14   *OR* 49(2):1059; *AS* 3(1):228 (former slave). On Wilson in Georgia, see James Pickett Jones, *Yankee Blitzkrieg*, 160–83. For a different view, see Whites, *Crisis in Gender*, 132–35, 167, 176.

15   *Dispatch*, January 3, 1867.

16   Ibid,; Farrell, *Rituals and Riots*, 12–13; Wetherington, *New South*, 35, 150, 285–86.

17   *Dispatch*, January 2, 1868; Flynn, *White Land*, 29–37.

18   *Dispatch*, January 2, 1868; Drago, *Black Politicians*, 144; Bartley, *Modern Georgia*, 59.

19   *Dispatch*, January 2, 1868 (quotations); Mitchell, "Confederate Loyalties," 102–3.

20   Foner, *Reconstruction*, 387–91; *Dispatch*, October 28, 1875, September 6, 1877, April 1, 1875, May 28, 1874.

21   *Dispatch*, September 9, 1875.

22   *American Union*, August 16, 27, 1867.

23   Reidy, *From Slavery to Agrarian Capitalism*, 210; *American Union*, August 16, 27, 1867. Motivations for joining the Republican political ranks were similar to those of Union troops during the war. See Frank, *With Ballot and Bayonet*, 11–12.

24   Drago, *Black Politicians*, 24–25; *American Union*, May 7, 1869, August 23, 1867.

25   *American Union*, December 3, 1869, August 23, 1867; David Lasey to N. S. Hill, July 28, 1868, box 21, BRFAL. For a discussion of emancipationist and Union memories, see Blight, *Race and Reunion*.

26  *American Union*, May 7, 1869; L. Lieberman to C. C. Sibley, July 27, 1868, vol. 277, 53–57, BRFAL.

27  "A Colored Baptist" to Editor, *American Union*, April 16, 1869.

28  *American Union*, August 16, 1867, April 16, 1869, March 16, 1871 (quotations); Reidy, *From Slavery to Agrarian Capitalism*, 210.

29  *Dispatch*, September 9, 1875. For a different view, see Whites, *Crisis in Gender*, 166.

30  *American Union*, August 11, 1871; Mitchell, "Confederate Loyalties," 101.

31  *Dispatch*, December 11, 1873.

32  Wallace Leigh Harris, *Pulaski and Bleckley Counties*, 1:127; U.S. Census, 1860, Ga., Pulaski County Slave Schedule, 1, MC; Hahn, *Nation under Our Feet*, 268–71; McDonald and Lawson, *Passing of the Pines*, 26; Farrell, *Rituals and Riots*, 36–37.

33  Robertson, *Soldiers*, 21; McPherson, *For Cause*, 53–55; *Hawkinsville Dispatch*, January 2, 1868; DAR-H, *History of Pulaski County*, 350–51, 392; Henderson, *Roster*, 4:839, 2:45; Hahn, *Nation under Our Feet*, 270–72.

34  Henderson, *Roster*, 2:45; Wallace Leigh Harris, *Pulaski and Bleckley Counties*, 1:91, 147, 173; DAR-H, *History of Pulaski County*, 332.

35  Henderson, *Roster*, 2:45; Wallace Leigh Harris, *Pulaski and Bleckley Counties*, 1:91, 147, 185; DAR-H, *History of Pulaski County*; *Dispatch*, January 2, 1868, September 24, 1874. According to the latter issue, which called for a reunion of local Confederates, Reverend McCall was still riding "Old Kite," the cavalry mount that had served him well in the war.

36  R. G. Dun and Co., GA26, 145, Harvard University ("Man of means"); U.S. Census, 1860, Ga., Pulaski County Slave Schedule, 15–16, MC; DAR-H, *History of Pulaski County*, 316–17; Wallace Leigh Harris, *Pulaski and Bleckley Counties*, 1:97, 102, 126; Bozeman, "Reminiscences," private collection.

37  Foner, *Reconstruction*, 425–26; Wallace Leigh Harris, *Pulaski and Bleckley Counties*, 1:561–62; U.S. Congress, House, *Condition of Affairs in Georgia*, 65–66; Thompson, "Moral Economy," 95; Hahn, *Nation under Our Feet*, 270.

38  *Dispatch*, September 30, October 7, 1869; Wallace Leigh Harris, *Pulaski and Bleckley Counties*, 1:561–62; Flynn, *White Land*, 12–13; Whites, *Crisis in Gender*, 165–67.

39  *Morning News*, September 10, 1873. See also "R. E. Construction" to Editor, *American Union*, April 12, October 29, December 3, 1869, January 7, 1870, and February 23, 1871.

40  Hahn, *Southern Populism*, 214–16; Michael P. Johnson, *Patriarchal Republic*, 65–66; Fitzgerald, "Radical Republicanism and the White Yeomanry," 580–84, 587–96.

41  *Dispatch*, October 1, 1874; J. H. Hollinquist to Lamar Cobb, January 23, 1865, Cobb-Erwin-Lamar Papers, box 3, UGA; *American Union*, July 30, August 27, 1869.

42  *Dispatch*, October 2, 1873, October 1, 1874; U.S. Census, 1860, Ga., Pulaski County Slave Schedule, 33, MC; Wallace Leigh Harris, *Pulaski and Bleckley Counties*, 1:128. On the diverse nature of local Republican leadership, see Otto H. Olsen, "Reconsidering the Scalawags," 313–14. On the importance of the antebellum militia as a foundation for paramilitary organization during Reconstruction, see Hahn, *Nation under Our Feet*, 268–71.

43  Wallace Leigh Harris, *Pulaski and Bleckley Counties*, 1:103–4; Myrick, *Wilkinson County, Georgia, 1860*, 129; Acord and Anderson, *An Index for the 1860 Federal Census of Georgia*, 522, 797, 1004; Howell, *1860 Federal Census for Houston County*, 27, 32; *Dispatch*, June 4,

1874; *Georgia State Gazetteer, 1881–82*, 312; Joel R. Griffin to Governor R. B. Bullock, December 16, 1868, box 57, GIC-GDAH.

44  *Dispatch*, March 26, April 9, 1874; *Macon Telegraph*, June 7, 1865. On Jelks's Confederate service, see Wallace Leigh Harris, *Pulaski and Bleckley Counties*, 1:132.

45  *OR* 49(2):986; "Orion" to Editor, *Georgia Weekly Telegraph*, April 9, 1866.

46  *Atlanta Constitution*, July 31, 1868; *American Union*, August 28, 1868; Bartley, *Modern Georgia*, 45–47.

47  *Journal of the House of Representatives of the State of Georgia*, 1868, 218; Foner, *Reconstruction*, 454–55; *Manual and Biographical Register of the State of Georgia, for 1871–2*, 97; Wallace Leigh Harris, *Pulaski and Bleckley Counties*, 1:126.

48  *Dispatch*, February 23, 1871; Foner, *Reconstruction*, 454–55; *American Union*, February 23, 1871.

49  Drago, *Black Politicians*, 51–53, 93; White to Editor, *Dispatch*, September 9, 1875; *American Union*, November 6, 1868; Foner, *Reconstruction*, 432. On the paramilitary nature of white attacks, see Hahn, *Nation under Our Feet*, 265–76.

50  Thompson, "Moral Economy," 126–27; Journal, 1868, Hawkinsville Agent, 38, entries for March 13 and April 18, 46–47, BRFAL. See, e.g., the burning of John D. Wynn's barn, the poisoning of his two mules, and the stabbing of his mare at Jacksonville in *Dispatch*, August 2, 1877. On the tradition of wrecking, see Farrell, *Rituals and Riots*, 26–27. Such actions seem to be similar to "leveling" threats toward the rich in England, but they were instead aimed at freedmen and Republicans of all classes, especially blacks just beginning to accumulate significant property.

51  *Dispatch*, October 10, 1872. For similar incidents, see Jacqueline Jones, "Encounters, Likely and Unlikely."

52  Salter to Hon. J. E. Bryant, December 2, 1868, in *Condition of Affairs in Georgia*, 66.

53  *American Union*, October 22, December 3, 1869.

54  *Morning News*, September 10, 1873. C. T. Trowell ("Douglas before Memory") notes that Barber sold out and moved to Appling County in 1873.

55  *American Union*, October 22, December 3, 1869; S. F. Salter to J. E. Bryan, November 4, 1868, in *Condition of Affairs in Georgia*, 65–66.

56  *American Union*, December 3, 1869; L. Lieberman to N. S. Hill, June 29, 1868, Letters Sent, BRFAL.

57  Pollock to Hill, November 26, 1867, Letters Received, Macon, box 21, BRFAL. See also Reidy, *From Slavery to Agrarian Capitalism*, 154, 205, and *Manual and Biographical Register of the State of Georgia, for 1871–72*, 97.

58  *Atlanta Constitution*, August 27, 1868; Drago, *Black Politicians*, 22, 31.

59  L. Lieberman to E. A. Ware, n.d., Letters Sent, BRFAL.

60  *American Union*, December 4, 1868.

61  N. S. Hill to J. R. Lewis, December 3, 1868, Macon, Letters Received, December 1865–March 1869, BRFAL; *American Union*, December 4, 1868.

62  "R. E. Construction" to Editor, *American Union*, January 7, 1870.

63  *American Union*, July 14, 1868; L. Lieberman to N. S. Hill, June 27, 1868, Hawkinsville Agent, BRFAL.

64  *American Union*, July 14, 1868; L. Lieberman to N. S. Hill, June 27, 1868, Hawkinsville Agent, BRFAL.

65  *American Union*, July 14, 1868; L. Lieberman to N. S. Hill, June 27, 1868, Hawkinsville Agent, BRFAL.

66  L. Lieberman to N. S. Hill, June 27, 1868, Hawkinsville Agent, BRFAL.

67  *American Union*, July 14, 1868 (quotation); Clements, *Irwin County*, 437–38.

68  Foner, *Reconstruction*, 77–78. See also Blight, *Race and Reunion*.

69  Ford, "Rednecks and Merchants," 297–98; Hahn, *Nation under Our Feet*, 318–54.

70  *Dispatch*, December 12, 1872, February 27, May 15, 1873, August 5, 1875.

71  *Macon Star*, quoted in *Dispatch*, January 14, 1875, and *Dispatch*, April 29, 1875, September 13, 1877.

72  *Dispatch*, January 2, 1868.

73  *Dispatch*, September 8, 1870, September 14, 1871, June 26, 1873 (quotation); Hahn, *Nation under Our Feet*, 324.

74  *Morning News*, June 19, 1873; *Dispatch*, November 21, 1872, June 18, December 3, 1874. John McBurrows also appears in accounts as John McBurris, John Burrus, and possibly John Swain.

75  *Dispatch*, June 26, 1873, and June 18, 1874 (quotations); U.S. Census, 1870, Ga., Pulaski County Population Schedule, 354, 376, MC; Hahn, *Nation under Our Feet*, 320–23.

76  *Dispatch*, June 26, 1873, January 15, June 18, 1874.

77  "Panter-Fork" to Editor, *Atlanta Constitution*, September 24, 1868; *Dispatch*, December 13, 1877, January 3, 1878.

78  Bartley, *Modern Georgia*, 78–82; Bozeman, "Reminiscences," private collection; *Dispatch*, June 7, 1877.

79  *Dispatch*, September 20, December 13, 1877.

80  "Locating the State Capital—Milledgeville Our Choice" and "Wiregrass" to Editor, *Dispatch*, September 20, November 22, 1877; Bartley, *Modern Georgia*, 80–81.

81  "The Prejudice of the Negro," *Dispatch*, December 13, 1877.

82  *Manual and Biographical Register of the State of Georgia, for 1871–2*, 38; U.S. Census, 1860, Ga., Pulaski County Slave Schedule, 38, MC; Wallace Leigh Harris, *Pulaski and Bleckley Counties*, 1:90; *Dispatch*, June 1, 1871, December 20, 1877 (first quotation), July 18, 1878 (second quotation).


Epilogue

1  *Dispatch*, February 16, 1871, May 14, 1874.

2  Wetherington, *New South*, xvii–xxiii; *Dispatch*, June 18, 1874.

3  *Eastman Times*, April 9, 1873; Cobb, *Dodge County*, 84; Talley, "Dodge Lands and Litigation," 242–43.

4  *Eastman Times*, April 9, 1873.

5  Ibid.; Wetherington, *New South*, 123–24; Wilson, *Baptized in Blood*, 85–86.

6  Talley, "Dodge Lands and Litigation," 242–43; Wetherington, *New South*, 82–83.

7  *CRSG* 2:124–25.

8  Wetherington, *New South*, 224–25; Petition of H. J. McLeod et al., to the Senate and

House of Representatives of the State of Georgia, June 7, 1872, Telfair County Loose Records, GDAH; Cobb, *Dodge County*, 25–26; *Dispatch*, August 11 (quotation), August 4, November 3, 1870.

9   *CRSG* 2:124–25; *Eastman Times*, January 31, 1873, April 9, 1874, January 24, 1878; Foner, *Reconstruction*, xxv, 460–61; *Dispatch*, May 2, 1872; Ayers, *Promise of the New South*, 123–31.

10  *Eastman Times*, April 9, 1874.

11  *Dispatch*, February 1, 1872, and "Alpha" to Editor, May 15, 1873 (quotation); Cobb, *Dodge County*, 42, 167, 224–26.

12  *Dispatch*, April 16, 1874, "Alpha" to Editor, January 1, 1874, and May 15, 1873. J. N. Talley ("Dodge Lands and Litigation," 240–43) provides the best account of the title history.

13  John W. McRae to W. W. Paine, August 11, 1876, box 3, folder 42, Paine Papers, GHS; "Interrogatories of Daniel McRanie in the Ejectment Cause for Lots No.s [*sic*] 111 & 112, 14th Dist. Dodge" and "Testimony of Daniel McRanie," both in folder 57, box 4, ibid.; *Dispatch*, January 1, May 7, 1874; Cobb, *Dodge County*, 233–34.

14  *John A. Kelly et al. vs. . . . Georgia*, 1–4; Henderson, *Roster*, 5:210; *OR* 46(2):1315–17.

15  *John A. Kelly et al. vs. . . . Georgia*, 14, 21–22, 26–29, 34–35, 44, 46–48, 51–55.

16  Ibid., 28–29, 32–35.

17  *Dispatch*, December 20, 1877, July 11, 1878; A. G. P. Dodge to Walter T. McArthur, March 14, 1878, folder 34, box 3, Paine Papers, GHS. Essentially the plain folk were "fighting against disintegration" again. See Escott, *After Secession*, 196–225.

18  *Dispatch*, July 18, August 15, 1878; Henderson, *Roster*, 5:304. See Wetherington, *New South*, chaps. 5 and 6, on local deforestation and the subsequent expansion of cotton cultivation.

# BIBLIOGRAPHY

*Manuscript and Archival Material*

Duke University, William R. Perkins Library, Special Collections, Durham
    S. H. Latimer Papers
Georgia Department of Archives and History, Atlanta
    Adjutant General's Incoming Correspondence, Record Group 22-2-17
    Adjutant General's Letter Books
    Adjutant General's Muster Rolls
    Cedar Creek Baptist Church Minutes, Wilcox County, 1853–86
    Civil War Miscellany, Personal Papers
    Civil War Unit Card Files
    File II, Record Group 4-2-46
    William W. Fisher Diary
    Friendship Baptist Church Minutes, Wilcox County
    Governor's Incoming Correspondence, Record Group 1-1-5
    Irwin County Inferior Court Minutes, 1852–78
    Kirkland Collection
    Macon and Brunswick Railroad Officers' Correspondence
    Pleasant Primitive Baptist Church Minutes, Berrien County
    Pulaski County Inferior Court Minutes, 1860–65
    Pulaski County Ordinary, Loose Records
    William H. Smith Diary
    Telfair County Inferior Court Minutes, 1832–69
    Telfair County Loose Records, File 2
    Wilcox County Ordinary, Loose Records
    J. C. Wilkes, "Wilkes Family Recollections" (typescript)
Georgia Historical Society, Savannah
    William W. Paine Papers
Hargrett Rare Book and Manuscript Library, University of Georgia, Athens
    Joseph E. Brown Papers
    Howell Cobb Papers
    Cobb-Erwin-Lamar Papers
    Nathaniel Gibbs Letters
    Thomas E. Lee Letters

Harvard Business School, Baker Library, Cambridge
    R. G. Dun & Co. Collection, Credit Reporting Ledgers
Huntington Library, San Marino, California
    Eldridge Collection
    James Leath Journal
Jacksonville Public Library, Jacksonville, Florida
    Colonel Greenleaf Dearborn: Letters of an Indian Fighter, 1836–46. Transcribed by his
    wife, P. A. S. Dearborn. Typescript copies of October 22, November 10, and December 3,
    1836, letters, provided by C. T. Trowell.
Laurens County Historical Society, Dublin, Georgia
    McRae and McMillan Store Ledgers
National Archives, Atlanta Branch
    Records of the District Courts of the United States, Georgia, Southern District, Record
    Group 21
National Archives, Washington, D.C. (microfilm)
    Amnesty Papers, Record Group 94
    Letters Received, Confederate Secretary of War, Record Group 109
    Manuscript Census, Seventh Census of the United States, 1850
    Manuscript Census, Eighth Census of the United States, 1860
    Manuscript Census, Ninth Census of the United States, 1870
    Records of the Adjutant General's Office, Record Group 94
    Records of the Bureau of Refugees, Freedmen, and Abandoned Lands,
    Record Group 105
Private Collections (copies provided by Keith Bohannon)
    F. H. Bozeman, "Reminiscences of F. H. Bozeman," 1915 (typescript)
    Pate Family Letters
Pulaski County Courthouse, Hawkinsville, Georgia
    Pulaski County Inferior Court Minutes
    Pulaski County Probate Records, 1855–60
    Pulaski County Register of Free Persons of Color, 1840–65
    Pulaski County Superior Court, Tax Digest, 1857
    Pulaski County Superior Court, Will Book B, 1855–1906
Southern Historical Collection, University of North Carolina, Chapel Hill
    Duncan Malloy Papers
Washington Memorial Library, Macon, Georgia
    R. N. Taylor Papers


*Published Primary Materials*

Acord, Arlis, and Martha S. Anderson et al., comps. *An Index for the 1860 Federal Census of
    Georgia.* N.p., 1986.
Bartram, William. *Travels through North & South Carolina, Georgia, East & West Florida. . . .*
    Edited by Mark Van Doren. New York: Dover Publications, 1928.
Berlin, Ira, Barbara J. Fields, Thavolia Glymph, Joseph P. Reidy, and Leslie S. Rowland. *The*

*Destruction of Slavery*. Ser. 1,, vol. 1, of *Freedom: A Documentary History of Emancipation, 1861–1867*. Cambridge: Cambridge University Press, 1985.

Botkin, B. A. *A Treasury of Southern Folklore*. Reprint, New York: Bonanza Books, 1980.

Brisbane, A. H. "Detailed Report of General Brisbane, Dated June 30, 1849, Addressed to Richard Keily, Esq." In *A Brief Description and Statistical Sketch of Georgia*, by Richard Keily. London: J. Carroll, 1849.

Candler, Allen D., comp. *The Confederate Records of the State of Georgia*. 6 vols., Atlanta: State Printer, 1909–11.

Chestnut, Mary. *Mary Chestnut's Civil War*. Edited by C. Vann Woodward. New Haven: Yale University Press, 1981.

"Circular Letter." *The Primitive Pulaski Association . . . , 1872*. N.p.

*Fifth Annual Report of the President and Directors and Reports of Standing Committees of the Savannah Cotton Exchange, . . . 1877*.

*Fourth Annual Report of the President and Directors of the Macon & Brunswick Railroad Co., to the Stockholders*. Macon, Ga.: Telegraph Steam Power Press, 1862.

Freehling, William W., and Craig M. Simpson, eds. *Secession Debated: Georgia's Showdown in 1860*. New York: Oxford University Press, 1992.

*Georgia State Gazetteer and Business Directory, 1881–82*. Atlanta: A. E. Sholes, 1882.

Hall, Basil. *Forty Etchings: From Sketches Made with the Camera Lucida, in North America, in 1827 and 1828*. Edinburgh: Cadell and Co., 1830.

——. *Travels in North America in the Years 1827 and 1828*. 3 vols. Graz, Austria: Cadell and Co., 1829.

Henderson, Lillian, comp. *Roster of the Confederate Soldiers of Georgia, 1861–1865*. 6 vols. Hapeville, Georgia: Longino and Porter, 1959–64.

Howell, Addie Paramore, comp. *1860 Federal Census for Houston County, Georgia*. Warner Robins, Ga.: Central Georgia Genealogical Society, Inc., 1986.

Hundley, Daniel R. *Social Relations in Our Southern States*. 1860. Reprint, Baton Rouge: Louisiana State University Press, 1979.

Johnson, Robert Underwood, and Clarence Clough Buel, eds. *Battles and Leaders of the Civil War*. 4 vols. New York: Century, 1887.

*Journal of the House of Representatives of the State of Georgia*. 1868.

*Journal of the State Convention Held in Milledgeville in December, 1850*. Milledgeville: R. M. Orme, State Printer, 1850.

Keily, Richard. *A Brief Descriptive and Statistical Sketch of Georgia*. London: J. Carrall, 1849.

Kemble, Frances Anne. *Journal of a Residence on a Georgian Plantation in 1838–1839*. New York: Harper and Brothers, 1862.

*Macon and Brunswick Railroad Company*. N.p., 1876[?].

*Minutes of the Primitive Baptist Pulaski Association, Held with Big Creek Church, Pulaski County, Ga. on the 4th, 5th, and 6th Days of September, 1847*.

*Minutes of the Primitive Baptist Pulaski Association, Held with the Brushy Creek Church, Irwin County, Georgia, 27th, 28th and 29th October*. Hawkinsville, Ga.: Pulaski Times Print, 1860.

*Minutes of the Seventeenth Annual Session of the Primitive Baptist Pulaski Association, Convened with Beaver Creek Church, Houston Co. Ga., October 27–29, 1855*.

*Minutes of the Twenty-Fourth Annual Session of the Primitive Baptist Association, Held with the Beaver Creek Church on the 12th, 14th, and 15th September, 1863.*

*Minutes of the Twenty-Fifth Annual Session of the Primitive Baptist Pulaski Association, Held with the Mount Beazor Church, on the 10th and 12th September, 1864.* Macon, Ga.: Burke, Boykin and Company, 1864.

*Minutes of the Thirty-Third Annual Session of the Pulaski Primitive Baptist Association, Held with Providence Church, Worth County, Georgia, October 5th, 6th, and 7th, 1872.*

Olmsted, Frederick Law. *A Journey in the Back Country.* London: Mason Brothers, 1860.

——. *A Journey in the Seaboard Slave States, with Remarks on Their Economy.* New York: Dix and Edwards, 1856.

Rawick, George P., gen. ed. *The American Slave: A Composite Autobiography.* 19 vols., 12 vols. in supplement. Westport, Conn.: Greenwood Publishing Co., 1977.

Richardson, Simon Peter. *The Lights and Shadows of Itinerant Life: An Autobiography of Rev. Simon Peter Richardson.* Nashville: Methodist Episcopal Church, South, 1901.

Sherwood, Adiel. *A Gazetteer of Georgia: Containing a Particular Description of the State, Its Resources, Counties, Towns, Villages, and Whatever Is Usual in Statistical Works.* Atlanta: J. Richards, 1860.

Southern Historical Association. *Memoirs of Georgia: Containing Historical Accounts of the State's Civil, Military, Industrial and Professional Interests, and Personal Sketches of Many of Its People.* Atlanta: Southern Historical Association, 1895.

St. Clair-Abrams, A. *Manual and Biographical Register of the State of Georgia, for 1871–2.* Atlanta: Plantation Publishing Co.'s Press, 1872.

Stephens, Alexander H. *A Constitutional View of the Late War between the States: Its Causes, Character, Conduct and Results.* Philadelphia: National Publishing Co., 1868–70.

Stevens, Mildred Taylor. *Family Letters and Reminiscences.* N.p., n.d.

White, George. *Statistics of the State of Georgia: Including an Account of Its Natural, Civil, and Ecclesiastical History. . . .* 1849. Reprint, Spartanburg, S.C.: Reprint Co., 1972.

Wills, Charles W. *Army Life of an Illinois Soldier.* Washington, D.C.: Globe Printing Co., 1906.

Zettler, Berrien M. *War Stories and School-day Incidents for the Children.* New York: Neale, 1912.


*Government Documents*

*Georgia Acts and Resolutions.* 1853–75.

*John A. Kelly et al. vs. the State of Georgia and W. A. Allagood, Sheriff, Telfair County, Georgia.* Macon: News Printing Co., 1895[?].

*Statistics of the United States in 1860.* Washington, D.C.: GPO, 1866.

*Testimony Taken by a Joint Committee of the Two Houses of the Legislature of Georgia upon the Condition of the Macon and Brunswick Railroad, in January and February 1874.* N.p.: J. H. Estill, 1874.

U.S. Bureau of Soils. *Soil Survey of Dodge County, Georgia.* Sixth Report, 1904. Washington, D.C.: GPO, 1905.

U.S. Census Office. *Seventh Census of the United States, 1850.* Washington, D.C.: GPO, 1854.

——. *Eighth Census of the United States, 1860*. Washington, D.C.: GPO, 1864.

——. *Ninth Census of the United States, 1870*. Washington, D.C.: GPO, 1872.

——. *Tenth Census of the United States, 1880*. Washington, D.C.: GPO, 1883.

U.S. Congress. *Affairs of Southern Railroads*. 39th Cong., 2d sess. Washington, D.C.: GPO, 1867.

——. House. *Condition of Affairs in Georgia*. 40th Cong., 3d sess., H. Misc. Doc. 52. Washington, D.C.: GPO, 1868.

——. House. *Elections in Georgia, North Carolina, and South Carolina*. 40th Cong., 2d sess. Washington, D.C.: GPO, 1868.

U.S. Department of Agriculture. *Report of the Commissioner of Agriculture for the Year 1866*. Washington, D.C., 1867.

U.S. Department of the Interior. *Report on Cotton Production in the United States*. 47th Cong., 2d sess. Washington, D.C.: GPO, 1884.

U.S. War Department. "Survey of the Ocmulgee River, Georgia." *House Ex. Doc.* 215, 51st Cong., 1st sess. Washington, D.C.: GPO, 1890.

——. *The War of the Rebellion: A Compilation of the Official Records of the Union and Confederate Armies*. 70 vols. Washington, D.C.: GPO, 1902.


*Newspapers and Periodicals*

*American Union* (Macon), 1867–72

*Atlanta Constitution*, 1868–75

*Brunswick Advertiser and Appeal*, 1885

*Christian Index*, 1855–65

*Confederate Veteran*, 1897

*Eastman Times*, 1873–77

*Georgia Journal and Messenger* (Macon), 1858–65

*Georgia Weekly Telegraph* (Macon), 1866

*Hawkinsville Dispatch*, 1867–77

*Macon Southern Confederacy*, 1865

*Macon Daily Telegraph*, 1865

*Milledgeville Southern Cultivator*, 1860

*Milledgeville Southern Recorder*, 1850–65

*Milledgeville Union Recorder*, 1852–61

*Savannah Daily Herald*, 1865

*Savannah Daily Morning News*, 1860–77

*Savannah Republican*, 1861

*Telfair Enterprise*, 1907

*Valdosta Times*, 1895


*Maps and Atlases*

Bonner, William G. "Bonner's Map of the State of Georgia, with the Addition of Its Geological Features." Savannah, 1849.

Colton, J. H., pub. "Colton's Georgia." New York, 1860.

Cowles, Capt. Calvin D., comp. *Atlas to Accompany the Official Records of the Union and Confederate Armies*. 2 parts. Washington, D.C.: GPO, 1891–95.

Johnson, A. J. *Johnson's Georgia and Alabama*. New York: Johnson and Ward, 1863.


*Books, Articles, Dissertations, and Theses*

Abzug, Robert H., and Stephen E. Maizlish, eds. *New Perspectives on Race and Slavery in America: Essays in Honor of Kenneth M. Stampp*. Lexington: University Press of Kentucky, 1986.

Ambrose, Stephen E. "Yeoman Discontent in the Confederacy." *Civil War History* 8 (1962): 259–68.

Arnold, Sue Lynn Stone. "Expressions of Grief in South Central Kentucky, 1870–1910." M.A. thesis, Western Kentucky University, 1983.

Ash, Stephen V. *Middle Tennessee Society Transformed, 1860–1870: War and Peace in the Upper South*. Baton Rouge: Louisiana State University Press, 1988.

——. *When the Yankees Came: Conflict and Chaos in the Occupied South, 1861–1865*. Chapel Hill: University of North Carolina Press, 1995.

Ayers, Edward L. *In the Presence of Mine Enemies: War in the Heart of America, 1859–1863*. New York: Norton, 2003.

——. *The Promise of the New South: Life after Reconstruction*. New York: Oxford University Press, 1992.

——. *Vengeance and Justice: Crime and Punishment in the 19th Century American South*. New York: Oxford University Press, 1984.

Bailey, Anne J. "In the Far Corner of the Confederacy: A Question of Conscience for German-Speaking Texans." In *Southern Families at War: Loyalty and Conflict in the Civil War South*, edited by Catherine Clinton, 211–27. New York: Oxford University Press, 2000.

——. *War and Ruin: William T. Sherman and the Savannah Campaign*. Wilmington, Del.: Scholarly Resources, Inc., 2003.

Bailey, Fred Arthur. *Class and Tennessee's Confederate Generation*. Chapel Hill: University of North Carolina Press, 1987.

Baker, Jean H. *Affairs of Party: The Political Culture of Northern Democrats in the Mid-Nineteenth Century*. Ithaca, N,Y.: Cornell University Press, 1983.

Barney, William L. *Flawed Victory: A New Perspective on the Civil War*. New York: Praeger Publishers, 1975.

——. "Resisting the Republicans: Georgia's Secession Debate." (Review Essay.) *Georgia Historical Quarterly* 77 (Spring 1993): 71–83.

——. *The Road to Secession: A New Perspective on the Old South*. New York: Praeger Publishers, 1972.

——. *The Secessionist Impulse: Alabama and Mississippi in 1860*. Princeton, N.J.: Princeton University Press, 1974.

Bartley, Numan V. *The Creation of Modern Georgia*. Athens: University of Georgia Press, 1990.

Bearman, Peter S. "Desertion as Localism: Army Unit Solidarity and Group Norms in the U.S. Civil War." *Social Forces* 70 (December 1991): 321–42.

Beringer, Richard E., Herman Hattaway, Archer Jones, and William N. Still Jr. *Why the South Lost the Civil War*. Athens: University of Georgia Press, 1986.

Berlin, Jean V. "Did Confederate Women Lose the War? Deprivation, Destruction, and Despair on the Home Front." In *The Collapse of the Confederacy*, edited by Mark Grimsley and Brooks D. Simpson, 168–93. Lincoln: University of Nebraska Press, 2001.

Berry, Stephen W., II. *All That Makes a Man: Love and Ambition in the Civil War South*. New York: Oxford University Press, 2003.

Billings, Dwight B., Jr. *Planters and the Making of a "New South": Class, Politics, and Development in North Carolina, 1865–1900*. Chapel Hill: University of North Carolina Press, 1979.

Blair, William. *Virginia's Private War: Feeding Body and Soul in the Confederacy, 1861–1865*. New York: Oxford University Press, 1998.

Blassingame, John W. *The Slave Community: Plantation Life in the Antebellum South*. New York: Oxford University Press, 1972.

Blight, David W. *Race and Reunion: The Civil War in American Memory*. Cambridge: Harvard University Press, 2001.

Bode, Frederick A. "A Common Sphere: White Evangelicals and Gender in Antebellum Georgia." *Georgia Historical Quarterly* 79 (Winter 1995): 775–809.

——. "The Formation of Evangelical Communities in Middle Georgia: Twiggs County, 1820–1861." *Journal of Southern History* 60 (November 1994): 711–47.

Bohannon, Keith S. "The Northeast Georgia Mountains during the Secession Crisis and Civil War." Ph.D. diss., Pennsylvania State University, 2001.

——. "They Had Determined to Root Us Out: Dual Memoirs by a Unionist Couple in Blue Ridge Georgia." In *Enemies of the Country: New Perspectives on Unionists in the Civil War South*, edited by John C. Inscoe and Robert C. Kenzer, 97–120. Athens: University of Georgia Press, 2001.

Boles, John B. "Foreword: Revisiting the Plain Folk of the South." In *Plain Folk of the South Revisited*, edited by Samuel C. Hyde Jr., ix–xix. Baton Rouge: Louisiana State University Press, 1997.

Bond, Bradley G. "Herders, Farmers, and Markets on the Inner Frontier: The Mississippi Piney Woods, 1850–1860." In *Plain Folk of the South Revisited*, edited by Samuel C. Hyde Jr., 73–99. Baton Rouge: Louisiana State University Press, 1997.

——. *Political Culture in the Nineteenth-Century South: Mississippi, 1830–1900*. Baton Rouge: Louisiana State University Press, 1995.

Brooks, Charles E. "The Social and Cultural Dynamics of Soldiering in Hood's Texas Brigade." *Journal of Southern History* 67 (August 2001): 535–72.

Bryan, T. Conn. "The Churches in Georgia during the Civil War." *Georgia Historical Quarterly* 33 (1949): 283–302.

——. *Confederate Georgia*. Athens: University of Georgia Press, 1953.

Bryant, Jonathan M. *How Curious a Land: Conflict and Change in Greene County, Georgia, 1850–1885*. Chapel Hill: University of North Carolina Press, 1996.

Burkley, Nola Margaret. "Floyd County, Georgia, during the Civil War." Ph.D. diss., Florida State University, 1998.

Burnham, Walter Dean. *Presidential Ballots, 1836–1892*. Baltimore: Johns Hopkins University Press, 1955.

Burton, Orville V., and Robert C. McMath Jr., eds. *Class, Conflict, and Consensus: Antebellum Southern Community Studies*. Westport, Conn.: Greenwood Press, 1982.

Bynum, Victoria E. *The Free State of Jones: Mississippi's Longest Civil War*. Chapel Hill: University of North Carolina Press, 2001.

———. *Unruly Women: The Politics of Social and Sexual Control in the Old South*. Chapel Hill: University of North Carolina Press, 1992.

Campbell, Edward D. C., Jr., and Kym S. Rice, eds. *A Woman's War: Southern Women, Civil War, and the Confederate Legacy*. Charlottesville: University Press of Virginia, 1996.

Campbell, Jacqueline Glass. *When Sherman Marched North from the Sea: Resistance on the Confederate Home Front*. Chapel Hill: University of North Carolina Press, 2003.

Carey, Anthony Gene. *Parties, Slavery, and the Union in Antebellum Georgia*. Athens: University of Georgia Press, 1997.

Carlson, David. "The 'Loanly Runagee': Draft Evaders in Confederate South Georgia." *Georgia Historical Quarterly* 84 (Winter 2000): 589–615.

Cashin, Joan E., ed. *The War Was You and Me: Civilians in the American Civil War*. Princeton, N.J.: Princeton University Press, 2002.

Chalker, Fussell M. "Irish Catholics in the Building of the Ocmulgee and Flint Railroad." *Georgia Historical Quarterly* 54 (Winter 1970): 507–16.

———. *Pioneer Days along the Ocmulgee*. Carrollton, Ga.: Thomasson Printing, 1970.

Cimbala, Paul A. *Under the Guardianship of the Nation: The Freedmen's Bureau and the Reconstruction of Georgia, 1865–1870*. Athens: University of Georgia Press, 1997.

Clements, J. B. *History of Irwin County*. 1932. Spartanburg, S.C.: Reprint Co., 1989.

Clinton, Catherine. "Bloody Terrain: Freedwomen, Sexuality, and Violence during Reconstruction." *Georgia Historical Quarterly* 76 (Summer 1992): 313–32.

———. *The Plantation Mistress: Woman's World in the Old South*. New York: Pantheon Books, 1982.

———. *Tara Revisited: Women, War, and the Plantation Legend*. New York: Abbeville Press, 1995.

———, ed. *Southern Families at War: Loyalty and Conflict in the Civil War South*. New York: Oxford University Press, 2000.

Clinton, Catherine, and Nina Silber, eds. *Divided Houses: Gender and the Civil War*. New York: Oxford University Press, 1992.

Cobb, Addie Davis. *History of Dodge County*. 1932. Reprint, Spartanburg, S.C.: Reprint Co., 1979.

Coclanis, Peter. "Slavery, African-American Agency, and the World We Have Lost." *Georgia Historical Quarterly* 79 (Winter 1995): 873–84.

Cole, Arthur Charles. *The Whig Party in the South*. 1913. Reprint, Gloucester, Mass.: Peter Smith, 1962.

Collins, Bruce W. "Governor Joseph E. Brown, Economic Issues, and Georgia's Road to Secession, 1857–59." *Georgia Historical Quarterly* 71 (Summer 1987): 189–225.

Coulter, E. Merton. *Georgia: A Short History*. Chapel Hill: University of North Carolina Press, 1947.

Crowley, John G. *Primitive Baptists of the Wiregrass South, 1815 to the Present*. Gainesville: University Press of Florida, 1998.

Daughters of the American Revolution, Hawkinsville Chapter. *History of Pulaski County, Georgia*. Atlanta: Walter W. Brown Publishing Co., 1935.

Davis, Burke. *Sherman's March*. New York: Random House, 1980.

Davis, William C. *Battle at Bull Run: A History of the First Major Campaign of the Civil War*. Garden City, N.Y.: Doubleday, 1977.

DeBats, Donald A. *Elites and Masses: Political Structure, Communication and Behavior in Ante-Bellum Georgia*. New York: Garland Publishing Co., 1990.

DeCredico, Mary A. *Patriotism for Profit: Georgia's Urban Entrepreneurs and the Confederate War Effort*. Chapel Hill: University of North Carolina Press, 1990.

Degler, Carl N. *The Other South: Southern Dissenters in the Nineteenth Century*. New York: Harper and Row, 1974.

Doherty, Herbert J., Jr. "Union Nationalism in Georgia." *Georgia Historical Quarterly* 37 (March 1953): 18–38.

Donald, David Herbert, Jean Harvey Baker, and Michael F. Holt. *The Civil War and Reconstruction*. New York: Norton, 2001.

Doyle, Don H. *Nations Divided: America, Italy, and the Southern Question*. Athens: University of Georgia Press, 2002.

——. *New Men, New Cities, New South: Atlanta, Nashville, Charleston, Mobile, 1860–1910*. Chapel Hill: University of North Carolina Press, 1990.

Doyon, Roy R., and Thomas W. Hodler. "Secessionist Sentiment and Slavery: A Geographic Analysis." *Georgia Historical Quarterly* 73 (Summer 1989): 321–43.

Drago, Edmund L. *Black Politicians and Reconstruction in Georgia: A Splendid Failure*. Athens: University of Georgia Press, 1992.

Durrill, Wayne K. *War of Another Kind: A Southern Community in the Great Rebellion*. New York: Oxford University Press, 1990.

Dyer, Thomas G. *Secret Yankees: The Union Circle in Confederate Atlanta*. Baltimore: Johns Hopkins University Press, 1999.

Eaton, Clement. *A History of the Old South*. New York: Macmillan, 1954.

Escott, Paul D. *After Secession: Jefferson Davis and the Failure of Confederate Nationalism*. Baton Rouge: Louisiana State University Press, 1978.

——. "The Context of Freedom: Georgia's Slaves during the Civil War." *Georgia Historical Quarterly* 58 (1974): 79–104.

——. " 'The Cry of Sufferers': The Problem of Welfare in the Confederacy." *Civil War History* 23 (September 1977): 228–40.

——. "Joseph E. Brown, Jefferson Davis, and the Problem of Poverty in the Confederacy." *Georgia Historical Quarterly* 61 (1977): 59–71.

——. "The Moral Economy of the Crowd in Confederate North Carolina." *Maryland Historian* 13 (Spring–Summer 1982): 1–17.

Ethridge, Robbie. *Creek Country: The Creek Indians and Their World*. Chapel Hill: University of North Carolina Press, 2003.

Evans, W. McKee. *Ballots and Fence Rails: Reconstruction on the Lower Cape Fear*. Chapel
Hill: University of North Carolina Press, 1966.

Fahs, Alice. *The Imagined Civil War: Popular Literature of the North and South, 1861–1865*.
Chapel Hill: University of North Carolina Press, 2001.

Farrell, Sean. *Rituals and Riots: Sectarian Violence and Political Culture in Ulster, 1784–1886*.
Lexington: University Press of Kentucky, 2000.

Faust, Drew Gilpin. "Altars of Sacrifice: Confederate Women and Narratives of War." In
*Divided Houses: Gender and the Civil War*, edited by Catherine Clinton and Nina Silber,
171–99. New York: Oxford University Press, 1992.

——. "Christian Soldiers: The Meaning of Revivalism in the Confederate Army." *Journal of
Southern History* 53 (February 1987): 63–90.

——. "The Civil War Soldier and the Art of Dying." *Journal of Southern History* 67 (February
2001): 3–38.

——. *The Creation of Confederate Nationalism: Ideology and Identity in the Civil War South*.
Baton Rouge: Louisiana State University Press, 1988.

——. *Mothers of Invention: Women of the Slaveholding South in the American Civil War*. New
York: Vintage Books, 1997.

Fitzgerald, Michael W. "Radical Republicanism and the White Yeomanry during Alabama
Reconstruction, 1865–1868." *Journal of Southern History* 54 (November 1988): 565–96.

——. *The Union League Movement in the Deep South: Politics and Agricultural Change during
Reconstruction*. Baton Rouge: Louisiana State University Press, 1989.

Flynn, Charles L., Jr. *White Land, Black Labor: Caste and Class in Late Nineteenth-Century
Georgia*. Baton Rouge: Louisiana State University Press, 1983.

Foner, Eric. *Reconstruction: America's Unfinished Revolution, 1863–1877*. New York: Harper
and Row, 1988.

Ford, Lacy K. *Origins of Southern Radicalism: The South Carolina Upcountry, 1800–1860*.
New York: Oxford University Press, 1988.

——. "Popular Ideology of the Old South's Plain Folk: The Limits of Egalitarianism in a
Slaveholding Society." In *Plain Folk of the South Revisited*, edited by Samuel C. Hyde Jr.,
205–27. Baton Rouge: Louisiana State University Press, 1997.

——. "Rednecks and Merchants: Economic Development and Social Tensions in the South
Carolina Upcountry, 1865–1900." *Journal of American History* 71 (September 1984): 294–
318.

Formwalt, Lee W. "Planters and Cotton Production as a Cause of Confederate Defeat:
Evidence from Southwest Georgia." *Georgia Historical Quarterly* 74 (Summer 1990):
269–76.

Foster, Gaines M. *Ghosts of the Confederacy: Defeat, the Lost Cause, and the Emergence of the
New South, 1865 to 1913*. New York: Oxford University Press, 1987.

Fox-Genovese, Elizabeth. *Within the Plantation Household: Black and White Women of the
Old South*. Chapel Hill: University of North Carolina Press, 1988.

Frank, Joseph Allan. *With Ballot and Bayonet: The Political Socialization of American Civil
War Soldiers*. Athens: University of Georgia Press, 1998.

Franklin, John Hope. *The Militant South, 1800–1861*. Cambridge: Belknap Press of Harvard
University, 1956.

Fraser, Walter J., Jr., and Winfred B. Moore, Jr., eds. *From the Old South to the New: Essay on the Transitional South*. Westport, Conn.: Greenwood Press, 1981.

Fredrickson, George M. *The Black Image in the White Mind: The Debate on Afro-American Character and Destiny, 1817–1914*. New York: Harper and Row, 1971.

Freehling, William W. *The Reintegration of American History: Slavery and the Civil War*. New York: Oxford University Press, 1993.

———. *The South vs. the South: How Anti-Confederate Southerners Shaped the Course of the Civil War*. New York: Oxford University Press, 2001.

Freehling, William W., and Craig M. Simpson, eds. *Secession Debated: Georgia's Showdown in 1860*. New York: Oxford University Press, 1992.

Gallagher, Gary W. *The Confederate War: How Popular Will, Nationalism, and Military Strategy Could Not Stave Off Defeat*. Cambridge: Harvard University Press, 1997.

Genovese, Eugene D. *The Political Economy of Slavery: Studies in the Economy and Society of the Slave South*. New York: Random House, 1967.

———. *Roll, Jordan, Roll: The World the Slaves Made*. New York: Random House, 1972.

———. "Yeoman Farmers in a Slaveholders' Democracy." *Agricultural History* 49 (1975): 331–42.

Gilmour, Robert Arthur. "The Other Emancipation: Studies in the Society and Economy of Alabama Whites during Reconstruction." Ph.D. diss., Johns Hopkins University, 1972.

Glatthaar, Joseph T. *The March to the Sea and Beyond: Sherman's Troops in the Savannah and Carolinas Campaigns*. New York: New York University Press, 1985.

Goodman, Paul. "White over White: Planters, Yeomen, and the Coming of the Civil War: A Review Essay." *Agricultural History* 54 (1980): 446–52.

Gorman, Kathleen Lynn. "When Johnny Came Marching Home Again: Confederate Veterans in the New South." Ph.D. diss., University of California at Riverside, 1994.

Grimsley, Mark. *The Hard Hand of War: Union Military Policy toward Southern Civilians, 1861–1865*. Cambridge: Cambridge University Press, 1995.

Grimsley, Mark, and Brooks D. Simpson, eds. *The Collapse of the Confederacy*. Lincoln: University of Nebraska Press, 2001.

Groce, W. Todd. *Mountain Rebels: East Tennessee Confederates and the Civil War, 1860–1870*. Knoxville: University of Tennessee Press, 1999.

Gross, Jennifer Lynn. " 'Good Angels': Confederate Widowhood in Virginia." In *Southern Families at War: Loyalty and Conflict in the Civil War South*, edited by Catherine Clinton, 133–53. New York: Oxford University Press, 2000.

Hahn, Steven. *A Nation under Our Feet: Black Political Struggles in the Rural South from Slavery to the Great Migration*. Cambridge: Belknap Press of Harvard University, 2003.

———. *The Roots of Southern Populism: Yeoman Farmers and the Transformation of the Georgia Upcountry, 1850–1890*. New York: Oxford University Press, 1983.

———. "The Yeomanry of the Nonplantation South: Upper Piedmont Georgia, 1850–1860." In *Class, Conflict, and Consensus: Antebellum Southern Community Studies*, edited by Orville Vernon Burton and Robert C. McMath, Jr., 29–56. Westport, Conn.: Greenwood Press, 1982.

Hallock, Judith Lee. "The Role of the Community in Civil War Desertion." *Civil War History* 29 (June 1983): 123–34.

Harper, Roland M. "Development of Agriculture in Lower Georgia from 1850 to 1880." *Georgia Historical Quarterly* 6 (June 1922): 97–121.

Harris, J. William. *Plain Folk and Gentry in a Slave Society: White Liberty and Black Slavery in Augusta's Hinterlands*. Baton Rouge: Louisiana State University Press, 1998.

——. "Portrait of a Small Slaveholder: The Journal of Benton Miller." *Georgia Historical Quarterly* 74 (Spring 1990): 1–19.

Harris, Wallace Leigh, comp. *History of Pulaski and Bleckley Counties, Georgia, 1808–1956*. 2 vols. Macon: J. W. Burke Co., 1957.

Harvey, Paul. " 'Yankee Faith' and Southern Redemption: White Southern Baptist Ministers, 1850–1890." In *Religion and the American Civil War*, edited by Randall M. Miller, Harry S. Stout, and Charles Reagan Wilson, 167–86. New York: Oxford University Press, 1998.

Herring, John Lewis. *Saturday Night Sketches: Stories of Old Wiregrass Georgia*. Tifton, Ga.: Sunny South Press, 1978.

Hettle, Wallace T. "An Ambiguous Democrat: Joseph Brown and Georgia's Road to Secession." *Georgia Historical Quarterly* 81 (Fall 1997): 581–92.

Heyrman, Christine Leigh. *Southern Cross: The Beginnings of the Bible Belt*. Chapel Hill: University of North Carolina Press, 1997.

Hill, Louise Biles. *Joseph E. Brown and the Confederacy*. Chapel Hill: University of North Carolina Press, 1939.

Hilliard, Sam Bowers. *Hog Meat and Hoecake: Food Supply in the Old South, 1840–1860*. Carbondale: Southern Illinois University Press, 1972.

Holt, Michael F. *The Rise and Fall of the American Whig Party: Jacksonian Politics and the Onset of the Civil War*. New York: Oxford University Press, 1999.

Hubbard, Charles M. *The Burden of Confederate Diplomacy*. Knoxville: University of Tennessee Press, 1998.

Hubbs, G. Ward. *Guarding Greensboro: A Confederate Company in the Making of a Southern Community*. Athens: University of Georgia Press, 2003.

Hummel, Jeffrey Rogers. *Emancipating Slaves, Enslaving Free Men: A History of the American Civil War*. Chicago: Open Court, 1996.

Hyde, Samuel C., Jr. "Backcountry Justice in the Piney-Woods South." In *Plain Folk of the South Revisited*, edited by Samuel C. Hyde Jr., 228–49. Baton Rouge: Louisiana State University Press, 1997.

——. *Pistols and Politics: The Dilemma of Democracy in Louisiana's Florida Parishes, 1810–1899*. Baton Rouge: Louisiana State University Press, 1996.

Inscoe, John C. *Mountain Masters, Slavery, and the Sectional Crisis in Western North Carolina*. Knoxville: University of Tennessee Press, 1989.

Inscoe, John C., and Robert C. Kenzer, eds. *Enemies of the Country: New Perspectives on Unionists in the Civil War South*. Athens: University of Georgia Press, 2001.

Johnson, Michael P. "A New Look at the Popular Vote for Delegates to the Georgia Secession Convention." *Georgia Historical Quarterly* 56 (Summer 1972): 259–75.

——. *Toward a Patriarchal Republic: The Secession of Georgia*. Baton Rouge: Louisiana State University Press, 1977.

Joiner, Edsel A., comp. *Pioneer Families of Telfair and Dodge Counties*. Cochran, Ga.: 1968.

Jones, Jacqueline. "Encounters, Likely and Unlikely, between Black and Poor White Women in the Rural South, 1865–1940." *Georgia Historical Quarterly* 76 (Summer 1992): 333–53.

Jones, James Pickett. *Yankee Blitzkrieg: Wilson's Raid through Alabama and Georgia*. Athens: University of Georgia Press, 1976.

Jordan, Ervin L., Jr. *Black Confederates and Afro-Yankees in Civil War Virginia*. Charlottesville: University Press of Virginia, 1995.

Joyner, Charles. *Down by the Riverside: A South Carolina Slave Community*. Urbana: University of Illinois Press, 1984.

Kennett, Lee. *Marching through Georgia: The Story of Soldiers and Civilians during Sherman's Campaign*. New York: HarperCollins, 1995.

Kenzer, Robert C. *Kinship and Neighborhood in a Southern Community: Orange County, North Carolina, 1849–1881*. Knoxville: University of Tennessee Press, 1987.

———. "The Uncertainty of Life: A Profile of Virginia's Civil War Widows." In *The War Was You and Me: Civilians in the American Civil War*, edited by Joan E. Cashin, 112–35. Princeton, N.J.: Princeton University Press, 2002.

Kerber, Linda K. *Women of the Republic: Intellect and Ideology in Revolutionary America*. Chapel Hill: University of North Carolina Press, 1980.

King, J. Crawford, Jr. "The Closing of the Southern Range: An Exploratory Study." *Journal of Southern History* 48 (February 1982): 53–70.

Kolchin, Peter. *American Slavery, 1619–1877*. New York: Hill and Wang, 1993.

Krug, Donna Rebecca Dondes. "The Folks Back Home: The Confederate Home Front during the Civil War." Ph.D. diss., University of California at Irvine, 1990.

Kulikoff, Allan. "The Transition to Capitalism in Rural America." *William and Mary Quarterly*, 3rd ser., 46 (January 1989): 120–44.

Laderman, Gary. *The Sacred Remains: Attitudes toward Death, 1799–1883*. New Haven: Yale University Press, 1996.

Laver, Harry S. "Rethinking the Social Role of the Militia: Community-Building in Antebellum Kentucky." *Georgia Historical Quarterly* 68 (November 2002): 777–811.

Lebsock, Suzanne. *The Free Women of Petersburg: Status and Culture in a Southern Town, 1784–1860*. New York: Norton, 1985.

Linderman, Gerald F. *Embattled Courage: The Experience of Combat in the American Civil War*. New York: Free Press, 1987.

Link, William A. *Roots of Secession: Slavery and Politics in Antebellum Virginia*. Chapel Hill: University of North Carolina Press, 2003.

Litwack, Leon F. *Been in the Storm So Long: The Aftermath of Slavery*. New York: Knopf, 1979.

———. " 'Blues Falling Down Like Hail': The Ordeal of Black Freedom." In *New Perspectives on Race and Slavery in America: Essays in Honor of Kenneth M. Stampp*, edited by Robert H. Abzug and Stephen E. Maizlish, 109–27. Lexington: University Press of Kentucky, 1986.

Lonn, Ella. *Desertion during the Civil War*. 1928. Reprint, Lincoln: University of Nebraska Press, 1998.

Lowitt, Richard. *A Merchant Prince of the Nineteenth Century: William E. Dodge*. New York: Columbia University Press, 1954.

Luraghi, Raimondo. *The Rise and Fall of the Plantation South*. New York: New Viewpoints, 1978.

Magdol, Edward, and Jon L. Wakelyn. *The Southern Common People: Studies in Nineteenth-Century Social History*. Westport: Greenwood Press, 1980.

Malone, Ann Patton. "Piney Woods Farmers of South Georgia, 1850–1900: Jeffersonian Yeomen in the Age of Expanding Commercialism." *Agricultural History* 60 (Fall 1986): 51–84.

Mann, Floris Perkins, comp. *History of Telfair County: From 1812 to 1949*. Macon, Ga.: J. W. Burke Co., 1949.

Massey, Mary Elizabeth. *Refugee Life in the Confederacy*. Baton Rouge: Louisiana State University Press, 1964.

Mathews, Donald G. *Religion in the Old South*. Chicago: University of Chicago Press, 1977.

McCurry, Stephanie. "'The Brothers' War?': Women, Slaves, and Popular Politics in the Civil War South." Paper presented at the Southern Association of Women Historians, Southern Historical Association Annual Meeting, Fort Worth, Tex., November 5, 1999.

——. *Masters of Small Worlds: Yeoman Households, Gender Relations, and the Political Culture of the Antebellum South Carolina Low Country*. New York: Oxford University Press, 1995.

——. "'The Soldier's Wife': White Women, the State, and the Politics of Protection in the Confederacy." In *Women and the Unstable State in Nineteenth Century America*, edited by Alison Parker and Stephanie Cole, 15–36. College Station: Texas A & M Press, 2000.

McDonald, Forrest, and Grady McWhiney. "The South from Self-Sufficiency to Peonage: An Interpretation." *American Historical Review* 85 (December 1980): 1095–1118.

McDonald, JoAnna M. *We Shall Meet Again: The First Battle of Manassas (Bull Run), July 18–21, 1861*. New York: Oxford University Press, 2000.

McDonald, Mary Lou L., and Samuel Jordan Lawson III. *The Passing of the Pines: A History of Wilcox County, Georgia*. 3 vols. Roswell, Ga.: W. H. Wolfe Associates, 1984.

McInvale, Morton R. "'All the Devils Could Wish For': The Griswoldville Campaign, November, 1864." *Georgia Historical Quarterly* 60 (Summer 1976): 117–30.

McNeill, William J. "A Survey of Confederate Soldier Morale during Sherman's Campaigns through Georgia and the Carolinas." *Georgia Historical Quarterly* 55 (1971): 1–25.

McPherson, James M. *Battle Cry of Freedom: The Civil War Era*. New York: Oxford University Press, 1988.

——. *For Cause and Comrades: Why Men Fought in the Civil War*. New York: Oxford University Press, 1997.

——. *What They Fought For, 1861–1865*. New York: Anchor Books, 1995.

McWhiney, Grady. *Cracker Culture: Celtic Ways in the Old South*. Tuscaloosa: University of Alabama Press, 1988.

Miller, Elinor, and Eugene D. Genovese, eds. *Plantation, Town, and County: Essays on the Local History of American Slave Society*. Urbana: University of Illinois Press, 1974.

Miller, Randall M., Harry S. Stout, and Charles Reagan Wilson, eds. *Religion and the American Civil War*. New York: Oxford University Press, 1998.

Mitchell, Reid. "Christian Soldiers? Perfecting the Confederacy." In *Religion and the American Civil War*, edited by Randall M. Miller, Harry S. Stout, and Charles Reagan Wilson, 297–309. New York: Oxford University Press, 1998.

———. "The Creation of Confederate Loyalties." In *New Perspectives on Race and Slavery in America: Essays in Honor of Kenneth M. Stampp*, edited by Robert H. Abzug and Stephen E. Maizlish, 93–108. Lexington: University Press of Kentucky, 1986.

———. *The Vacant Chair: The Northern Soldier Leaves Home*. New York: Oxford University Press, 1993.

Mohr, Clarence L. *On the Threshold of Freedom: Masters and Slaves in Civil War Georgia*. Athens: University of Georgia Press, 1986.

Moore, Albert B. *Conscription and Conflict in the Confederacy*. New York: Macmillan, 1924.

Murrell, Amy E. " 'Of Necessity and Public Benefit': Southern Families and Their Appeals for Protection." In *Southern Families at War: Loyalty and Conflict in the Civil War South*, edited by Catherine Clinton, 77–99. New York: Oxford University Press, 2000.

———. "Union Father, Rebel Son: Families and the Question of Civil War Loyalty." In *The War Was You and Me: Civilians in the American Civil War*, edited by Joan E. Cashin, 358–91. Princeton, N.J.: Princeton University Press, 2002.

Newby, I. A. *Plain Folk in the New South: Social Change and Cultural Persistence, 1880–1915*. Baton Rouge: Louisiana State University Press, 1989.

Noe, Kenneth W., and Shannon H. Wilson. *The Civil War in Appalachia: Collected Essays*. Knoxville: University of Tennessee Press, 1997.

Olsen, Christopher J. *Political Culture and Secession in Mississippi: Masculinity, Honor, and the Antiparty Tradition, 1830–1860*. New York: Oxford University Press, 2000.

Olsen, Otto H. "Reconsidering the Scalawags." *Civil War History* 12 (1966): 304–20.

Owsley, Frank Lawrence. *Plain Folk of the Old South*. Baton Rouge: Louisiana State University Press, 1949.

Paludan, Phillip Shaw. *Victims: A True Story of the Civil War*. Knoxville: University of Tennessee Press, 1981.

Parks, Joseph H. *Joseph E. Brown of Georgia*. Baton Rouge: Louisiana State University Press, 1977.

Peeples, Dale Hardy. "Georgia Railroads: Civil War and Reconstruction." M.A. thesis, University of Georgia, 1961.

Perman, Michael. *Emancipation and Reconstruction, 1862–1879*. Arlington Heights, Ill.: Harlan Davidson, 1987.

Phillips, Ulrich Bonnell. *Georgia and State Rights: A Study of the Political History of Georgia from the Revolution to the Civil War, with Particular Regard to Federal Relations*. Washington, D.C.: GPO, 1902.

Rable, George C. *Civil Wars: Women and the Crisis of Southern Nationalism*. Urbana: University of Illinois Press, 1989.

———. *The Confederate Republic: A Revolution against Politics*. Chapel Hill: University of North Carolina Press, 1994.

———. "Despair, Hope, and Delusion: The Collapse of Confederate Morale Reexamined." In *The Collapse of the Confederacy*, edited by Mark Grimsley and Brooks D. Simpson, 129–67. Lincoln: University of Nebraska Press, 2001.

———. "Hearth, Home, and Family in the Fredericksburg Campaign." In *The War Was You and Me: Civilians in the American Civil War*, edited by Joan E. Cashin, 85–111. Princeton, N.J.: Princeton University Press, 2002.

Ransom, Roger L., and Richard Sutch. *One Kind of Freedom: The Economic Consequences of Emancipation*. New York: Cambridge University Press, 1977.

Rapport, Sara. "The Freedmen's Bureau as a Legal Agent for Black Men and Women in Georgia, 1865–1868." *Georgia Historical Quarterly* 73 (Spring 1989): 26–53.

Reidy, Joseph P. *From Slavery to Agrarian Capitalism in the Cotton Plantation South: Central Georgia, 1800–1880*. Chapel Hill: University of North Carolina Press, 1992.

Richard, Patricia L. *Busy Hands: Images of the Family in the Northern Civil War Effort*. New York: Fordham University Press, 2003.

Richards, Leonard L. *"Gentlemen of Property and Standing": Anti-Abolition Mobs in Jacksonian America*. New York: Oxford University Press, 1970.

Riley, James A. "Desertion and Disloyalty in Georgia during the Civil War." M.A. thesis, University of Georgia, 1951.

Roark, James L. *Masters without Slaves: Southern Planters in the Civil War and Reconstruction*. New York: Norton, 1977.

Robertson, James I., Jr. *Soldiers Blue and Gray*. Columbia: University of South Carolina Press, 1998 (paperback edition).

——. *Stonewall Jackson: The Man, the Soldier, the Legend*. New York: Macmillan, 1997.

Rose, Anne C. *Victorian America and the Civil War*. New York: Cambridge University Press, 1992.

Rosenberg, Ellen M. *The Southern Baptists: A Subculture in Transition*. Knoxville: University of Tennessee Press, 1989.

Rothstein, Morton. "The Antebellum South as a Dual Economy, A Tentative Hypothesis." *Agricultural History* 41 (October 1967): 373–82.

Schama, Simon. *Landscape and Memory*. New York: Alfred A. Knopf, 1995.

Scott, Anne Firor. *The Southern Lady: From Pedestal to Politics, 1830–1930*. Chicago: University of Chicago Press, 1970.

Silber, Nina. *The Romance of Reunion: Northerners and the South, 1865–1900*. Chapel Hill: University of North Carolina Press, 1993.

Smith, George G. *The History of Georgia Methodism from 1786 to 1866*. Atlanta: A. B. Caldwell, 1913.

Smith, Julia Floyd. *Slavery and Rice Culture in Low Country Georgia, 1750–1860*. Knoxville: University of Tennessee Press, 1985.

Stampp, Kenneth M. *The Peculiar Institution: Slavery in the Ante-Bellum South*. New York: Random House, 1956.

Storey, Margaret M. *Loyalty and Loss: Alabama's Unionists in the Civil War and Reconstruction*. Baton Rouge: Louisiana State University Press, 2004.

Stover, John F. "Georgia Railroads during the Reconstruction Years." *Railroad History* 134 (Spring 1976): 56–65.

Summers, Mark W. *Railroads, Reconstruction, and the Gospel of Prosperity: Aid under the Radical Republicans, 1865–1877*. Princeton, N.J.: Princeton University Press, 1984.

Sutherland, Daniel E. "Guerrilla Warfare, Democracy, and the Fate of the Confederacy." *Journal of Southern History* 68 (May 2002): 259–92.

——. *Seasons of War: The Ordeal of a Confederate Community, 1861–65*. New York: Free Press, 1995.

———, ed. *Guerrillas, Unionists, and Violence on the Confederate Home Front*. Fayetteville: University of Arkansas Press, 1999.

Talley, J. N. "The Dodge Lands and Litigation." *Report of the Forty-Second Annual Session of the Georgia Bar Association*, edited by Harry S. Strozier. Macon: J. W. Burke Co., 1925.

Tatum, Georgia Lee. *Disloyalty in the Confederacy*. Chapel Hill: University of North Carolina Press, 1934. Reprint, New York: AMS Press, 1970.

Thomas, Emory M. *The Confederacy as a Revolutionary Experience*. Englewood Cliffs, N.J.: Prentice-Hall, 1971.

———. *The Confederate Nation, 1861–1865*. New York: Harper and Row, 1979.

Thompson, E. P. "The Moral Economy of the English Crowd in the Eighteenth Century." *Past and Present* 50 (February 1971): 76–136.

Thornton, J. Mills, III. *Politics and Power in a Slave Society: Alabama, 1800–1860*. Baton Rouge: Louisiana State University Press, 1978.

Tripp, Mary Ellen. "Longleaf Pine Lumber Manufacturing in the Altamaha River Basin, 1865–1918." Ph.D. diss., Florida State University, 1983.

Trowell, C. T. "Douglas before Memory, 1854–1905: A Study of Everyday Life in a South Georgia Town." 1996. (Typescript copy provided by author.)

Varon, Elizabeth R. *We Mean to Be Counted: White Women and Politics in Antebellum Virginia*. Chapel Hill: University of North Carolina Press, 1998.

Wallenstein, Peter. "Rich Man's War, Rich Man's Fight: Civil War and the Transformation of Public Finance in Georgia." *Journal of Southern History* 50 (February 1984): 15–42.

Ward, Warren P. *Ward's History of Coffee County*. 1930. Reprint, Spartanburg, S.C.: Reprint Co., 1978.

Weitz, Mark A. *A Higher Duty: Desertion among Georgia Troops during the Civil War*. Lincoln: University of Nebraska Press, 2000.

Wells, Tom Henderson. *The Slave Ship Wanderer*. Athens: University of Georgia Press, 1968.

Wetherington, Mark V. *The New South Comes to Wiregrass Georgia, 1860–1910*. Knoxville: University of Tennessee Press, 1994.

Whites, LeeAnn. *The Civil War as a Crisis in Gender: Augusta, Georgia, 1860–1890*. Athens: University of Georgia Press, 1995.

Wiener, Jonathan M. "Class Structure and Economic Development in the American South, 1865–1955." *American Historical Review* 84 (October 1979): 970–92.

———. *Social Origins of the New South: Alabama, 1860–1885*. Baton Rouge: Louisiana State University Press, 1978.

Wiley, Bell Irvin. *The Life of Johnny Reb: The Common Soldier of the Confederacy*. 1943. Reprint, Baton Rouge: Louisiana State University Press, 1993.

———. *The Plain People of the Confederacy*. Baton Rouge: Louisiana State University Press, 1943. Reprint, Gloucester, Mass.: Peter Smith, 1971.

Wilkinson, Warren, and Steven E. Woodworth. *A Scythe of Fire: A Civil War Story of the Eighth Georgia Infantry Regiment*. New York: William Morrow, 2002.

Williams, David. *Rich Man's War: Class, Caste, and Confederate Defeat in the Lower Chattahoochee Valley*. Athens: University of Georgia Press, 1998.

Williams, David, Teresa C. Williams, and David Carlson. *Plain Folk in a Rich Man's War: Class and Dissent in Confederate Georgia*. Gainesville: University Press of Florida, 2002.

Wilson, Charles Reagan. *Baptized in Blood: The Religion of the Lost Cause, 1865–1920*. Athens: University of Georgia Press, 1980.

Woodman, Harold D. *King Cotton and His Retainers: Financing and Marketing the Cotton Crop of the South, 1800–1925*. Lexington: University Press of Kentucky, 1968.

Woodward, C. Vann. *Origins of the New South, 1877–1913*. Baton Rouge: Louisiana State University Press, 1951.

Wooster, Ralph A. "The Georgia Secession Convention." *Georgia Historical Quarterly* 40 (March 1956): 21–55.

——. "Notes on the Georgia Legislature of 1860." *Georgia Historical Quarterly* 45 (1961): 22–36.

——. *The People in Power: Courthouse and Statehouse in the Lower South, 1850–1860*. Knoxville: University of Tennessee Press, 1969.

Wright, Gavin. *Old South, New South: Revolutions in the Southern Economy since the Civil War*. New York: Basic Books, 1986.

——. *The Political Economy of the Cotton South: Households, Markets, and Wealth in the Nineteenth Century*. New York: Norton, 1978.

Wyatt-Brown, Bertram. "The Antimission Movement in the Jacksonian South: A Study in Regional Folk Culture." *Journal of Southern History* 36 (November 1970): 501–29.

——. *The Shaping of Southern Culture: Honor, Grace, and War, 1760s–1880s*. Chapel Hill: University of North Carolina Press, 2001.

——. *Southern Honor: Ethics and Behavior in the Old South*. New York: Oxford University Press, 1982.

# INDEX

Fort Sumter: attack on, 85, 86, 114, 127, 195
Fountain, Elender. *See* Gibbs, Elender
Fourteenth Amendment, 267
Fraser, James, 235–36
Fredericksburg, Battle of (1862), 136, 139, 304
Freedmen's Bureau, 253, 269, 284, 285; as
    enforcing power for freedmen/women,
    249, 255, 256, 279; reporting violence
    against blacks, 251, 252, 283; unable to
    protect freedmen, 286
Frier, Joshua, 56, 72, 74, 75, 77
Frier family, 48, 54
Fuller, Samuel, 28, 63, 100, 164, 181, 236; and
    Abbeville Resolutions, 213, 215–16; and
    Griswoldville, 204, 206; as leader of State
    Rights Guards, 90–91, 94, 97, 98, 136; as
    Southern Democrat, 65–66, 97, 99
Fussell, Jacob, 163
Fussell, Jacob, Sr., 54
Fussell, William, 26, 38

Gardner, W. M., 116
General Order No. 108, 279
Georgia Cavalry, 87; 4th, 214–15, 228; 10th
    Confederate, 119, 220, 279, 283, 293; 22nd
    Battalion (State Guards), 273; demobiliza-
    tion of U.S., 266; Georgia Hussars (Savan-
    nah), 89; Wheeler's cavalry unit, 207, 208,
    209, 222; Wilcox Grays (State Guard cav-
    alry company), 198, 204, 207
Georgia constitutional convention (1877),
    291, 292
Georgia constitution of 1868, 291
Georgia Hussars (Savannah), 89
Georgia Infantry Regiments: 8th, 113–17, 142,
    234, 236, 320 (n. 15), 337 (n. 39); 8th, casu-
    alties, 116, 117–18, 142; 10th, 119, 142, 320
    (n. 15); 20th, 119, 139, 142; 23rd, 86, 119,
    126, 142; 31st, 86, 142; 49th, 119, 122, 123,
    142, 143; 49th, after war, 246, 265, 274, 303;
    49th, casualties, 1, 137, 139, 142, 188, 191;
    49th, deserters, 131, 142, 216, 220–21; 49th,
    officer elections, 133–34, 135; 49th, organi-
    zation, 321–22 (n. 40); 49th, religious

revivalism in, 139–41; 49th, substitute hir-
    ing in, 130, 131, 142; 50th, 99, 142, 224, 265,
    321–22 (n. 40); 61st, 88, 142, 176; deserters,
    131, 142, 203, 216, 220–21, 337 (n. 39); elec-
    tion of officers, 132–36; as foundation of
    Confederate army, 93; at Gettysburg, 136–
    37, 150, 161, 184, 189, 190, 195, 205, 228,
    238–39, 304; hiring substitutes, 130–32,
    135, 142, 150; kin folks together in, 93, 320
    (n. 15); Macon Guards, 87; motivations
    for staying at front, 144–45; numbers in
    service, beginning of war, 85, 98; physi-
    cal/sanitary conditions causing sickness/
    disease, 119–26; plain folk as company
    officers in, 94–95; planters as leaders in,
    94–95, 98–100; political allegiances of
    commanders, 97; professional men in,
    95–97, 99, 100–101; and religion, in face
    of death, 137–41; and slaves, proposed use
    of in army, 143, 303; veterans, amputees/
    disabled, 234–37. *See also* Casualties, in
    Georgia Infantry; Coffee County Guards;
    Confederate army; Georgia Militia; Geor-
    gia Rangers; Georgia Reserves; Irwin
    County Volunteers; Irwin Cow Boys;
    Pulaski Blues; Pulaski Greys; Pulaski
    Rangers; Pulaski Volunteers; State Rights
    Guards; Telfair Volunteers; Wilcox
    County Rifles
Georgia invasion, 3, 129, 130, 153, 176, 180,
    198, 199, 201–4, 218, 230; after fall of
    Atlanta, 208–9, 211, 212, 219, 220, 222, 305;
    Atlanta, fall of, 206–7, 208, 219; cutting
    off troops at home, 220; Griswoldville,
    Georgia Militia attack, 202, 207–11, 219,
    305; weather conditions, 222
Georgia Land and Lumber Company
    (GL&LC), 297, 299, 300; and land acquisi-
    tion, dispossessing plain folk, 302, 303
Georgia Light Artillery, Dawson's Battery,
    86, 119, 138, 157, 296; and Griswoldville,
    207, 209
Georgia Militia, 151, 219; 7th, 204–5, 207–11,
    212; and Griswoldville, 207–11. *See also*

Georgia Reserves; Wilcox Grays (State Guard cavalry company); Wilcox Home Guards

Georgia Platform (1850), 57, 64, 67, 72, 74

Georgia Rangers, 86, 87, 93, 105, 118, 119, 193–94, 320 (n. 15); veterans, 265, 273, 274, 275. *See also* Georgia Infantry Regiments: 10th

Georgia Reserves: 5th, 203, 208–11, 212, 275; Griswoldville, 208–11. *See also* Georgia Militia

Gettysburg, Battle of (1863), 134, 136–37, 139, 145, 150, 181, 205, 228, 304; casualties at, 137, 141, 161, 184, 189, 190, 195, 238–39

Gibbs, Elender, 159–60, 168

Gibbs, John, 46, 47, 124

Gibbs, Nathaniel, 151, 159–60, 169

Gibbs family, 123, 143, 159, 232

Goodson, Alvey, 92, 118, 148, 190

Goodson, Amantha, 92, 118, 148

*Governor Troup* steamboat, 214, 226

Grant, Ulysses S., 145, 284; election to presidency, 281

Grant Clubs, 265, 270, 283, 284, 292

Grantham, Daniel, Sr., 46

Grantham, Henry, 128–29

Grice, Washington, 273–74

Griswold, Samuel, 208

Griswoldville, Georgia Militia attack at, 202, 207–11, 219, 305; aftermath of, 211–12, 215, 230; casualties of, 210–11

Gum Swamp neighborhood, 19, 22; and anti-Confederates, in last year of war, 223, 276

Harpers Ferry, 114. *See also* Brown, John: and Harpers Ferry raid

Hatton, William, 100, 125, 184, 193

Hawkinsville, Ga., 12, 23, 82; African-American businessmen, 256; climate, 124; lack of federal troops in, soon after war, 278–79; as market town, 17, 19, 43; merchants, and regional pride, 59, 61, 96, 321 (n. 35); merchants during panic of 1873,

244–46; militia elections, 1836, 50; Orange Hill Cemetery, 1, 191; population, 4, 13; and railroads, 61; Reconstruction, attitude toward, 261–62; slaves in, 38; steamboats at, 25, 166; troop farewell at, 105, 274

Henderson, Manassah, 46, 47, 197, 228, 229, 230, 243; and secession, 75, 77, 80, 82

Hendley, John A., 279, 283

Hill, A. P., 138, 139, 274

Hill, Benjamin, 61, 62, 79

Hilliard, James K., 74, 77, 96

Hobbs, Anderson, 279–80

Hollinquist, J. H., 203, 222–23, 224

Home manufactures by women, 105–6, 109–10; in black versus white belt neighborhoods, 107–8

Homestead Laws, 245, 247

Hood, John, 207

Horne, Mary, 101, 102

Horne, Orran, 61, 95, 97, 101, 226, 300; on Committee of Seven, 273–74; and Henry, his slave, 92–93, 193–94; leading Georgia Rangers, 87, 92–93, 119, 194

Howard's Grove, Va., 113–14

Humphreys, James, 109, 135, 220; leading Telfair Volunteers, 100–101, 134, 159, 160, 162, 205, 303; mobilizing, in Telfair County, 100–101, 104, 127–28; as physician, 124, 134; returning home, exempt as physician, 153, 164

Hyman, John James, 139, 140

Indigent Soldiers Family Fund, 153, 157, 160, 167, 169, 238; slaveless plain folk on, 168, 205

Intermarriage between planters and plain folk, 5–6, 22, 48

Irish railroad workers, 40, 41–42, 58

Irwin County, 6, 14, 298; anti-Confederate takeover of Irwinville, 213–14, 215, 216, 217, 227, 230, 239; and Compromise of 1850, 57; county office-holding in, 47, 48; economic conditions (1875), 237–38; election precincts, in slaveholders' homes, 46,

Macon, Ga., 12, 24, 232; defense of, 208; Democratic convention (1873) at, 272–73; as mustering point, 86, 93

Macon and Brunswick Railroad, 14, 24, 39, 42, 61–62, 95, 284; extended into Dodge County, 297–98, 301

Macon Guards, 87

Magdol, Edward, 3

Male authority, 31–32, 35, 46, 47, 49

Malloy, Caroline, 37, 101, 193, 250, 253

Malvern Hill, Battle of (1862), 206

Manassas, First Battle of (1861), 2, 114–18, 119, 146, 152, 189; 8th Georgia action in, 116, 117, 236; 8th Georgia casualties at, 2, 116, 117–18, 148, 152, 189, 190

Manassas, Second Battle of (1862), 131, 198

Manning, Harriette, 1, 24, 191–92, 193, 232

Manning, Sallie, 252–53

Manning, Seaborn, 7, 100, 154, 232; death, 1, 191–92; as leader of Pulaski Greys, 98, 99, 133, 218, 321–22 (n. 40); as leader of 49th Georgia, 1, 133; as planter-merchant, 87, 94, 97; slaves on plantation of, 29, 193; wealth of, 23–24

Manning, William, 18, 24, 26, 27, 48, 54, 56, 99

Masculinity and white supremacy, 7, 51, 56, 70, 84, 145, 147–48, 150, 155, 262–65, 266–67, 287

Mason, Charles, 185–86, 188

Mason, Daniel, 2, 7, 92, 118, 120

Mason, Wilbur, 275

Masons (Masonic Order), 59, 60, 95, 136, 167, 188, 198–99

Mathews, Arnold, 284–85

Mayo, William, 74, 76

McBurrows, John, 289, 290, 291

McCall, Charles, 234–35

McCall, David, 94–95

McCall, George, 105, 196, 274, 344 (n. 35)

McCrimmon, Christiana, 159, 160

McCrimmon, John, 159, 160

McCurry, Stephanie, 4

McDonald, Charles, 58

McDowell, Irvin, 114, 117

McDuffie, James Y., 86, 94, 119, 193

McDuffie, Norman, 19, 28, 57, 61, 110, 226, 273, 275, 282–83, 293

McDuffie, Thomas J., 208, 210

McDuffie, W. M., 141

McGriff, Thomas "Tobe," 74, 76, 182–83

McLean, Hugh, 62, 76–77

McLennan, Alexander, 136

McLeod, Daniel, 74, 76

McPhail, Edwin R., 129–30, 325 (n. 42)

McRae, Alexander, 89

McRae, Daniel F., 204–6, 208, 209–10, 211, 212

McRae, Duncan, 60, 90

McRae, Ga., 297, 299, 300

McRae, Malcolm N., 62, 89

McRae and McMillan country store, 18, 108

Meade, George G., 279

Measles, 124

Mechanicsville, Battle of (1862), 136

Merritt, Simon, 61, 81, 235, 254–55

Mexican War (1846–48), 87, 93, 273

Militia District elections, 50–51

Milledgeville, Ga., 47, 53, 67, 129; measure to be returned as state capital, 291–92; state convention on secession (1861), 70–80, 228; Union convention (1850) at, 56–57, 68

Mobley, W. P., 203, 212

New Hope Primitive Baptist Church, 35, 36, 53, 75, 76, 198–99

Nullification crisis, 52

Ocean Pond, Fla., Battle of (1864), 121

Ocmulgee and Flint Railroad (Canal Company), 39–42

Ocmulgee River, lower region: anti-Confederates, in last year of war, 203, 215, 219, 221–23, 276–77, 298, 335 (n. 4); men and boys joining army, 149; black versus white belt, 8, 12–15, 24, 26, 164–65; black versus white belt, after war, 247, 297–99;

black versus white belt, home manufactures, 107–8; black versus white belt, substitute hiring, 131; black versus white belt,
at 'war's end, 203, 204, 215; class structure
of people of, 31; Confederacy, withdrawal
of support from, 202–3, 211–30; counties
of, 6, 13–15, 297–300, 308 (n. 11); as Democratic stronghold, 59–60; landscape of,
eighteenth to nineteenth century, 11–13;
mobilization in beginning of war, 85–90,
110–11; in 1864, 202–7; plain folk, as
majority whites in, 4, 15; religious affiliations, 34–38; and secession, 6–7, 69–80,
298; settlements of, 14; slaves lives in, 29–
31; slave population, 148–49, 164–65; slave
population, freed, 232; soil fertility, 16–17,
19, 23, 24, 168; steamboat traffic, 23, 24, 25;
traditional support for Union, 71–72, 77;
white belt crops, 15–19; white belt fear of
slave revolt, 161–62
Ocmulgee River ferry, 81
Orange Hill Cemetery, Hawkinsville, 1, 191
Overstreet, W. B., 155–56, 161–62, 223–24
Owsley, Frank L., 3

Pafford, Rowan, 75, 77, 78
Paine, William, 28, 56, 57, 59, 62, 68, 80, 91,
    184; conscription, opposition to, 127;
    opposing planter Democrats, 50–51, 54–
    55; opposition to secession, 45, 46, 60, 71–
    72, 73, 78; support of war, 85
Panic of 1857, 60–61
Panic of 1873, 243–44, 246, 249, 274, 288
Pate, John, 134, 191, 245–46, 249, 321–22
    (n. 40)
Pate, Thomas C., 304
Patton, Henry, 254–55
Paulk, Dennis, 218, 219
Paulk, George, 36, 48, 53
Paulk, Jacob, 36, 247
Paulk, James, 36
Paulk, Reason, 131, 153, 246
Peanuts: as crop, 166
Pearson, Benajah, 224–25

Perry, Virgil, 277–78
Petersburg, Va., 235, 303
Phelps, Dodge, and Company, 297, 300
Phillips, Epson, 249–50
Phillips, Exum, 249–50, 251
Phillips, Pleasant, 208–9
Phillips, Richmond, 250–51
Pierce, Franklin, 58
Piney woods region, Ga.: anti-Confederates,
    in last year of war, 203, 213–14, 215, 219,
    221–23, 276–77, 298, 335 (n. 4); balloting
    for secession convention, 73–78, 81, 89–
    90; calling for end of war, 3, 212–13, 215–
    16; community activities, 34; Confed-
    eracy, withdrawal of support, 202–3, 211–
    30; conscription, opposition to, 127, 128,
    129; cotton, selling to Yankees, 226–27, 339
    (n. 63); cotton cultivation impinging on,
    11–13; and death, 179–81; defined, 6; as
    Democratic stronghold, 69; deserters,
    203, 213–14, 215–19, 221–25; "domestic
    security" issues, late 1850s, 60, 63–65, 66,
    82; emigration from, after war, 288–91;
    financial ruin after war, 235, 245, 246;
    food shortages, 213, 220; forest industry,
    296–97, 299, 300–303, 304–5; and Georgia
    invasion, 201–4; home front conditions,
    148–54, 154–61; home front security
    issues, 128, 148–49, 154, 202–3; household
    structure, changes with war, 161–64;
    inferior courts, and oversight of soldiers'
    families, 152–54, 157, 169, 177–78; labor
    shortage, due to soldiers leaving, 158–60,
    169–70; lack of military preparedness, 85–
    86; lack of natural immunity in soldiers
    from, 121; loyalist neighborhoods, 226;
    men at home, 7–8, 149–54, 161–64, 167–
    69; mobilization, 85–90, 110–11, 319
    (n. 10); mobilization, in last year of war,
    202–5; mobilization, second wave, 97–98,
    321–22 (n. 40); mobilization versus home
    front defense, 202–3; mobilizing, outside
    of home area, 87, 89; new economy of,
    after war, 288, 296–305; officer veterans,

playing similar role after war, 273–75; politics of (1830s to 1850s), 52–53, 54, 59–60; politics of (1850s), 59–61; politics of (1871), 261–62; poverty, after surrender, 234, 235, 238–39, 240, 258–59; prosperity versus poverty after war, 245–46; recession of 1857, 60–61; religious activities, 34–38; rural economy unraveling during war, 169–72, 174; seceding, 2–3, 6–7, 8, 45–47, 60–61, 65–66, 68–80; soldiers returning home, 143–44, 163–64, 220–21, 232; veterans preserving white supremacy values in, 271–73

Plain folk: black labor, rejected after war by, 242; black voter registration, reaction to, 267–68, 271; buried far from home, 1–2, 137, 189–91, 195; cotton, rejected as crop after war by, 3, 240–43, 244–45; cotton cultivation by, 5, 18–20, 21, 42–43, 310–11 (n. 20); county office-holding, 47; crop lien system, rejection of, 241, 243–45, 247, 248; death, living with, 136–46, 179–91, 192–94, 195–99; defined, 3–4; demoralization after war, 236–37; emigrating to Texas, after war, 288–89; fear of being "slaves" to Yankees, 7, 55–56, 70, 83, 145, 147–48, 202, 206, 299, 301–2, 305; fear of freed black insurrection, 284; fear of slave revolt, 41, 63–65, 66–67, 70, 143; fear of slave revolt, against women, 155–56, 161–62, 165; Griswoldville, Georgia Militia attack, effect of on, 211–12; hiring substitutes for army service, 130–32; homestead laws, rejection of, 247; housing, 20, 33; independence/self-sufficiency after war, 238–45, 246–48; intermarriage with planters, 5–6, 22, 48; as junior officers in army, 94, 133; local government, ideas on who votes/rules, 263–65; men at home, 149–54, 161–64, 175–78, 202, 213; new economy after war, reactions to, 301–4, 347 (n. 17); personal honor, 206; versus planters, 12–13, 17–18; and planters, deference to, 46–47, 70, 73, 95, 110, 133–36; and planters, slavery uniting, 31, 55–56, 65, 70, 84, 133; and planters, united against Radicalism, 275–76; political influence, decline of after war, 299; politics of, 46–51, 52–55; politics of (1850s), 57–63; politics of before 1860 election, 68–69; professional families, 4; professional men, 74, 76, 77, 95–96; race consciousness of, 2, 4–5, 8, 58, 84, 245, 262–63, 276; race consciousness versus class consciousness, 65–66; Radicalism, rejection of, 261–63, 264, 266, 267–68, 272, 273, 292–93, 295, 299, 302, 305; and railroads, 39–42, 61–62; Reconstruction, justification of violence by, 263, 272, 275, 276, 285; Reconstruction, rejection of, 261–63, 268, 276, 279; secession, moving toward, 65–66, 69–70, 72–73; secession, supporting, 6–7, 8–9, 80, 309 (n. 12); secession, voting for, 45–46; secession convention, balloting for, 73–78, 81, 89–90; slaveholding, 21–22, 26, 30–31, 47, 90, 136, 185, 311 (n. 24); slaveless, 15–16, 22, 32, 58; slaveless soldiers, 90, 92, 95, 133, 205; slaveless and labor shortage during war, 89, 168; slaveless and poverty with men leaving, 158–60, 168; slaveless, proportion of, 42, 47, 73, 184–85, 333 (n. 14); and slavery, support of, 4–5, 8, 58, 66; slaves, freed, competition from, 249, 287; slaves, freed, hostility toward, 252; and Southern nationalism, 80, 82, 85, 89, 97, 100, 171–72, 202, 205–6; Southern nationalism, dying for, 150–51, 180, 185–88, 199; state capital, measure to move from Atlanta back to Milledgeville, 291–92; values of home and family, 82–84, 93, 101–4, 145, 154–55; values of masculinity and white supremacy, 7, 51, 56, 70, 84, 145, 147–48, 150, 155, 262–65, 266–67, 287; values of regionalism and egalitarianism, 58, 72–73; veterans, amputee/disabled, 234–37; veterans and violence against blacks, 279. *See also* Ocmulgee River, lower region; Piney woods region, Ga.; Women

Planter elite: conspicuous consumption, after war, 248–49; convention on secession (1861), delegates, 73–74; death, living with, 183–84, 191–92; former slaves, relationship with, 249–52, 253, 256, 257–58; and hiring substitutes for army service, 131; intermarriage with plain folk, 5–6, 22, 48; and livestock herding, 27; military leadership of, 1, 98–99, 133, 154; mobilization and participation, end of war, 204; outfitting/supplying soldiers, 106–7; plain folk, united with over slavery, 31, 55–56, 65, 70, 84, 133; power and influence of, 22–23, 26, 35–36, 46–47, 48, 50–53; and railroads, 39; Reconstruction, violence during, 275; slaveholding, 22–24, 26, 37, 38, 47, 73; slave management during war, 166–69; women as owners during war, 166–68; women learning cloth production during war, 108–9. *See also* Ocmulgee River, lower region; Piney woods region, Ga.

Pneumonia, 124–25

Pridgen, William, 46, 47

Primitive Baptists, 32, 34–38, 95, 140–41, 181, 229; excommunications, 53, 198–99; maintaining social order, 53; and Masons, 60, 198–99; opposition to evangelicalism in Confederacy, 197–98; political leanings of, 53–54, 72, 73, 76; Union supported by, 53–54, 65, 75, 77, 196–99; values of, 53–54, 241, 247–48

Pulaski Blues, 91, 96, 119, 124, 157, 192, 195. *See also* Georgia Infantry Regiments: 31st

Pulaski County, 6, 14, 298; anti-Confederates, late in war, in backwoods of, 222–23, 276–77; men and boys joining army, 328 (n. 6); artillery battery from, 86, 119, 138, 157, 207, 209, 296; black belt in northern, 13–15, 22–23, 26; Committee of Seven, 272, 273–75; and Compromise of 1850, 57, 59; corn production, 17, 18; cotton cultivation, 11–12, 18–19, 23–24; crop lien system, 238; Dodge County formed from

backwoods of, 297–300; draft evasion, 128; freedmen voter registration in, 265–66; home manufactures, in domestic economy, 108; on Indigent Soldiers Family Fund list, 157, 158; livestock raising, 26; and Macon and Brunswick Railroad, 62; mobilizing, 81–83, 86; mobilizing, second wave, 119; paramilitary whites in, 276–77; planters in, 22–23, 47, 57, 59, 74, 93, 118, 119, 256, 308 (n. 10); politics of (1830s to 1850s), 54; politics of (late 1850s), 58–59, 61, 62; presidential election (1860), 69, 97; Primitive Pulaski Association, 198; secession, representatives to state convention on, 79, 182–83, 274; secession, support for, 47, 76, 79, 81; slaves in, 30–31, 164–65; soil fertility, 17, 23, 24; transition from slavery to free labor, 238, 256; Trippville neighborhood, 218, 219, 276–78; veterans, 84, 265, 274, 278, 296; white belt in southeastern, 13–15

Pulaski County Inferior Court, 50, 165; corn regulations, 172–73, 212; and draft evasion, 128–29, 219; oversight of soldiers' families, 152–54, 156–57, 173

Pulaski Greys, 98, 99, 122, 157, 218, 234, 321–22 (n. 40), 325 (n. 42); at Battle of Cedar Mountain, Va., 191; casualties, 188, 191; deserters, 131; disease/sickness in, 126; officer elections, 133–34, 136; substitute hiring in, 130, 131. *See also* Georgia Infantry Regiments: 49th

Pulaski Rangers, 152, 157, 185

Pulaski Volunteers, 86, 157; action after First Manassas, 236; backgrounds of, 82–83, 91–92; boredom of camp, 119; casualties, 126, 184; casualties, First Manassas, 2, 116, 117–18, 148, 152, 189, 190; casualties, from disease, 120–21, 126, 184; disease/sickness in, 114, 118, 120–21, 124; first actions, 114; first bivouac, at Sutton's plantation, 82, 83, 85, 113; flag presentation to, 101; Manassas, First Battle of (1861), 115–19; mobilization, 81–83, 85, 87, 93; officer elections,

87; returning home, 150, 165; saying good-
bye to, 105, 274; substitute hiring in, 131,
150; Virginia, arrival in, 113, 320 (n. 15). *See
also* Georgia Infantry Regiments: 8th

Race consciousness: versus class consciousness, 65–66; of plain folk, 2, 4–5, 8, 58, 84,
245, 262–63, 276
Radicalism, 287; and class, attempts to
exploit differences, 271–72, 275–76; constitution (1868) inspired by, 291; demand to
include freedmen in local government,
265; Democrats mobilizing to defeat, 268,
272–73; freedmen turning away from, in
desperation, 291; local authorities, rejection of, 279; plain folk, rejection of, 261–
63, 264, 266, 267–68, 272, 273, 292–93, 295,
299, 302, 305; planters, rejection of, 282–
83, 292–93; and Trippville neighborhood,
276–78; white anti-Confederates, 277–78
Radical Reconstruction, 266, 292; plain folk
rejection of, 268, 279; seeking state police
force to protect blacks, 279; threat to
white supremacy, 275
Railroads, 14, 24, 55, 58, 61–62, 95, 224, 284;
Macon and Brunswick Railroad extension
into Dodge County, 297–98, 301; Ocmulgee and Flint Railroad (Canal Company),
39–42
Reconstruction: black state congressman
during, 284; and forest industry, 301; martial law in South, 265; mock funeral procession putting to rest, 261–62; new
county created, 297–300; plain folk, rejection of, 261–63, 268, 276, 279; and plain
folk justification of violence, 263, 272, 275,
276, 285; and planter involvement in violence, 275; in South, in context of Confederate defeat, 262–63; violence during,
262–63, 279, 343 (nn. 5, 10); voter registration of freedmen, 265–66, 267–68, 271
Reconstruction Acts: demand to include
freedmen in local government, 265; white
denouncing of, 268

Reed, Easter, 21, 30, 101–2, 179, 180, 194, 252,
257
Reeves, Willis, 57, 59
Reid, George, 36, 53, 72, 74–75, 76, 143, 197,
198–99, 213
Reid, George (son), 75, 143, 199
Reid, Henry, 75, 198, 199
Religion: affiliations in Piney woods region,
Ga., 34–38; and death, dealing with, 137–
41, 186, 195–98; and planters, 35–36;
revivalism in Confederate army, 139–41;
and slaves, 37; used in mobilization, 104–5
Republican Party, 65–66, 68, 70, 150; and
African Americans, 265, 267–68, 269–70,
278, 279, 343 (n. 23); and African Americans, violence against, 280, 283, 284–85; in
Dodge County, 299; efforts to displace
Southern patriarchy, 263; fear of eman-
cipation brought by, 72, 82–83; and Ku
Klux Klan intimidation/violence, 280;
mobilization of black voters, 267–68, 269–
70, 278, 279, 343 (n. 23); physical attacks on
members, 275, 276, 281, 282, 283; plain folk
rejection of, 276; white anti-Confederates
supporting, 213–14, 276–78
"Republic of Irwin," 239–41, 244–45, 246,
248, 261–62, 302
Rice production, 17–18, 176
Richardson, Simon Peter, 37, 38
Richardson Methodist Episcopal Camp
Ground, 38
Richmond, Va., 113, 114, 117, 124
Rollins, Joseph, 143, 276
Ryan, Thomas, 61, 83, 92, 95, 97, 190; background, 93–94; leading Pulaski Volunteers, 81, 82, 87, 113, 120, 134, 236; Ma-
nassas, First Battle of (1861), 115, 116, 118

Salter, Seaborn F., 277–78, 279, 281, 283, 293
Savannah, Ga., 12, 85
Savannah and Gulf Railroad, 224
Scarborough, Aden, 152
Scarborough, Jesse, 91, 118, 152, 192
Scott, Winfield, 93